Six Wings: Men of Science in the Renaissance

by GEORGE SARTON

Six Wings

MEN OF SCIENCE
in the RENAISSANCE

illustrated with contemporary portraits

INDIANA UNIVERSITY PRESS
1957
BLOOMINGTON

THE PATTEN FOUNDATION

Mr. Will Patten of Indianapolis (A.B., Indiana University, 1893) made, in 1931, a gift for the establishment of the Patten Foundation at his Alma Mater. Under the terms of this gift, which became available upon the death of Mr. Patten (May 3, 1936), there is to be chosen each year a Visiting Professor who is to be in residence several weeks during the year. The purpose of this prescription is to provide an opportunity for members and friends of the University to enjoy the privilege and advantage of personal acquaintance with the Visiting Professor. The Visiting Professor for the Patten Foundation in 1954-55 was

PROFESSOR GEORGE SARTON

Preface

It was a great honor to be selected to deliver the Patten Lectures of 1955, and I am grateful to the Patten Foundation, not so much for having invited me as for having invited (in me) a historian of science. The number of people who understand the value of the studies to which I have devoted my life is still very small. I am grateful also because these lectures and the many interviews deriving from them created a spiritual bond between the lecturer, on the one hand, and the teachers and students of Indiana University, on the other. I humbly hope that the lectures did not disappoint my audience and that *Six Wings* will be strong enough to lift and exhilarate its readers.

Though most of my energy throughout the years has been spent in the study of ancient and mediaeval science, I have never been far away from the Renaissance. Not to mention my Harvard lectures, which obliged me to come back to it every alternate year, and my editorship of *Isis* and *Osiris,* I gave a lecture in a Renaissance symposium at Mount Holyoke College (1929), another at the Metropolitan Museum (1952), three more as a Rosenbach Fellow at the University of Pennsylvania, and a sixth at the American Philosophical Society in Philadelphia (1953).[1]

Moreover, in my investigations on ancient and mediaeval science, I was always anxious to establish the date of first publication in printed form, when the tradition of any particular work was fixed and that work finally saved for posterity. These first publications were often incunabula or sixteenth-century editions, and I was thus

obliged to study Renaissance printing and to become acquainted
with the early typographers.

The author of a monograph on a small subject may be expected
to say everything that is known or knowable about it, and to say it
with precision; that is his duty. It would be ridiculous to nourish
such expectations with respect to the author of a broad synthesis
or to reproach him because he does not know everything or because
he has forgotten to say this or that.

The whole of science during a period of a century and a half
(1450-1600) is a subject of tremendous magnitude. To measure its
size, consider the third volume of my *Introduction to the History
of Science*. This is a complete but condensed survey of science in a
single century (the fourteenth), yet it covers 2,192 pages. We may
assume that the number of scientific events doubled in the fifteenth
century and trebled in the sixteenth (a moderate assumption; the
increase was probably much larger); a summary of science in the
period 1450-1600, if done on the same scale as my Volume 3, would
cover at least 8,768 pages.

It is clear that in a book less than one-twentieth this size, it is
impossible to treat the whole of Renaissance science. Even if the
summary were reduced to the very bones (thus becoming incomprehensible), completeness would still be out of the question. The best
that can be done is a sketch illustrating some aspects of scientific
efforts in that period. I have tried to do this, and because of my
long experience, it may be that my sketch will have some validity
and include divers items of novelty or weight.

What would be the good of completeness anyhow? Except for a
few scholars who plan to devote their whole lives to the understanding of the Renaissance, the endeavor to be complete and to say
everything worth saying is hopeless and deadly. If you wanted to
know France, would it be wise to visit every town and village?
Would it not be better to stay as long a time as possible in a few of
them and to look around? Well, that is just what I am aiming at. In
this book we shall meet a few men of science of the Renaissance
period and try to know them well enough to imagine all the others.

The only trouble (and it is a serious one) is that our selection
is somewhat artificial. Our views of the past are always falsified,

because time has acted like a sieve, and what has been permitted to reach us is not a representative sample. Almost all the mediocre things have been sifted out. We may be certain that great artists, philosophers, scholars, and saints were not more numerous then than they are now. I am thinking of the people for whom scholarship, art, wisdom, or religion was not a job to be enjoyed and exploited but a mission to be carried through at any cost. Then, as now, the majority of people were mediocre; they wanted to live as comfortably as possible, to sell their work and what they called their "devotion" at the highest price. There is nothing wrong in that, nothing criminal, but it is petty.

We are obsessed by the mediocrity of our own times, while the past which has come to us has been cleaned up, and our attention is restricted to the best people, or sometimes to the worst, but in any case to outstanding figures. Any comparison between the highly selected past and the total present is therefore misleading and dangerous. Bearing that always in mind, there is no harm in enjoying the great paintings and the great books of the Renaissance.

My description of science during that period is typical of my lifelong teaching at Harvard and elsewhere. I have not tried to teach science; there was no time for that, and it was not my business. I am not and have never been a science instructor, but a humanist, a man deeply interested in all the humanities of science, and above all, in the personalities of scientific investigators. It is very strange, by the way, that this kind of humanism is less common in science than in other fields. People interested in art are curious to know all they can concerning the artists, the creators of beauty; is not that natural enough? And is it less natural for a scientist to want to know all that he can about the lives, as well as the works, of his predecessors? Unfortunately, some scientists are merely technicians who want to master the facts, theories, and tricks of their branch of science and have no time or curiosity left for anything else. That is not enough.

Scientific work is criticized from the technical angle and that is as it should be, but we need something more than technical criticism. Consider again the artists. Few people are able to criticize them on purely technical grounds, but that does not matter, because the criticism that is most valuable to the artist is not technical but much broader—it is human. What is the meaning of this or that symphony, of this or that painting? What does it add to our conscience or to our feelings? Or to take another homelier example, if we are given food, do we attempt to criticize it in technical terms, do we investigate the recipe? No, our criticism is focused upon the goodness of the meal. Did it please our bodies and refresh our souls, or did it not?

The cook needs such criticism and so does the musician and the sculptor, the chemist and the geometer. One of the main purposes of the history of science is to provide such criticism and to develop the humanities (as against the technicalities) of scientific efforts. Saints strive for goodness and justice, artists search for beauty, and men of science for truth. How do they do it? And why? How do their efforts combine and help one another? How do the branches of science hold together? These are the questions—human questions, not technical ones—which we are trying to answer.

In order to keep my account within reasonable bounds and yet sufficiently diversified, I have not allowed myself to speak too much of some of the giants, men like Erasmus, More, Stevin, Vives, and Viète, who might have stolen the show and with whom some of my readers are already familiar. It was better, I thought, to leave more space for lesser men, whose humbler contributions were nevertheless of great importance. These men came not from one country but from every country of western Europe. The Renaissance did not begin everywhere at the same time, and it did not always begin in Italy; some initiative was taken in other countries, such as Portugal or Flanders.

The Renaissance was international, and the history of science in every period is independent of political, racial, or religious boundaries. The quest for knowledge has always been international or supranational, even more fundamentally so than the quest for beauty or salvation. The Italian artists could have created all of their masterpieces just as well if the Germans, the Flemings, and the English had not existed. On the contrary, scientific discoveries always implied the collaboration of many nations. No scientific achievement can ever be explained within the limits of a single country. This is made clear in my summary, in spite of the fact that it is necessarily restricted to the Western world. If I had been able to speak of India, China, and Japan, I would have shown many curious relationships, but my space is too short to do justice even to the West, and hence I had to abandon the East. A scientific discovery may be made anywhere. "The wind bloweth where it listeth and thou hearest the sound thereof, but canst not tell whence it cometh and whither it goeth" (*John* 3:8).

Proper names cause many difficulties. In the case of places, I have generally preferred to give the modern names with which the reader is more familiar; there is no point in adding to his perplexities. As to persons, the difficulties are due mostly to the coexistence of Latin with many vernaculars, whose growth could not be repressed. The authors who wrote in Latin were obliged to Latinize or Hellenize their names and, in many cases, the Latin or Greek name is the one that is best remembered, as well as the easiest to index. Consider, for example, the names of Erasmus, Copernicus, Melanchthon, Tragus, Dodonaeus, Clusius, Faber Stapulensis. Sometimes the vernacular name has stuck, such as Brahe, Cardano, Stevin; that was the case, of course, for writers who preferred to use the vernacular, such as Paré, Palissy, and Luther. In some cases the original name was Latinized and a new common name was derived from the Latin. For example, Chauvin was Latinized Calvinus, hence the common name Calvin; Cleynaerts became Clenardus, hence Clenard. The possibilities are endless. Whichever form I chose, I have tried to use it consistently.

This book is illustrated with authentic portraits. The importance of portraits can hardly be exaggerated. A good portrait of a man tells us more about him than the longest descriptions. Think of portraits as revealing as those of Descartes by Frans Hals, Galileo by Susterman, or Pope Paul III Farnese by Titian. Such portraits are rare, of course, but the early printers gave us many engravings that can be fully trusted, because they appear in books published during the author's lifetime or very soon after his death. If the author and his friends accepted the portrait as genuine, we are safe in doing the same.

People have always attached so much importance to portraits that when no genuine portrait was available they were ready to accept anything as a substitute. The wish was father of the portrait. This fallacy was magnified by the engravers. There are Renaissance collections of portraits in which genuine portraits are indiscriminately mixed up with fanciful ones. The authors of these collections did not seem to realize that portraits of Plato and Archimedes (not to mention Adam and Eve) were essentially different from portraits of their contemporaries made from life; the difference was as great as that between a lie and the truth. Some of the outstanding scholars not only of the Renaissance but of today are victims of this kind of illusion; while they insist on the need of accuracy in words, they are ready to sacrifice it where portraits are concerned.[2]

Each portrait in this book is genuine, and the proof of its genuineness is given in its legend.

Bibliographical references are restricted to the essential, or to novelties which the reader would have no other opportunity of checking.

And now I come to the final point, which should perhaps have been the first. Why is this book entitled *Six Wings?* This is not an idle fancy of mine but the continuation of a very old tradition. It can be traced back to the Old Testament, but I was made aware of it thanks to a mediaeval writer, Immanuel Bonfils of Tarascon, who flourished c.1340-77,[3] and was best known because of his astronomical tables entitled *Kanfe nesharim* (wings of eagles, *Exodus* 19:4); as these tables were divided into six parts they were more generally called *Shesh kenafayim*. This was an illusion to the six wings of the seraphim *(Isaiah* 6:2), and Immanuel himself was called *Baʻal kenafayim* (master of the wings).

My title is thus a reference to the famous astronomical tables compiled in Tarascon (Bouches-du-Rhône) in 1340-65, and beyond them to the seraphim "each one of whom had six wings; with twain he covered his face and with twain he covered his feet, and with twain he did fly."

GEORGE SARTON

Cambridge, Massachusetts
April 16, 1955

NOTE: Professor Sarton died on March 22, 1956, and was therefore unable to read the proofs of this book or to prepare the index.

Contents

Illustrations

Six Wings: Men of Science in the Renaissance

First Wing

THE FRAME OF THE RENAISSANCE:
EXPLORATION AND EDUCATION

 As THIS BOOK is devoted to the history of science during
the Renaissance, it is necessary to explain briefly what the
history of science is. Many people, even educated people,
do not know what it is, and how could they, considering
their misunderstanding of science? They often confuse
science with technology, the fruits of which are abundant and rich
beyond the dreams of avarice. I do not like this confusion because
I think of science as the well-ordered gathering of knowledge concerning the universe and ourselves; I think of it as a sacred con-
templation and a spiritual fulfillment. Technology is science applied
to the business of life. Its fruits are innumerable; most of them are
good, but many are bad—the exploitation of men, their enslave-
ment to machines, their idolatry of gadgets, and finally such devilish
creations as atomic bombs.

The history of science includes some parts of the history of technology, yet it is essentially a different subject.

For example, the historian of science must speak of the genesis
and first realization of the great inventions, but he will not try to
explain their technical development. He will explain the invention
of printing, the steam engine, the dynamo, the internal combustion
engine, etc., but he must leave to the historian of technology any
account of the very complex growth of each and the endless ramifica-
tions to which each of them gave birth. Each key invention is like the
seed of a gigantic tree. The history of science may be defined as the
story of the gradual unveiling of objective truth and of the conquest
of matter by mind; it describes the age-long and endless struggle for

1

freedom of thought—freedom from violence, intolerance, error, and superstition.

The history of science is one of the essential parts of the spiritual history of mankind, the other main parts being the history of art and of religion. It is not more important or more enlightening than these other parts, but it differs from them in that the development of knowledge is truly cumulative and progressive. Our knowledge is vastly superior to that of our ancestors; on the other hand, the saints of today are not closer to God, nor are modern artists closer to beauty, than their predecessors. Hence, if we would explain the progress of mankind, the history of science should be the very axis of our explanation.

The history of science provides the axis, or, let us say, the armature of the history of mankind. The armature is essential but insufficient. A man needs a good skeleton to be sure, but that is not enough; he needs blood and flesh, and even that is as nothing, he needs feelings and thoughts; then only is he complete.

My work has always been inspired by that ideal. I am primarily a historian of science, but the history of science has never satisfied me in itself; I always needed and gave away much more.

As I have promised to tell the history of science during the Renaissance, or at least to throw light upon some of its outstanding episodes, it is well also to explain when and where the Renaissance occurred. I dislike that word Renaissance, because it is a kind of weasel. In February 1952 the Metropolitan Museum organized a symposium on the Renaissance, at the end of which the six scholars who had taken part in it and their guide and moderator realized that they were not agreed on its chronology. But the misunderstanding is deeper. It is not enough to say that many renaissances have occurred in various places and times; we might claim that there has almost always been a renaissance of one kind or another going on in some part of the world. In this book the word "Renaissance" is simply a brief way of referring to the period from about 1450 to about 1600 in western Europe, or, to replace dates by deeds, from the Western discovery of printing to the death of Giordano Bruno.

The period might be stretched at both ends; the Renaissance began a century earlier in Italy, with Petrarch and Boccaccio, and it lingered for many more years in other countries. It would be tempt-

ing to use as its terminal the year 1616, which witnessed the death
of those two giants, Cervantes and Shakespeare.[1] Another terminal,
if one wants a great book and the *De Magnete Magneticisque
Corporibus* (1600) of William Gilbert is not deemed great enough,
is the *Dialogo dei due massimi sistemi del mondo* (1632) of Galileo.
This would let in too large a part of the seventeenth century, however, even though it might be argued that the *Dialogo* is to some
extent an epitome of Renaissance thought.[2] Similar things would
happen whatever period were chosen; there would always be antici-
pations of it in earlier periods and remembrances of it in later ones.

Moreover, no period is valid for all nations or for the whole of any
single nation, because the men and women living at any one time
are never spiritual contemporaries. Some of our own contemporaries
have not yet reached the Renaissance; they are still living in the
Middle Ages. Others are not even as advanced as that; they are still
in the Stone Age. It is because of such disparities that our technical
inventions are so frightening. Our ancestors were uneasy when guns
were used by children. Our own fears are deeper; we shudder to
think that atomic bombs might fall into the hands of men who in
every respect except technology are still barbarians.

Our definition of the Renaissance (i.e., 1450 to 1600) may seem
artificial, but it is easy to remember and it is not arbitrary. Whatever
one might say about its ceiling (1600), I am convinced that it would
be impossible to find a more adequate floor (1450), so far as western
Europe is concerned. The discovery of printing was one of the great
turning-points in the history of mankind, and it was of special importance for the history of science. It changed the very warp and
woof of history, for it replaced precarious forms of tradition (oral
and manuscript) by one that was stable, secure, and lasting; it is as
if mankind had suddenly obtained a trustworthy memory instead of
one that was fickle and deceitful. It is not enough to make a discovery, for if it fails to be transmitted, it is almost as if it had never
been; it is not enough to write a scientific treatise, it must be preserved. If it be lost, as were a great many ancient and mediaeval
treatises, it is of no use to us. We need the text, a faithful and permanent text, and that became possible only when printing was established by the middle of the fifteenth century.

To return to the Renaissance, it was, among other things, a revolt
against mediaeval concepts and methods. Of course every generation

reacts against the former one; every historical period is a revolt against its predecessor. Yet in this case the revolt was sharper than usual. It is not sufficiently realized that the Renaissance was not simply a revolt against scholasticism; it was also directed against Arabic influences (especially those represented by Avicenna and Averroës).[3] The anti-Arabic drive was already in full swing in Petrarch's time. Such a revolt and struggle for independence were symptoms of growing strength. The revolt was successful, but not complete; there are still many Arabic elements in our language and culture.

Fear of novelties was characteristic of the Middle Ages.[4] The Renaissance was more tolerant of them, and sometimes went out of its way to find them. Each novelty created trouble, but as they impinged on the mind with increasing frequency, one got used to them and distrusted them less; one ended by liking them. In most cases, however, the novelties were rather superficial. For example, the Renaissance artists discovered the beauty of the human body, but that had never been completely forgotten.[5] They discovered the beauties of ancient art, new accents in poetry, new rhythms in music; they discovered ancient books and were anxious to publish them. All that was very exhilarating.

In the field of science, the novelties were gigantic, revolutionary. This explains why timid people are afraid of science. Their instinct is sound enough; nothing can be more revolutionary than the growth of knowledge. Science is at the root of every social change. The Renaissance scientists introduced not a "new look" but a new being. The novelty was often so great that one could hardly speak of a Renaissance or rebirth; it was a real birth, a new beginning.

The Renaissance was a transmutation of values, a "new deal," a reshuffling of cards, but most of the cards were old; the *scientific* Renaissance was a "new deal" in which many of the cards were new. This will be shown simply and all too briefly in this book. I feel rather as though I were required to paint a series of immense frescoes in a very short time. Well, the frescoes will be painted as well as I can and I invite you to contemplate them, one after another.

THE DISCOVERY OF THE EARTH

One of the most remarkable achievements of the beginning of the twentieth century was the tectonic synthesis of the Austrian geologist,

Edward Suess (1831-1914), in *Das Antlitz der Erde*.[6] This was an elaborate survey of the "face of the earth," the whole earth, a description of all the irregularities of its crust, the mountains, the seas and lakes, the valleys, the river beds and deltas—an attempt to explain the deformations and foldings which led to the earth's present appearance. When one uses that book or simply dips into it, it is hard to realize that in the middle of the fifteenth century, at the time when the Renaissance is supposed to begin, man's knowledge of the "face of the earth" was still restricted to a very small portion of it, and even in that portion was very superficial. One of the great tasks to be accomplished was the discovery of the earth.

The forerunner was Henry the Navigator (Dom Henrique o Navegador, 1394-1460), and in this respect the Renaissance was heralded not by Italians but by Portuguese. Their initiative was followed gradually by the other nations of western Europe. It is not necessary to recite those heroic deeds, for everybody is familiar with them. A few names and dates will suffice to awaken your memories: Bartholomeu Diaz (1488), Christopher Columbus (1492), Vasco da Gama (1498), Amerigo Vespucci (1497-1504), Magellan (1519-22). These men were the greatest of the first generation of explorers and navigators, but they were followed by many others, too many to be named. The Renaissance was truly the golden age of geographical discovery. By the year 1600 the surface of the known earth was doubled. Was not that an achievement of incredible significance? The earth was doubled! It was not only a matter of quantity, but one of quality as well. New climates, new aspects of nature were revealed, new plants, new animals, new men and women.[7]

Ancient and mediaeval navigation had been largely coastal; mariners did not sail many days out of sight of land. They knew the seas but not the Ocean except as a barrier. The Ocean was now conquered, and they learned to know also the Arctic regions, the deserts, and the tropics.

The psychological reverberation of such new vistas was immense. A man of today can recall the deep emotions he felt when he found himself for the first time in the middle of the ocean, or in the heart of a tropical jungle, or when he tried to cross a desert or a glacier. These discoveries, which are fundamental for each of us individually, were made for the whole of mankind in the fifteenth and sixteenth centuries.

It is significant, however, that the rediscovery of the Old World (such as India and China) impressed scholars far more deeply than the revelation of a world in the Americas that was entirely new. One would have expected the poets of Europe to hail the appearance of the New World, but they did not, or their literary efforts[8] were too puny for remembrance. On the other hand, the Portuguese exploits in Asia inspired the greatest epic of the age, *Os Lusíadas* (1572) by Camões. This is easy to understand, for to scholars who had no idea of anthropology the American Indians could not be as interesting as the real Indians. The meaning of American culture could not be understood by the historians of that time, whose models were Greek and Roman, whereas the explorers and conquerors of Asia were constantly "recognizing" men and things which had never been completely hidden from them. The sophisticated men of India and China did astonish them often, but their exotic cultures could be explained without too great difficulty in Western terms.

This reveals the duality of the Renaissance, which will stare us in the face throughout this book. The humanists were rediscovering geography in ancient books, mathematical geography in Eratosthenes, tables and maps in Ptolemy, historical geography in Strabon, physical geography in Aristotle and Pliny. The discussion of ancient localities, regions, and nations was one of the favorite games of humanists, and under their auspices, geography became one of the auxiliary sciences of philology. That was not bad. It was as important to realize where great events had happened as when, how, and why. One of the best examples of humanistic geography had been given, just before the curtain of the Renaissance rose, by Giovanni Boccaccio in his geographical dictionary, *De montibus, sylvis, fontibus, fluminibus, stagnis seu paludibus, et de diversis nominibus maris liber* ("On mountains, forests, springs, rivers, ponds and marshes, and on the various names of the sea").[9] Boccaccio exhibited a remarkable curiosity about natural phenomena, but his main interests were literary, historical, and mythological. One would have thought that the breath-taking discoveries of the navigators and the conquistadores would have turned attention from the little books of men to the great book of Nature, but this happened much less often than one might expect. More weight was given to Strabon's words than to those of Columbus or Vasco da Gama, and the expedition of the Argonauts was considered more interesting than Magellan's.

These tendencies were somewhat corrected in the new schools led by the Jesuits, who improved mathematical teaching and were more realistic than their predecessors, but the Jesuit schools did not bear many fruits before the seventeenth century.[10] Until the end of the nineteenth century, and perhaps in some places until yesterday, geographical teaching remained a part of belles lettres rather than of natural history. When I was a student in the Athénée (high school) of Ghent, the teaching of history and geography was entrusted to the same man, and these two subjects were supposed to complement one another (as they do of course in a common sector called historical geography). It was not yet understood that geography must be primarily the description of the earth. It complements history, but it is different in nature from humanistic studies. Geography studies the world in its flatness, while history investigates its chronological sequence. The two subjects represent orthogonal sections, horizontal and vertical. The geographer invites us to contemplate the side-by-sidedness of things, the historian their one-after-anotherness; both contemplations are necessary and complementary.

We must always bear in mind that during the Renaissance there were two kinds of geographical knowledge and two kinds of geographical discovery. The first was comparable to the excavation of ancient statues or the interpretation of forgotten manuscripts; it was the rediscovery of ancient geography. The other was the unveiling of unknown parts of the earth's surface. We have already spoken of the discovery of the Americas and of the reinterpretation of India and China, but genuine discoveries could be and actually were made in the very heart of Europe; the high Alps, which had remained largely unknown, were now explored with increasing enthusiasm.

This was a new world in the heart of the old one. The severity and danger of the Alpine climate had deluded mediaeval minds into believing that the high mountains were the abode of gnomes and devils. In this they were less advanced than the Buddhists of India, China, and Japan, who regarded mountains as sacred, and built temples on their slopes and at the very summits.[11] The earliest Alpine expeditions began very timidly in the fourteenth century, but did not assume any importance before the sixteenth century; by the end of that century some forty-seven summits had been reached.[12] Two main purposes could be served in Alpine expeditions; the first was aesthetic or religious, the second was scientific. One might risk one's life in difficult ascents in order to drink in the beauty of nature and the sublimity of God's works, or in order to understand the mysterious climate obtaining at high altitudes, and to observe the shape of the mountains and the plants and animals that inhabited them. The first man to combine in himself both purposes was Leonardo da Vinci.

This introduces one of the greatest heroes of the Renaissance, whose activities marked a climax of the Italian Renaissance as well as the beginning of the French one. Leonardo moves us deeply, first because of the Oriental proclivities that are one of the aspects of his mysterious genius, and second because of his scientific tendencies. He was a man without academic learning, whose attention, therefore, was not focused on books but rather on nature. He was concerned with new discoveries, not with rediscoveries.

The sixteenth century was a golden age of Alpinism. It is very curious that Alpinism almost died out during the seventeenth century and did not begin again in earnest until the end of the eighteenth.[13]

THE NEW EDUCATION

Any renaissance must express itself in the field of education, for when men begin to think and feel in a new way, some of them are eager to modify teaching methods in proportion to their own spiritual change. It is true that men with a strong creative urge often are not interested in education or have no time and energy left for it. Leonardo's unconcern was such that he did not try to publish his views or even to put his abundant notes in order. Of course he was an educator in spite of himself, in the sense that every artist and investigator is. There were genuine educators, however, born educators as we call them, whose mission was less to discover than to explain, less to find new treasures than to communicate their own heritage to their successors.

Unfortunately the great majority of new schools was informal, and the teacher of genius could hardly emerge from the local and temporal circumstances that limited his activities. For example, one of the most lovable teachers of the fifteenth century, Vittorino da Feltre, established in Mantua, in 1423, a school of virtue and happiness, the Casa Giocosa, which did not survive him. It was a personal creation, Vittorino's masterpiece, which his patron, the marchese Giovanni Francesco Gonzaga, was unable to stabilize and perpetuate. The same misfortune happened to educators of the Renaissance; there were among them many great teachers but they were not given the possibility of creating durable schools. Let me introduce three of them: two Englishmen, More and Ascham, and the Spaniard, Vives.

Before doing so I must offer a preliminary remark in order to obviate criticism. Did any great teacher ever have a successor worthy of himself? And was it not more natural as well as easier for the successor to destroy or modify traditions rather than to continue them? Maybe, but in many cases the existence of institutions guaranteed the transmission of ideas and methods even across periods of sterility caused by the lack of genius. Men of genius are needed for the sake of creation; institutions are equally needed for the sake of continuity and permanence.

Sir Thomas More (1478-1535)—or let us give him, as we may now, a much rarer and nobler title, Saint Thomas More—was born in the City of London in 1478. During his college years in Oxford he became familiar with representatives of the "new learning" (which meant Greek learning) such as Colet, Grocyn, and Linacre,[14] and he would fain have followed in their footsteps, but his father, Justice Sir Thomas, wanted him to make law his career. Toward the end of the century he became acquainted with Erasmus, who influenced him deeply in many ways. His *Epistola ad Martinum Dorpium*[15] was a defense of Erasmus' *Moriae encomium* and of the new learning; his masterpiece, *Utopia,* (Louvain, 1516)[16] revealed not only his piety and love of education and learning, but also his consciousness of social wrongs. It is a satire on English (or European) conditions, for life in Utopia is the reverse in almost every respect of English life. More gives an elaborate description of the good society, which brotherhood, universal education, and religion combined with toleration would make possible. Not only was he one of the first defenders of the education of women, but he suggested that women be admitted to the priesthood. The religion of the Utopians was so pure that they had no fear of science, indeed from their point of view the pursuit of science was a part of religion. This imaginative and generous book inspired innumerable thinkers, not only "utopians," but good men and women, lovers of justice and culture, everywhere.[17]

As Ascham is not so well known as More, our account of him must be a little longer. Roger Ascham (c.1515-68) hailed from the North Riding of Yorkshire and was encouraged by his first patron to devote much effort to the study of archery. At St. John's in Cambridge he distinguished himself so well as a classical scholar that he was appointed secretary to the ambassador of Charles V. Later he was a tutor and friend of the unfortunate Lady Jane Grey (executed in 1554), and was Latin secretary to Queen Mary and Queen Elizabeth. The fact that he held the same office under both queens proves that he was considered indispensable. His reputation is largely based upon his *Scholemaster* (published posthumously in London in 1570), which contained various educational novelties; for example, he advised teachers to be gentle and persuasive and condemned the use of flogging. He recognized the honesty and utility of the English language but denied its eloquence; for him Latin and Greek were the only learned tongues, English was good for humbler purposes.[18] The "Schoolmaster" was a teacher of Latin, yet Ascham was clear-sighted enough to defend English. As long as the maternal language was forsaken by learned men and abandoned to the ignorant, it was bound to deteriorate. That must not happen. His earlier and more original work, *Toxophilus* (London, 1545), addressed to the "Gentlemen of England," was also written in English, because "the best men in the realm use it and he is willing to sacrifice his own interest to the good of the unlatined gentlemen and yeomen of England."[19]

Toxophilus or the Schole of Shootynge, a dialogue between Toxophilus (the lover of archery) and Philologus, had greater and more immediate influence upon English schools than the *Scholemaster.* It advocated the educational value of archery, and the practice of that sport was almost certainly established in St. Albans, Harrow, and other Elizabethan schools because of Ascham's defense of it. Not only was archery encouraged in the schools of England, it was realized that sport was an essential part of education. It is not enough for boys to study, they must be taught to pray and play together. *Toxophilus* had also some influence upon English literature, if it be true that it was the model for Izaak Walton's *Compleat Angler* (London, 1653).

The idea that the practice of a sport is good not simply for the body but also for the mind was an excellent innovation. The selection of archery is extremely interesting, because we have an Arabic treatise on archery written by an anonymous Moroccan about the beginning of the sixteenth century. The sport was encouraged also by Zen Buddhists in Japan as a means of religious and moral discipline. A comparison of the English, Arabic, and Japanese books on archery would be very instructive because of their points in common, and even more so because of their divergences.[20]

Luis Vives (1492-1540),[21] the Spanish contemporary of More and Ascham, a little younger than the former and older than the latter, was much like them in his appreciation of the classics and his desire for a new education, yet he was different from them in one essential characteristic. In spite of travel abroad and much commerce with foreigners, More and Ascham were English to the very core. Vives, born in Valencia, Aragon, in 1492, was a cosmopolitan; he studied in Paris, and lived in Bruges, Louvain, and Oxford. He was a fellow of Corpus Christi in the last-named city, but his longest residence was in Bruges, where he spent his adolescence and the end of his life and died in 1540. Like Erasmus, he was a true European, a citizen not of any country but of the Christian and Latin world.[22]

His literary output was considerably larger than that of his English contemporaries, because he was more exclusively a scholar than they could be. More was a lawyer and high magistrate, Ascham was engaged in diplomatic and curial services. Vives was a professional, while they were amateurs giving to scholarship only the time left free from other duties. His first important work, a commentary on the *Civitas Dei* of St. Augustine (Louvain, 1521) raised him to the level of Erasmus and Budé, and they constituted a kind of scholarly triumvirate during the first half of the sixteenth century.[23] He was profoundly disturbed by the political chaos of Europe and the Turkish peril, and many of his writings were devoted to explaining the need of international peace.[24] He was not afraid of admonishing kings, such as Charles V, John III of Portugal, Henry VIII, and Pope Adrian VI, in the name of suffering humanity. The *De institutione feminae christianae* (Louvain, 1523) was the first book

LUIS VIVES (1492-1540). Portrait by Philippe Galle (1537-1612) in *Virorum doctorum de disciplinis benemerentium effigies XLIIII* (Antwerp: Plantin, 1572), portrait B2. This is not strictly a contemporary portrait, but it is the earliest dated one and is trustworthy. Abdón M. Salazar, "Iconografía de J. L. Vives durante los siglos XVI, XVII y XVIII," *Boletín de la Real Academia de la Historia,* tomo 133, 305-44, 10 pls., Madrid, 1953.

showing the necessity of educating women; it was frequently re-printed and translated.[25] Various other books were devoted to education: *De ratione studii puerilis* (Oxford, 1523); *De disciplinis libri XX (Bruges, 1531)*, one of the greatest pedagogical treatises of the Renaissance;[26] *Linguae latinae exercitatio* (Bruges, 1538), the last book published in his lifetime. We must also mention his *De subventione pauperum* (Bruges, 1526), one of the first attempts to deal with the problem of poverty (and God knows it was needed in those days)[27] and his *De anima et vita* (Bruges, 1538), which has been called the first modern treatise on psychology, anticipating Bacon and Descartes.[28]

He was the first, or one of the first, to insist that good education implied active participation of the students, and he insisted upon meeting their physical needs (gymnastics, games) and the necessity of employing professional teachers, trained in normal schools. History, he claimed, should not be focused upon dynasties and wars but upon the development of thought. His treatises meant for an international audience were all written in Latin, but he recognized the necessity of using the vernacular for good teaching. This is one of the paradoxes of Renaissance culture: in spite of the immense development of classical studies and the existence of innumerable treatises written in Latin for the whole republic of letters, the main vernaculars were getting stronger and more ambitious every year. The story of Renaissance English, so well told by Richard Foster Jones,[29] could be told apropos of the other European vernaculars. The classical Renaissance witnessed the triumph of Spanish, Portuguese, Italian, French, German, etc., as well as that of English.

To return to Vives and to conclude, he was the greatest pedagogue of his time, who addressed the whole of western Europe. He conceived ahead of Comenius[30] a system of education extending from the cradle to the grave, and realized that the whole of it must be centered upon moral and religious growth and lead to the building of character.

The efforts which we have described, those of Vittorino, More, and Ascham, and even those of Vives, were very instructive and inspiring, but in spite of their merit they were not as constructive as they might have been if they had been implemented, preserved, and transmitted by adequate institutions.

There was an educational institution, however, which although of mediaeval origin should be mentioned here because it flourished throughout the Renaissance: the group of schools established by a monastic order, the Brothers of Common Life, started in Holland by Geert Groote (d. 1384). The movement that they originated has been called *Devotio moderna;* their ideals are illustrated by their main literary product, the *Imitatio Christi,* a masterpiece of mediaeval thought.[31] The Brothers were tremendously interested in education. Their schools were perhaps too monastic, and they did not concern England and the Romance countries but only the region of their birth, the Rhineland and other German lands. Their main purpose was to reconcile the humanities with Christianity; they could do this only on a mystical plane, but they did it very well and their ideas were not only mystical but also practical.

By the middle of the fifteenth century the Brothers had already founded some 150 schools in the Netherlands and Germany. These remained the best organized schools in Europe until their gradual replacement by the Jesuit schools. Some of their alumni spread their influence widely. It will suffice to evoke the memory of Nicholas of Cusa, Rudolph Agricola, Adrian VI, and Erasmus.[32] Moreover, they influenced also two men who were not their alumni, Martin Luther and Ignatius of Loyola, and through them, in very different directions, an infinity of other people.[33] The Jesuit schools that appeared toward the end of the Renaissance were better schools: first, because they could exploit the experience that the Brothers had accumulated; second, because they appreciated the value of scientific education; and finally, because of their improved organization and discipline.

Two of the Brothers' alumni deserve our attention: Nicholas of Cusa, who loved them, and Erasmus of Rotterdam, who was irritated by them. The first, who was one of the heroes of the Renaissance in many fields, does not really belong to our story, except as a forerunner. Nicholas Krebs was born at Cues on the Moselle in 1401, was educated by the Brothers of Common Life in Deventer, continued his studies in Heidelberg, Padua, and Cologne, took a conspicuous part in the Council of Basel (1432-36), was made a cardinal in 1448, vicar general of Rome in 1452, and died at Lodi, Umbria, in 1464. In his main work, bearing the excellent title *De docta ignorantia* (learned ignorance) (1439-40), he explained the essential relativity and imperfection of human knowledge. He was a man full of learning, wisdom, and tolerance and the Reformation might have been averted if his advice had been heeded and if his humanity had been shared by a larger number of bishops and cardinals. He even went so far as to suggest that all religions are essentially one in spite of many practical divergences, God having sent special prophets to each people in order that each might receive the religious instruction best fitted to its needs. This is almost incredible, and proves that Nicholas was ahead not only of his own time but of ours. Nevertheless the fall of Constantinople[34] prompted him to publish, in 1459, an arraignment of Islam, *Cribatio alchoranis.*

Nicholas was in many respects a forerunner of Erasmus, but he was also a man of science, as will be shown later. All in all, he was perhaps the greatest man of the first half of the fifteenth century, as Leonardo was of the second.

Nicholas of Cusa is an excellent symbol of the transition between the Middle Ages and the new age; Desiderius Erasmus (1466-1536), born two years after Nicholas' death, was a true child of the Renaissance. He shared Nicholas' toleration, but in a different way, the former being a great administrator as well as an original thinker and a man of science, while the latter was primarily a humanist, a defender of the *bonae litterae.* He was not as intensely religious as Nicholas—this was perhaps the chief reason for his dislike of the Brothers' methods—yet he would have liked to preserve the unity of the Church, and he was opposed to the firebrands of both sides. Born in Rotterdam in 1466, he spent his childhood and youth in Holland. In 1495 he went to Paris, and from that time on there were few years when he did not travel in France, England, Italy, Switzerland, Germany, or the Netherlands. His love of peace (religious and civil) equaled his love of learning. He was one of the greatest teachers of the Greek and Latin humanities, the editor of many ancient texts, and the author of original books of considerable popularity. He also wrote innumerable letters, which mirror the republic of letters in the first half of the sixteenth century.[35] From among his many works it will suffice to mention the *Adagia* (Paris, 1500);[36] his masterpiece, the *Moriae encomium* (Paris, 1510/11);[37] and the first edition of the Greek New Testament together with a revision of the Latin Vulgate (Basel, 1516).[38] His main pacifist book, the *Querela pacis,* was issued by the same publisher, Froben, in the same year (Basel, 1516).[39]

Among the many aspects of Erasmus' personality, I should like to speak of one which I found very suggestive, namely, his deep interest in St. Jerome (IV-2),* the translator of the Bible into Latin, the scholarly saint and the patron saint of Christian humanists. Some of his letters prove that as early as 1500 Erasmus was already playing with the idea of editing all of St. Jerome's writings, and he actually collected them in an edition of monumental size.[40] This predilection for St. Jerome enables us to understand Erasmus' character as opposed to that of his younger contemporary and adversary, Luther. The latter expressed their fundamental difference of opinion and temperament as follows: "I prefer Augustine to Jerome in the same proportion as Erasmus prefers Jerome to Augustine," and in his table talk of 1533 he exclaimed, "I hate Erasmus from the bottom of my heart."[41]

Humanists paid very little attention to the plastic arts; this is true of many of them, such as Montaigne, but especially so of Erasmus, who was primarily a Christian moralist and philologist, but neither a poet nor a lover of art. He was not at all an ascetic, but he was austere, disliking the extravagance of artists as well as that of the Ciceronians. Art for art's sake would have been incomprehensible to him. He was deeply religious and preferred order to disorder, gentleness to violence, and objective truth to fantasy. Yet, paradoxically enough, in spite of his neglect of art, his influence upon the development of Flemish art was not inconsiderable. This is revealed in the paintings of Quentin Metsijs[42] of Antwerp, who initiated, among other things, a new Hieronymian tradition. His portrait of St. Jerome in his study (1515) was repeated by many artists; it expressed an Erasmian ideal, the holiness of scholarship.[43]

The difference between these two great men might perhaps be summarized in this way: Luther was concerned with Christian education but not (as Erasmus was) with Christian humanities; Luther was a propagandist and a fighter, while Erasmus was simply a scholar, unwilling to fight, or even to assert himself unkindly, in this respect a prototype of Goethe.

---

* The abbreviations IV-2, XI-1, etc., used throughout this book, stand for "second half of fourth century," "first half of eleventh century," etc.

He remained steadfastly outside the scramble, failed to attend the Diet of Worms (1521), where Luther made his stand, and the Confession of Augsburg (1530), in spite of Charles V's invitation. His fame and influence were greater than those of any other scholar until Voltaire and Goethe centuries later. He was honored by kings, as were Titian by Charles V and Michelangelo by Julius II. Toward the end of his life, however, his mind was darkened by many calamities. Thomas Münzer, the Anabaptist, was beheaded in 1525; his printer and friend, Johann Froben, died at Basel in 1527; Louis Berquin was roasted to death in Paris in 1529; Huldreich Zwingli was slain on the battlefield at Kappel (Zürich canton) in 1531; and the worst shock of all was the execution of his good friends, John Fisher and Thomas More, in London in 1535. He passed away in despair and loneliness on July 11/12, 1536. Kindness and tolerance had failed; religious wars would darken the end of the Renaissance.

The main source of division in the sixteenth century was the Reformation and the religious wars which followed it, wars conducted in the name of Christ but without mercy. When I was a young man I found it almost impossible to conceive of such cruelties and horrors, but alas! I know better now, for the two world wars and especially the second one have enabled us to have a fuller understanding of man's inhumanity. There is progress, however, that we do not kill one another in the name of Christ but in the name of Stalin; the nightmare of other people's heterodoxy has been replaced by that of Soviet Communism.

There is no time or room for me to discuss the various reformations and counter-reformations, but we must bear in mind that Luther's revolutionary deed of 1517[44] was not by any means a bolt out of the blue. Criticism of the Church had been going on for centuries and much of it had been contributed by her most faithful members.[45] The events of 1517 and the following years were unavoidable; when a difference of potential is allowed to increase indefinitely, a discharge must occur sooner or later, and the later it comes the more violent it is bound to be.

What interests us here is the effect of the Reformation upon education. The schools of the Brothers of Common Life reached only a minority of children. From the Protestant point of view this was very insufficient; every Christian should be able to read the Scrip-

tures by himself. To make it possible to fulfill that religious duty
two preparatory steps were needed: the Scriptures must be translated into the vernacular of every country; and so far as possible all
children must be taught to read. Therefore Martin Luther was very
deeply concerned with public education. Schools were established
in many German cities and their availability to children was gradually increased; it has been claimed that the public school system
of the German Protestant states was the first model of our own. The
inspirer and organizer of that system was Philip Melanchthon (1497-
1560), whose influence was so pervading and lasting that he has fully
deserved the title given to him, Praeceptor Germaniae.[46]

PHILIP MELANCHTHON (1497-1560), aet. 30. Copper engraving by Albrecht Dürer,
1526.

The movement to translate the Bible was one of the most fertile results of the Reformation; it was itself the cause of innumerable battles and persecutions. The Catholics who maintained that it was sinful to translate it forgot that the Latin text, the Vulgate, was itself a translation;[47] the sacredness of the original texts, Hebrew and Greek, had been transferred by the Church to the Latin version. Clerics were not expected to read God's words in Hebrew and Greek, and the people, who could not read Latin, were not permitted to read them at all. The struggle between Catholicism and Protestantism thus became a conflict between, on the one side, Latin humanism and eloquence, hierarchical authority, sacredness, and mystery, and on the other, the vernaculars, individualism, political and economic democracy, freer trades and industries. In the course of time Protestantism was a better cutting edge for the development of science. These statements, compressing an extremely complex situation into a few words, are oversimplified, but they indicate that the terrible conflict of the sixteenth century transcended religious issues even as our conflict with Soviet Communism transcends economic issues.

The most pregnant discovery of the Renaissance was that of printing, and the Church was the first patron of the master printers and of the "chapels."* By a strange twist of fate, printing became the best tool of the Protestants, because it made possible the great diffusion of Bibles in many languages. The price of each copy of the Bible or of the New Testament and Psalms was enormously reduced when it was possible to issue these books not in single units, but by hundreds or thousands.

The fight for supremacy between each vernacular and Latin was not restricted to the Bible but extended gradually to every field of knowledge. Many Catholics who obeyed the Church and did not try to read the Bible (the very idea had not occurred to them; it has not yet occurred to many of them to this day) were itching to use their mother tongue for other purposes. In every nation there arose great vernacular writers, such as Rabelais and Montaigne in France, both of them Catholics, who fought for the independence of the growth

---

* The word "chapel" means a printer's workshop, because the first English shop of that kind was established by William Caxton (1422?-91) in a chapel attached to Westminster Abbey. Later the word chapel was used to designate the body of journeymen printers in a printing house (their guild or union).

of their language. Their fight was difficult at the beginning, but it became gradually easier, and before the end of the sixteenth century their advance was irresistible. In 1549 Joachim du Bellay published a brave manifesto, *Défense et illustration de la langue française;* the "Pléiade" of poets using that language was organized around their leader Pierre de Ronsard (1524-85), and the battle was won.[48] This does not mean that Latin was discarded; far from it. The majority of books written exclusively for scholars and learned men continued to be written in Latin. This had a great advantage in that Latin books published, say, in Paris or Lyon could reach immediately not only the scholars of France but also those of the whole republic of letters.

This is another paradox of the Renaissance. We often think of it as the renaissance of classical humanism, and so it was. The Latin and Greek literatures were investigated more deeply than they had ever been before and the period boasted some of the greatest classical scholars the world has ever known. A few of them, such as Erasmus, Budé, and Vives, have already been named. And yet if the vernacular literatures had not arisen, the triumph of Latin and Greek might have spelled the end of literature; the humanism of dead languages would have flourished and languished, but no new humanism would have been ready to take its place.

The reason for this is very simple. No genuine style can be created except with a living instrument, the language that one has learned from his mother's lips and uses in complete innocence and freedom, without bothering about grammar or dictionary. One may consult these occasionally, of course, but it is impossible to write fluently and beautifully, or to speak at all, if one's need of them is continuous or too frequent. Good speech and good writing must flow as water from a source; each personality has a style of its own; great personalities have a great style. They are constantly recreating and enriching the language they are using.

Now all this was impossible in Latin, except in the case of a very few individuals, such as Erasmus, for whom Latin had become a natural language. I imagine that Erasmus could speak Dutch, and less well other vernaculars like German, English, French, and Italian, but his genuine mode of expression in speech and script was in Latin.[49] It is probable that many monks, especially oblates who had been brought up in monasteries since childhood,[50] knew Latin as one knows a maternal language; high eccelesiastics might be obliged to use the Latin language, in speech and script, so much that it was to them a living language; the same might be the case for doctors provided they remained unmarried and childless. In all other cases the vernacular was too strong for equal competition and soon dominated. A good example is that of Montaigne, who was educated in Latin by a German pedagogue who knew no French; until the age of 13 he used Latin almost exclusively; then the circumstances of life obliged him to speak French more and more. At the time of writing his *Essais* he could still read Latin with ease, yet he preferred to read Plutarch not in Latin but in the French translation of Jacques Amyot (1513-93).[51] It would have been well-nigh impossible for him to write the *Essais* in Latin, or if he had managed to do so, with the greatest difficulty, his translation would have been stilted and starched. The world would have lost one of the masterpieces of French literature.

The fact is that no language can be truly alive that is not used by women. Latin was spoken only by men, and the number of men able to use it spontaneously was steadily decreasing.

According to Professor Jones,[52] "of all the factors making for the use of English [before the Restoration] the invention of printing seems to have been the most important." I am certain that the same statement could be made about French in the sixteenth century, and it is highly probable that it would apply also to other vernaculars.[53] In these cases, printing was valuable not only for the sake of publicity and self-confidence, but also for the sake of stabilization. As each vernacular grew up and was considered worthy of expressing philosophical and scientific ideas, it was necessary to create an adequate vocabulary, and printing helped to establish it. New words were introduced in such quantities that some purists were offended, but their protests were ineffectual. We can observe the same thing going on today in such languages as Arabic and Hebrew. Hundreds of new words are needed, and the latest dictionary becomes obsolete after a few years. The same is true also, to some extent, of our own language, for its very life implies constant transformations, not only the addition of new words to designate new objects but also grammatical twists. We hardly notice these changes because they are relatively few in number, and we accept them unconsciously; we are not aware of the growth of our language because we are growing with it, but if a Rip van Winkle reappeared after an absence of fifty years, he would have trouble reading the newspapers.

The web of the Renaissance was extremely complex, because there were incessant conflicts in many directions; the Reformation vs. Catholicism, oceanic vs. coastal navigation, the new World vs. the Old, vernaculars vs. Latin, printing vs. manuscript, the moderns vs. the ancients, etc. In the following chapter we shall witness other conflicts, equally deep and exciting, often irritating, caused by scientific discoveries and by technical inventions.

Second Wing

MATHEMATICS AND ASTRONOMY

So MANY mathematical books were published in Europe during the Renaissance that it is impossible to speak, even briefly, of more than a few of them. To begin with, there were many editions in Greek of the old classics, also Latin translations (a Latin version was generally published before the Greek original), and numerous commentaries. Some of the commentaries on Euclid, Archimedes, Apollonios, and Pappos included original investigations of the first importance.[1] Then a large number of new books on arithmetic, of various degrees of profundity, were published in many countries in various languages. The great majority were in Latin, but a good many appeared in vernaculars for the reasons explained above. In every country, especially in the cities, there was a growing class of intelligent men—businessmen and gentlemen, even gentlewomen—who were educated and eager for more learning, but who knew little Latin or none at all. They needed books on arithmetic in their own language, and they were not long satisfied with the rudiments.

Some of these vernacular books were very elaborate: they were not restricted to arithmetic but included also some geometry and algebra.[2] One of the earliest and most ambitious was the Italian *Summa de arithmetica, geometria et proportionalita* by the Franciscan brother Luca Pacioli (Venice: Paganinis, 1494). We shall come back to it presently.

The best general account of Renaissance mathematics is still, I believe, the one included in Moritz Cantor's *Vorlesungen zur Geschichte der Mathematik*.[3] This is only a small part of an enormous work. The best treatment of any topic is often found not in a monograph exclusively devoted to it but in a work covering a larger field. Cantor has been corrected and completed on many single topics, but his account is still the best survey of the whole field.[4] His learning was great and his wisdom was equal to it.

EARLY PERSPECTIVE

Historians of painting never fail to discuss the new conception of perspective that was due to Florentine artists of the fourteenth century and also, in a smaller degree, to Flemings and Germans. The Florentine tradition is the best documented; it can be represented by a golden chain, the main links of which are Brunelleschi, Alberti, Uccello, Piero della Francesca, and Leonardo da Vinci. The first, Filippo Brunelleschi (1377?-1446) was the founder of Renaissance architecture and the creator of one of the most beautiful churches in the world, Santa Maria del Fiore. He is said to have been the first to make a systematic study of perspective, and the statement is very plausible.[5] Leon Battista Alberti (1404-72), who was also an architect as well as a painter, organist, and writer, described in his *De re aedificatoria* (c.1435) a contrivance called *velo* to facilitate the drawing of objects in their true perspective. It is possible that Brunelleschi was the first investigator and Alberti the first writer.

A book on perspective is ascribed to Paolo Uccello, the painter (1397-1475). Was that book actually written? At any rate, it has not come down to us, but we have a drawing of his of a *mazzocchio* (a complicated polyhedrical tore used as a head ornament) which proves that he was familiar with the subject. Another painter, Piero della Francesca (1420?-92), devoted much attention to stereometry and perspective and composed, late in life (c.1485), a treatise entitled *De prospettiva pingendi*. It was originally written in Italian but was soon translated into Latin and the translation was corrected by the author. He introduced into perspective the notion of the vanishing point.

Finally, Leonardo da Vinci brought these ideas to their climax. He was interested not only in linear but also in aerial perspective, a subtler matter involving the consideration of shadows, colors, albedo, and various intangible qualities.[6] So far as we can see in his manuscript notes and in the posthumous *Trattato della pittura*,[7]

SIR THOMAS MORE (1478-1535), aet. 49. Portrait completed by Hans Holbein the Younger (1497-1543) in 1527, one of the first (if not the very first) portraits painted by him after his arrival in England. More was then chancellor of the Duchy of Lancaster and had not yet succeeded Cardinal Wolsey as Lord Chancellor (1529). *Copyright The Frick Collection, New York.*

ERASMUS (1466-1536), aet. 65. The Erasmian iconography is very rich. Many portraits of him were painted by three great artists—Holbein, Dürer, and Quentin Metsijs— and by others. Fifteen portraits are reproduced in Emil Major, *Erasmus* (Basel: Frobenius, 1926). The one shown above was painted by Holbein, c.1531; it was in the Pierpont Morgan collection and later on loan at the Metropolitan Museum, New York. *Courtesy of Robert Lehman. Photograph by the Metropolitan Museum.*

Above: FRA LUCA PACIOLI, aet. c.50. Painting by Jacopo de' Barbari (Venice, c.1450-1516) in Museo Nazionale, Naples. The younger man is probably Guid'Ubaldo di Montefeltro (1472-1508), duke of Urbino, whom Julius II (Pope 1503-13) appointed Gonfaloniere della Chiesa. The book on the right is inscribed LI R LUC BUR (*liber reverendi Lucas Burgensis*), a reference to Fra Luca's *Summa* (Venice, 1494). Hence the portrait was painted after 1494, but not long after. R. Emmett Taylor, *No Royal Road: Luca Pacioli and His Times* (University of North Carolina Press, 1942; reviewed in *Isis*, 34: 428), pp. 200-205. *Anderson, Rome.*

Right: TYCHO BRAHE (1546-1601), aet. 40. Portrait made in 1586 by Tobias Gemperlin, engraved by J. de Gheyn of Amsterdam. First published in Brahe's *Epistolae astronomicae* (Uraniborg, 1596).

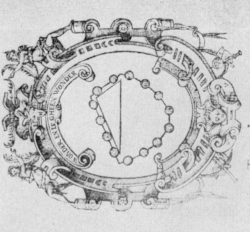

DE
BEGHINSELEN
DER WEEGHCONST
BESCHREVEN DVER
SIMON STEVIN
van Brugghe.

TOT LEYDEN,
Inde Druckerye van Chriftoffel Plantijn,
By Françoys van Raphelinghen.
cIɔ. Iɔ. LXXXVI.

Above: SIMON STEVIN. Portrait by an unknown painter (Library of the University of Leiden). See *Isis*, 21: 244, 287 (1934). The inscriptions read, "Simon Stevin, born Bruges 1548, died The Hague 1620. Eminent mathematician, counselor to His Highness Maurice Prince of Orange." *Right:* Stevin's *Statics* with its motto, "The wonder is no wonder." The same motto is used on his three mechanical treatises printed in Leiden, 1586. *Courtesy of Royal Library, Belgium.*

CONRAD GESNER, aet. 48. Portrait painted by Tobias Stimmer (1539-84) in 1564. The original is preserved in the Museum Allerheiligen, Schaffhausen, Switzerland.

GIAMBATTISTA DELLA PORTA (c.1535-40—1615). Portrait at the age of 64, hence c.1599-1604. In *De distillatione*, printed by the Camera apostolica in Rome, 1608. *Courtesy of Harvard Library.*

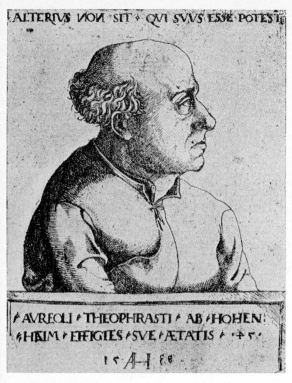

ALTERIVS NON SIT + QVI SVVS ESSE POTEST

+ AVREOLI + THEOPHRASTI + AB + HOHEN +
+ HEIM + EFFIGIES + SVE + AETATIS + 45 +

1 + A + 1 + 88 +

Nascitur 19 Feb A° 1526   CAROLVS CLVSIVS

PEREG.   ATREBAS

SIMPLIC   SCRIPTOR

Consilio Pylium, Chironem vincit in herbis,
Atq; Titum antiqua Clusius Historia.

N 113

Above, left: PARACELSUS, aet. 45. Engraved b
Augustin Hirschvogel in 1538. Another wood
cut (1540, aet. 47) by the same artist is repro
duced in Paracelsus' *Labyrinthus medicorur
errantium* (Nuremberg: Valentinus Neuberg
1553).

Above, right: LOBELIUS (1538-1616), aet. 77
Matthias de l'Obel (Lobelius) holding a flow
er; oval in rich architectural frame. Engrave
in 1615 by Francis Delaram (d. London 1627
aet. 37). *Department of Prints, British Mu
seum.*

Below: CLUSIUS (1526-1609). Engraving mad
during his lifetime. The inscription around i
reads, "Carolus Clusius of Arras, writer o
simples, traveler, born February 19, 1526." I
the Dutch book by Joh. Theunisz, *C. Clusiu
(Amsterdam, 1939; reviewed in *Isis*, 40: 363
there are three other portraits of him, aet. 49
59, and 75. This last one was published at th
beginning of *Clusii Rariorum plantarum his
toria* (Antwerp: Plantin, 1601). The portrai
here reproduced is not dated but by compari
son with the other portraits must have beer
made in the last decade of the sixteenth cen
tury.

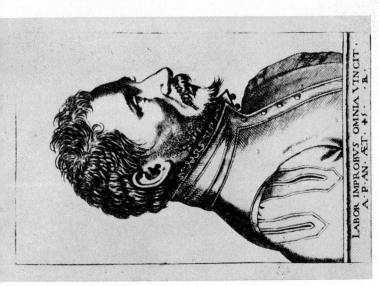

AMBROISE PARE (1510?-90), aet.-45-51. Portrait in the first edition of the *Anatomie Universelle* (Paris: Jehan le Royer, 1561). The motto printed under the portrait appears here for the first time. Another portrait of Paré, aet. 72, was published in his *Discours de la numie* (Paris: Gabriel Buon, 1582). On the basis of the indication given in the book of 1561, Paré was born c.1516; according to that of 1582 he was born in 1510. Janet Doe, *A Bibliography of Paré* (University of Chicago Press, 1937), frontispiece, pp. 46-69, 77, 89.

LUIGI CORNARO (c.1475-1566). Portrait painted c.1560 when Cornaro was at least 85. First believed to be by Titian (1477-1576), it is now ascribed to Tintoretto (1518-94). It is in the Galleria Pitti, Florence. *Alinari.*

LEONARDO DA VINCI (1452-1519). Self-portrait drawn with red chalk toward the end of his life (Torino, National Library). *Alinari.*

Leonardo was the first man in the West to combine the study of linear perspective with that of aerial perspective.

It is significant that these five men were Florentines, except Piero della Francesca; Piero was born in Umbria, but he had spent at least ten years (c.1439-50) in Florence. Three of them were architects, and all were painters or at least very familiar with drawing and painting.

Albrecht Dürer (1471-1528), a little younger than Leonardo, independently developed similar ideas on linear perspective, which were printed within his lifetime (Nuremberg, 1525). As to the practice of perspective by many other northern artists, Flemish and German, their paintings need no credentials. Obviously they knew the art as well as their Italian contemporaries.

TRIGONOMETRY

Linear perspective implied a certain amount of mathematical knowledge, but not a great deal. The best mathematical work was done in other fields, such as trigonometry and algebra.

Trigonometry had been built up on a Greek-Indian foundation in a series of Arabic treatises, the climax of which was the *Kitāb shakl al-qaṭṭāʿ* of Naṣīr al-dīn al-Ṭūsī (XIII-2). This work was written too late to become available to Western mathematicians, who had to work on the same foundation as Naṣīr al-dīn himself. Thus, so far as the West was concerned, Greco-Arabic trigonometry was continued in Hebrew by Levi ben Gerson (c.1321) and in Latin by Richard Wallingford (d. 1335). Levi's treatise was translated into Latin by Peter of Alexandria in 1342, and it was from that treatise, and not from Richard's, that later work stemmed. Trigonometry was carried further by the Austrian Georg von Peurbach, whose efforts were brought to fruition by Regiomontanus (1436-76) in his treatise *De triangulis omnimodis libri quinque,* published half a century after his death.[8] For all practical purposes Regiomontanus' treatise of 1533 may be called the foundation of modern trigonometry.

Trigonometry was needed chiefly for astronomical purposes, and as instruments were improved and observations were refined, astronomers required trigonometrical tables of ever greater precision. The Tyrolian Georgius Rhaeticus (1514-67) calculated tables of sines with a radius of 10^{10} (and later with a radius 10^{15}) for every $10''$, and began the computation of tables of tangents and secants

carried to the same degree of accuracy; though he employed several
computers for a dozen years he died too early to finish them. They
were completed and published in 1596 by his pupil, Valentin Otho
(1550?-1605).[9] A revised edition of them was published in Frankfort
in 1613 by Bartholomaeus Pitiscus (1561-1613). It is said that Pitiscus
was the first to use the word trigonometry. What matters more is
that Rhaeticus and Pitiscus raised trigonometry to a higher theoretical plane and created a mathematical instrument of a precision
inconceivable up to that time.

Pitiscus seems to have taken us out of the Renaissance, but he
has not, for his tables were still relative to the angles themselves.
Logarithmic tables of trigonometrical functions were first published
by Edmund Gunter of London in 1620. The Renaissance was definitely pre-logarithmic. Seventeenth-century mathematics is distinguished by a succession of gigantic discoveries—logarithms, analytic
and projective geometry, differential and integral calculus—which
the Renaissance mathematicians could no more than adumbrate.

It is sad to think that the immense efforts of Rhaeticus, Otho, and
Pitiscus were largely wasted, because their tables became useless in
1620. But they had enjoyed themselves and their achievement will
always deserve admiration.

ALGEBRA

Let us now turn to algebra, which was a much older discipline
than trigonometry. A complete historical outline would oblige us to
go back to Sumerian days.[10] Much work was done on the Babylonian-
Greek foundation by Jewish and Arabic algebraists, the greatest of
whom was the Persian poet, 'Umar al-Khayyām (XI-2), who classified
quadratic and cubic equations and managed to solve many of them.
The transmission of Arabic algebra was similar to that of trigonometry, in that it occurred through Latin and Hebrew channels
before the Arabic climax had been reached. The Arabic algebra
transmitted to the Latin West did not include 'Umar's discoveries.
The double introduction of pre-'Umarian algebra occurred in 1145,
which witnessed the Latin translation by Robert of Chester (XII-1)
of the treatise by al-Khwārizmī (IX-1) and the Latin translation by
Plato of Tivoli (XII-1) of the Hebrew treatise of Abraham bar
Ḥiyya (XII-1).

The first original Latin treatise on algebra was the *Liber abaci*

of Leonardo Fibonacci of Pisa (XIII-1) in 1202. After that, progress
was very slow; the next great step was made by Immanuel Bonfils
of Tarascon (XIV-2), then a greater one by the Frenchman, Nicolas
Chuquet, a Parisian, who flourished in Lyon, c.1484. In that year
and place he completed his treatise, *Le Triparty en la science des
nombres,* which included pregnant ideas, such as the comparison of
two progressions, arithmetic and geometric (germ of the logarithms);
a clearer understanding of equations and their roots, negative as
well as positive; the use of positive, negative, and null exponents,[11]
and some rules of the exponential calculus.[12] Unfortunately Chuquet's treatise remained unpublished until four centuries later.[13]
Even if it had been published, it would not have been understood.

The fact that Chuquet's *Triparty* remained unprinted, though
it appeared at a time when printing was already in full swing, is
significant of the lack of alertness of the early typographers in the
scientific domain.[14] In this case there was a remarkable aggravation.
Another Frenchman, Estienne de la Roche, dict Ville Franche, published *Larismetique & Geometrie,*[15] in which he named as his masters Chuquet and Pacioli, and it has been concluded that he incorporated the substance of their works in his own. This is true only
in a superficial way.

I have examined carefully the two editions (1520, 1538) in the
perfect copies preserved in the Harvard Library, but without attempting to compare the texts, except in a general way. Both are
divided into two parts. The first part, dealing with arithmetic, is
copied from the *Triparty,* sometimes literally; part two, dealing with
commercial arithmetic, is largely derived from Pacioli, but the end
of it (which might be called part three) considers geometric applications. Then follow, in the second edition only (1538), a large number of tables compiled by Gilles Huguetan of Lyon (one of the pub-
lishers of the book, Gilles et Jacques Huguetan frères). So far from
incorporating the substance of the *Triparty* in this book, La Roche
left out the significant novelties enumerated above.

Hence the exponential calculus made three false starts: in the
Algorismus proportionum of Nicole Oresme (before 1360), in the
Derek ḥilluq of Immanuel Bonfils (before 1377), and in the *Triparty*
of Chuquet (1484). These three works were published respectively
in 1868, 1936, and 1887. We may as well say that so far as the growth
of mathematics is concerned, they were not published at all, for

these late editions were of historical interest but had no value whatsoever for practical purposes.

In his pillage of the *Summa* of Luca Pacioli, Estienne de la Roche was more fortunate. Fra Luca de Borgo Sancti Sepulchri (as Pacioli was often called) was born in Tuscany. His *Summa de arithmetica geometria proportioni e proportionalita*[16] was a mathematical encyclopaedia. He could not complain of being pillaged by others, because he himself had borrowed shamelessly from earlier writers; some of the very best materials came from Leonardo da Pisa (XIII-1). The book was so comprehensive and clear and contained so many useful novelties (novel at least in printed form, such as double-entry bookkeeping and other methods of commercial arithmetic),[17] and it was distributed so well (in the best market, Venice) that it exerted a great influence on textbook writers throughout Latin Europe. In that respect we may consider it one of the outstanding books in mathematical history.

Let us return, however, to creative algebra and consider its main tradition, that of Italy, which can be summarized with the names of Scipione del Ferro, Tartaglia, Cardano, Ferrari, and Bombelli.

The first four of this quintet constituted the most singular team in the whole history of science. They illustrate the Italian Renaissance in its perversity as well as in its greatness. Their collective achievement was the solution of cubic and biquadratic equations, and implicitly a deeper understanding of equations in general. Before telling that story and introducing the persons involved, it is well to explain the extraordinary climate in which they worked. Mathematical interest had been greatly stimulated, especially in Italy, by the art of printing. Some 214 mathematical books were published in Italy between 1472 and 1500, a period of less than thirty years.[18] New mathematical needs were steadily growing in the shops, banking houses, workshops, mines, military and naval organizations, and universities; mathematical calculations had to be performed by merchants, contractors, public and private administrators, physicians, and above all by astrologers.

The revival of algebra, the higher mathematics of that time, was creating a kind of fever. It was then the custom for professors to challenge their colleagues to take part in public debates and discussions. If one of them discovered how to solve a kind of equation, say, $x^3 + ax = c$, he would be able to solve every problem leading to it; it was as if he had a secret key that opened many doors. But he would face a dilemma. Should he publish his discovery and be honored for it? That would be very fine, but he would lose the exclusive possession of his precious key. If he kept his secret in order to exploit it in public debates, he would earn another kind of fame and also money,[19] but his discovery might be repeated and published by one of his rivals.

Hence the actual disputation was as full of risks and surprises as a boxing match. Victory in any such contest called for many qualities: it was not enough to have sole possession of a key, one must be able to find the keyhole rapidly (that is, to recognize the adaptation of a problem to a given equation), and not least, one must be able to defend oneself in debate and to browbeat one's adversaries. In the Italian climate of the Renaissance, a good deal of eloquence and acting were mixed up with the arguments and the public disputations were often highly dramatic. Moreover, the men taking part in these disputes were often indelicate, petulant, brutal, and unscrupulous.[20] The disputations, or challenges, that revolved around the cubic equations are the best specimens of their kind; in fact, they are the only ones that are well documented.[21] The custom was continued for a long time, however (not only in Italy), but more quietly and with greater decorum. The latest example known to me dates from 1658,[22] but of course challenges are implicit in many scientific publications and always will be.

We may now tell briefly how the equations of the third and fourth degrees were gradually solved. Pacioli had remarked that the solution of these equations was as hopeless as the quadrature of the circle. Yet Scipione del Ferro (d. 1526), who was professor of mathematics at Bologna for thirty years, found (c.1505-15) a way of solving the equation (A) $x^3 + ax = b$, that is, a cubic without an x^2 term; he did not publish his solution but showed it to his favorite pupil, Antonio Maria Fiore, and later his papers were inherited by his son-in-law and successor, Annibale della Nave, who taught in Bologna until 1550. Neither Fiore nor Nave bothered to publish it.

On February 12/13, 1535 Niccolò Tartaglia of Brescia (c.1506-1559), having been challenged by Fiore, discovered a new solution of (A) and also a solution of the equation (B) $x^3 + ax^2 = c$, that is, a cubic without a term in x. He won the challenges ad hoc and was for a time the champion algebraist of Italy.[23] He refused to publish his method but was imprudent enough to communicate it as a secret to Geronimo Cardano (1501-76), who promised under oath not to reveal it but finally published it (with due credit, however, to Tartaglia) in the *Ars Magna*[24] (Nuremberg, 1545), the first great treatise devoted exclusively to algebra.

Cardano went much further than Tartaglia. He not only gave the solutions of equations (A) and (B) but showed how to reduce the general cubic to the form (A) by eliminating the term in x^2, and he enumerated thirteen forms of cubics having positive roots. It is interesting to recall that 'Umar Khayyām had also recognized thirteen forms of cubic equations.[25] Cardano admitted negative roots, though he called them fictitious (the positive roots being "real"), but he failed to recognize imaginary roots in spite of the fact that he would not disregard computations involving the square roots of negative numbers. Thus he discussed the irreducible case[26] and had an idea of the number of roots to be expected in a cubic; he also had some inkling of the relationships between the roots and the coefficients of an equation, for he found that the sum of the roots of a cubic equation is equal to the coefficient of x^2 with a minus sign (that is, if the coefficient of x^3 is one). This discovery is almost unbelievable when we remember that in those days equations were not written in the simple form used today; hence even easy deductions were difficult to make. Cardano was also able to solve a particular biquadratic equation and his pupil, Lodovico Ferrari of Bologna (1525-65), found a general solution.

In order to measure the achievements of these four men in little more than half a century, it will suffice to recall that they had reached the limit of the algebraic possibilities attainable with any kind of instrument, let alone with their wretched symbolism. Only equations of degrees 1 to 4 are susceptible of general solutions; those of degrees 1 and 2 were solved in antiquity, those of degrees 3 and 4 in the sixteenth century. Some optimists were inclined to think that equations of the fifth and even higher degrees could be solved in a general way; it would be very difficult, of course, but a general solution would eventually be found. It was finally realized that the solution of the quintic and higher equations was as impossible, to use Pacioli's comparison, as the quadrature of the circle, but it took a long time to establish that conclusion. The later illusion was destroyed before the ancient one. In 1826 the Norwegian mathema-

NICCOLÒ TARTAGLIA. Woodcut on the cover of his *Quesiti et inventioni* (264 pp., Venice: printed by Venturino Ruffinelli at the author's expense, 1546). *Courtesy of Harvard Library.* The same portrait occurs on the title page of *La prima parte del General Trattato di numeri e misure* (Venice: Curtio Troiano, 1556), reproduced in *Rara Arithmetica* (1908, p. 277), and in a later edition of the *Quesiti* (256 pp., Venice, 1554). There is another portrait of Tartaglia on the title page of his *Travagliata inventione* (Venice: Bascarini, 1551) and his *Ragionamenti* ad hoc (Venice: Bascarini, 1551).

tician, Niels Abel, proved rigorously that general algebraic equations of the fifth and higher degrees cannot be solved by radicals. In 1882 the German, Ferdinand Lindemann, proved that π is transcendental.[27]

TARTAGLIA AND CARDANO

Who were these mathematicians of the Renaissance? We have no time to get acquainted with all of them; let us draw a sketch of Tartaglia and a more elaborate one of Cardano.

Niccolò Tartaglia was born in Brescia (not very far from Milan) in 1506. His parents were too poor to provide for his education, and he was a self-taught mathematician. He did so well, however, that he became a professor of mathematics in Venice, where he died in 1559. His lack of education hardly mattered so far as mathematics was concerned, but it was manifest in his insufficient knowledge of Latin. He took part in many "challenges," and was boastful, quarrelsome, and jealous.

Geronimo Cardano, born in Milan in 1501, was a man of the same type, but more so. He belonged to a better family than Tartaglia, but was an illegitimate child; according to his own statement his arrival in this world was unwelcome, as his mother had tried to cause an abortion but had failed. His childhood was miserable, and at the age of 19 he left his tyrannical father[28] and went to study in Pavia and Padua. He obtained his M.D. at 25 but was not admitted to the College of Physicians in Milan because of his illegitimacy. The next seven years (1526-32), the happiest of his life, were spent in Sacco, near Padua, where he was a country doctor. He had time enough for studies, not only medical and mathematical but of every kind, for his curiosity was insatiable. His first important book was an elaborate treatise on theoretical arithmetic, *Practica arithmetice & Mensurandi singularis* (Milan, 1539). Arithmetical theory led him occasionally into algebra, and therefore this may be included among the early algebraical treatises. The book was so successful that it attracted the attention of the great Nuremberg printer, Johannes Petreius, who offered to publish his other books. His masterpiece, the *Ars Magna*, was published by Petreius in Nuremberg in 1545. As we have already seen, it was the major publication on the new algebra as it had developed in the middle of the sixteenth century.

His popular fame was based upon other books, such as those devoted to astrology or to moral subjects like his *De consolatione*

(Venice: H. Scotus, 1542)[29] and *De sapientia* (Nuremberg: Petreius, 1544),[30] or medical books, to which I shall come back in another chapter, but above all upon the *De subtilitate rerum* (Nuremberg: J. Petreius, 1550), which was a best-seller in many languages, and its continuation *De rerum varietate* (Basel, 1557). These two books are typical of Cardano's versatility and ingenuity. They explain physics and cosmology (a mixture of rational and practical ideas with occultism), describe various gadgets, etc. Their success was natural, for they provided the kind of pabulum of which the learned men of that time were fond, science but not too much of it, and tempered with a sufficient amount of nonsense and magic.

GERONIMO CARDANO, aet. c.38. Woodcut on the cover of the *Practica arithmetice* (Milan, 1539). *Courtesy of Harvard Library*. The following words are inscribed around the portrait: "Nemo propheta acceptus in patria."

By 1560 Cardano was recognized as the most illustrious mathematician, physicist, and physician of Europe; in medicine he was considered to be at least the equal of Vesalius. The Tarpeian rock is ever close to the Capitol, however. His elder son, Giambattista, a doctor in Pavia, murdered his wife and was executed in 1560. The father was disgraced and was obliged to resign his professorship in Pavia, but such was his prestige that two years later he was elected professor of medicine in Bologna. But his troubles were not over. His younger son, Aldo, turned out to be a scoundrel who went so far as to burglarize the paternal home in 1569.[31] The nadir of Cardano's misfortunes was reached in 1570, when he was accused of heresy,[32] arrested, and jailed. The treatment meted out to him was relatively lenient, but he lost his chair and was obliged to leave Bologna; he was forbidden to lecture or to publish books. He took refuge in Rome, where he was surprisingly well received by the College of Physicians and awarded a pension by Gregory XIII.

During these last years of retirement and meditation under the Pope's wing, he wrote the *De vita propria*,[33] one of the strangest autobiographies ever published, many fragments of which are almost unbelievable. One cannot help suspecting that Cardano's imagination colored his narrative; he had never been very trustworthy, and confessions written at the end of a life full of calamities cannot be believed without reservations. He died in Rome in 1576; we must be grateful to Gregory XIII for having eased the final years of the old man's tumultuous pilgrimage.[34]

One more remark anent Cardano's autobiography. In spite of his personal misfortunes he realized the privilege of having lived in an age full of marvelous novelties. The four main achievements, according to him, were the discovery and exploration of the world (the ancients knew but one-third of it), firearms and pyrotechnics, the compass, and printing.[35]

This sketch cannot describe all the extravagances of Cardano's life or the extraordinary scope of his activities. He left 138 printed books and 111 more in manuscript, in spite of having burned a good many. His books and manuscripts were bequeathed to his faithful pupil, Rodolfo Silvestri. Many of the manuscript works were published a century later in the magnificent *Opera omnia*.[36]

A few words about the other pupil, Lodovico Ferrari (1522-65), whose arrival in Cardano's household, in 1536, was considered by the latter as a blessing. And well it might, for it must have been difficult, even in those days, to find a servant who was also a mathematical collaborator! Lodovico, then 14, was a poor boy and his first duties were those of a servant, but he soon became a secretary and scientific assistant. Unfortunately the boy was as extravagant as his master, and ungovernable. He was successively a lecturer on mathematics, a tax assessor to the governor of Milan, and a secretary to the Cardinal of Mantua; eventually he became rich enough to retire in Bologna. He continued to help his old master in his many difficulties, but died prematurely before him. It is said that he was poisoned by his sister or by her lover. He gained renown by achieving a solution of the biquadratic equation, which was included in the *Ars magna* and still bears his name.

To return to the main hero of the cubic saga, Cardano. As we know him through Tartaglia's writings and his own, and above all through his autobiography, he was one of the most complex personalities who ever graced the human comedy. He disarms us by enumerating not only his own good qualities but also his bad ones. He is willing to confess to every vice, and one cannot help feeling that he is exaggerating them, and boasting even as he does when he speaks of his virtues, merits, and genius. He was vain, arrogant, crafty, treacherous, jealous and grudging, lascivious and obscene, lying, quarrelsome, greedy, vindictive, superstitious (we have all that information on his own authority); one is tempted to add, like Marot, "au demeurant, le meilleur fils du monde," for he was one of the greatest mathematicians of all time, and upon that he does not insist, at least not in his final confessions. Perhaps, as he looked back over his life, the *Ars magna* seemed less important than his other writings, chiefly the nonsensical ones, the mixtures of magic and astrology, with gadgetry and medicine, which the world had acclaimed.

The confessions of an old and broken man must be handled with caution; it must be added, however, that his confidences are sufficiently confirmed by other statements (his own, Tartaglia's, or others) to seem plausible. He did not shock his contemporaries as he would ours, because he was only an exaggerated specimen of a not uncommon type. The quarrels between mathematicians, physicians, and men of letters were frequent and sordid, and their spirit and their manners were very much alike. Many of them were ready to shout, "I know more than you do, I am better than you." Such conceit was common in the sixteenth century; it was aggravated by social calamities, such as the religious wars, plagues, and untold miseries, and by the almost universal belief in astrology, magic, and witchcraft. We can understand it because that spirit is not yet completely eradicated; a few men are living in our day who are vain enough to nourish such feelings, and a very few who are stupid enough to express them.

Leibniz, who flourished about a century and a half after Cardano, delivered a judgment which we may accept as final because of its weight and generosity. "Cardano was a great man with all his faults; without them, he would have been incomparable."[37]

Before leaving these mathematicians, whose behavior was so different from those with whom we are acquainted today, let us give a few other instances of their genius. Tartaglia's views on ballistics will be discussed in the following chapter. He wrote a *General trattato dei numeri*,[38] which is one of the outstanding books of the age. Vol. 1 (1556) is a very elaborate arithmetic; its many problems illustrate admirably the life of the people and the customs of merchants. The title page of that volume bears Tartaglia's portrait. He showed how to calculate the coefficients of a binomial development (when the exponent is a positive integer); in other words, he showed how to compute the exponents of $(a + b)^n$ knowing those of $(a + b)^{n-1}$. This is an excellent example of recondite knowledge that was many times discovered, lost, and rediscovered, until the matter was fully understood. 'Umar al-Khayyām (XI-1)[39] had a glimpse of it; then also Chu Shih-chieh (XIV-1),[40] who spoke of it as an ancient method and started the Japanese tradition as well as restarting the Chinese one.

In the sixteenth century the same empirical method reappeared many times under slightly different forms. The cosmographer, Petrus Apianus (1495-1552), showed it in the first edition of his German arithmetic, *Eyn Newe und wolgegründte Underweysung aller Kauffmannsz Rechnung* (Ingolstadt, 1527)—indeed, it is illustrated on the title page, which proved that he thought it of some importance. It appears again in the *Arithmetica integra* of Michael Stifel (Nuremberg, 1544), in the *De numeris et diversis rationibus* of Johann Scheubel (Leipzig, 1545), in the *General trattato* of Tartaglia (Venice, 1556), and finally in the *Traité du triangle arith-*

métique of Blaise Pascal (Paris, 1665).[41] This final publication introduced the method in mathematical literature, and many people believe that Pascal's triangle was an original discovery without antecedents. The discovery may have been original so far as Pascal was concerned, but it had moved capriciously from mind to mind; it had been "in the air" for centuries.

Among Cardano's treatises that were published posthumously is the *Liber de ludo aleae,* which deals with games of chance and may be called the first treatise on probability.[42] As games of chance are immemorial, it is not surprising that some inquisitive minds should ask questions about their hazards even as they did about fortune. Are any methods of divination valid for the game of life? And if so, could one not conceive methods of divination applying to games of chance? What is surprising is that the notion of probability, applied to gambling, occurred so late. The earliest mention of probability in world literature appeared c.1379 in the commentary on Dante's verse (*Purgatorio,* VI: i)—"Quando si parte il giuoco della zara"— by Benvenuto de' Rambaldi (XIV-2).

"When the game of zara ends," said Dante, "the loser is sad. . . ." Benvenuto's discussion of this was imperfect, but it was the first to be written down.[43] Cardano's treatise was considerably more, however; it was a gambler's handbook revealing one of the darkest corners of his experience. He was not only an inveterate gambler but also a professional one, knowing all the tricks of the trade and for a time living by them. He was acquainted with false dice and marked cards, and knew other methods of cheating, including those depending on legerdemain or fascination. What is more important, he discussed the first principle of probability and defined it as we do (the ratio of favorable cases to all cases). Instead of beginning the history of the calculus of probabilities about the middle of the seventeenth century with the Chevalier Georges de Méré and Fermat's correspondence with Pascal, we must now begin it with Cardano a century earlier.[44] Cardano's use of his main vice for scientific investigations is typical of the man. Being a physician, he claimed that gambling was a chronic disease which deserved to be studied like any other, but it was a disease that he loved.

In my account of cubic equations, I wrote them in the usual way for the reader's convenience, but the mathematicians of the sixteenth century did not use our system of notation. They had to write about mathematics in literary language or else use symbols that were fragmentary, arbitrary, and insufficient. Indeed, one of the great advances of the mathematical Renaissance was the creation of syncopated and later of symbolic algebra. Syncopated algebra formed a natural transition; instead of describing an equation by means of a long sentence, mathematicians learned to use some kind of shorthand. Gradually the shorthand gave way to symbols. This was a complicated evolution, a detailed account of which would be very long indeed.[45] We now realize that it would have been impossible to proceed faster, because clear symbols cannot be introduced ahead of clear ideas; it was only later, much later, when the necessity of symbols was well understood, that newer branches of mathematics could be published immediately with appropriate symbols, and even then the symbols required modification at least as often as the theory itself was modified.[46]

The history of mathematical symbols is extremely complex, because it began very early (in early Babylonian and Egyptian days), yet moved very slowly and capriciously. It is difficult to say when algebraical equations were written just as we write them now; the main efforts were made during the Renaissance, though the fruits thereof did not mature until later. Each symbol (say, $+$, $-$, $\times$, $:$, $=$, $\pm$, $>$, $<$, etc.) was introduced separately, one in Italy, another in Germany, a third in England. Seldom did one introduction suffice. Moreover, the significance of each symbol was not immediately and unambiguously clear. For example, $+$ might mean plus as we do now when we say the length of a stick is "10 feet plus" (it is somewhat more than 10 feet); or it might mean addition as in $a + b$, and it took a long time to understand that if b was a negative quantity it was still an addition. Finally, one had to explain how the symbols affected each other, to make sure that they were not ambiguous, and to ascertain whether the operations they represented were (or were not) associative, commutative, or transitive. When we examine a chronological series of algebras printed not only during the Renaissance but also during the seventeenth century and even later, we find nowhere the modern equation, but a series of equations each of which is (or is not) more modern than the preceding one. A fuller explanation would be exceedingly tedious; those who need it will find it in Cajori's indispensable book.

The first stage of Renaissance algebra, described above, was largely concerned with the solution of cubic and biquadratic equations and the adumbration of a general theory of equations. A longer history than mine would have introduced algebraists of many nations; nevertheless, it may be conceded that the protagonists were Italian. The new stage, covering the second half of the sixteenth century and the first years of the seventeenth, was astonishingly cosmopolitan, for the four protagonists belong to three nations: Ramus and Viète were Frenchmen, Bombelli an Italian, and Stevin a Fleming.

RAMUS

The oldest of these is the least important from the purely algebraic point of view, but he acquired a great European (and even American) fame in the following centuries as a logician, pedagogue, and philosopher as well as mathematician; his reputation was perhaps greater than he deserved, but it must be taken into account and respected. Pierre de la Ramée (1515-72), better known under his Latin name Ramus,[47] was born in Picardy, the scion of a noble but impoverished family of Burgundian origin. He studied at the College of Navarre in Paris, and the scholastic, Aristotelian teaching to which he was subjected aroused in him a violent reaction. We may note in passing that the most original scientific minds of the Renaissance developed the same kind of reaction and for the same reason. The healthy growth of genuine science implies not a ready-made system of knowledge, established on the basis of static authorities and buttressed with dialectics, but, on the contrary, something close to a *tabula rasa,* leaving abundant room for new observations of nature, experiments, and careful deductions. The history of sixteenth-century science (as opposed to learning) is to a large extent a history of growing anti-Aristotelianism, preparing gradually the post-Renaissance revolution to be accomplished by Bacon, Descartes, and Galileo.

At the time of his final examination, in 1536, the young iconoclast had the courage or the impudence to defend the thesis "Quaecumque ab Aristotele dicta essent, commenticia esse": (all the things that Aristotle said are wrong!) That was a bit strong, and one wonders how he got away with it. It is true that the judges could not appeal to Aristotle's authority without begging the question; yet they seem to have been almost incredibly tolerant. In spite of this ominous start, his

PETRUS RAMUS (1515-72). Portrait made shortly before his death at the age of 58. From a microfilm of the *Testamentum Petri Rami* (Paris: Jean Richer, 1576), which I owe to the courtesy of the Rev. Walter J. Ong, S.J., of St. Louis. A similar portrait exists in the Cabinet des Estampes, Bibliothèque Nationale, Paris. Both portraits were published posthumously but they are trustworthy.

career was, on the whole, very successful; he became a professor at the Collège Royal[48] and managed to publish a very large number of books.

He must have been a difficult person to live with, for he never hesitated to adopt a new doctrine if it seemed better to him, and to defend it in plain, not to say aggressive, terms.[49] Thus, in spite of the fact that his few protectors were Catholics, he became a Protestant. This sealed his fate at the time of the St. Bartholomew Massacre. It should be noted, however, that he was not murdered on the first night (August 24, 1572) but three days later when the worst was over. Many people hated him because of his non-conformism and perhaps because of his arrogance, and his murderers may have killed him to gratify private grudges.[50] On the other hand, it is certain that his martyrdom increased enormously his spiritual authority in Protestant countries.[51] His influence was not restricted to Protestant circles, however; many Catholics were exposed to it and accepted it with more or less reluctance. "Ramism" was a dominant philosophy or intellectual attitude in the seventeenth and eighteenth centuries; professors of philosophy in the Protestant universities of Germany were "Ramists" for a considerable time.[52]

Ramus has taken us far away from algebra, but before returning to it we must say a few words about his work in general. Four of his books were dedicated to his main patron, Charles de Lorraine, Cardinal de Guise (1525-74), and one to Catherine de' Medici (1567). His *Aristotelicae animadversiones* in twenty books was first printed in Paris in 1543 and many times afterward. Many of his books are devoted to dialectics, grammar (Latin, Greek, and French), commentaries on Cicero, Virgil, and Quintilian, and translations of Aristotle's *Politics,* Euclid's *Elements,* and Plato's *Epistles.* His first mathematical book was an *Arithmetica* dedicated to Cardinal Charles de Lorraine (Paris, 1555), often reprinted. He published another *Arithmetica* together with a *Geometria* in Basel in 1569; later editions of it reproduced the original text. Other mathematical books contained the arithmetic alone, or arithmetic with geometry, or arithmetic with algebra (all in Latin), and some added explanations by Lazarus Schoner or Rudolph Snel. A more ambitious work was the *Prooemium mathematicum ad Catherinam Mediceam, reginam, matrem regis*[53] (introduction to mathematics, dedicated to Queen Catherine de' Medici, mother of the king) (Paris, 1567); a French version of it was published in the same year. This was considerably expanded under a new title, *Scholarum mathematicarum libri unus et triginta*[54] (thirty-one books of mathematical teaching) (Basel, 1569).

As regards the solution of cubic equations, Ramus had the idea of bringing that "new" problem close to the ancient ones of the duplication of the cube and the trisection of the angle;[55] he concluded that the first of these ancient problems implied the solution of all cubics in which the radical in Tartaglia's formula is real, but the latter included only those leading to the irreducible case.[56] This gives us a higher notion of his merit than the mass of textbooks bearing his name. Nevertheless one cannot help feeling that his influence was largely that of a prominent teacher and fertile writer,[57] rather than of a creative thinker.

RAFAEL BOMBELLI

The last of the sixteenth-century Italian mathematicians to investigate the cubic and biquadratic equations, Bombelli, was as quiet a man as his predecessors were wild and excitable.

We know very little about Rafael Bombelli, not even the dates and places of his birth and death, but he called himself "cittadino Bolognese." A noble family of that name flourished in Bologna in the first half of the thirteenth century, was exiled for Ghibellinism[58] at the end of it, and did not return until the beginning of the sixteenth century. Bombelli, a scion of that family, may have been born in Bologna at the beginning of the sixteenth century; he was certainly educated there. He studied mathematics and hydraulic engineering at the University of Bologna and was employed by Mgr. Alessandro Rufini, bishop of Melfi, to drain marshes in Tuscany. When that work was interrupted, he devoted his time to mathematics and produced one of the most original works of the century, bearing the curious title *L'Algebra . . . divisa in tre libri con la quale ciascuno da sè potra venire in perfetta cognitione della teoria dell'Aritmetica* (algebra . . . divided into three books, thanks to which anybody will be able to obtain by himself a perfect knowledge of the theory of arithmetic) (Bologna: G. Rossi, 1572).[59] The title shows that the respective meanings of algebra and arithmetic were not yet properly defined. The purpose of his *Algebra,* indeed, was to explain the principles of arithmetic, algebra being conceived as a kind of higher arithmetic. In a sense this was not incorrect, but it was misleading.

The book represented the climax of the efforts described above, all of which had been accomplished in nothern Italy (Bologna, Padua, Milan). It was fitting that the final treatise should be written by a son of Bologna. The most significant among many noteworthy items was his discussion of cubic and biquadratic equations, which was clearer and more methodical than those of his predecessors, and his notations were a definite improvement. Following the German, Michael Stifel (1487-1567), who was himself standing upon Cardano's shoulders, he invented a relatively simple way of writing equations. He was the first to use continued fractions systematically—for example, to extract square roots.

He proved the reality of the three roots of a cubic when the application of the Tartaglia-Cardano rule led to the "irreducible case" involving imaginaries. His solution of cubic (and biquadratic) equations was so well ordered that Leibniz selected his treatise for their study and considered him an outstanding mathematician ("egregium certe artis analyticae magistrum"); Huygens meant to praise Leibniz highly when he wrote him, "Vous avez plus fait que Bombelli. . . ."[60]

Bombelli composed his treatise on algebra about the middle of the century. Then he started to rewrite it for publication in two volumes. This took him considerably longer than he had foreseen. For example, having found a Greek manuscript of Diophantos in the Vatican, he and a friend, Antonio Pazzi, translated it (five books out of seven), and this new material was introduced into his text. The treatise printed in 1572 contained three books; books I and II are the same as in the Ms. of c.1550, but book III, as printed, included 143 Diophantine problems. At the end of book II Bombelli announced the publication of the second volume to be devoted to geometry. It is probable that he died not long after 1572.

The Ms. of the whole work remained unknown in the Biblioteca dell' Archiginnasio in Bologna until it was discovered some twenty-five years ago, and edited and published by Ettore Bortolotti.[61] This resurrection of Bombelli's work in our own day increased his prestige considerably. In book IV Bombelli discussed problems of linear algebra, the geometrical representation of irrationals, and the geometrical construction of algebraical problems; in book V he dealt with problems of plane geometry, regular and semi-regular polyhedra, the representation of powers by segments, and the consideration of negative segments and even of negative areas. In short, Bombelli was not less original as a geometer than as an algebraist. Bortolotti goes so far as to say that his geometry marks the separation between the geometrical algebra of the ancients and modern analytical geometry.[62]

There were various other algebraists (and trigonometrists) in those days, not only in Italy but also in France, England, Germany, and the Netherlands. We shall speak only of two, who were perhaps the greatest of all, the Frenchman Viète and the Fleming Stevin.

FRANÇOIS VIETE

It is clear that Tartaglia, Cardano, and Ferrari were not "gentlemen"; their French contemporary, Viète, was one, and rather a solemn one. François Viète (Vieta in Latin) was born at Fontenay-le-Comte (Poitou, Vendée) in 1540 and died in Paris in his sixty-third year.[63] He was trained as a lawyer and became a member of the Parlement de Bretagne,[64] that is, a high magistrate. This very honorable function left him plenty of time for a hobby and his hobby was mathematics. He was thus an "amateur" mathematician, one of the greatest;[65] so far as essentials are concerned that does not matter, but the amateur is often a better man than the professional and more deeply devoted to his self-chosen task.

Viète did for algebra in France what Bombelli did in Italy but did it better and on a larger scale. He was also more of a humanist than his Italian colleagues. Bombelli wrote in Italian, the implication being that he could not write in Latin; on the contrary, Viète was a very good Latin scholar, conscious of his scholarship and a little pedantic. He coined many new terms of Greek derivation.[66] It was a great privilege for him to be able to exercise his genius in two fields, trigonometry and algebra, which were then in a critical stage, just before maturity. He compiled trigonometrical tables and wrote a good many mathematical tracts, the bibliography of which is exceedingly difficult. Since Viète was a man of means and a patrician, as indifferent to publicity as Cardano was eager for it, his many books were issued privately in Tours or Paris, in very small editions which he distributed to his friends.[67]

Viète was more of an inventor than a teacher. He did not try to explain his ideas very well; maybe he could not, but I suspect that in many cases he preferred to be esoteric and obscure. Most of his works were published in the last quarter of the sixteenth century, but their rarity and obscurity diminished their influence. Viète's genius did not appear in full light until it was explained by his secretaries, Pierre Aleaume of Orléans and Nathaniel Torporley (1602) and by commentators, such as the Frenchman I. L. de Vau-Lézard (1630), the Scots James Hume (1636) and Alexander Anderson (1615), and above all the Dutchman Frans Van Schooten, who published *Vietae Opera Mathematica* (Leiden: Elzevir, 1646). This single folio, which he edited with the help of Marin Mersenne and Jacobus Golius, contains sixteen treatises, that is, everything of importance except the trigonometrical tables. Note that Viète's editors and interpreters belonged to four different nations, and there were probably others in other countries.

Viète's first important publication was his *Canon mathematicus* (Paris, 1579), trigonometrical tables which contained so many errors that he destroyed every copy he could lay hand upon; needless to say, that book is exceedingly rare, and its reimpression in 1609 is also very rare.[68] In these tables Viète abandoned sexagesimal fractions and replaced them by decimal fractions, the fractional part being printed in smaller type than the integral and separated from the latter by a vertical stroke.[69] We shall come back to this presently apropos of Stevin. Most of his books appeared in the last decade of the century.[70] The *Effectionum geometricarum canonica recensio* (1593) treats of algebraic geometry, solutions with ruler and compass, leaving cubic equations out. In a supplement to this work (*Supplementum geometriae*, 1593) he shows that every cubic equation can be solved by the determination of two mean proportionals or the trisection of an angle (see Ramus above). This was equally true of a biquadratic equation, because he had shown in the *De aequationum recognitione* that every biquadratic can be reduced to a cubic. In *Variorum de rebus mathematicis responsorum liber VIII*[71] (Tours, 1593) he discusses the angle of contingence, which is not a tangible angle but a vanishing one (he calls it "cornicularis, ceratoeides").

The pamphlet entitled *Pseudomesolabum et alia quaedam adiuncta capitula* (1596) was written to refute an unnamed adversary (Joseph Scaliger),[72] who thought he had solved the quadrature of the circle and nourished other mathematical fancies. In it Viète shows that

$$\sqrt[3]{2} = \sec 37° 30'$$

(sec 37° 28′ would be a better approximation; Viète was a prodigious analyst but not a good computer).

His most important geometrical work was the *Apollonius Gallus* (1600), which deserves a longer explanation. A great Belgian mathematician, Adrianus Romanus[73] of Louvain, issued, in 1593, a challenge to his colleagues all over the world to solve an equation of the 45th degree. Henri IV called upon his mathematician, Viète, who in a very short time found a way to reduce that awesome problem to a simpler one, and solved it! Using trigonometrical methods, he found not only one root but twenty-three; he could not find the others because they involved negative sines, which were meaningless to him.[74] In his turn, in the *Apollonius Gallus,* he challenged Adrianus to solve another problem, namely, to draw a circle tangent to three given circles. Adrianus proved his own mastery with an elegant solution by means of two hyperbolas; but the solution could not be constructed with ruler and compass, and Viète replaced it with a better one.[75]

Adrianus, being a generous man and not a jealous one like Tartaglia, was so impressed by Viète's genius that he left Louvain and traveled to France to express his admiration and improve their acquaintance. Upon his arrival in Paris he found that Viète was in Poitou, and journeyed all the way there to meet him. They spent a month together.[76]

Viète's fame among mathematicians was much increased by his astounding answer to Adrianus' challenge; but his popular fame had been well established before that, under Henri III, by a challenge of a very different kind. Philip II of Spain used to send secret messages to his armies in the Low Countries; many of these were intercepted but the code was so difficult that nobody could read them.[77] Since Viète was employed as a royal councilor by Henri III, the king submitted the matter to him. The interpretation of a secret code is a mathematical problem that must have appealed to Viète's imagination; he was not long in finding the key and all the Spanish messages were decoded, read, and acted upon. According to De Thou, the Spaniards could not believe that their secret had been disclosed in a rational way and scattered the rumor in Rome and elsewhere that Henri III had been helped by magical means.

Viète is often cited as a pioneer in that field which is of so much value to military intelligence and to secret services in general. This is an exaggeration. The struggle between cipherers and decipherers is almost as old as the struggle between arms and armor. People have always tried to write secret messages when openness was dangerous, and their enemies have tried equally hard to discover their true meaning. At the beginning, the means of concealment were very simple; the cryptographic art improved gradually and the methods of decipherment were improved in proportion. There were at least two authors of cryptographic treatises before the Renaissance, the Italian Leon Battista Alberti (1404-72) and the German Johannes Trithemius (1462-1516); a more elaborate work, the *Traicté des chiffres* by Blaise de Vigenère (Paris, 1586), appeared in Viète's own time and must have caused much talk and speculation. Trithemius' *Polygraphia,* first published in Oppenheim in 1518, was often reprinted and a French version of it was published in Paris in 1561.[78] We may be sure that Viète was acquainted wih Trithemius and Vigenère, but his mathematical genius made it relatively easy for him to lift the cryptographic art to a much higher level.

There has been some discussion of Viète's religion. He was undoubtedly a Catholic, but like his contemporaries, Montaigne and De Thou, he realized that in the civil wars the evils were evenly divided. It would be too much to say that these men had Protestant leanings, but they could understand the Protestant point of view with a certain amount of sympathy. His main patron was a Vendeian lady, Catherine de Parthenay,[79] to whom some of his books were dedicated.[80] She was an ardent Protestant leader; her first husband was one of the heroes and martyrs of the St. Bartholomew massacre (1572), and later she withdrew to La Rochelle and was the very soul of its resistance in 1627-28.

Without attempting an analysis of his several works, we shall now indicate Viète's main mathematical contributions. We might begin with trigonometry, which was perhaps his first passion. He compiled elaborate tables. He knew the formulas expressing $\sin nx$ and $\cos nx$ in function of $\sin x$ and $\cos x$. The notion of polar triangles adumbrated by Naṣīr al-dīn al-Ṭūsī (XIII-2) was explained by him and made full use of (1593).[81]

His main contribution to algebra was the explanation of what he called *"logistica speciosa"*[82] (vs. *logistica numerosa*), that is, the use of letters for known as well as for unknown quantities. This introduced two advantages: first, greater generality, and second, preservation of the elements of the calculus, which in the case of numbers would disappear in the totals. He had some knowledge of the relations between the coefficients and roots of an equation; he knew how to increase, decrease, multiply, and divide the roots of an equation by a given quantity, and how to eliminate the power $(n - 1)$ in an equation of the nth degree. His rejection of negative roots (not to mention imaginary ones) made it impossible for him, however, to formulate a general theory of equations.

This particular error was corrected by Albert Girard of Lorraine (1590?-1633?) in his *Invention nouvelle en l'algèbre* (Amsterdam, 1629), and the theory of equations was formulated by the Englishman Thomas Harriot (1560-1621), whose *Artis analyticae praxis* appeared only in 1631 (London). Harriot and Girard were younger contemporaries of Viète and published their treatises at a time when Viète's views had been clarified by his interpreters;[83] moreover, Harriot enjoyed the assistance of Nathaniel Torporley, who had been Viète's secretary. Harriot and Girard have taken us beyond the sixteenth century, yet their works might be considered not improperly as delayed fruits of the Renaissance.

Another merit of Viète's work must not be forgotten. He expressed π in the form of an infinite series

$$2/\pi = \cos 90°/2 \cdot \cos 90°/4 \cdot \cos 90°/8 \cdots$$

$$= \sqrt{\tfrac{1}{2}} \cdot \sqrt{(\tfrac{1}{2} + \tfrac{1}{2}\sqrt{2})} \cdot \sqrt{[\tfrac{1}{2} + \tfrac{1}{2}(\sqrt{\tfrac{1}{2}} + \tfrac{1}{2}\sqrt{\tfrac{1}{2}})]} \cdots .$$

This was the first infinite series in literature and Viète was lucky; it was convergent.

Viète was one of the greatest mathematicians of the Renaissance, certainly the greatest in France. Huygens counted him as one of his three masters, the two others being Galileo and Descartes, but we have seen that he also admired Cardano and Bombelli, and this reminds us that the statement sometimes made by French historians of science, that Viète was the creator of algebraic symbolism and of the new algebra, is certainly untrue. He prepared the way for Descartes and hastened the standardization of algebra and trigonometry, but many others were doing the same thing in different ways. The creation of the new algebra was a very complex business implying the conscious or unconscious collaboration of mathematicians of many countries. A detailed analysis would show that of the many sixteenth-century algebraists, some were superior in one respect, others in another.

It has been claimed by Joseph Bertrand[84] that Viète was a geometer rather than an algebraist; the letters that he introduced in his arguments represented lines and the homogeneity that he imposed on his equations was due to his considering each of them as a geometrical problem. He applied geometry to algebra in the Greek style rather than algebra to geometry. His main algebraic discoveries were obtained by trigonometrical means. There is much truth in this. Viète had revealed himself as a new Apollonios. Yet according to his own statements, and to the titles of most of his books, he considered himself primarily an analyst or algebraist. He was ready to use any approach, geometrical or trigonometrical, that was promising, but his main purpose was the solution of equations.

The general solution of equations below the quintic was one of the greatest achievements of the sixteenth century; it was a collective achievement of international (west European) scope. Its international nature will be illustrated once more in a final section devoted to the Fleming Stevin.

SIMON STEVIN

Simon Stevin was born eight years later than Viète and lived nine years longer; hence his life projected further into the seventeenth century than Viète's, but his main work was done in the sixteenth century. He was born in Bruges in 1548 and was active for a time in Antwerp as cashier and bookkeeper; later he was employed in the financial service of his native country. It is rare in any age to find a man entering the mathematical field by way of accountancy. After 1571 he traveled in Prussia, Poland, and Scandinavia, and finally established himself in the northern part of the Netherlands, which had already shaken off Spanish domination and the Catholic Inquisition. In 1581 we find him in Leiden, and in 1583 he was matriculated as a student of the university in that city. That was rather late to begin, but he was very well prepared and went fast. A few years later he was already teaching mathematics at the University of Leiden, and in 1593, upon the recommendation of Prince Maurice of Nassau, who had been one of his pupils, he was appointed by the States General as "castrametator," i.e., quartermaster

general of the Dutch armies, a very high position which he held
until his death. In 1600 he helped to organize mathematical teaching at the engineering school of Leiden, and later Maurice of
Nassau appointed him as a member of his council and superintendent of the financial administration.

Stevin's duties were wider than his title of castrametator would
suggest. He was the mathematical, technical, and financial adviser
of the Prince of Nassau and of the Dutch government. It has been
suggested that Stevin had become a Protestant and for this reason
established himself in Holland and not in his native country. That
is possible but cannot be proved. It is certain that one could be a
good Catholic and yet hate the methods of the Inquisition, the
intolerance and religious fanaticism that the Spaniards had introduced into Belgium; it is probable that Stevin spent the best part of
his life in Holland because he preferred to be in a free country than
to live under foreign domination at the mercy of informers and
inquisitors.

Stevin's interest in financial matters was natural enough considering the experience of his youth. His first publication was a table
for the computation of compound interest (in Dutch, Antwerp,
1582). This was not the first table of its kind; Stevin himself recognized as the inventor Jean Trenchant (Lyon, 1558),[85] but Trenchant's
table was much less elaborate than Stevin's, which covered ninety-two
pages. We may say that Stevin's were the first printed tables sufficiently expanded to be of use to bankers, merchants, or administrators; of course, such tables were so necessary to business men that
they must have existed in manuscript form. The nonexistence or
extreme rarity of such manuscripts in our libraries is easy to explain;
they were used so much that they were torn to pieces or became so
dirty as not to be worth keeping.

Stevin deserves credit for two other innovations. He insisted on
the separation of princely or government accounts from personal
ones, and on the application of the Italian method—double-entry
bookkeeping—to both (1608). He worked out these ideas in great
detail and recommended their adoption to Prince Maurice and also
to Henri IV's minister, Sully.[86]

His algebraical ideas might be dismissed rapidly with the statement that they were variations on a sixteenth-century theme, comparable to those of Stifel, Cardano, Viète, and others, but some items

are so original that they require mention, however brief. He advanced the general theory of equations by remarking that signs could be attached to numbers [$a + (-b)$ is the same as $a - b$] and that though some terms of an equation are missing, it may be still considered complete. He suggested that it was better to treat equations in a purely algebraical way, free from geometrical considerations (1585). Negative roots, which had perplexed so many mathematicians, may be considered as the positive roots of another equation obtained by the substitution of ($-x$) for x. Hence every equation of the second degree whose roots are real has two roots (1585).

He gave rules for the solution of numerical equations of any degree. Given the equation $f(x) = 0$, if $f(a) > 0$ and $f(b) < 0$ there is at least one root between a and b. He showed how the decimals of a root can be obtained by successive approximations, but remarked that in some cases the true value cannot be reached though one can obtain as many decimals of it as one may wish and come indefinitely near to it (1594).

I have enumerated those important ideas somewhat hastily because I am anxious to speak of Stevin's greatest mathematical achievement: his ability to introduce simplifying conventions. For example, every equation is complete, if we simply assume that some of its coefficients are null; a subtraction is simply the addition of a negative number, a division is multiplication by a reciprocal. Thus does a man of genius brush away difficulties.

His greatest triumph in that line was his vindication of decimal fractions in 1585.[87] It is difficult to imagine today that decimal numbers and the decimal calculus were practically unknown before that time, in spite of the fact that all the integers were built on a decimal basis. The belatedness of that discovery, to wit, that numbers of the form $a10^n$ should be written in the same style irrespective of whether n is positive or negative, is the more astounding in that the early Sumerians had already made a similar discovery with regard to sexagesimal fractions.[88] Our ancestors accepted these fractions (they are still with us) but not the far more important idea of a numeral system in which integers and fractions were dealt with in the same way. Until the end of the Renaissance[89] the only fractions in general use were plain fractions like 3/5 or 87/141,[90] sexagesimal fractions (these were the most frequent),[91] and the duodecimal fractions implied in Roman metrology and money. The pound (*libra*) was divided into twelve ounces (*unciae*); we still have them! The monetary unit, the *as*, was also divided into twelve fractions. These duodecimal fractions were not used much, however, because special names were given to each fraction of the *libra* and of the *as* and one used those names. One did not speak of 1/12, 2/12, 3/12, 4/12, etc., but of *uncia, sextans, quadrans, triens, quincunx, semis, septunx, bes, dodrans, dextans,* and *deunx*.[92]

Though everybody was using decimal integers and no others, it did not occur to anybody to think of decimal fractions! Viète, it is true, used decimal fractions in his *Canon* of 1579, and even asserted their superiority over sexagesimals, but Stevin was the first to explain the matter clearly and fully; and by extending decimalization to weights, measures, and money, he gave to decimals their fullest meaning and utility.

With the simple-mindedness of true genius Stevin was the first to understand that if decimal fractions, measures, and coins were used together with decimal integers, not only would fractions be considerably easier, but one might forget them. If you don't like 1.52 meters, just say 152 centimeters; if you don't like 19.65 francs, just say 1,965 centimes. The fractions have vanished.[93] If you have to add, subtract, multiply, or divide decimal numbers, treat them as if they were integers and in the end move the decimal point to its new position. That is all. Stevin's genius is even more obvious if we reflect that what he understood so well in 1585 is not yet understood in 1956 by a number of presumably intelligent people.

Stevin's notations were not as fortunate as his ideas. For example, what we would write very simply 8.937 he wrote 8(0) 9(1) 3(2) 7(3),[94] which was rather cumbersome, the more so because it caused some ambiguity between his algebraic and his decimal symbols. It is possible that he wanted the ambiguity, for he considered his decimal notation as an exponential one. To return to the same number, his notation meant $8(1/10)^0 \cdot 9(1/10)^1 \cdot 3(1/10)^2 \cdot 7(1/10)^3$; it is strange that when he had gone so far it did not occur to him that the notation 8.937 was much simpler and clearer. This is an excellent illustration of a not uncommon occurrence; a man of genius makes a great discovery but stops short of the last step which would crown it. In this respect, Viète was ahead of him; his notation, 8/937, was much simpler, but his ideas lacked vigor and remained undeveloped.

This suggests a final comparison between these two giants, Viète and Stevin. The first belonged to the gentry; his education was the best obtainable in those days, and he became an ornament of the *"noblesse de robe"* (the gentleman of the robe, the magistrates). The latter's origin was much humbler and his early education was sufficient only to make of him a cashier, a clerk; he was intelligent, however, and ambitious and entered Leiden University at the age of 35. In mathematics, they were both self-taught explorers of the unknown. Viète was aristocratic and pedantic; he was more anxious to exhibit the depth of his thoughts than to make them accessible to others. His favorite language was Latin with plenty of Greek or difficult terms. Stevin, an engineer and a practical man, was eager to explain his views; his favorite language was his native Dutch. He was not afraid of declaring that Dutch was the best language for scientific purposes, superior in that respect to Greek and Latin.[95] Such illusions are common enough. Every man is tempted to fancy that his language is the best; it certainly is the best for him, because it is the one of which he can make the cleverest use. Yet it took some courage, as well as originality, to make such a declaration. Viète, Ramus, and other scholars of the same ilk were often pompous and pedantic, and what is much worse, their imagination was restrained by decorum and conformity. Neither of them would have dared to write such a treatise as Stevin's *Disme* (*Tithe*) of 1585; it was too simple. It had the simplicity of natural and untrammeled genius.

There is an immense contrast between the mathematical and the geographical triumphs of the Renaissance. The motives of the early navigators, explorers, and conquistadores were mixed, as all human motives are, but in them base motives were stronger than noble ones. Some of them might think of increasing geographical knowledge, but most were dreaming of material conquest, of wealth and power. The mixture of motives is nowhere more shocking than in the field of religion. The early Portuguese and Spanish navigators and their patrons were inflamed with the holy desire to extend the realm of Christianity; they felt themselves to be crusaders and missionaries fighting for Christ's sake. Yet they found it perfectly natural to hunt down the natives like wild animals, to rob them and rape their women; sometimes they would baptize them as Christians and then enslave them. Such a mixture of good and evil is intolerable, but the most astounding part of it is that the majority of the colonizing nations were unaware of it. They thought that all was well, that their rulers were Christian kings, their conquistadores heroes of the purest kind; those who died during the perpetration of their crimes were considered martyrs. The Renaissance was the beginning of the (modern) colonial age. The peoples of the Hispanic peninsula showed the way and their example was followed by the other civilized and Christian nations.

The mathematicians were not angels or saints—some of them were rascals—but at least they did not try to murder, exploit, or enslave their fellowmen. Their transgressions were petty, while their fundamental purpose was noble and holy. Their conquests were spiritual ones, conquests of pure reason, the scope of which was infinite.

ASTRONOMY

The main astronomical event of the Renaissance was the publication in 1543 of Copernicus' treatise *De revolutionibus orbium coelestium*. This is indeed one of the outstanding landmarks in the whole history of science. Copernicus did not come unheralded out of the blue; he had been foreshadowed more than eighteen centuries before by two Greeks, Heracleides of Pontos (IV-2 B.C.) and Aristarchos of Samos (III-1 B.C.) But their wise prophecies were disregarded by other Greeks, Hipparchos of Nicaia (II-2 B.C.) and Ptolemy (II-1), whose theories were built upon a better mathematical foundation. The Ptolemaic conception of the universe, with the earth standing still at the center of the world, was the orthodox theory from, say, 150 to 1543, with the following qualification. As many astronomers, especially Arabs, multiplied and improved their observations and prepared better tables, there were growing discrepancies between the calculated and the observed positions of the stars and planets. It was clear that Ptolemaic astronomy needed correction. This suggested that the theory of epicycles and eccentrics which Ptolemy had used should be replaced by the older theory of homocentric spheres sponsored by Aristotle. During the Middle Ages, especially in the twelfth century and later, there was an almost continuous tussle between the Ptolemaists pure and simple, on the one hand, and the Aristotelians on the other.[96]

New cosmological ideas were nursed by philosophers, e.g. Nicholas of Cusa, who were trying to compromise. The earth cannot be in the center, because the universe is infinite and infinity has no center; the earth is a star made of the same substance as the others and having motions of its own. It has been claimed that Cusanus was a forerunner of Copernicus;[97] this is very misleading, but one might perhaps call him a forerunner of Giordano Bruno. Fortunately he was more prudent than Bruno and the Church less impatient then than it was later. Leonardo da Vinci seems to have nourished ideas of the same kind, but he hardly expressed them. Copernicus could have had no knowledge of Leonardo's meditations; he may have been aware of Cusanus' views, but the main sources of his theory were the early Greek writings and the observations made by himself and by many other astronomers of his own age.

COPERNICUS

The algebraic discoveries related above took place in western Europe and especially in France and Lombardy. Copernicus lived in another world, central Europe.

Nicolas Copernicus[98] was born February 19, 1473 in Thorn on the Vistula, half way between Danzig and Warsaw. His father died early, but Nicolas was tutored and protected by an uncle, Lucas Watzelrode (1447-1512), who eventually became bishop of Ermeland.[99] Lucas, who had been educated in Italy recognized his nephew's intelligence and promoted his education. Nicolas spent four years (1491-94) at the University of Cracow, and later four years (1496-1500) in Bologna. During his absence his powerful uncle managed to have him appointed a canon[100] of the Frauenburg cathedral. In 1500 Nicolas gave mathematical lectures in Rome and the following year he returned to Ermeland. His stay at home was short; its main purpose was probably a reassessment by uncle and nephew of the work done and to be done. Nicolas was sent back to Italy and completed his studies in Padua and Ferrara; in the latter city he obtained his doctorate in canon law (1503). In 1506 he was back in Ermeland, never to leave it again. The bishop, his bene-factor, required his presence, for Nicolas was his physician as well as his main assistant in the government of the diocese.[101] Therefore Nicolas remained in Heilsberg, the bishop's see, until the latter died in 1512; then he returned to Frauenburg and remained there until his own death in 1543.[102]

COPERNICUS (1473-1543). An early portrait of him is represented with small variations in various woodcuts. In the three with which I am acquainted Copernicus
holds a lily of the valley in one hand. A copy of this engraving is preserved in the
Czartoryski Museum, Cracow (other versions in the Jagellonian Library, Cracow,
and in the Bartynowski Collection, Cracow). Discussion of Copernicus iconography
by Ernst Zinner, *Entstehung und Ausbreitung der Coppernicanischen Lehre*
(Erlangen, 1943; reviewed in *Isis*, 35: 61; 36: 261-66), pp. 455-84. The portrait
here reproduced belongs to Zinner's type IV.

The main periods of his life may be summarized as follows:

1491-94   University of Cracow
1496-1500   University of Bologna
1501-05   Padua, Ferrara
1506-12   Heilsberg
1512-43   Frauenburg

It was his fate to be born, live, and die in a disputed territory—
the eastern march of Germany or the western march of Poland.[103]
Hence he was called a German or a Pole as conditions might require.
Primarily he was neither a Pole nor a German, but a Catholic, and
his best language was Latin. Moreover, however good the education he had received in Cracow before his twenty-first year, he
obtained his main education in Italy, where he spent the ten most
impressionable years of his life (1496-1505, aet. 23-32).

Copernicus' first alma mater, the University of Cracow, was not
a new institution; it dated back to 1364, though it became important
only in 1397.[104] At the time when Copernicus was a student the
principal teacher of mathematics was Albert Brudzewski (1445-95),
but there were various others, enough for discussion and stimulation.

Among the Italian teachers the one who influenced him most was
Domenico Maria da Novara (1454-1504), a practical astronomer and
a keen critic of astronomical theory. Under the direction of these
men, Copernicus read all the standard astronomical books then
available. In Cracow he had already studied the *Alphonsine Tables*
(XIII-2), the *Tabulae directionum* of Regiomontanus,[105] and the
Epitome in Almagestum begun by Georg von Peurbach and completed by Regiomontanus (Venice, 1496). He knew the version of the
Almagest translated from Arabic into Latin by Gerard of Cremona
(Venice, 1515), and had the pleasure of holding in his hands shortly
before his death the first edition of the Greek text (Basel, 1538).[106]

Copernicus was essentially a man of one great book, the publication of which marked the culmination as well as the end of his life.

The astronomical teaching that he had received at the University
of Cracow under Albert Brudzewski and others was as good as was
available anywhere. He became familiar not only with books but
with instruments and their use. We may be sure that he was already
dissatisfied with the orthodox views before he left his native country,
for no intelligent man could study astronomy without becoming

aware of their shortcomings and of the contradictions to which they led. His education was completed and his doubts amply confirmed in Bologna. His own ideas were matured after his return home, probably in Heilsberg (1506-12), and received their final development in Frauenburg, where he could probably devote more time to his vocation.

It is not necessary to explain the details of the Copernican reformation. It was a revival of the old Aristarchian ideas, with which he was familiar, strengthened by the empirical knowledge that had accumulated in the meantime and by the observations of his teachers and himself.[107] The sun is the center of the solar system; the earth is a planet like the others; all the planets move in circles, or more exactly in epicycles (circles whose centers move along other circles); the moon moves on an epicycle that is itself moving on another epicycle. His ideas were revolutionary in that they placed the sun instead of the earth in the center, but they were conservative in that he preserved the circular motions. He was not enough of a mathematician to think of something better than eccentrics and epicycles. One might suppose from his language that he believed in the physical reality of the "spheres" that were said to carry the planets, but this is misleading; he merely wanted to explain the epicycles as clearly as possible, and he could not have believed in the material existence of these "spheres" any more than did the Greek astronomers.[108]

Another essential part of the Copernican doctrine was the daily rotation of the earth around a central axis instead of the almost inconceivable rotation of the fixed stars around the same axis.[109]

The first exposition of his views was written[110] under the title *Commentariolus;* it was not printed but a few copies were sent to his friends.[111] It was a non-technical account that promoted the writing of his great treatise in at least two ways. In the first place, it attracted the attention of Clement VII (Giulio de' Medici, Pope 1523-34); and in 1536 Nicolas Schönberg, cardinal of Capua, wrote a letter to Copernicus encouraging him to complete his task (this letter was printed at the beginning of the *De revolutionibus*). In the second place, it awakened the enthusiasm of a young mathematician, Rhaeticus, who traveled from Wittenberg to Frauenburg for the sole purpose of meeting Copernicus.

Rhaeticus' intervention was providential. Georg Joachim Rhaeticus (1514-76) was forty years younger than Copernicus; he was born in Feldkirch (Tirol-Voralberg), almost as far away from the eastern Baltic as a German place could be, in an Austrian, not a Slavonic, land. He studied in Zurich and Wittenberg and was a professor there when he heard of Copernicus' endeavor. He was a Protestant, while Copernicus was a Catholic. When he visited the latter in 1539, coming straight from Wittenberg,[112] he was like a Muslim coming from Mecca, yet Copernicus welcomed him and persuaded him to lengthen his stay. The two men lived and worked together for more than two years (1539-41).

Was the first draft of the *De revolutionibus* already written at the time of Rhaeticus' arrival? We do not know, but it certainly went through several drafts, and the final composition was hastened because of the enthusiasm of the younger man; it may have been completed with his collaboration. A miracle of love and truth-seeking had occurred in an age of hatred (I wish we could witness a similar miracle in our own day). Copernicus and Rhaeticus, the old and the young (66 vs. 25), the Pole and the Austrian, the Catholic and the Lutheran, thought only of science and worked together like father and son. The *Narratio prima*,[113] written by Rhaeticus in Copernicus' name, was the first explanation of the new ideas to appear in print. It was published in Danzig in 1540, then again in Nuremberg in 1541. The second edition in one of the printing centers of Europe assured excellent publicity and the success of the opuscule must have stimulated Copernicus to hasten his larger work.

We must be grateful to Rhaeticus for giving the old man the courage, the will, and strength to complete his great work. Rhaeticus' relationship to Copernicus is somewhat like that of Halley to Newton. Without Halley it is probable that the *Principia* (1687) would not exist, and without Rhaeticus the *De revolutionibus* might have remained unfinished and unpublished.

Copernicus' book is so important that it is worth while to recount how it was finished and printed.

When Rhaeticus left Frauenburg in 1541 he took with him two chapters (1, 13-14) dealing with plane and spherical trigonometry and published them separately at Wittenberg in 1542.[114] Was the rest of the manuscript finished at that time? If not, it was completed soon afterward. Copernicus gave it to his friend, Tiedemann Giese, bishop of Culm,[115] who transmitted it to Rhaeticus; the latter entrusted it to the famous printer, Johannes Petreius in Nuremberg. Rhaeticus, being obliged to go to Leipzig, was unable to see it through the press; it was edited by his friend, Andreas Osiander, a Lutheran theologian and mathematician. An advance copy of the printed folio reached Copernicus on his deathbed on May 24, 1543; he saw it and handled it, and died a few hours later.

The only manuscript that has come down to us was revised at various times and includes many corrections, additions, and cancellations, some of which were probably made during Rhaeticus' stay in Frauenburg. It changed hands many times. From 1614 to c.1641 it was in the possession of Jean Amos Komenský (Comenius); then it entered the famous private library of the Nostitz family in Prague, where it was practically forgotten until the middle of the last century.[116] The printed text is somewhat different from that of the manuscript, which suggests that a fair copy was made from it for the printers and was probably soiled and destroyed in the course of printing.

The great book as we have it begins with a few words of caution which Osiander[117] had thought it necessary to add, in which he warns the reader that the fundamental hypotheses of the book, the centrality and immobility of the sun and the mobility of the earth, are simply mathematical hypotheses, bases of calculation, not concerned with the Christian faith. Then follows the letter of Cardinal Schönberg (Rome, November 1, 1536). Finally comes Copernicus' long dedication to the Very Holy Father, Paul III,[118] in which he explains the circumstances that have guided his mathematical investigations, the encouragements he has received not only from ancient philosophers but also from living prelates, bespeaks the Pope's kind judgment and begs him not to be influenced by irrelevant criticism: "Mathematics is written for mathematicians; if I am not mistaken they will agree that my work adds to the glory of the ecclesiastical republic of which Your Holiness is the prince."

The tables included in the De revolutionibus of 1543 were imperfect; better ones prepared by Erasmus Reinhold (1511-53) appeared a few years later under the title Tabulae Prutenicae or Prussian Tables.[119] This Reinhold was a colleague of Rhaeticus in Wittenberg. In 1536 Melanchthon had caused two mathematical chairs to be established in that university, one for higher mathematics and astronomy, which was entrusted to Reinhold, and one for elementary mathematics, which was given to Rhaeticus (then aged 22).

There are thus three men who deserve special praise for their early assistance to Copernicus: Andreas Osiander, Erasmus Reinhold, and

Georg Joachim Rhaeticus, who were respectively 45, 32, and 29 in 1543. The youngest of these, who worked two years with Copernicus, was the greatest.

It would be unfair to Rhaeticus to think of him only as a devoted and competent assistant to Copernicus. He was one of the leading trigonometricians of the heroic age. He defined tangents and cotangents as ratios and prepared very elaborate tables of sines, tangents, and secants. The computations required for his tables were so enormous that he could not complete them even with the assistance of other computers. The work was far advanced by 1575, when a young man, Valentin Otho (1550?-1605), appeared and was accepted as a collaborator. In the following year the two men traveled together to Kaschau in Hungary,[120] where Rhaeticus fell very ill and after a week died in the arms of his young friend. Otho inherited the tables as well as the responsibility of having them published, for they were so vast that no printer could handle them without a substantial grant in aid. They appeared twenty years after Rhaeticus' death under the title *Opus Palatinum de Triangulis* (2 vols., folio, Neustadt, 1596).[121]

I have referred to Copernicus as a man of one book. St. Thomas Aquinas is said to have remarked, "Timeo hominem unius libri" (I fear the man of one book); I do not know exactly what he meant but he probably referred to a man who reads one book over and over, as some Jewish doctors read the Talmud. Copernicus is the supreme example of a man who devoted half of his life[122] to the composition of a single book, through which he became immortal. The Copernican astronomy was an idea of his youth that was realized and developed in his maturity; it was eternalized in printed form just as he was beginning his own eternal life.

I have taken special pains to show that while he was aided by a Protestant mathematician, he received the greatest encouragement from prelates: his good uncle the bishop of Ermeland, the Cardinal of Capua, the bishop of Culm, the bishop of Fossombrone, and two Popes, Clement VII and Paul III. His book was published under the highest Catholic auspices.

It is, therefore, not strange that the first clerical attacks came not from the Catholic side but from the Lutheran. The leader was Melanchthon, who called Copernicus "ille Sarmaticus Astronomus qui movet terram et figit Solem"[123] (the Sarmatian astronomer who moves the earth and fixes the sun). This statement reveals that

Melanchthon, who hailed from Baden in southwestern Germany, considered the hated Copernicus to be Sarmatian, a non-German, a Slav. When Copernicus' fame was securely established in the nineteenth century, the Germans changed their minds and claimed he was one of their brethren. The reader will draw his own conclusions. A man of Copernicus' stature belongs to the whole world.

Lutherans shared Melanchthon's attitude. The master himself, Martin Luther, showed his incomprehension by referring to Copernicus as the new astrologer. "The fool will overturn the whole art of astronomy,"[124] he said, and in a sense he was right in his wrongness, for Ptolemaic astronomy was overturned forever.

After a while Catholics joined the Protestants in the fray, and Biblical fundamentalists of both sides vied with one another in denouncing the arch-heretic who belied the Holy Scriptures. Giordano Bruno, whose Copernicanism was aggravated by pantheistic tendencies, added venom to the quarrel. He was arrested in 1593 by order of the Inquisition, imprisoned for seven years, excommunicated, and burned at the stake in Rome on February 17, 1600.

In the second half of the seventeenth century most men took the same position as Osiander, that heliocentricism was simply a mathematical hypothesis. After the experiences of Bruno and Galileo, a good deal of prudence was necessary. Gassendi[125] declared that the Copernican system would be the best if it were consistent with the Scriptures; that was a clever way of stating a scientific conclusion without endorsing it. Two plus two make four, God willing! The situation was much simpler for the people who, however learned they might be, had no scientific knowledge. For example, in Montaigne's eyes scientific conclusions had no more validity than philosophical opinions. To him the difference between Copernicists and Ptolemaists was comparable to the difference between Stoics and Epicureans.[126] In a great many scientific textbooks of the seventeenth century, and even of the eighteenth, the Ptolemaic and Copernican hypotheses were presented as alternative explanations; the authors were careful to add, however (as Gassendi had done), that the second hypothesis, however brilliant it might seem, could not be seriously envisaged because it was condemned by the Church.

TYCHO BRAHE

The history of science illustrates repeatedly an eternal conflict between men of different types; it is not simply the conflict between theory and practice, synthesis and analysis, general views and precise measurements. Copernicus was not a practical astronomer, and he did not bother about the niceties of astronomical observation; his book must have irritated the astronomers who did not care so much for theories as for good tables. The tables of the *De revolutionibus* were very insufficient; the *Prussian Tables* of Erasmus Reinhold (1551) were much better, yet imperfect.

There was living at that time in Denmark a young man, Tyge (or Tycho) Brahe (1546-1601),[127] who was an astronomical observer of outstanding ability. His first recorded observation was made as early as 1563 (aet. 17); observing a close approach of Jupiter and Saturn, he was shocked because the prediction derived from the *Alphonsine Tables* (XIII-2) was a whole month wrong, while that of the *Prussian Tables* was many days in error. In 1572 (aet. 26) he discovered a new star in Cassiopeia and observed the gradual changes of magnitude during the sixteen months of its appearance; he showed that it was not a meteor but a real star and belonged to the region of the fixed stars at the end of space.[128]

To Tycho Brahe, who was primarily an observer, the weaknesses of the Copernican tables were soon obvious, yet his opposition to Copernicanism was very largely a matter of prejudice. How could one account for the lack of parallactic motions in the stars? The only way out would be to assume that they are almost infinitely distant. Would that not be an immense waste of space?[129] The earth was too sluggish to move around as Copernicus suggested. Brahe was also restrained by Biblical evidence, for he was a faithful Lutheran. Copernicus' system was hardly less complex than Ptolemy's; it required 34 cycles or epicycles[130] against Ptolemy's 40, which was not a great economy.

Brahe's contempt for Copernican theory was aggravated by the fact that he himself had little theoretical ability.[131] He realized, and insisted, that accurate observations constituted the foundation of all astronomical knowledge. Hence it was necessary to make more and better observations, to devise and build better instruments, and to make the best use of them. This implied not only an abundance of precautions but also a very careful study of the instruments in order to discover their mechanical defects and to allow for them in the computations; one had to allow also for other permanent causes of error, such as atmospheric refraction.

His great purpose was already well outlined in his mind when he was about thirty, but the realization of it would require considerable expenditure. It was very lucky for him, therefore, that in 1576 he acquired a generous patron, Frederick II (king of Denmark 1555-88), who gave him an island, Hveen, not far from Copenhagen,[132] and enabled him to build there a palatial observatory. This observatory, which Brahe called Uraniborg, was one of the most famous places of its kind in the world; Brahe drew the plans for it, equipped it with the best instruments (devised by himself), and even added a printing shop for its publications.[133]

The best Arabic astronomers, as well as Regiomontanus, had understood the need for frequent observations, but Brahe was probably the first to realize the necessity for continuous observations and to make them possible. This required regular assistants who were trained observers or trustworthy computers, and royal patronage enabled him to hire them. Nobody before his time had conducted astronomical research with so much efficiency. The organization of every modern observatory derives from Uraniborg,[134] though the instruments used there have been developed far beyond Brahe's possibilities and even his conceptions. For example, his observations, which were remarkably precise, were made with the naked eye without lenses of any kind.

Another observatory was functioning at about the same time in Cassel, where it was established in 1561 by Wilhelm IV (1532-92), landgrave of Hesse. It was not as well planned or as well used as Uraniborg, but it was remarkably good. Brahe was in touch with Wilhelm IV and with his astronomer, Christopher Rothmann,[135] and his rivalry with them was the best of stimulants.

Brahe was so busy with his observations that he had no time to set forth his views in print, and he was anticipated by his former assistant, Reymers Bär of Ditmarsch in Holstein, whose *Fundamentum astronomicum* (1588) came like a thunderbolt.[136] Not only did "Ursus" steal the Tychonian system, but he modified it in an essential point, for he admitted the diurnal rotation of the earth. Ursus was a betrayer as well as a robber!

One of Brahe's first achievements in Uraniborg was his very careful observation of the comet of 1577.[137] He was able to prove that the comet was at least three times as far away as the moon (which showed that comets are not necessarily sublunar, meteorological objects), and that it revolved around the sun at a distance greater than Venus (which made the hypothesis of material spheres untenable). He observed many other comets but his account of this one was the most elaborate; the comet itself attracted universal attention.

Brahe observed systematically a large number of stars and prepared a catalogue, which he planned to publish in the first volume of a great astronomical treatise, *Astronomiae instauratae progymnasmata*. This work was begun in 1588, and much of it was printed in 1592, but it was still incomplete at the time of his death[138] and was published by Johann Kepler in 1602. It included a catalogue of 777 stars, to which Kepler added 228. A similar catalogue was being prepared at Cassel; it was meant to include 1,032 stars, but was never finished. It is interesting to compare these two contemporary catalogues, which can be done easily by consulting Flamsteed's *Historia coelestis Britannica,* where the stellar coordinates of the landgrave and of Tycho are printed side by side.[139]

To give an idea of the precision of Brahe's observations it will suffice to say that in the case of his nine fundamental stars the error was less than 1'; this was chiefly due to his imperfect knowledge of atmospheric refraction. He found the longitude of the sun's apogee to equal 95° 30' with an annual motion of 45" (against Copernicus' estimate of 24", and the correct value 61"). His estimate of the length of the tropical year was only 2" too small. He determined the precession of the equinoxes exactly (51") and finally rejected the false idea of trepidation, which had sidetracked astronomers for twelve centuries, that is, from the time of Theon of Alexandria (IV-2).[140] Considering the quality of his instruments, such precision is almost uncanny.

Brahe had good reasons as well as bad ones for distrusting Copernican astronomy. At the end of the patient years of work at Uraniborg (1576-97) his distrust was completely justified by his observations. Thus did history repeat itself. Just as Hipparchos and Ptolemy had been obliged to reject the heliocentric theory of Aristarchos, so Brahe was obliged to reject the heliocentric theory of Copernicus. Unfortunately he could not offer a new theory of greater validity.

Brahe was not an attractive personality; he was arrogant and inconsiderate of others. Instead of showing gratitude to his royal protector and endearing himself to the government, his own subordinates, and the peasants of Hveen, he made himself obnoxious by various abuses and by bad manners. He had already lost favor with his patron, Frederick II, and when the latter died his situation worsened. During the minority of Christian IV (king 1588-1648, but crowned only in 1596) he had to face the growing hostility of the regents; his fiefs were taken away from him one by one, and life and work in his beloved Hveen became impossible. He was obliged to move to Copenhagen, then out of the country, and later to Rostock and Wandsbeck (near Hamburg). In the castle of Wandsbeck he was the honored guest of Henrik Rantzau, governor of Holstein, who was an astrologer[141] and had an observatory of his own. While at Wandsbeck he published a splendid album, *Astronomiae instauratae mechanica*,[142] describing and illustrating his old observatory and his instruments, and used it as a means of obtaining the interest and protection of other sovereigns, such as Maurice of Nassau, stadholder of the Dutch Republic (1587-1625) and Rudolf II, Holy Roman Emperor (1576-1612), both of whom were generous patrons of science.[143] The latter gave him his imperial protection and called him to his court, but as the plague was raging in Prague, Brahe stopped a few months in Wittenberg, where he was lodged in the house which had been Melanchthon's. He finally arrived in Prague in June 1599. Rudolf II received him with the greatest honors and assigned to him the castle of Benatky, some twenty miles out of the city, where Brahe established a new observatory, set up his instruments, and resumed his activities.

In spite of Rudolf's generosity, exile was hard and Brahe often thought regretfully of the golden days of Uraniborg. Yet fortune smiled at him once more when she sent him a young assistant called Johann Kepler (1571-1630). At the time of his arrival in Prague, in January 1600, Kepler was 29 years old and was himself in exile. He had been professor at the University of Graz and mathematician of Styria, but he was a Protestant and the Archduke Ferdinand had vowed to drive every heretic out of his province.[144] The two banished men worked together as well as they could. Brahe's overbearing manners were perhaps a little tempered by misfortune, and they were compensated by Kepler's gentleness and obedience.

Their immediate collaboration did not last long, for Brahe died on October 24, 1601, after a short illness. He had been in Bohemia for two and a half years and Kepler had been working with him for less than two. This was more than enough for the younger man to understand thoroughly the methods of the older and to be able to use his notes with relative ease.[145]

At Rudolf's orders Brahe received an honorable and splendid funeral. He was perhaps the first man of science to be so honored.[146]

Brahe was one of the greatest astronomers of all time, but he was less admirable as a man. He was a nobleman in an age when nobles were considered to belong to a higher level of humanity, and his self-conceit on that account, as well as on account of his own merits, was excessive. While Copernicus was gentle, liberal, tolerant, and fearless, Brahe was arrogant, self-willed, irritable, intolerant, contemptuous of others, narrow-minded, chockful of prejudices, revengeful, and timorous. The other side of the medal was well shown by Johann Jessen of Wittenberg,[147] whose praise includes the following *cri du coeur*: "He coveted nothing but time."[148] This is characteristic of the born man of science, which Brahe undoubtedly was; for him there was nothing more precious than time, limited and inexorable.

In spite of his rejection of Copernican astronomy, Brahe admired Copernicus very much, had a portrait of him in the library, and kept one of his instruments in the observatory.[149] He was different from Copernicus, however, in every respect. The latter wrote one great book; Brahe wrote several, but in a sense he failed to complete his own *magnum opus*, which would have remained fragmentary but for Kepler's genius and piety. It was paradoxical, however, that Kepler could save Brahe from oblivion only by reversing his fundamental ideas. Instead of establishing the Tychonian system and completing the destruction of the Copernican one, Kepler resurrected the latter and gave it a more perfect form.

During his years of immediate collaboration with Brahe, Kepler had begun to use the latter's observations on Mars. After Brahe's death he inherited all his master's records; but much to his vexation the instruments never were available to him. Brahe had been unable to derive a good theory from his incomparable observations, but this was done by Kepler in the *Astronomia nova de motibus stellae Martis* (Prague, 1609), the *Harmonice mundi* (Linz, 1619), and other works. His treatise of 1609 revealed the first two laws of planetary motion, and the third one was expounded in his book of 1619.

Kepler revived the heliocentric theory[150] but replaced circular trajectories by elliptical ones. The final heliocentric system was thus created by the genius of three very different men, Copernicus, Brahe, and Kepler—a Pole, a Dane, and a German.

There is no time to speak of the mathematical aspects of Brahe's

work, but an exception must be made for the discovery of prosthaphairesis,[151] that is, of formulas that made it possible to add and
subtract trigonometrical ratios instead of multiplying them, thus
replacing a long and difficult computation by a short and easy one.
The discovery was of very great practical value in those days. It had
been made a long time before by Ibn Yūnus (XI-1),[152] but had fallen
into oblivion until the difficulties of trigonometrical computers led
to its rediscovery in the sixteenth century. This rediscovery may have
been made independently in many places; it has been ascribed to
Johann Werner, Rhaeticus, Joost Bürgi (mathematician of the landgrave of Hesse), and Ursus. It may be found also in the *Canon
mathematicus* of Viète (1579). That book may have reached Uraniborg, but it is quite possible that the discovery was made there anew
not by Brahe but by Paul Wittich of Breslau, who was assisting him
in 1582. Of course Brahe was quick to realize that it was a labor-
saving device of the first order.

Prosthaphairesis is now completely forgotten, but it was an in-
estimable blessing for a time. It was no longer needed after the appearance of tables giving the logarithms of trigonometrical functions;
the first table of this kind was published by Edmund Gunter of London in 1620.

Brahe's best reason for rejecting Copernicanism was his inability
to detect stellar parallaxes, in spite of the fact that his observations
were extremely precise, say within the range of half or even a quarter
of a minute. He could not possibly conceive that the stars were so
much farther away than the sun. The first astronomer to measure a
stellar parallax was another Dane, Ole Römer, who found one in
1701-1704 (which was erroneous) and was so pleased with his result
that he described it under the title *Copernicus triumphans*. James
Bradley, in 1729, did not find a parallax but discovered the aberration of light instead.[153] The first parallax was measured only in 1838,
237 years after Brahe's death, by Friedrich Wilhelm Bessel (parallax
of 61 Cygni, 0.3"); the second by Thomas Henderson, who measured
at Cape Town the parallax of the brightest and nearest star of
heaven, Alpha Centauri, and overestimated it 1".[154] No star has a
parallax as high as one second.[155]

Brahe could not imagine the possibility of such enormous distances
as are measured or estimated today, and hence it was reasonable for
him to reject the heliocentric hypothesis on that ground alone. His

rejection would have been as admirable as Copernicus' acceptance, if he had not weakened his case by silly arguments. At present we are so used to fantastic distances expressed in parsecs, light years, or light-centuries, that we must make an effort to recapture Brahe's incredulity. The universe has been extended so far above and below our size that man, the earth, and the solar system lie midway between the two extremes of astronomical and microscopic measurement (say between a radius of 10^{-13} cm. and one of 10^{27} cm.)

THE GREGORIAN CALENDAR

The adoption in 1582 of a new calendar, the one in use today, was an important event, though it hardly deserves to be called a landmark in mathematics. Yet many people seem to think that it was the fruit of exceptional mathematical efforts, and therefore it may be well to speak of it in this chapter.

The difficulty of constructing a calendar is due to the necessity of combining three units of time—the day, the month, and the year—that have no common measure. Some kind of compromise must be found. The difficulty was increased by the introduction of a fourth unit, the week, incommensurable with the month and year. The week, a legacy of the astral religion, was introduced about the time of Christ or not long before; it is an arbitrary unit so far as astronomy is concerned, but it is very useful for the common needs of life and many religious rites are organized on a weekly basis.

The Julian calendar had been established by order of Julius Caesar, in 45 B.C., on the assumption that the year contained 365¼ days. To the normal year of 365 days it thus sufficed to add one more day every fourth year, in order to harmonize the calendar with the equinoxes. This appreciation of the year's length in days was too long, however, by 11¼ minutes, a difference that is seemingly insignificant but adds up to a full day in 128 years; in thirteen centuries the discrepancy amounted to ten days.

According to canon law Easter was to be celebrated on the first Sunday after the full moon following the equinox. Paschal dates continued to be reckoned as if the equinox occurred on March 21, although in the sixteenth century the actual date was March 11. Hence Easter might arrive as much as a month late, in May.

It is not surprising then that the need of reforming the calendar was felt chiefly by clerics who were concerned with computing the

date of Easter. The history of that reformation would include a long
list of Christian scholars, such as Bede the Venerable (VIII-1),
Robert Grosseteste (XIII-1), Roger Bacon (XIII-2), Jean de Meurs
(XIV-1), Firmin de Beauval (XIV-1), Nicephoros Gregoras (XIV-1),
and Albert of Saxony (XIV-2).[156] As the difference between the real
and assumed dates of the equinox increased, the need of calendar
reform became more urgent. Many popes took a special interest in
the matter, which was discussed at various Church councils. Pierre
d'Ailly (1350-1420) reported at the Council of Constance (1414-18)
and Nicholas of Cusa at the Council of Basel (1431-49). Regiomontanus was called by Sixtus IV to help solve the problem, and
died at Rome in 1476. Paul of Middelburg (1446-1533) submitted a
large memoir[157] on the subject to the Fifth Lateran Council (1512-
17); the same Council consulted two Polish astronomers, Martin
Biem[158] (c.1470-1540) and Copernicus. It was Gregory XIII's glory
to accomplish the reform that had been delayed for centuries.

A new project was published by the Calabrian, Luigi Lilio, in
1577,[159] and after Lilio's death it was completed by Clavius. Christopher Clavius was a German Jesuit (Bamberg 1537–Rome 1612), who
obtained considerable prestige from his elaborate editions of Euclid
and his many textbooks. He dominated mathematical studies in the
Jesuit colleges, which were then the best in the world; his textbooks
were standard in all of them and through his pupils he became the
mathematical teacher of Europe. Not only that, but Matteo Ricci
caused some of his treatises to be translated into Chinese.[160]

Briefly, the new calendar was devised by Lilius and Clavius and
sanctioned by Gregory XIII in 1582;[161] it may justly be called the
Gregorian calendar. Clavius' mathematical prestige was a great help
in establishing it and silencing the opposition, and non-mathemati-
cians were inclined to believe that his invention of the new calendar
was sufficient proof of his mathematical genius. As a matter of fact
it involved only simple arithmetic and common sense. Clavius was
not a great mathematician, but he was the most influential teacher
of the Renaissance.[162]

The Gregorian reform implied two steps:

(1) In order to correct the existing confusion, the Pope ordered
that the morrow of St. Francis' day (October 4) should be reckoned
as October 15, 1582 (the vernal equinox would thus be restored from
March 11 to March 21).

(2) The average Julian year was too long; the average Gregorian year is shortened by the suppression of a few leap years.[163] In the Julian calendar every year whose number was divisible by four was a leap year; thus there were 100 leap years in four centuries. In the Gregorian calendar three of these were canceled, making only 97 leap years in 400. It was decided that century years would be leap years only when the first two figures were divisible by four (1600 and 2000 are leap years; 1700, 1800 and 1900 are not). The average length of the mean tropical year was thus reduced from 365.25 to 365.2425 days. The old Julian intercalation caused a lag of 3.1132 days in 400 years; in the Gregorian calendar this was reduced to 0.1132 day in the same period, or 1.132 days in 4,000 years (this could be obviated eventually by cancelling the leap years 4000, 8000, etc.)

The Gregorian calendar was excellent, but unfortunately it was introduced too late. If it had been proposed before the Reformation, it would have been easily accepted by the whole of Christendom, but it had become impossible for the Protestants to accept it or for the Pope to coerce them. It was hard enough for good Catholics to go to sleep on October 4, 1582 and wake up on October 15, but for Protestants such a Babylonian imposition was intolerable. The reform was accepted in Spain, Portugal, and part of Italy on the same day as in Rome; in France, in December 1582; in Catholic Germany in 1583.

The Protestant nations of Germany refused to consider it for more than a century; it was finally accepted at the Imperial Diet of Regensburg in 1700. England held out until 1752.[164] As Voltaire put it, "The English mob preferred their calendar to disagree with the Sun than to agree with the Pope and they refused to accept a reform for which one should have been grateful to the Grand Turk if he had proposed it." Poor Bradley was badly treated by his countrymen for his participation in the reform, which they regarded as a kind of treason.[165]

Orthodox Russia never did accept the Gregorian calendar, which was introduced only after the Revolution, on January 31, 1918.

The Protestants were generally unwilling to pay any attention to the Popish calendar, but Brahe, who understood the improvement, used the New Style from July 22, 1599 on.[166] On the other hand, while the Catholics accepted the new calendar (they had to under pain of excommunication) some of them grumbled. Clavius' main opponent was none other than François Viète, the most illustrious mathematician of his time, in comparison with whom Clavius was a pigmy. It may be that jealousy was a motive; at any rate, he devised another kind of calendar and denounced the Gregorian one.[167] Another kind of opposition in Catholic circles was natural enough. Many people were disgruntled because of the change in their habits and chiefly because of the "loss" of ten days of their lives. It is amusing to read Montaigne's sarcasms on the subject.[168]

ASTROLOGY

To appreciate correctly the scientific spirit of any period it is necessary to have some knowledge not only of its positive achievements but also of its adulterations and deviations. The two outstanding deviations in the Renaissance were astrology and alchemy; the latter will be dealt with in the next chapter. Astrology dominated not only the minds of the vulgar and uneducated but also those of astronomers, even Brahe and Kepler. Both of them drew horoscopes and were presumably sincere in their astrological beliefs. On the other hand, so far as I know Copernicus showed no such weakness. This illustrates once more the infinite variety and complexity of personalities. The great merit of Brahe and Kepler was their precise observations and their respect for facts, yet they accepted the astrological nonsense without a shadow of proof. On the contrary, Copernicus remained aloof from it. In this respect at least the theorist was superior to the conscientious observers.

It is not necessary to retrace in detail the previous history of the astrological aberration. The first reference to it in Western literature may be in the Hippocratic treatise, *Regimen IV (De victu IV* or *De insomniis)*, though I doubt that interpretation. The astrological delusion grew out of Chaldaean and Egyptian fancies, and the Platonic *Epinomis*[169] provided a scientific foundation for it. During the Middle Ages and the Renaissance everyone's thinking was colored more or less by astrological beliefs.

It should be noted, however, that the opinions of learned men were generally mixed. Between outspoken believers in astrology and its very few outspoken opponents there was a wide gamut of compromises. Men like Giovanni Pico della Mirandola, Jacques Lefèvre d'Etaples, Johann Reuchlin, Johannes Trithemius, and Thomas Erastus did not hesitate to attack astrology, but their attacks were almost always qualified. During the last year of Charles VIII's rule (1498) one Simon de Phares wrote a collection of astrological biographies in which he criticized many of the adepts.[170] The collection is interesting because it includes many men of science as well as astrologers.

The same ambiguity prevailed in the sixteenth century. There were few physicians or mathematicians who did not believe in astrology, and many were engaged in astrological pursuits of one kind or another. If an astronomer was not a professor in a university he had no source of income but that provided by horoscopes or astrological advice. Many princes, bishops, and governors employed "mathematicians," whose main duties were of an astrological nature.

Astrologers (or believers in astrology) were ruling in every field. Consider the following (named in chronological order of birth years): Agrippa von Nettesheim, Paracelsus, Geronimo Cardano, Nostradamus,[171] John Dee, Jean Bodin, Cornelius Gemma,[172] Giambattista della Porta, and Robert Fludd.[173] The superstitious notions of these men were combined with admirable achievements in many diverse fields.

Take, for example, comets. We have seen that Brahe's study of the comet of 1577 was a landmark in astronomical history. There is, however, a tremendous literature on this comet, and much of it is primarily astrological; public curiosity on the subject was insatiable.[174]

There were many other Renaissance comets. That of 1472 is famous because it was studied by Regiomontanus (1436-76), the greatest practical astronomer before Copernicus; it was the first comet whose orbit was investigated in a competent manner.[175] The most important comet, however, from the point of view of Renaissance folklore was that of 1456, which threw terror into men's hearts because it followed so closely upon the heels of the catastrophe of 1453, the fall of Constantinople and the end of the Byzantine empire. Fears of the comet, the Devil, and the Turks were all mixed up together. The Spaniard Calixtus III (Pope from 1455 to 1458) preached a new crusade against the Turks, and the fears induced by the comet were used in his propaganda. It was said (wrongly) that he introduced the words, "From the Turk and the Comet, good Lord, deliver us" into the Litany.[176]

However interesting the comet of 1456 may be as a source of folklore, its scientific interest was far greater when its identity with Halley's comet was realized. In his *Astronomiae cometicae synopsis* (1705) the English astronomer Edmund Halley (1656-1742) announced that the orbit of the comet of 1682, which he had observed, was nearly identical with those of the comets of 1607 (observed by Kepler) and of 1531, and he prophesied that the same comet would reappear not later than 1759; it did actually reappear in that year. This was the first periodic comet to be discovered; it proved that comets were heavenly bodies, whose behavior, like that of the planets, was subject to natural laws. Halley's prophecy and its vindication put an end to the superstitions regarding comets. Periodic passages of Halley's comet have been traced back to 240 B.C., and it appeared in 1066 (battle of Hastings), 1145, 1223, 1301, 1378, 1456, 1531, 1607, 1682, 1759, 1835, and 1910.[177] However, the Renaissance astronomers, even Kepler, did not know this, and superstitious beliefs about comets continued to flourish until 1705, or even until 1759.[178] Indeed, they are still current in backward nations and among benighted individuals in the most civilized countries.

GEMATRIA

Another form of superstition to which Renaissance scholars and mathematicians were addicted was gematria, i.e., giving mystical values to numbers and finding future dates in words. This was implied in neo-Platonic arithmetic, and was highly developed during the Middle Ages by Jewish cabalists and Muslim occultists.[179]

The practice of gematria was encouraged by the fact that Greek, Hebrew, Arabic, and Roman letters have numerical values. One aspect of Renaissance thought, not discussed here, was the translation of Hebrew cabalistic writings into Latin. That Judeo-Christian movement was begun in Spain by Pablo de Heredia (1405-86) and continued by the Italians Pico della Mirandola[180] and Paolo Rici of Pavia (physician to Maximilian, Emperor 1493-1519), the Germans Johann Reuchlin and Agrippa von Nettesheim, and others. One of the oldest cabalistic treatises, the *Sefer Yeẓirah* (book of creation), was translated into Latin by Guillaume Postel (Paris, 1552) and by Johannes Pistor (*Ars cabalista*, vol. 1, Basel, 1587).[181] Through one or another of these books the poison of gematria found its way into the minds of sixteenth-century scholars.

One example of that kind of nonsense must suffice. Michael Stifel of Esslingen (Württemberg) (1487-1567) was one of the most distinguished German mathematicians. He improved algebraic symbolism and was one of the few who invented Pascal's triangle; he also adumbrated the idea of logarithms by means of some rules of the exponential calculus and by comparing arithmetical with geometrical series. He received his early education in an Augustinian monastery, but after his conversion by Luther he became a religious fanatic, predicted the end of the world, and behaved in such a manner that he was thrown into jail. He claimed that Leo X (Giovanni de' Medici, Pope 1513-21) was the Beast of the Apocalypse and proved it by means of gematria. The number of the Beast was 666 (Revelation 13:18). Now if we write Leo DeCIMVs (Decimus), the capital letters represent $50 + 500 + 100 + 1 + 1,000 + 5 = 1656$. Take out M, which stands for *mysterium,* and add X because he was Leo X. Then the total is $50 + 500 + 100 + 1 + 5 + 10 = 666$. Q.E.D.

It is hard to reconcile such stupidity with the mathematical genius that informed Stifel's books. Perhaps his mind had been deranged by excessive bigotry. But many other men of the period were as crazy as he. Nevertheless the cryptographic wisdom of these fools was held in great respect by the contemporary public.

All kinds of superstition and occultism were encouraged by the social elite, headed by emperors, kings, and princes. A good example is Catherine de' Medici (1519-89), widow of Henry II, regent of France from 1560 to 1574, and mother of three kings. A stupid and unscrupulous woman, she was mainly responsible for the massacre of St. Bartholomew, and she did not hesitate to order other crimes when it seemed expedient.[182] She was extremely superstitious and relied heavily on the advice of quacks, as did many of her subjects. Life in France in the second half of the sixteenth century and the first quarter of the seventeenth was full of hatred and terror. The atmosphere of Paris and other cities, and even of the countryside, was poisoned by irrational fears.

Another example is Rudolf II,[183] Holy Roman Emperor from 1576 to 1612, who was a great patron of astronomers, astrologers, and alchemists. We shall come back to him in the next chapter.

As to the Popes, the most inclined to astrology were perhaps Leo X (Pope 1513-20) and Paul III (1534-40).[184] Both were enlightened men, however, who appreciated learning and science; Paul III was

Copernicus' patron. It should be added to the credit of the Catholic Church that it took considerable pains to oppose astrology as well as other superstitions, but these evils were so widespread in every class of society that they could not be eradicated. The Faculty of Theology of the University of Paris had become one of the main organs of Catholic orthodoxy. It delivered a heavy blow at astrology by solemnly condemning it in 1494. Yet this did not greatly disturb the astrologers, for they then constituted the most powerful "scientific" group in Christendom; in case of trouble, there were always civil or ecclesiastical princes ready to protect them.

Besides astrology and gematria, there was an abundance of other superstitions—alchemy, divination, magic, occultism, witchcraft— which are almost impossible to classify for they were all tangled together.[185] They represent the shady side of the Renaissance. Much creative work was done in the scientific field, much more in the field of the arts, but superstitions were as ubiquitous as the mud of the streets and the dirt of the houses. We must remember this, but we need not insist on it too much. The history of science is a very large subject, but the history of superstition is infinite. The former is instructive and encouraging, the latter is repetitious and futile; it can prove nothing except the imbecility of the human mind.

Third Wing

PHYSICS, CHEMISTRY, TECHNOLOGY

I. Physics

IN APPRAISING Renaissance achievements in the physical arts and sciences, the first man we have to deal with is the German, Nicholas of Cusa. In the middle of the fifteenth century, when the Renaissance begins, he was perhaps the greatest man in the Christian world; and he was not an Italian, but a German. The awakening did not take place only in Italy, as the textbooks say; it occurred also in Portugal and Spain, the Low Countries and Germany. Nicholas Cusanus came from Cues on the Moselle, a little below Treves (Trier). He was an individual of extraordinary complexity, and so great that we can never see the whole of him; every time my studies bring me back to him I discover something new and remarkable.[1]

Nicholas had the knack of giving his books significant titles. His philosophical synthesis was called *Docta ignorantia* (learned ignorance), which sums up in two words his condition and ours. Another great work, written in 1450, was entitled *Idiotae libri IV* (the idiot or the ignorant).* We are all idiots in some field, and some of us are idiots in every field. Book IV of the *Idiot* deals with static physical experiments, and lays great stress on the necessity of quantitative methods, measurements of weight and time. Every astronomer realized that unless his measurements of time and location were made as accurate as possible, his knowledge of the stars and planets

---

* *Idiotes* in Greek originally meant a private person, an individual. Later it came to mean one who has no professional knowledge, a layman. The "idiot" is the fresh man, which does not mean that every freshman is an ass, but simply that he is fresh, untrained, and ignorant.

77

was worth nothing. Cusanus was the first to realize that the same held true in every other branch of science.

The advancement of knowledge has been made possible by increasing accuracy of measurement. Cusanus did not see this as clearly as Kelvin,[2] who lived in the nineteenth century, but in his time he was remarkable for seeing it at all. He used the balance for physical, physiological, and even mathematical investigations. He used a clepsydra to measure the frequency of the pulse and of breathing in normal and pathological conditions. He devised experiments to measure humidity and invented a bathometer (to measure the depth of water), a part of which could be released at the bottom and rise to the surface.[3] No doubt such ideas were in the air and occurred to others (Alberti, for example); but Cusanus was the first, or one of the first, to express them. This shows his many-sidedness, for he was in fact an "idiot," i.e., a layman, in physics; by profession he was an ecclesiastical administrator. He was a prince of the Church but also a philosopher, a man of science with bold ideas, a forerunner of Erasmus.

Mention of the clepsydra raises the fundamental question: how did Cusanus and his successors in the sixteenth century measure time? Tycho Brahe, who as an astronomer had particular need of accurate timepieces,[4] had mechanical clocks indicating minutes and seconds, but they were not accurate enough for his purposes; they had mechanical defects and were influenced by the weather. He was so little satisfied with them that he used a mercury clepsydra when greater accuracy was needed. This shows that even toward the end of the Renaissance chronometry was still in its infancy. Cusanus lived a century earlier; in his day fairly accurate measurements of brief periods of time could be made with various types of clepsydra, but such methods were very cumbersome.

Mechanical clocks, however crude, were beginning to be sufficiently reliable for the simple needs of everyday life. Being driven by a weight, they had to remain in the same position. The device of using spiral springs for motive power made possible the manufacture of portable clocks or watches. The invention of the first watches (very heavy and bulky ones) is ascribed to a Nuremberg clockmaker, Peter Henlein (c.1505); being spherical or egg-shaped, they were nicknamed Nuremberg eggs.[5] These watches were less accurate than the wall clocks, clepsydras, and sundials. But sundials were difficult to place and to use and their indications of time were rough at best. The clepsydras were very inaccurate, except when they were used with extreme care as was done by astronomers.

The invention of the pendulum by Leonardo da Vinci, and its development in Italy during the sixteenth century, represented an advance, but this was of little practical value until the theory and practice of pendulums were established by Galileo and chiefly by Huygens, which takes us far beyond the Renaissance. Huygens' great work on pendulum clocks, *Horologium oscillatorium*, did not appear until late in the seventeenth century (Paris, 1673).

In short, the problem of measuring time was not satisfactorily solved, either theoretically or practically, during the Renaissance. Many of the clocks, watches, clepsydras, and sundials made in this period were beautiful instruments, which have found a place in our museums, but they were not accurate timepieces.[6]

MECHANICS

Mechanical theory may be said to begin with Aristotle and Archimedes; as it was an integral part of philosophy, its development was scarcely interrupted during later times, but its mediaeval history is that of a long incubation.[7] Not until the Renaissance did the theory of mechanics become independent of scholasticism and achieve mathematical clearness. The emancipation and clarification of theoretical mechanics was an Italian achievement, like the progressive solution of cubic and biquadratic equations. Indeed, some of the early mechanicians were also algebraists, which is not surprising; but the principles of mechanics were more difficult to disentangle than those of algebra. The story of sixteenth-century mechanics has not yet been told with sufficient completeness.[8]

In the development of the theory of equations the first steps were taken by Italians, but credit for the climax was shared by one Italian, Bombelli, with foreigners, chiefly Viète and Stevin. In mechanical theory the sixteenth-century preparation was almost exclusively Italian but in the climax Galileo shared the honors with a foreigner, the Fleming Stevin. Actually Stevin preceded Galileo, for his main work on statics and hydrostatics was published in 1586, more than half a century before Galileo's, which appeared in 1638.[9] Stevin is definitely a man of the Renaissance, while Galileo belongs to the following generation, half way between Stevin and Descartes; he

was one of the seventeenth-century inheritors of the mediaeval incubation and the Renaissance clarification.

The appearance of Stevin's work in 1586 was astounding, because
his inventions were derived not so much from the sixteenth-century
Italian tradition as from the much older one stemming from
Archimedes. The Italian chain described above was a short one; that
to which Stevin belonged was much longer—Archimedes, Stevin,
Galileo—, extending over nineteen centuries and a half. I do not
know to what extent, if at all, Stevin used the sixteenth-century
Italian writers, but he stood solidly on Archimedes' shoulders.[10]

Three of his books appeared in 1586, all printed in Dutch by
Christopher Plantin in Leiden:[11] *De Beghinselen der Weeghconst*
(principles of statics), *De Weeghdaet, Praxis artis ponderariae* (applications of statics), and *De Beghinselen der Waterwichts* (principles
of hydrostatics). The three booklets were like three parts of one book,
each with its own title page; they could be sold separately or bound
together.[12] The three title pages were alike except for the title, all
having the same woodcut and motto. The woodcut represented an
inclined plane surrounded by a chain. This was the famous "mental"
experiment which Stevin had used to prove the law of equilibrium
on an inclined plane, assuming as a postulate the impossibility of
perpetual motion. The experiment was perfectly simple, and yet so
convincing that Stevin was utterly astonished. We all experience
that feeling when we discover that something that looked extremely
difficult is really simple if tackled in the right way; it is as though
one braced oneself to pick up a heavy suitcase and found it was light as
a feather. Hence Stevin added the motto, "Wonder en is gheen wonder" (the wonder is no wonder)—a curious and tantalizing phrase.

Besides his proof of the law of equilibrium on an inclined plane,
Stevin's books of 1586 contained other novelties: a new proof of the
conditions of equilibrium of a horizontal lever with unequal arms,
the parallelogram of forces, the decomposition of a single force into
two normal components, a "statical axiom" approaching the principle of virtual displacement, and the representation of forces by
vectors. In the third book, dealing with hydrostatics, he restated the
principle of hydrostatic equilibrium, the laws of hydrostatic pressure
and their application to communicating vessels; and he stated before
Pascal the hydrostatic paradox (the proposition that any quantity of
water, however small, may be made to counterbalance any weight,

however great). He also adumbrated the notion of the metacenter of a floating body.

All of this was, or might have been, derived straight from Archimedes. We need not assume that Stevin did not know the Italian textbooks of his own century; he probably knew some of them, but he knew Archimedes much better. The title "Archimedes of his time" or "the new Archimedes" has often been given to mechanical inventors by ignorant people who had no idea of Archimedes' mechanical genius and thought of him only as a Greek Edison.[13] The title was never given to Stevin, who truly deserved it.

Archimedes and Stevin dealt only with statics. This is typical of their genius. Dynamics was not unknown; it was at least as old as Aristotle, but it implied so many assumptions that it was very speculative. The notion of *impetus* had been introduced in the first half of the sixth century by Simplicios and Philoponos, but nothing had come out of it until seven centuries later. During the thirteenth and fourteenth centuries there was a new efflorescence of mechanical thinking, yet much confusion remained between the idea of *impetus* and what we call *momentum* and *inertia*. The subject became of greater practical importance during the Renaissance because of the development of firearms.

Gunpowder was probably invented before the end of the thirteenth century, but at first no one understood the implications of the invention.[14] Firearms were invented in the fourteenth century. Small cannon were used in the second quarter of that century but were very inefficient. Later they were improved, and their use became increasingly common; for example, during the siege of Constantinople (1453) the defenders used heavy artillery built by a Hungarian renegade, Orban, who was in the service of Muhammad the Conqueror. More and better guns were constructed during the sixteenth century. In fact, military engineering in all its forms (arms, armor, fortifications, and the means of attacking and defending them) was the main field of technical invention throughout the Renaissance. The outstanding figure of that period, Leonardo da Vinci, was a military engineer as well as a painter and a thinker. Nevertheless firearms continued to be inefficient for centuries. As late as 1776 Benjamin Franklin could still advocate the use of pikes, bows, and arrows!

The use of guns called for knowledge of the best way of hitting a

target; hence a new branch of mechanics, called ballistics,[15] grew up
during the first half of the sixteenth century. Many writers have
spoken of the mediaeval forerunners whose work stimulated Galileo;
to them should be added the military technicians and students of
ballistics, among them our old friend, Niccolò Tartaglia.

The first publications on ballistics were Tartaglia's *Nova scientia*
(Venice, 1537) and his *Quesiti e inventioni diverse* (various queries
and inventions) (Venice, 1546), which was dedicated, oddly enough,
to Henry VIII of England. The second of these deals not only with
ballistics but with artillery in general, the foundry of guns, the
making of gunpowder, the use and especially the training of guns,
and the manufacture and use of bombs. Not only were these books
the first of their kind, but they were often reprinted, and remained
popular and authoritative in military circles until almost the end
of the seventeenth century: to be precise, until the publication of
François Blondel's *L'art de jeter les bombes* (Paris, 1683).[16] This
may seem strange, because Galileo had established dynamics on a
new basis in 1638,[17] but military men were not physicists.

Before Tartaglia's time, it was generally believed that the trajectory of a projectile consisted of three parts, two straight lines
united by a curved line. The projectile first moved in the direction
given it by its projector and finally in the natural vertical direction
enforced by gravity. Tartaglia argued that such motion was impossible. The projectile was influenced by gravity from the beginning of its flight; it lost speed in the initial direction because of this
and because of air resistance, while the speed of its fall tended to
increase. But the speed of a body cannot increase and decrease at
the same time. Hence the trajectory was not a curve joining two
straight lines; it was curved throughout. He observed that there was
a conflict between the speed of projection and the speed of fall; the
greater the initial speed, the smaller was the influence of gravitation.
He made experiments with guns and found that the maximum
range was obtained when the gun's inclination was 45°. Other experiments of his concerned the influence of the charge, the length of
the barrel, the weight and diameter of the projectile, and the caliber
of the gun.[18]

This work was not particularly important except for the fact that
Tartaglia's method was experimental and his experiments were the
first of their kind. The next real step forward in ballistics did not

occur until two centuries later, with the discovery by Benjamin
Robins of the ballistic pendulum.[19]

OPTICS

The tradition of Ibn al-Haitham (XI-1), known to the Latins as
Alhazen, provides an excellent example of the appreciation of ancient and mediaeval science during the Renaissance.[20] The most important optical treatise of ancient and mediaeval times was the *Kitāb
al-manāzir*, written by Ibn al-Haitham in Cairo before 1039. It was
translated into Latin by Gherardo of Cremona (XII-2) and exerted
a deep influence upon Arabic, Latin, and Hebrew writers. Its influence was felt not only by mediaeval writers like the Pole, Witelo,
and the Englishmen Roger Bacon and John Peckham (all thirteenth
century), but also later ones, even as late as Kepler (d. 1630).

The earliest of these optical writings to reach the printed form
was the *Perspectiva communis* of Peckham (1482).[21] Witelo was first
edited by Collimitius and Peter Apian (Nuremberg, 1535, reprinted
1551). The great textbook of Alhazen was not printed until much
later. It was edited by the German, Friedrich Risner (d. 1580) in his
book *Opticae thesaurus* (Treasury of optics) (1572).[22] Risner's book
included the Latin translation of the *Kitāb al-manāzir*, very probably Gherardo's translation, plus the third edition of Witelo's optics.
Thus Alhazen was revealed to Renaissance scholars in printed form
ninety years later than Peckham and thirty-seven years later than
Witelo. Risner was a Hessian, but he lived in Paris, being a protégé
of Ramus; it was probably the latter who persuaded him to dedicate
his *Opticae thesaurus* to the Queen, Catherine de' Medici, and thus
ensure its publication. It is not certain whether Ramus could have
seen the book published in Basel in August 1572, for he was one of
the victims of the St. Bartholomew purge on August 24, organized
by the good queen. Risner continued the optical studies that he had
begun with Ramus, after the latter's murder, but they were not published until many years after his own death.[23] In the meantime
Kepler had published his *Ad Vitellionem paralipomena quibus
Astronomiae pars optica traditur* (Frankfurt, 1604). This may be
said to end the direct Alhazen tradition in Latin,[24] while Kepler's
Dioptrice (Augsburg, 1511) was the vigorous beginning of modern
optics.

Many of the optical ideas ascribed to Renaissance physicists can be traced back to Ibn al-Haitham. A good example is the *camera obscura*, which was reinvented by Kamāl al-dīn al-Fārisī and by Levi ben Gerson (both XIV-1), ingeniously applied to astronomical purposes by the latter, and reinvented again by Daniello Barbaro (1568) and by Giambattista della Porta.[25] As Henry Crew put it, "The principal interest which here attaches to the *camera obscura* lies in the fact that it is somewhat the connecting link between the single lens and the telescope. It is, in fact, the next step after the solution of the ancient question put by Aristotle as to why a square hole in the side of a darkened room gives a round image of the sun, a solution first given by F. Maurolycus (1494-1577)."[26]

Another example is the rainbow, which is mentioned in Genesis (9:14-17). Hence all Biblical commentators had to speak of it, but the first to attempt a scientific explanation was Ibn al-Haitham. Better explanations were offered by his Muslim and Christian successors in the thirteenth and fourteenth centuries;[27] some of these are almost as satisfactory as that of Descartes (two refractions and one reflection of light in the water drops; no explanation of colors), and actually superior to the explanation given by Marco Antonio de Dominis in 1611.[28]

The history of optics, and especially of such topics as the *camera obscura* and the rainbow, illustrates the extraordinary vigor of the Ibn al-Haitham tradition. His treatise, written in Arabic in the first half of the eleventh century, influenced a whole school of Muslim physicists down to the fourteenth century, while its Latin translation influenced every Latin optician from Vitelo and Peckham in the thirteenth century to Kepler in the seventeenth.

Another optical book, perhaps the most remarkable of the sixteenth century outside the Alhazen tradition, is the *Photismi de lumine** of Maurolycus. Francesco Maurolico, born of Greek ancestry at Messina in 1494, was primarily a mathematician, and has been called the greatest geometer of his century.[29] He was one of the outstanding teachers of mathematics in the Renaissance. His knowledge of Greek made it easy for him to study the mathematical classics, and he translated many of them into Latin. Modern mathematics of the late Renaissance and the seventeenth century was

---

* The Greek *photismos* means illumination as from a star. Henry Crew's translation, "light concerning light," is very good.

essentially derived not from mediaeval but from Greek mathematics. Maurolycus was one of the small number of men who made that resurrection possible. He lived in Messina, then in Naples and Rome, but returned to his native island, to Palermo and later Messina, where he taught mathematics and died at an advanced age in 1575.

He was in Messina in 1571, when the fleet of the Holy League led by Don Juan of Austria came into that port. Maurolycus was asked to predict the weather, and gave full instructions, which were followed by Don Juan and enabled him to defeat the Turkish fleet at the battle of Lepanto, October 7, 1571. Maurolycus was lucky; such long-range weather forecasts would not be possible today!

The greatest part of his *Photismi* was already written by 1554, and the whole work was completed at the end of 1567,[30] that is, before the publication of Risner's *Opticae thesaurus*. It does not follow that Maurolycus was not acquainted with Alhazen's book, because he might have read a manuscript of it, or the Alhazen tradition might have reached him indirectly. However, his own *Photismi* was very different; it was composed in the Greek mathematical style with which he was familiar.[31] Its full title describes its contents: "Light concerning Light, consisting of A Chapter on Shadows & Reflection followed by Three Books on Refraction of which the first deals with transparent bodies, the second with the rainbow, the third with the structure of the human eye & the forms of spectacles."

Maurolycus' *Photismi* may have been the best optical book of the Renaissance, but as it remained unpublished it could not exert any influence before 1611. The most popular book on optics in the sixteenth century was, unfortunately, of a very different and inferior kind, the *Magia naturalis* (natural magic) (1558) of Giambattista della Porta. The best one, after the *Photismi*, was the *De refractione* (1593) by the same author.

Joannes Baptista (Giambattista) della Porta was one of the most famous scientific writers of his age, and a typical figure among the scientists of the period. He was born in Naples about 1535-40 and died there in 1615. A precocious lad, he started early to read all the Latin books he could lay his hands on, especially those which circulated under the name of Arnold of Villanova (XIII-2) and those of his older contemporary, Cardano (1501-76). He traveled widely, visiting libraries, collections, and workshops and becoming acquainted with dilettanti and artisans. He was a classical scholar, a physician and physicist, an oculist and occultist, a student of natural history and natural magic, a physiognomist and alchemist. Although a man of immense learning, he lacked common sense; he was as erratic and mystical as Cardano, and in very much the same way. In addition he was a fertile playwright, the author of some thirty comedies, half of which are still extant. His plays, which derived from Plautus and from the Italian *novelle,* exerted some influence on the English stage, for some of them were well known in England.[32] Thomas Middleton's *No Wit, No Help like a Woman's* was based on Della Porta's comedy *La Sorella.*

According to his own statement, Della Porta began his main "scientific" work at the age of fifteen. This was the *Magia naturalis sive de miraculis rerum naturalium* (natural magic, or miracles of the world of nature)[33]—a queer mixture of physics with various kinds of magic, the magical ingredients being so numerous that the book was censured and put on the *Index expurgatorius.* The *Index* was used to condemn not only heretical books but also many that propagated magic and occultism; one must give credit to the Catholic Church for its incessant fight against superstitious tendencies.[34]

The *Magia naturalis* was largely a compilation of the abundant mediaeval literature on secret lore, to which Della Porta had added much of the chemical and physical knowledge that had accumulated in the fifteenth and sixteenth centuries, together with notions that had occurred to him in the course of his readings and meditations. The book contains many good ideas and good intentions, which, alas, are drowned in an ocean of nonsense. It resembles Cardano's *De subtilitate rerum* (Nuremberg, 1550) and *De rerum varietate* (Basel, 1557); these three works, published in the same decade, are typical of the incredible fermentation of ideas that was taking place, which to a large extent was unsound and morbid. One can hardly praise a man for a wise saying if it is hopelessly entangled with superstitions, or for an invention if it is lost in a hotchpotch of fantasies. The very title of Della Porta's book is an indication of intellectual confusion. *"Magia naturalis"* was white magic as opposed to black magic; it symbolized a generous aspiration after truth, which Della Porta could not fulfill because of his immoderate dreams and uncritical attitude. It would take a century of patient effort before *magia naturalis* could become *philosophia naturalis.*

To understand his state of mind, we must remember that even now we often speak of the marvels and mysteries of science.[35] Many a scientific vocation has been awakened by such marvels, but none had a chance of flowering without incessant criticism and austere, honest, patient investigation.

The *Magia naturalis* was Della Porta's best known book, but he wrote many others: on secret writing,[36] on orchards and the care of fruit trees,[37] on architecture and husbandry,[38] and on physiognomy.[39] In his *Phytognomonica*[40] he draws many fanciful analogies between plants and animals, illustrated with woodcuts—for example, an aconite root is compared with a scorpion, or a lobster and a walnut with a *foetus in utero*. In other books he discussed hydraulic engines;[41] mathematics; mnemonics,[42] a topic that fascinated mediaeval scholars; "celestial physiognomy;"[43] chemistry and alchemy;[44] and meteorology.[45]

His serious work on optics is entitled *De refractione optices parte libri IX* (Naples, 1593). It deals with refraction in general, lenses, the anatomy of the eye and the refraction of light into it, binocular vision, the nature of light, and the rainbow. It includes some novelties; for example, he tried to determine the focal length of a concave mirror. On the basis of this treatise Della Porta has been called, erroneously, the father of modern optics. He could not have known Maurolycus' book, which was not printed until 1611, but he was well acquainted with Risner's *Opticae thesaurus,* and did not improve on it.

Della Porta's case is tragic, for he had some understanding of the experimental method, and might have done far better work had he not been sidetracked by the massiveness of his erudition (much of it unsound) and by an unwieldy imagination. He was keenly interested in natural phenomena and even more in unnatural ones, and his excessive love of marvels betrayed him at every step. He tried to explain these mysterious things in rational terms, but failed repeatedly, because he started at the wrong end and with the wrong spirit. Various inventions were ascribed to him, such as the *camera obscura* and spectacles, which were much older, and the telescope, which was invented in his lifetime but not by him.

His scientific and pseudo-scientific work was almost as abundant as Cardano's, but unredeemed by the mathematical discoveries of the latter. His best work seems to have been in the field of natural

history and horticulture rather than in physics. He gathered so
many curiosities, natural and other, in his estate near Naples that it
became a museum; and he organized what might be called a botanical garden. His museum attracted visitors from many countries, for
example, the French dilettante, Fabri de Peiresc,[46] but we must
assume that it was not better than other Renaissance collections of
the same kind. As natural history and anthropology were still undeveloped and unsystematic, these early "museums" were merely
exhibitions of marvels and curiosities with little scientific value.[47]

SPECTACLES

Spectacles were invented toward the end of the thirteenth century,
probably in northern Italy; there are various proofs of their use in
the fourteenth century, but they were still relatively rare.[48] According to a Latin letter of his, Petrarch began to use glasses when he
was 60 (in 1364). In one of his poems Charles d'Orléans (1391-1455)
refers to "lunettes" that facilitate reading. The early spectacles were
often very expensive, mounted in gold and adorned with jewels.
Hence mention of them is found in wills and account books.[49]

Although printed texts were easier to read than manuscripts, the
invention of printing brought about a rise in literacy and stimulated the habit of reading, so that it led to an increased demand for
spectacles. During the sixteenth century references to them became
more numerous in optical books like those of G. B. della Porta and
Maurolycus, and in medical books.[50] After that we may assume that
every book dealing with eye diseases refers to the use of spectacles.[51]

The earliest known representation of spectacles occurs in a Tre-
viso fresco by Tommaso da Modena, dated 1352. A very remarkable
example was given by Jan Van Eyck in the Virgin of Canon Van
der Paele, completed in 1436 (Museum of Bruges), a lovely painting
and an astounding composition. Raphael's portrait of Leo X, Pope
1513-21 (Palazzo Pitti, Florence) shows him holding a concave glass.
There is also a woodcut by Hans Burgkmair (1473-1531). The list
might be lengthened considerably.

It is clear that in the sixteenth century spectacles came to be
regarded as symbols of learning and wisdom, even of sanctity. There
are a number of paintings or engravings showing ancient sages and
saints with glasses on their noses or in their hands. Among the
worthy people thus represented I have noticed Pythagoras and

Virgil, the Evangelists SS. Peter and Paul, St. Jerome and St. Augustine, and even the infant Christ.[52]

The trade in spectacles developed during the sixteenth century chiefly in Venice, Regensburg, Augsburg, Nuremberg, and other commercial centers. The grinding of lenses did not assume any importance before the seventeenth century. The making and selection of spectacles remained empirical until the middle of the last century. People often used them from snobbish motives, which explains Goethe's strong prejudice against people who wore them.[53]

NAVIGATION

The art of navigation had been enormously stimulated by the great geographical discoveries. Ocean navigation required considerably more knowledge than the coastal navigation of earlier times.[54] Some of the needs were merely technological, like more seaworthy ships equipped with better rudders and sails; others required the help of men of science of various kinds: meteorologists, magneticians, astronomers, and cartographers. Let us consider a few of the problems that cried for solution.

First, weather predictions. There is a considerable literature *ad hoc* in the fifteenth and sixteenth centuries, most of it astrological, some anti-astrological—all very inadequate, not to say worthless. We have already told the fanciful story of Maurolycus' weather forecast that helped Don Juan's fleet to win the battle of Lepanto (1571). Scientific meteorology was utterly impossible at a time when one could not yet measure temperature, and when the very concept of atmospheric pressure was nonexistent.[55]

The first navigation on the high seas was that of Bartholomeu Dias (1450?-1500), who circumnavigated the Cape of Good Hope in 1487-88. Columbus' historic voyage followed in 1492. Neither of them had much need of the science of navigation in their first voyages, because they did not know exactly where they were going. During the following century, as it became necessary to return as directly as possible to definite harbors, there was urgent need for navigational aids. In order to steer for his destination the sailor had to be able to determine the ship's position at any time and to locate it on a map (to take the ship's bearings and to prick the chart). Methods of performing these operations were very slow in developing, and during the Renaissance only rough solutions of the problem were achieved.

To determine the ship's position one must know two coordinates, the latitude and the longitude. The latitude could be measured approximately without too much difficulty. One needed only tables giving the declination of the sun and planets, and an instrument to "shoot the sun." Tables existed, even in printed form: witness those of Regiomontanus (1494), Alfonso X el Sabio (1483), Giovanni Bianchini (1495), and Zacuto (1496).[56] The Alphonsine Tables dated back to 1272 (not 1252), but all the others were contemporary products. The dates of publication are not too important, however, for these tables were used in manuscript form before they were printed and also afterward. It is probable that the tables most used by the early navigators were Zacuto's; they were certainly used by the Portuguese junta in spite of the fact that the German Martin Behaim was a member of it.[57] On the other hand, the Alphonsine Tables continued to be reprinted even as late as 1641, in Madrid, but that was a real aberration because the Rudolphine Tables of Kepler were already available (Ulm, 1627).[58]

As to the instruments, the astrolabe went back to the Arabs and even to the Greeks, the Jacob's Staff had been invented by Jacob ben Maḥir ibn Tibbon (XIII-2) or by Levi ben Gerson (XIV-1), and there were modifications of these fundamental types, such as quadrants, cross staffs, and arbalesters. The astrolabes and quadrants were instruments not only of observation but of calculation, by means of various diagrams engraved upon them.

The determination of longitude was far more difficult. The difference of longitude of two places is given by the difference of local time in the observation of a definite astronomical event, but how could one know exactly the time of the other locality? The simplest way of doing so was to carry a clock keeping the time of the other place; this was suggested as early as 1530 by Gemma Frisius, but good clocks were not constructed until the eighteenth century (1759), and were not commonly available until the middle of the nineteenth century or even later.[59] The only practical way, then, of determining longitude was to time an eclipse and compare the result with the Nuremberg time in Regiomontanus' *Ephemerides* or with the Salamanca time in Zacuto's *Almanach perpetuum*. Even on such special occasions (for eclipses did not occur every day) the results were poor. For example, an attempt to determine the longitude of Mexico City by timing two eclipses of the moon was in error by 25½ degrees, and that was on land; imagine the results one would have obtained at sea.[60]

The navigators were thus obliged to deduce the ship's bearings from the latitude and dead reckoning. Knowing the ship's speed and direction at different times of day, they could theoretically trace their itinerary on the map. This method was full of uncertainties, however. They had no way of measuring the ship's speed; the log was first described by William Bourne in a *Regiment for the Sea* (London: T. Hacket, 1574); it was hardly known before the following century and the early types were very inadequate. Even with a better log, it was almost impossible to evaluate properly the drift of the ship, the action of currents (as yet unknown), variable winds, and the effect of reduced speed or of tacking. Dead reckoning was a gamble; like the Yankee clippers of a much later age, the sailors of the Renaissance navigated "by guess and by God." In the report of his fourth journey Columbus accuses his pilots of making a mistake of more than 20°.[61] As late as the eighteenth century errors of 10° were not uncommon. In 1741 Commodore Anson,[62] a sailor of long experience, spent more than a month endeavoring to round Cape Horn to the westward and found, after long efforts, that owing to an unexpected easterly current he was still on the eastern side of it! Whenever possible, navigators stuck to the coast lines. At the end of the seventeenth century Mediterranean navigation was still, to a large extent, coastal under the guidance of regional pilots.

THE COMPASS

The directive property of a magnetic needle was discovered by the Chinese, who failed to apply it to any rational purpose.[63] It is probable that Arab sailors were the first to take advantage of it in navigation. The earliest references to the compass are found not in Arabic or Persian but in Hebrew and Latin writings of the twelfth and thirteenth centuries. We may assume that some kind of compass was used by various sailors, Muslim and Christian if not Chinese, before that time; but these sailors were hardly literate and, in any case, they had no reason to publish their discovery and very good ones for keeping it secret. The first technical description of the compass, its properties and uses, was given by Peter the Stranger

(XIII-2) in 1269, in Latin. Peter's *Epistola* remained virtually unknown until about 1520. It was first printed by Silber in Rome not long after that year under the name of Ramon Lull (XIII-2), *De virtute magnetis*.[64] The first edition under Peter's own name was the *De magnete seu rota perpetui motus* (Augsburg, 1558).[65] According to Peter, the magnet was directed *virtu Dei* or *nutu Dei*, yet he had some vague notion of the terrestrial force inducing the virtue of particular magnets.

The combination of the wind rose with the magnetic needle was achieved in the fourteenth century and in the following centuries compasses were made and sold by professional instrument makers, for example, in Nuremberg and Augsburg. It would seem that some knowledge of magnetic declination had already been obtained.[66] At any rate, one of the earliest compasses that has been preserved is in the Ferdinandeum of Innsbruck (Tirol-Vorarlberg, province of Austria). It was probably made for the Emperor Friedrich III (r. 1440-93); it dates from 1451 and indicates a declination of 11°E.

Christopher Columbus rediscovered declination during his first crossing of the Atlantic, on September 13, 1492.[67] He made more observations *ad hoc* on the return from his second journey to America, and concluded that the declination varied from place to place, and that at some places it was nil. This suggested a new method of determining the ship's position. To put it in our own language, if it were possible to trace on the charts lines of equal declination (isogonic), the ship's position could be determined by the intersection of a parallel and an isogonic line. This was a beautiful dream, and in their despair over measuring longitude, it was natural that navigators should cherish it.

We must not anticipate, however; it is certain that Columbus' discovery or rediscovery of declination in 1492 increased the interest in terrestrial magnetism, especially in the Spanish world. In 1525 a pharmacist of Seville, Felipe Guillen, constructed an instrument combining a sundial with a compass and specially adapted to the measurement of declination *(bujula de variación)*. The first printed discussion of declination occurred in the *Tractado del esphera y del arte del marear* (Seville, 1535) by Francisco Falero (or Faleiro), a Portuguese in Spanish service. Pedro Nuñez improved Guillen's instrument and developed Falero's theory in his *Tratado da sphera* (Lisbon, 1537),[68] but the magnetic observations of declination re-

mained very imperfect. Some of the best were included in the
roteiros (rutters, *routiers*) of João de Castro, dated 1538-41.[69] There
continued to be discordances, however, and as late as 1545 Pedro de
Medina skeptically remarked that the observed declinations might
be simply the results of bad measurements.[70]

The discovery of a dip of the needle (inclination) was announced
by Georg Hartmann (1489-1564) in a letter to Albert, duke of
Prussia, in 1544.[71] Hartmann was the first also to observe changes of
declination on land (6°E in Rome, 10°E in Nuremberg, etc.) The
idea of spatial variation of declination was thus reinforced.

The first to speak of the magnetic pole was Girolamo Fracastoro
in 1530, then Gerhard Mercator (1512-94) in *De ratione magnetis
circa navigationem* (Louvain, 1546); the first to mention two poles
was Livio Sanuto in 1588 (*Geografia*, Venice, 1588).[72]

James Clarke Ross discovered in 1831 the north magnetic pole at
70°5'N, 96°46'W, and ten years later came close to the south magnetic
pole, c.75°S, 154°E. In 1905 Roald Amundsen showed that the position of the north magnetic pole had changed considerably since 1831.
It is now established that the positions of the magnetic poles are not
fixed and that the magnetic data of every place are always changing.

The first magnetic map was prepared by Edmund Halley and
published in his memoir, *Description and uses of a new and correct
sea chart of the whole world shewing the variations of the compass*
(London, 1701).[73]

One of the best magnetic books of the century was written by an
English instrument-maker, Robert Norman: *The new Attractive*
(London: Richard Ballard, 1581). The discovery of the inclination
was announced in the title, which is too long to be quoted in full.
Norman's discovery of the dip in 1576 was the first to be published
(Hartmann's remained in manuscript until 1831). Both he and
Hartmann discovered it in the same way; a well balanced needle
lost its equilibrium when magnetized. Norman's treatise was dedicated to William Borough (1536-99), comptroller of the navy, who
added an appendix entitled *A discourse of the variation*[74] *of the
compasse, or magneticall needle*. Norman's book with Borough's
appendix was reprinted in 1585, 1596, and 1614.

Another Englishman of a very different kidney was William Barlow (d. 1625), archdeacon of Salisbury, who published *The Navigator's supply* (London, 1597) and *Magneticall advertisements* (Lon-

don, 1616), and was praised as a forerunner of Gilbert. There was some contemporary controversy on the subject. Barlow and Gilbert corresponded and each may have given new ideas to the other, but Gilbert was undoubtedly the greater man.

De Havenvinding (Leiden, 1599) of Simon Stevin was the last sixteenth-century treatise on terrestrial magnetism. It was widely read not only in the original Dutch (Dutch was then a more important language than it is today), but also in Latin, English, and French.[75] The English version, *The haven-finding art,* includes a table giving the declination, latitude, and longitude of forty-three places. The longitudes, by the way, are often wrong, the average error amounting to 6°. According to Stevin himself, the data concerning declination had been collected by his singular countryman, Petrus Plancius, theologian and geographer.[76] Plancius had discovered or rediscovered the idea that lines of equal declination might provide a second locus instead of the elusive longitudes and, if charted, enable sailors to determine their position. Stevin was less optimistic but recognized the value of declination measurements in navigation. Other physicists shared these hopes, e.g., Giambattista della Porta in his *Magia naturalis.*[77] They were carried to the point of extravagance by Guillaume Le Nautonier in 1603.[78]

We should remember that mecometry (or measurement of longitude by the compass) was dependent upon the assumption that the declination was constant in any place. This was stated by Gilbert (1600) in dogmatic form: "Variatio uniuscujusque loci constans est." (*De magnete* IV, 3). In the *De sectore et radio* of Edmund Gunter (London: W. Jones, 1623) different values of the declination of sundry places were given; this helped the discovery of secular variation by the English mathematician, Henry Gellibrand, in 1635.[79]

WILLIAM GILBERT

The story of how knowledge of terrestrial magnetism developed during the Renaissance has been told in some detail because of its intrinsic importance and also because it was one of the very few fields of scientific endeavor in which tangible progress was made. I must now tell the climax of that story, which was the publication at the very end of the period of one of the greatest books of science, William Gilbert's *De magnete, magneticisque corporibus, et de magno magnete tellure; Physiologia nova plurimis et argumentis et experimentis demonstrata* (254 pp., 29 cm., London: Peter Short, 1600).[80] This very ambitious title would read in English, "On the magnet, magnetic bodies, and the great magnet (the earth); new physiology explained with many arguments and experiments." The word "physiology" has its old meaning of natural science or philosophy.

According to the title page the author was William Gilbert of Colchester, physician in London. According to the very long epitaph on his monument in Holy Trinity, Colchester, Gilbert died on November 30, 1603 (December 10, N.S.) in the sixty-third year of his life.[81] It has generally been concluded that he was born in 1540. The epitaph is erroneous, for according to a horoscope of his, preserved in the Bodleian, he was born in 1544, on May 24. He matriculated in 1558 at St. John's College, Cambridge, being then 14, which was the normal age. He obtained his M.A. in 1564 and then studied medicine. A readership in medicine had been established in Cambridge by Thomas Linacre (1460?-1524). Gilbert won his M.D. in 1569 and then traveled to Italy for postgraduate work. It is highly probable that he studied in Padua under Fabricius.[82] After his return to England he became a fellow of the Royal College of Physicians.[83] This was the beginning of a very distinguished medical career; he was chief physician to Queen Elizabeth and for a very short time to King James; in the meanwhile, he had been elected President of the Royal College of Physicians in 1600. Being a man of substance, he was able to conduct expensive magnetic experiments, and being a man of prestige he attracted to his residence, Wingfield House (near the old St. Paul's), some of the leading men of science of his time.[84]

His greatest achievement, however, was the writing of his *De magnete,* to which he devoted the leisure and meditations of at least seventeen years; it was published in his fifty-sixth year. His social prestige was based upon his medical practice and his high position at the royal court; his immortal fame rests upon the *De magnete.*

The exceptional value of the *De magnete* is due to the fact that it was to a large extent based upon experiments that Gilbert had had the patience and tenacity to continue for seventeen years. He had acquainted himself with all the lore already available and had sifted it critically. On account of the highly mysterious nature of magnetism, a good many superstitions had gathered around it, and these he briefly recalled and rejected. He described the lodestone and determined its poles and what would be called today its "lines of force." After having detected the poles of an elongated magnet, he broke it and detected those of the fragments. He increased the power of attraction of his lodestones by "arming" them with steel caps (magnes armatus). Having made sundry experiments with a spherical lodestone, he was inspired to think that the earth itself was a gigantic magnet (sixth and last book). This bold hypothesis enabled him to explain the facts of terrestrial magnetism hitherto observed: first the general tendency of the compass to turn toward the north, then the declination and the inclination. By means of his terrella (as he called his spherical lodestone) he was able to duplicate the phenomena of terrestrial magnetism.

Incidentally, he remarked that the earth exerts upon the needle not a single force but a couple* of them (V, 5); this had been observed in 1581 by Robert Norman but was too subtle a phenomenon to be readily accepted. The idea of couple was adumbrated by Gilbert, but two more centuries were needed for its clear formulation. He assumed erroneously that the magnetic poles were identical with the geographic poles, and this vitiated his argument concerning the change in inclination and declination in different geographical positions. On the basis of experiments with a terrella he concluded that the dip would increase as one approached the pole.[85] An improved form of dipping needle might perhaps enable one to determine one's latitude.[86] The declination was more difficult to account for; he admitted that it was partly determined by the longitude but recognized (in both cases, inclination and declination) the existence of other forces, such as irregularities of the earth's surface, the proximity of non-magnetic water instead of land, magnetic iron deposits, etc. Hence he rejected the idea of mecometry, yet believed that magnetic forces were constant in each locality. If a piece of iron were submitted long enough in a suitable position to terrestrial magnetism, it would become a magnet.[87]

One of his most remarkable intuitions was that of what we call

---

* A "couple" is a pair of equal parallel forces acting in opposite directions but not on the same point; they produce a rotation, as in the magnetic needle. The idea of couple was introduced into mechanics by Denis Poisson (1701-1840) in 1804.

a field of force *(orbis virtutis)*. A magnet, and the earth itself, must be conceived as surrounded by a space through which the magnetic virtue is diffused and produces tangible effects (II, 7). He had the boldness to generalize this idea and apply it to the whole solar system. In the last book of *De magnete* he accepted the Copernican hypothesis and tried to give a magnetic explanation of planetary motions[88] and of the earth's rotation.

Though the work was devoted to magnetism, one of its chapters (II, 2) included a discussion of electricity *(de succini attractione)*. He was the first to make a clear distinction between electricity and magnetism. The basis of his distinction was erroneous, yet extremely interesting, if only because it showed that his experimental efforts had not been sufficient to overcome the scholastic tendency of his mind.[89] He related electricity to matter and magnetism to form; thus electricity binds the particles of a body together while magnetism gives it its shape, and in the case of the earth, the tendency to rotate around a properly oriented axis. Electrical attractions are caused by effluvia; the magnetism of a body is likened to a soul. The earth and planets are endowed with a kind of life (V,12). All this was metaphysics rather than physics, and proved his own deep inculcation not only with mediaeval dialectics but also with Neoplatonic philosophy.

The planetary views of Gilbert, as well as his sounder magnetic theories, were reexplained in English by Master Blundeville[90] in *The theoriques of the seven planets, shewing all their diverse motions and all other accidents, called passions, thereunto belonging . . .* (London: Adams Islip, 1602). His philosophical views were elaborated by Gilbert himself in the *De mundo nostro sublunari Philosophia nova,* and edited posthumously by his half-brother, William Gilbert the Younger. The edition (Amsterdam: Elzevir, 1651) was based upon two manuscripts belonging to William Boswell;[91] it is probable that other manuscripts had been in circulation before that. At any rate, Francis Bacon (1561-1620) had access to one of them. His severe judgment of Gilbert's achievement was largely due to the fact that he was so shocked by Gilbert's metaphysical fancies that he overlooked his first-class experiments. Gilbert was one of the first to vindicate the Baconian method of induction, but Bacon did not recognize this; he himself would have been unable to apply his own method as brilliantly as Gilbert did.

The history of science is full of stories illustrating the queer limitations of genius and the frequent inability of men of science to understand one another even when they stand closest.[92]

The main point to remember is that by the end of the sixteenth century, in spite of the fact that knowledge of terrestrial magnetism was still rudimentary, the cosmological implications of that knowledge were already perceived. A man of genius like Gilbert, in spite of his experimentalism, felt the urge to explain the universe in magnetic terms. The details of his interpretation were naturally incorrect, but its main import had been vindicated by the elaborate investigations carried out by students of terrestrial magnetism in many countries.[93]

Gilbert's book was the foundation of magnetic science, even as Vesalius' was the foundation of anatomy (in either case, foundation is very different from beginning). It was the first great scientific book by an Englishman. The second, by the way, was Harvey's on the motion of heart and blood, *De motu cordis et sanguinis* (1628). Both books appeared within one generation; both were in Latin, not in English.

CARTOGRAPHY

The reference above to a chart of isonogonic lines implied the existence of charts, and it is clear that the navigator could do nothing without them. What was the use of knowing his position at sea, if he could not "prick" it on the chart? His absolute position was of no concern to him; what he wanted to know was his position with reference to the harbors he came from and was bound for. It was only when he knew exactly the point (A) where his ship was and the point (B), his future landing, that he could "chart" his course.

All the early charts, the so-called *portolani* and their ancient forerunners, were coastal charts.[94] Oceanic navigation brought an urgent need for oceanic charts, but this entailed new difficulties. To sail from A to B one had to know the best route. Was it the great circle passing through these points or was it the loxodrome or rhumbline (a curve cutting all the meridians under the same angle)? The history of the loxodrome begins with the Portuguese Pedro Nuñez,[95] who was the first to conceive it clearly and to show that there were spiral curves coiling round but never reaching the poles

(1537). Nuñez was not able to draw a loxodrome correctly on a map, and there is no Portuguese map with correct loxodromes before Mercator. The latter's globe of 1541 was the first correct application of them to cartography.[96] The use of the Mercator projection made the drawing of loxodromes very easy, since they were projected as straight lines. The earliest example of this projection is Mercator's planisphere of 1568-69, but it was only approximately correct up to the latitude of 40°. The construction was empirical: Mercator probably noted where the loxodromes cut the meridians on a sphere and placed his parallels on the map accordingly.[97]

During the Elizabethan age, English interest in navigation was raised to a high pitch. Hence it is not surprising that further investigations in terrestrial magnetism, rhumblines and their projection were carried out in England. The first attempt to solve the problem with greater rigor (as much as this could be done without the resources of the calculus) was made by the mathematician, Edward Wright (1558?-1615). Wright's principles were applied with acknowledgment by Thomas Blundeville: *Brief description of universal mappes and cardes* (London, 1589) and without acknowledgment by Jodocus Hondius (Amsterdam, 1597). Wright finally published them together with tables *ad hoc* in his *Certaine errors in navigation arising either of the sea chart, compasse, cross staffe and tables of declination of the sunne and fixed starres detected and corrected* (London: Sims, 1599).

Though we are concerned mainly with sea charts, the Renaissance produced a great profusion of maps of all kinds. A few examples must suffice. As early as 1451 it was claimed (by a competent man, Flavio Biondo, in his *Italia illustrata*) that in 1341 Petrarch and Robert of Anjou had drawn a map of Italy.[98] This would have been the first of its kind, not a *portolano* but a true land map; but we have no other evidence of its existence. In the second quarter of the fifteenth century excellent cartographic work was being done in Austria, chiefly by Reinhardus Gensfelder and other men whose center was in Klosterneuburg. Their main accomplishment was the first map of central Europe.[99] It helps to understand the creation of a map of Germany, c.1491, by Nicholas of Cusa.

It is probable that more early land maps of other countries will gradually be discovered, though it is very doubtful whether any will be as ancient as those of Klosterneuburg. The earliest Portuguese maps are a century younger.[100] English maps can be traced to at least 1566.[101]

The compilation of land maps necessitated geodetic measurements. Peter Apianus realized that the earth is not a perfect sphere. In 1525 Jean Fernel measured the distance from Amiens to Paris and their difference of latitude (both places are almost on the same meridian; Paris is 2′ east of Amiens). In 1533 Gemma Frisius explained the principles of triangulation (he was the man who had advocated in 1530 the transportation of timepieces for determining longitudes). Apianus' *Cosmographia* was first published in 1524 (Landshut: Weyssenburg); the second edition, in 1533 (Antwerp: Arnold Birckman), contained in an appendix Gemma's *Libellus de locorum describendorum ratione*. Apianus' treatise was very popular and was reprinted many times; if each edition included Gemma's *Libellus* the latter must have been very well known.[102]

The compilation of maps was enormously stimulated by the invention of printing and engraving, also by the revival of Ptolemaic geography, which was one of the main fruits of Renaissance scholarship. The *Cosmographia* of Ptolemy was printed eight times from 1475 to 1493 (Klebs 812-813), the first edition with maps was as early as 1477 (not 1462). During the sixteenth century not only were a great many maps engraved, but also whole atlases. The first great atlas was the *Theatrum orbis terrarum* by Abraham Ortelius, first published in 1570; another famous atlas was the creation of Mercator himself, after 1585. These two Flemings, Mercator (1512-94) and Ortelius (1527-98), are the main heroes of early printed cartography, and their atlases are among the great treasures of our libraries. These early maps were fascinating (like all good maps), because they provided in compact and synoptic form a large body of information of vital importance not only to geographers but also to statesmen and merchants; in addition, some of them are so beautiful that it is a joy to look at them.[103]

THE EARLY ITALIAN ACADEMIES

The famous school that Plato created in Athens in 387 B.C. lasted more than nine centuries, until 529.[104] It suffered many vicissitudes but kept the same name, Academy, still an honorable word not only in Greek but also in almost every other European language.

There were Platonic revivals in the Greek and Byzantine worlds but we do not hear of any revival of the Academy as a real institution. On the other hand, Cosimo de' Medici il Vecchio (1389-1464) created an Academy in Florence with the help of his protégé, Marsilio Ficino (1433-79). Ficino had a good knowledge of Greek and translated into Latin not only Plato but also Plotinos and Dionysios the Areopagite. He was an ardent lover of Plato and of ancient wisdom, but he was also a passionate Christian. The Academy of Florence became a center of Platonic discussion; Cosimo was its patron and Marsilio Ficino its high priest. It continued with a fair degree of success the mediaeval task of reconciling Platonism with Christianity, and it stimulated the study of Plato and Neoplatonism not only in Florence but also in the whole republic of letters. Platonism in the West was deeply influenced by Ficino's translations, commentaries, and separate writings. That influence was not wholly good, for Ficino was a great believer in astrology and other superstitions, to the extent that the Church accused him of magic in 1489.

His Latin version of Plato was printed by Alopa (Florence, 1485), then again by Torresanus (Venice, 1491) (Klebs 785.1-2). The Latin Plotinos was printed by Miscominus (Florence, 1492). Many other books of Ficino were published before 1500, the most interesting being the first edition of his letters (Venice, 1495, 1497) and the most popular, his treatise *De triplici vita* (7 editions from 1489 to the end of the century; Klebs 397.1-7). Let us examine it. What does the title mean, the treble life? The book is divided into three parts: I. *De sanitate tuenda*, a regimen for scholars (1482). II. *De vita producenda* (or *longa*), continuation of the regimen; how to live not only in good health but also a large number of years (1488). III. *De vita celitus comparanda,* celestial events and their influence upon human life (1489). How can the *anima mundi* help the souls and even the bodies of men? How can we capture astral virtues for our benefit? This is a very remarkable application of astrology to hygiene. It was stated in the proem to the whole book that mental health should be given priority over physical health. This double insistency, first on the spiritual life and second on the universal life, is typical of Ficino's philosophy. His astrological bent, derived from Stoicism and Plotinism, was moderated by his Christian faith and obedience to the Church. Hence he vacillated. In a treatise of 1477 *(Disputatio contra iudicium astrologorum)* he rejected the principles of judicial astrology; in the third part of his *De vita* (1489) his astrological beliefs were stronger, and yet when Giovanni Pico della Mirandola published his attack on astrology (1494), Ficino declared his agreement with him. The ambiguity of his attitude is easy to understand considering his Platonic and Plotinian training and his lack of scientific knowledge; it is to his credit rather than the opposite.[105]

The Platonic academy was probably the model and inspiration of the many other academies that flourished in Italy during the sixteenth century. The first to come to mind is the one conceived by Leonardo da Vinci, but unfortunately there is no proof that it was ever realized. The well-known drawing bearing the legend *Academia Leonardo Vici* (British Museum) is apocryphal.[106] Leonardo was a meditative and lonely man, not a founder of academies.

The creation of the other academies in Florence and other Italian cities is a witness to the new spirit that was blowing all over the country and to the healthy competition that existed between various cities or between great patrons of arts and letters. Most of those academies (or *accademie*) were literary, artistic, or philharmonic, but many were interested in the mysteries of science and natural magic. These had strange names, *Accademia degli Umidi,* or *Rozzi, Apatisti, Umoristi, Insensati.* They were somewhat in the nature of exclusive clubs whose members might indulge in discussions on science, magic, and other dangerous subjects without running the risks of misunderstanding and denunciation on the part of the ignorant and the bigots. They were generally secret to the extent that their members were given academic pseudonyms. This curious habit was adopted by the oldest German academy, the *Academia naturae curiosorum,* founded in Schweinfurt in 1652 (now the *Leopoldina-Carolina* of Halle an der Saale). The fellows of that illustrious company of men of science received secret names until as late as 1870.[107] By that time it had become a tradition, but we must assume that in the sixteenth century secret names were used as a protection. This was the more necessary because few of the dilettanti who belonged to these societies had any clear ideas concerning the limits of science; the overwhelming majority were indulging in astrological and alchemical dreams that the Church forbade. Ecclesiastical persecution was not very frequent but always possible; hence prudence was highly necessary. Some of these academies indulged in another dangerous game, anti-Aristotelianism. Thus Bernardino

Telesio (1509-88) founded the *Accademia Cosentina* (or *Telesiana*), whose purpose seems to have been the detection of Aristotelian errors in science.[108]

Many of the investigations sponsored by these academies were equivocal and of doubtful value, yet if they had done nothing but keep scientific curiosity awake, promote discussion, and stimulate research, they would have rendered great service. A good example of interaction between these societies and science is afforded by the career of Giambattista della Porta, the author of the *Magia naturalis*. After his return from a grand tour of Italy, Spain, and France with his brother, Gian Vincenzo, he founded in Naples the *Accademia degli Oziosi*. Soon afterward, in 1560, he founded in the same city another academy, the *Academia secretorium naturae* (or *Accademia dei segreti*). The name was a little suspicious and Della Porta was denounced to the Church authorities. Paul V (Pope 1605-21) summoned him to Rome and ordered him to close his academy. He was then elected a member of the *Accademia dei Lincei*, which functioned in Rome from 1603 to 1630 and then died because of indifference, hostility, and lack of leadership.[109] Thus Della Porta was a member, indeed a founder, of one or two of the early academies and finally a member of the earliest modern academy. It is highly probable that if one were to scan the first list of Lincei, one would find many who had been members of the early academies.

This illustrates the transition between the science of the Renaissance and the more modern science of the seventeenth century. The difference between the Renaissance academies and the modern ones was complex. The latter were more averse to elegant dilettantism, less confused in their understanding of science versus superstition, more conscious of the need of measurements and quantitative experiments, and perhaps less snobbish in the selection of their fellows. The same differences were found, more or less, in the literary and artistic academies. For example, the *Accademia della Crusca*,[110] founded in Florence in 1583, became more scientific and systematic in its great purpose, the defense and illustration of the Italian language. Its *Vocabulario*, published in 1612, was one of the fruits of the Renaissance.

I am not aware of the existence in other countries than Italy of similar academies fostering scientific endeavors. There were very probably societies or fraternities devoted to the arts, the drama, and pageantry; whether they were named academies or otherwise matters little, but their lack of scientific curiosity is significant. For example, in Flanders the "chambers of rhetoric" (*rederykerskamer, kamer van rhetorica, chambre de rhétorique*), which were already numerous in the fifteenth century, increased considerably in number and prestige during the sixteenth century. They were established in every city and in many of the villages. Their main activity was the production of morality plays (*zinnespelen*), comedies (*kluchten, esbatementen*), and pageants (*landjuwelen*). They improved literary education but had no interest in science.[111]

II. Chemistry

THE ONLY TECHNICAL art that was never inactive was the art of war, and in this period the main novelty was the making of firearms, gunpowder, and other materials used in bombs for the sake of killing other people or destroying their habitations. The making of gunpowder engaged the attention of many chemists or alchemists.

Chemists had been dragged into the art of war many centuries before through the use of inflammable materials such as Greek fire (VII-2), but the manufacture of gunpowder and its improvement increased their opportunities considerably. Most of their work was secret and anonymous, yet some discussion of it is found in a number of treatises on military technology.[112] By the end of the fifteenth century the technical problems of warfare had become so many and so complex that every ruler had to have a military engineer whose business it was to apply every bit of chemical and physical knowledge to the art of war, either offensive or defensive. Remember that the first and only position held by Leonardo da Vinci was that of military engineer to Lodovico Sforza Il Moro (duke of Milan, 1481-99); Leonardo held that position for eighteen years.

As we have seen, Niccolò Tartaglia's *Nova scientia* (Venice: Stephano de Sabio, 1537) was one of the first publications on ballistics. A few years later appeared the *Pirotechnica* of Vannoccio Biringuccio (Venice, 1540). Biringuccio is perhaps the best exemplar of the military and peaceful engineer of those days. The Petrucci family obtained a post for him in 1513 in the armory of Siena; in

1524 he held the monopoly of saltpeter production in the Sienese territories. He was military engineer to Alfonso I and Ercole d'Este and to Pier Luigi Farnese of Parma, and at the time of his death, in 1539, he was head of the foundry and director of munitions for Paul III.[113] Simon Stevin was military engineer to Maurice of Nassau, prince of Orange and stadholder of the United Provinces. This list could easily be lengthened. The point is that military engineering was one of the few technical professions of the Renaissance; it implied chemical and physical knowledge as well as experience in architecture and in the arts of fortification and sapping.

CHEMICAL INDUSTRIES

Among the chemical arts of peace, the most important was perhaps the art of distillation, which is best represented by the *Kunst zu distillieren* of Hieronymus Brunschwig of Strasbourg (d. very old, c.1512). The *Kunst zu distillieren* was first printed by Grüninger (Strasbourg, 1500)[114] and was admirably illustrated with many woodcuts. Brunschwig's book is divided into three parts: the first explains the technique, the second describes the herbs to be distilled and their virtues, the third deals with very much the same materials as the second but classified in a medical way. The first part is the most interesting; it contains many drawings of alembics. Some forms of distillation had been practiced in the West since the twelfth century,[115] but it is typical of the slowness of technical tempo that a method of continuous refrigeration was not invented until the middle of the sixteenth century.[116]

Another chemical craft was the making of glass objects, which dates back to Egypt, Mesopotamia, and Rome but enjoyed a revival in Venice during the Middle Ages, reaching a climax toward the end of the thirteenth century and a greater one during the sixteenth century.[117] A sophisticated ceramic art was introduced into Europe from the Islamic world in the fourteenth century and a kind of glazed or enameled earthenware (faïence or majolica) was made in Spain and in Italy during the following centuries. The art was well described by Cipriano Piccolpasso of Castel Durante in *Li tre libri dell'Arte del vasaio*, composed between 1556 and 1559 but not published until three centuries later.[118]

Other chemical arts might be mentioned, for almost every human activity—cooking, baking, building, mining, washing, dyeing, paper manufacture, etc.—has chemical implications, but I must make haste to speak of the greatest chemical industry, the preparation of alum. This is the first example of chemical industry on a relatively large scale, and its story is exceptionally full of political, economic, and religious vicissitudes.[119]

A kind of alum found in the oases was dug three or four thousand years ago by Egyptians, purified and used as a mordant in the dyeing of textiles. Later it was used to improve the surface of parchment or paper, but the textile applications remained the most important. From the tenth century on the main source of alunite (*alun de roche*) was in Asia Minor, where it was fairly abundant. This trade came to an end with the Turkish conquest in 1453, and there was for a time a real shortage of alum. Some deposits were found in Volterra in 1458 and finally caused a war between that city and Florence. About 1461 one Giovanni de Castro, who had much experience in the alum business, having been the agent in Constantinople for an Italian textile firm, discovered richer quantities of alunite at La Tolfa,[120] in papal territory. These deposits were exploited by the Popes (chiefly Pius II until 1464, then Paul II until 1471), who thus became the first chemical industrialists on a large scale.

By 1463 four mines were worked at Tolfa by 8,000 men. Instead of paying tribute to the Turks for alum, the Popes were able to set aside their vast alum profits for crusades against the infidels; for example, alum money was used to help Matthias Corvinus (king of Hungary 1458-90) and to equip the fleet that won the battle of Lepanto in 1571. This was all very well, but the European nations soon tired of paying high prices to the papal cartel and tried hard to find other sources. As infringers of the alum monopoly increased in number and boldness, the Popes did not hesitate to anathematize them. In 1506 Julius II issued an encyclical (the first to be published in printed form) that excommunicated and perpetually condemned all people who bought, sold, or conveyed Turkish or heretic alum. This was a dangerous game, which jeopardized not only Catholic alum but also the Catholic Church. In every nation new and greater efforts were made to obtain non-papal alum. Under Henry VIII the English bestirred themselves to find native alum, but their attempts were not very successful in spite of the cooperation of the mathematician, Robert Recorde.

It is a complicated story. The textile merchants needed a mordant for dyeing their wares. Until 1543 their needs were easily filled thanks to the Italian brokers established in Constantinople. After the fall of the great city, that flourishing business came to a stop. A new and greater alum industry was started by the Popes and their Medici bankers and reached its climax under Paul II. In the year of his death (1471) the profit was as high as 140,000 ducats, but then it began to decline. Many new things happened—the growth of nationalism, the Reformation, the industrial progress of northern countries—and the Popes were gradually driven out of the chemical industry and were obliged to concentrate their attention on ecclesiastical needs and political emergencies.

THE SECRETS OF ALCHEMY

A fu'l account of Renaissance chemistry should devote considerable space to its secret and mystical aspects, but this will not be done here. The word alchemy is as ambiguous as astrology, or even more so. There was no sharp distinction between practical chemical work, such as was done by the men purifying alum, and fanciful excursions into the unknown. The craftsmen handling chemical substances found that certain combinations produced astonishing transformations, and some of them indulged in immoderate dreams. Would it not be possible to change base metals into noble ones? Even the ancients had been aware of the possibility of coloring metals; could one not transform as well their inner substance? Baser metals could be improved as to their color and surface; a single drop of gold acting as a ferment would produce an iridescent purple.[121] Could it not be that a better kind of ferment or elixir, the "philosopher's stone," would accomplish miraculous changes? There is no need to describe all these aberrations, which became more complicated as time went on. Although their hopes remained unrealized, the alchemists proceeded to make even wilder claims, asserting that the "philosopher's stone" would help men to create not only silver and gold but also things of greater value, not only material wealth but also health, longevity, happiness, and virtue.[122]

The alchemists were protected by princes, kings, and Popes, all of whom hoped to obtain more and more gold not only for good works but also for material power, war, and ostentation, or simply to satisfy their greed. The most liberal patron of the alchemists has already been mentioned: the Holy Roman Emperor Rudolph II, who was king of

Hungary from 1572, king of Bohemia from 1575, German king from
the same year, and emperor from 1576 to his death in 1612. Rudolph
patronized astrologers, alchemists, and other soothsayers, but he
also patronized Tycho Brahe and Kepler and stimulated the development of the chemical arts.

The alchemical situation, we should never forget, was extremely
complex. Some of the alchemists were undoubtedly crooks, and
others were self-deluded quacks, but there was a large group of
craftsmen, like the makers of pigments, dyes, earthenware, and
paper, the enamelers, the glassmakers, and the druggists, most of
whom were presumably honest. The craftsmen could hardly be
accused of propagating false theories, because they had no theories
at all, only recipes. Between the craftsmen and the highbrow alchemists there was a whole gamut from mere empiricism to fantastic theoretical excesses.

I shall not waste time discussing gratuitous speculations or describing the tricks of those alchemists who ever were ready to exploit the
credulity of their fellow-men. Instead, I shall speak of two outstanding men, Paracelsus and Libavius, whose backgrounds and purposes
were very different. Paracelsus was the more imaginative, and in
spite of many shortcomings and aberrations he was one of the greatest men of the Renaissance.

PARACELSUS

Paracelsus, or to give him his full name, Philippus Aureolus
Theophrastus Bombastus Paracelsus von Hohenheim, was born in
Einsiedeln, Switzerland,[123] in 1493. His father, Wilhelm Bombast,
was a prominent physician in that village who had married a distinguished woman.[124] About 1502 he moved to Villach in Carinthia
(Austria), a much larger town located in a mining district that boasts
radioactive thermal springs. There he continued his medical practice
until his death in 1534. As Theophrastus was only nine years old at
the time of the family's exodus to Villach, he received most of his
schooling in that city. The Fugger of Augsburg[125] had established
a mining school there, and in that environment Theophrastus could
hardly help acquiring some knowledge of mineralogy, chemistry,
and metallurgy. He has told us himself that he was trained from his
childhood by good instructors who knew the secrets of the *adepta
philosophia* (alchemy). Moreover, at the age of 22, he worked for a

year in the Fugger mines and laboratories at Schwaz in the Tirol. It is not clear where he studied medicine or where he obtained his M.D., if he did obtain one. He probably received his basic medical training from his father. He was exceedingly restless, however, and his *Wanderlust* continued until his death in the city of Salzburg[126] in 1541.

After leaving Schwaz he served as an army surgeon in Denmark and Sweden and took part in other wars in the Venetian service (1521-25). In 1526 he was planning to practice in Strasbourg, and in his certificate of citizenship he was called M.D.[127] It is not clear whether he actually began medical practice in Strasbourg, for he received in the same year an invitation to be city physician (*Stadt-arzt*) in Basel and professor at the University. He obtained this remarkable appointment because he had been able to cure the famous printer and publisher, Johann Froben. He became acquainted also with Erasmus,[128] who was then living in Basel and was in close touch with Froben; it is possible that Erasmus' influence was added to that of his old friend to give the young man his great opportunity. At any rate, Paracelsus did not use that opportunity very wisely, for he soon began to criticize traditional medicine in the most violent manner and to make himself as obnoxious as possible to the faculty. Having been trained as a chemist before he began his medical studies, he remained primarily a chemist, and his hateful originality consisted precisely in this, that he applied chemical ideas to medicine. He was a chemist in medical clothing and the majority of his brethren in Aesculapius did not like that at all.

The Basel faculty challenged his M.D. and even questioned his medical knowledge, but the city council supported him and kept him in office. Instead of recognizing his danger and trimming his sails, the tactless Paracelsus abused his victory. In the following June (1527) he caused a Latin program of his lectures to be printed and posted and declared his intention of teaching medicine not after the old superannuated treatises but on the basis of nature and of his long experience (he was then 33!). This proclamation suggests comparison with the theses that Luther had nailed to the church door of Wittenberg ten years before (1517). In order to add emphasis, he threw Avicenna's *Canon* into the St. John's Day bonfire.[129] To top it all, he lectured not in Latin but in German, or rather in the Swiss dialect.[130] It is possible that having been brought up in a mining environment instead of an academic one he could not do otherwise, but this was a final provocation to his colleagues. It was much as if a medical professor of today should lecture in thieves' argot. Moreover, it was a betrayal of professional secrecy. Latin was the esoteric language used to prevent the dissemination of learning to people who were deemed unworthy of it, or who might make a bad use of it.[131]

It is not surprising that Paracelsus' stay in Basel was not very long, less than two years. He then resumed his vagrant life, never staying as long as a year in a single place. At the age of 35 he found himself a kind of outcast,[132] and his rejection by society caused him to become more truculent and abusive than ever, thus aggravating his social disgrace. In spite of poverty and insecurity he wrote a great many books, but he was unable to obtain publication for most of them; even when the public censors permitted it, academic and medical intrigues were strong enough to stop the printing. The worst period of poverty seems to have been the years 1531 to 1534. At the end of it he reached Innsbruck[133] in rags and was soon driven out. His reaction to such contumely was increased contempt for the medical education and practice of his day. He seems to have recovered a modicum of peace and comfort during the last years of his life, which ended in Salzburg in 1541. He was buried in the Hospital of St. Sebastian, where his tombstone can still be seen against the wall of the church. It bears a long epitaph in Latin, the second half of which reads: "Here is buried Philippus Theophrastus, distinguished Doctor of Medicine, who with wonderful art cured dire wounds, leprosy, gout, dropsy, and other contagious diseases of the body, and wished his goods to be distributed to the poor. In the year of our Lord 1541, the 24th of September, he exchanged life for death."[134]

This gentle epitaph is as misleading as most of them. It is not likely that Paracelsus was able to accumulate much property, but it is true that he bequeathed what he had to the beggars of Salzburg and Einsiedeln; there is no greater generosity than that of the poor. It is true that he was a skilful wound-healer, but it is unlikely that he cured leprosy, gout, dropsy, and "other contagious diseases." The greatest inaccuracy, however, could not yet be realized at the time of his death. Paracelsus was primarily not a doctor but a chemist, and he exerted a much deeper influence upon the progress of chemistry than on that of medicine.

One of two opposite mistakes has generally been committed in the judgment of Paracelsus' contribution to chemistry: the first is to give him credit for inventions that he was not the first to make, the second is to deny his originality altogether and to consider him a plagiarist.

He was brought up in a chemical environment, so to speak, for he spent the years of his youth and adolescence in mining towns, Villach and Schwaz, where as receptive an intelligence as his could not help absorbing some knowledge of chemistry and metallurgy. These good influences were partly offset by the bad effects of reading alchemical literature, for Paracelsus was unfortunately as familiar with the alchemical delusions as he was with the chemical crafts of his time. His queer ideas were the fruit of this combination. The chemical treatises ascribed to him are apocryphal, but he explained his chemical ideas in other works, such as the *De mineralibus*, the *De natura rerum*, and *Archidoxa*.

His main idea in these writings was that of the "three principles," which he did not invent, but developed and popularized. It did not imply a rejection of the old theories of four elements, four qualities, and four humors, but was an addition to them. The three principles were Sulphur, Mercury, and Salt; these were not elements, but rather hypostases of certain properties inherent in various forms of matter. Sulphur represented the principle of combustion; Mercury that of liquidity, fusibility, volatility; Salt that of incombustibility and non-volatility, the remnant of every chemical experiment. The Paracelsists or Spagyrists did not speak of one sulphur, mercury, or salt, but of many salts, sulphurs, and mercuries.

Paracelsus did not invent the three principles, for these generalizations had slowly matured in chemical laboratories. On the other hand, he did introduce them into chemical literature, where they held their place until the time of Boyle and even that of Lavoisier. This fact was eclipsed for a long time because Johann Thölde[135] published between 1599 and 1624 a series of books ascribed to a "Benedictine monk, Basilius Valentinus" whose ideas were very similar to those of Paracelsus but who lived a generation or two before him. The conclusion was that whatever credit had been given to Paracelsus must be transferred to Basilius, reducing Paracelsus to the status of a petty plagiarist. It is possible that such an accusation was partly the result of Paracelsus' intolerances; the many enemies he had made had found the best way of revenging themselves.

Paracelsus' arrogance, it was said, was not justified by any genuine superiority; it was rather a mark of quackishness and ignorance. It is now certain, however, that the books ascribed to Basilius Valentinus (and also to other authors, Johann and Isaac Hollandus) did not precede Paracelsus but followed him; these writings are forgeries, and the forgers, whoever they may be (Johann Thölde in the case of Basilius?) were cribbing from Paracelsus, not he from them. It is thus necessary to vindicate him as a chemist, because his ideas were stolen from him. We must do what we can to repair that injustice, although such errors can never be entirely extirpated. Basilius' praise is found in many books (not only ancient ones); one of the best ways of testing a man's knowledge of the history of chemistry is to question him on that very subject.

The similarities to be found in the books of Paracelsus, Basilius, Hollandus, and others are not necessarily the result of plagiarism; they are largely due to the fact that all these authors drank from the same sources, Neoplatonistic writings, the Qabbalah and earlier alchemical writings, such as the very popular ones that circulated under the names of Arnold of Villanova (XIII-2) and Ramon Lull (XIII-2).

When speaking of different forms of air, Paracelsus used the Greek word *chaos*.[136] This word had a strange fate. It was changed by one of Paracelsus' disciples, Jan Baptista Van Helmont (c.1577-c.1644), into gas, and the word gas has remained with us in many languages until today. In American English we use it not only for real gases but also for rock oil (petroleum)!

Paracelsus was called the founder of iatrochemistry (chemistry combined with medicine). As he put it, "Many have said of alchemy that it is for making gold and silver. But here such is not the aim but to consider only that virtue and power may lie in medicines." "The purpose is to make *arcana* and to direct them against diseases."[137] Paracelsus' influence on medicine was not great, but he gave a strong impetus to a new kind of alchemy. The difficulties inherent in his position half way between chemistry and medicine were aggravated by his boorishness, his bitterness, and, it must be added, by romantic and quackish tendencies. We shall see him in a better light if we remember that such tendencies were typical of the Renaissance climate, and we shall have more sympathy for him and understand him better if we compare him with some of his contemporaries, such as Geronimo Cardano and Giambattista della Porta.

He was very boastful as well as contemptuous of others (these two vices are often combined). One cannot help suspecting that he had not been well educated and was ignorant of many things. Indeed, his originality, like that of Leonardo da Vinci, was partly due to his ignorance and his lack of academic inhibitions. He wrote a number of theological books which happily for him remained unpublished until long after his death; he was a devoted Catholic until the end but his writings were sometimes widely divergent from orthodoxy. He was not a reformer and was as ready to criticize Lutheran usages as Catholic ones; but he was a born rebel in the religious field as well as in others, and he had to pay the heavy price which every nonconformist has to pay in any kind of society.

PARACELSUS' INFLUENCE

Paracelsus' influence on medicine will be discussed below; here we are concerned only with his influence on chemistry. His books caused a big splash in chemical and medical waters, and many chemists of the sixteenth and seventeenth centuries were his disciples. The number of Paracelsist books (most of them in his defense) is legion. He made many enemies but also many friends, and less than twenty years after his death scholars such as Dorn, Toxites, and Bodenstein were vying with one another to publish new editions of his works, translations, commentaries, and dictionaries.[138] The controversy over his ideas continued with undiminished zest in the seventeenth century and later. I should not be surprised if some Paracelsian Rip van Winkle reappeared in our own day; if he had a modicum of cleverness, he would soon gather a fair audience.

On account of its occult tendencies, Paracelsism has attracted the attention of hermetic, theosophical, and alchemical writers throughout the ages. There is thus a relatively large Paracelsian literature that is definitely not scientific. During romantic and critical periods there has been a marked recrudescence of Paracelsism, as in Germany at the beginning of the last century, and even more so during the Nazi nightmare.

The Paracelsus theme, sometimes combined with the Faust theme, has inspired many poets and musicians: Christopher Marlowe (1601), Goethe (1808, 1832), Robert Browning (1835), Hector Berlioz (1846),

Arthur Schnitzler (1899), and Erwin Guido Kolbenheyer (1917-30).
One of the characters in *Fathers and Sons* by Ivan Turgenev (1881,
chapter 20), a country doctor, refers to the many truths that Paracelsus discovered "in herbis verbis et lapidibus" (in herbs, words,
and stones). A man as queer, emphatic, and turbulent as Paracelsus
has a good chance of remaining alive in the imaginations of other
men.[139]

LIBAVIUS

Libavius, the last chemist of the sixteenth century, was remarkably well balanced, very different from Paracelsus and from the mass
of Paracelsian adepts. Andreas Libau was born at Halle an der
Saale, c.1540 (a year before Paracelsus' death). From 1588 to 1591
he was professor of history and poetry at the University of Jena.
Then he became city physician and director of the gymnasium of
Rothenburg ob der Tauber, and from 1607 to his death in 1616
he was director of the gymnasium of Coburg in Upper Franconia.

The list of his activities shows how undifferentiated the professions
were at the very end of the Renaissance. The best chemical work of
the century was done not by a professional chemist but by a professor of history and poetry (meaning Latin poetry), a physician,
and, in American language, an "educator" (that is, a school administrator). He had a taste for moderating disputes; he tried to find the
truth somewhere between the assertions of the contestants. Thus he
surveyed the dispute between the Peripateticists (Aristotelians) and
the Ramists and the one raging between Paracelsus' friends and his
enemies.[140] It was perhaps the latter that turned his attention to
chemistry. He began his chemical investigations with the advantage
of being relatively unprejudiced, made many experiments with an
open mind, and succeeded in finding new substances, such as the
spiritus fumans Libavii, ammonium sulphate, and the glass of antimony;[141] he observed the blue color produced in ammonia by copper, and prepared sulphuric acid in a new way. This list of little
discoveries might probably be lengthened. On the other hand, it
might be argued that in many cases he was not the first to make the
discovery ascribed to him, even when he was probably the first to
publish it. By the end of the sixteenth century, we must remember,
there were already hundreds, if not thousands, of chemists and
alchemists who were trying all kinds of combinations and chemical

operations and could not help creating and observing novelties. Libavius did not invent any new theory, but he was good at criticizing the theories of other people (this was probably due to his historical training) and suppressing exaggerations. He fought magic and superstitions, yet shared many of them (how could it be otherwise in his intellectual climate?). He pruned the books of Paracelsus but accepted some of his ideas, such as the three principles. His moderation is sufficiently proved by the fact that he was accused by each party (the Paracelsists and their opponents) of being a member of the other.

Libavius' *Alchemia* of 1597[142] was called by Father Kopp the first real textbook on chemistry.[143] Such a statement is highly controversial, especially if we remember that chemistry was still groping in darkness and would continue to do so for another century or two. It is significant that the title of his book was "alchemy," not "chemistry." With regard to the fundamental controversy on whether or not it is possible to transmute common metals into noble ones, Libavius was still on the alchemical side; he believed in the possibility of transmutation, yet recognized the primary claims of experimentation; experiments should be made repeatedly in many directions, in many ways, and as carefully as possible. He was engaged in alchemical contoversies not only with Riolan but also with Josephus Michelius of Lucca and with the Frenchman Nicolas Guibert.[144] These alchemical controversies of the late Renaissance were passionate because they were largely irrational; they were endless because they were utterly unrealistic. The proper definitions had not yet been agreed on; the true problems had not yet been formulated; every theory was disputable, every term was vague and ambiguous. Correct ideas were hopelessly mixed with fantasies, and facts with superstitions.

The *Alchemia* of 1597 is divided into two parts, the first, *De encheria*,[145] on chemical operations and manipulations, and the second, *De chymia*, three times as long, on the preparation of various substances by the methods set forth in the first.[146] He dealt with a large number of chemical entities, the index to which covers twenty pages.

It was a bold attempt to put order into the alchemical chaos, but it came too early, and it was not weighty enough to put a stop to alchemical delusions. The latter continued to hold the ground and to make chemical progress impossible for at least another century.

III. Technology

THE INVENTION OF PRINTING

IT HAS OFTEN been stated that the three main inventions of the Renaissance (or of the late Middle Ages) were the use of gunpowder in firearms, the use of the compass in navigation, and printing from movable type. It is remarkable that all three were anticipated in China, though the Chinese invention was purposeful and complete only in the third case. Chinese block printing can be traced back at least to the eighth century and possibly to the sixth,[147] and Chinese printing from type to the eleventh century.[148] A Chinese government press existed as early as 1236;[149] paper money was printed in China and as early as 1294 in Tabriz (in Arabic and Chinese).[150] Chinese methods of printing were imitated in Japan and Korea but remained unnoticed in the West. In his elaborate account of China, Marco Polo (XIII-2) did not speak of printing,[151] although he must sometimes have held paper money and other printed documents in his own hands. This is an excellent illustration of the fact that we notice only that which we know and understand.

The first attempts at xylography, or block printing, in the West did not occur until the last quarter of the fourteenth century. Xylography did not develop to any extent until the second quarter of the fifteenth century, and it was then largely restricted to the reproduction of pictures with brief legends.[152] Its further growth was almost completely checked by the Western reinvention of movable type about the middle of the fifteenth century. This reinvention was apparently entirely independent; we have no evidence that the early European printers were even aware that their problem had been solved in Asia.

The problem itself, namely, how to reproduce a text in many identical copies by mechanical means, became increasingly urgent in the fifteenth century because of the growing need for books in universities, business, administration, churches, and schools. Its solution, by the invention of printing from movable type and of engraving from copper plates, was one of the greatest accomplishments of the Renaissance and one of the most pregnant discoveries in all history.

The idea of printing from type was simple enough, but its practical realization was extremely complex; indeed, new devices for better printing are still being invented today. One of the first problems was to find satisfactory means of casting uniform type and to select the best kind of metal for that purpose. The first description of type-casting was given by Biringuccio in 1540;[153] by that time experiments had been going on for almost a century. The type metal that he describes was a mixture of tin, lead, and antimony. Then one needed chases (rectangular frames to hold the type), presses, suitable paper[154] and ink (ordinary writing ink was not suitable; printer's ink had to be greased with linseed oil); etc., etc. Printing was not a single invention, but many inventions directed to a single purpose.

It might be more correct to speak of a double purpose, for the invention of printing brought about two great improvements: it assisted the diffusion of knowledge by making it possible to produce many books cheaply; and it assisted scholarship by promoting the standardization of texts. Books were now accessible not merely to a few privileged persons but to thousands of people; and scholars could cite a book knowing that the reference could be found in hundreds of private and public libraries all over Europe.

The invention of engraving, which was developed at about the same time as early printing (the fifteenth and sixteenth centuries), made it possible to reproduce illustrations as well as texts. This was extremely important for science, as well as for artistic purposes. A portrait of a man, a drawing of a bird or a fish, a flower or a root, was often worth thousands of words. The use of illustrations obliged the author to be more precise than he could be, or wished to be, without them. This is not yet generally understood even by good scholars, many of whom do not realize the need of illustrations, or what is worse, use them carelessly and uncritically.[155]

Modern historians discussing the invention of printing are generally inclined to attach more importance to the diffusion of books than to their standardization. The latter, however, seems to have been the chief motive in producing the invention. This was certainly true in China. Printing appealed to the Chinese because it was the best way to give authenticity to a text, which was particularly desirable in the case of the classics, Buddhist texts, and currency. The Chinese wanted every important text to be transmitted in such a way as to guarantee its accuracy, its genuineness, and its immutability. Printing was the only solution, and the Chinese exploited it thoroughly.

We are not so sure about the Western reinvention, though the fact that the first printed book was the Holy Bible suggests that the Western purpose was the same as the Chinese. Printers were at first conservative, and devoted most of their attention to ancient texts.[156] Gradually, however, they began to publish new books. Unfortunately their selections were largely based, then as now, on commercial prospects. The early printers were businessmen; though not as cynical and tough as our contemporaries, they preferred to issue popular books rather than unpopular ones, and could not afford to print books that would not sell. The result was that they printed books of every kind, both good and bad.

The Roman Church was the first patron of the early printers, because it realized that printing afforded the best means of preserving the Holy Scriptures and other sacred books in their integrity. Unfortunately the new discovery opened other possibilities as well. The printers published the Bible not only in Latin for clerks, but also in vernacular translations. They published not only catechisms and devotional books approved by the Catholic Church, but also the books of the reformers. It is possible that the Reformation could not have been realized without the printers' help; certainly it could not have spread so far or so fast.[157] The "divine art," as it was called by contemporaries, favored the establishment and growth of vernacular languages, and their defense was often combined with that of the Reformation.

The press helped to diffuse not only reason and faith, truth and wisdom, but also superstitions such as astrology and other kinds of soothsaying. To that extent it helped to debase the minds of men and to retard progress. No invention is good or bad in itself; it depends on who uses it and for what purpose. The compass was useful to pirates as well as to honest sailors, firearms were the tools of aggression as well as of defense, and printing could be used for many purposes, good and evil. Old Aesop showed long ago that the tongue was both good and evil, and the same was true of the printing press, except that it amplified good and evil infinitely.

To return to science and learning, the printers guaranteed the preservation of a book and made possible for the first time the establishment of a standard text. Mediaeval scholars had sometimes taken pains to correct and edit a text, but they could not be sure that they had done their task well or that it would not be undone, for it was practically impossible to compare manuscripts and decide which were the more reliable.[158] Thanks to printing, it became possible to make exact references to books and, if errors were found, to point out and correct them. The memory of mankind was infinitely perfected and further progress, however slow, in the advancement of knowledge was assured.

It has often been claimed that Italy was the "incunabula,"[159] or cradle, of the Renaissance. This is certainly not true with regard to the incunabula themselves, the first of which were made in Germany. Important novelties did occur in Italy, but many others are found in other countries, such as Germany, Portugal, and the Netherlands.

The invention of printing opened up much greater vistas than could immediately be grasped by contemporary minds. The first printed account of this great invention appeared only a generation later.[160] The parallel invention of engraving was equally significant. The fruits of the invention of printing were so abundant that it was in itself a revival, a transmutation of values, and therefore it is justifiable to consider its advent as the beginning of a new age, the birth of the Renaissance.

VANNOCCIO BIRINGUCCIO

The Renaissance was an age of inventions, of technology. One of its coryphaei, Leonardo da Vinci, was an engineer, the inventor of many machines and gadgets. In many cases he had been preceded by other inventors, some of them almost a century earlier.[161] The number of inventions was so large that the need arose for analysis and synthesis of technological progress. The best way to give an idea of this exuberance is to describe the work of three leading men whose books represent sixteenth-century technology, as the books of Gesner and Aldrovandi represent the natural history of the same period.

The earliest of these three men, the only Italian, was perhaps the most original. Vannoccio was born in Siena in 1480; his father, Paolo Biringuccio, was an architect or a contractor in the service of the city. Thanks to the patronage of Pandolfo Petrucci, a leading patrician of Siena, Vannoccio was able to travel in northern Italy and Germany and to inspect various works and mines. In 1512 he lost his father and his patron, Pandolfo, but the latter's son, Borghese, continued to help or to employ him until 1515, when the Petrucci and their protégés were driven into exile. Vannoccio visited Rome, Naples, and Sicily. The favor of Clement VII (Pope 1523-34) made it possible for him to return to Siena in 1523 and to resume his position in the armory. Later he was military engineer and technical adviser to members of the Este and the Farnese families. The Farnese connection enabled him to enter the service of Paul III (Alessandro Farnese) and in 1538 he became the head of the papal foundry and arsenal. He did not hold that important position very long, however, for he died before April 30, 1539.

His immortality is insured by his treatise *De la pirotechnia*, published in 1540, a year after his death, by Curtio Navo in Venice, under the combined sponsorship of the Pope, the Emperor, and the Venetian Senate. Was a book ever launched under highei auspices? It is remarkable that such an honor was reserved for a technical work; this proves the high value that the great of the world attached to technology, to material power. On the other hand, considering the hoary antiquity of metallurgy,[162] it is even more remarkable that the first comprehensive textbook did not appear until 1540. The reason is simple: metallurgists were workingmen or at best craftsmen, who could not write or did not care to do so, while the learned men did not care about metallurgy.

It is probable that Biringuccio was not trained in any university; otherwise we should have heard of it in one way or another. His genius was that of a technician and industrialist, and there was no formal training for such men during the Renaissance. He had to train himself in the studios and workshops. He quickly realized that technical jobs do not pay except on a sufficiently large scale with the help of power-driven machinery. He was a typical businessman, whose main interest was in material gain; yet he was rational and rejected the superstitions of his day. On chemical questions he was definitely with the artisans and against the alchemists. In engineering, he laid stress on exact measurements.

The *Pirotechnia* is divided into ten books, as follows: 1. Minerals in general, ores of gold, silver, copper, lead, tin, iron. Steel and brass. 2. Quicksilver, sulphur, antimony, alum, arsenic, etc. 3. Assaying and preparing ores for smelting. 4. Separation of gold from silver. 5. Alloys. 6. Casting. 7. Melting. 8. Casting of small objects.

9. Various works of fire (alchemy in general, distillation, coining money, arts of the goldsmith, coppersmith, ironsmith, pewterer; type metal, first account of casting type; drawing metal wires, etc.). 10. Fireworks in warfare and festivals. A final chapter deals "with the fire that consumes without leaving ashes, that is more powerful than all other fires and that has as its smith the great son of Venus."[163] What fire is that? Love. This was a very Italian and very gallant way of bringing to a close the first metallurgical treatise.

Its success was not inconsiderable. The original edition of 1540 was followed by three other Italian editions (Venice, 1550, 1558, 1559) plus a fourth one, more than a century later (Bologna, 1678). Richard Eden (1521?-76) began an English translation in 1552. A French translation by Jacques Vincent was first published (posthumously) by Claude Frémy (Paris, 1556) and was twice reprinted (Paris, 1572, Rouen, 1627). The success of the *Pirotechnia* would have been greater, but for the appearance of Agricola's work sixteen years later. Agricola appealed to the same public as Biringuccio and could obtain more readers in Latin and German than the latter could in French (both were available in Italian).[164]

EARLY GERMAN BOOKS

Before speaking of Biringuccio's German rival, let us say a few words on two booklets that were published in German in the first quarter of the sixteenth century, that is, not only before Agricola's *De re metallica* but even before Biringuccio's *Pirotechnia*. They were the first fruits (in printed form) of Renaissance mining and metallurgy.[165]

The first of the two, the *Bergbüchlein*, was the first printed book in the field of mining. It was printed between 1505 and 1510, probably by Martin Landsberg in Leipzig. The title of the second edition (Worms: Peter Schöfern, 1518) defines its purpose so well that it is best to quote it in translation: "A well-planned, useful little book on how to prospect for and find the ores of the different metals, with illustrations of the lay of the terrain and an appendix of mining terms, which will prove most useful to young miners." It did not belie its title, for though it contained only twenty-four leaves it was a most useful book, or at any rate, the practical part was. It presented in simple terms the kind of knowledge a prospector would need, the tools he would require, the ores of the seven metals and

their occurrence and associations, etc. Among the miners' tools was
the compass, the use of which is not very well explained at the end of
chapter 3. The theoretical part was much weaker, being vitiated by
alchemical and astrological considerations.[166]

The *Bergbüchlein* was published anonymously, but the author
was Calbus of Freiberg, alias Ulrich Rülein von Kalba, who served
the city of Freiberg as physican and mayor and died at Leipzig in
1523. To the two editions already mentioned (Leipzig, 1505/10;
Worms, 1518) must be added a few others (Erfurt, 1527, s.a.l.;
Frankfurt a.M., 1533; Augsburg, 1534; Frankfurt, 1535). Seven editions in thirty years, all in German, in five or six different German
cities; that was not bad at all for a relatively small market.

The second of these books is the *Probierbüchlein*, the full title of
which would read in translation, "A little book on the assaying of
gold, silver, copper, and lead. Also on how to assay and work profit-
ably all kinds of metal. Compiled with great care for the benefit of
all mintmasters, assay masters, goldsmiths, miners and dealers in
metal." It completed the first book, appealing to a new group of
readers, goldsmiths rather than prospectors, and its first dated edition appeared in Magdeburg in 1524. It is possible that undated
editions were issued earlier but not much earlier; hence the *Probierbüchlein* is about ten years younger than its predecessor.

The compiler is unknown; we can hardly dignify him with the
title of author, for the *Probierbüchlein* is a collection of recipes,
put together without order and without style. The compiler was
obviously a man of experience but almost illiterate. The demand for
such a book was so great, however, that it was often reprinted.[167]
Various other German books on mining and assaying were published
in the sixteenth century, for which I must refer the reader to the
Sisco-Smith translation of 1949. All these books were eclipsed by the
De re metallica (1556) written by a great man, one of the outstanding scientific writers of the Renaissance. It is time to meet him.

GEORGIUS AGRICOLA

Georg Bauer, alias Agricola, was born at Glauchau in the Chemnitz circle, Saxony, on March 24, 1494. He was not, like Biringuccio,
a self-made metallurgist but a scholar who got his B.A. in Leipzig,
was a teacher of Latin and Greek and vice-rector of the school of
Zwicken; in 1520 he became the rector and was assisted by Johannes

Förster.[168] Two years later he was called to lecture at the University of Leipzig, and from 1524 to 1526 he visited Italian universities (Bologna, Padua?). While passing through Basel after his return he made the acquaintance of Froben and Erasmus. He was back in Zwickau before the end of 1526 and was appointed town physician in Joachimsthal.[169] The German cities where he spent most of his life, Joachimsthal, Chemnitz, Freiberg, etc., were all mining centers.[170] This helped to develop his intense curiosity about geology, mineralogy, and related physical and chemical subjects. In 1530-33 he traveled throughout the mining district, making observations and reading books that might help him to understand better this aspect of nature.

In 1533 he was appointed city physician of Chemnitz, where he remained until his death in 1555. The position of city physician, or the medical profession in general, was then the chief if not the only calling in which a man of science could earn his living. For this he had to be an M.D. or obtain a chair in a university; most scientists who entered the academic world did so through the medical door. During his Chemnitz years Agricola published many books, based on observations made throughout his life. We can speak only of one, his greatest, the De re metallica, which was already begun by 1529 and was finished in 1550, but was not published until after his death, in 1556. The delay was caused by the preparation of the woodcuts. By the middle of the sixteenth century every scientific writer realized the need for pictures to illustrate and explain his text.

Although he lived in a Protestant environment under a Lutheran prince, Agricola remained a staunch Catholic. It speaks volumes for his character that in spite of this, in an intolerant age, he was on good terms with leading Lutherans, such as Johann Förster, Johann Froben, Melanchthon, and Georg Fabricius.[171] He was in good favor with the electors of Saxony, and Duke Maurice appointed him burgomaster of Chemnitz; he held that office, the highest in the city, for four terms. A Catholic burgomaster would have been impossible in a Protestant city if he had not been respected and loved by the population. Yet at the time of his death, at the age of 62, a church funeral was denied to him and his remains had to be taken to Zeitz to be buried in the cathedral of that city. The good people of Chemnitz may have said that there are limits to toleration; they could put up with the living Agricola because of his generosity, but there was no reason why the dead infidel should be permitted to desecrate their sanctuary.

In his long dedication of the *De re metallica* Agricola explains to the electors-dukes of Saxony[172] the purpose of the book and outlines the history of the "metallic arts," which are as ancient and fundamental as the "agricultural arts." He intends, he says, to treat mining and metallurgy as a whole, as other scholars have treated husbandry. The literature is less abundant, however. His earliest source was Pliny's *Natural History* (I-2), his latest Biringuccio. "By reading his directions," says Agricola, "I have refreshed my memory of those things which I myself saw in Italy. . . ." In reality he cribbed from Biringuccio as well as from the little German books printed during his lifetime. He also made some use of the abundant alchemical literature in spite of his distrust and contempt for it. His main source of information, however, was the manual tradition that he had observed with his own eyes in Germany and Italy and the oral tradition that he had collected with his own ears.

His work, much larger and more comprehensive than Biringuccio's, was divided into twelve books. I. Introductory, general statements for and against the metallic arts. II. The miner, the finding of veins. III. Veins and stringers, seams in the rocks. IV. Delimitation of veins; functions of the mining officials. V. Digging of ore, surveying (the use of the compass is well explained in this book, as well as in book III). VI. Miners' tools and machines. VII. Assaying. VIII. Roasting, crushing and washing of ore. IX. Smelting. X. Separation of silver from gold, and of lead from gold and silver. XI. Separation of silver from copper. XII. Manufacture of salt, soda, alum, vitriol, sulphur, bitumen, and glass.

Toward the end of his dedication he declares: "I have not only described these things but have also hired illustrators to delineate their forms, lest descriptions which are conveyed by words should either not be understood by men of our own times, or should cause difficulty to posterity.[173] I have omitted all those things which I have not myself seen, or have not read or heard of from persons upon whom I can rely. That which I have neither seen, nor carefully considered after reading or hearing of, I have not written about. . . ."

The main value of the *De re metallica* lay in its cautious matter-of-factness and in its relative clearness. Agricola had read all that the ancients had to say about geology, discussed the problems involved with practical men, and reached his own conclusions. For example, he was convinced that waters had created underground channels in the rocks and that ores had been deposited in them from metallic solutions. This was a prefiguration of the Werner theory,[174] but less comprehensive and less dogmatic. He asserted that bismuth and antimony were metals. He described the many processes used by miners, but did not claim any one of them as his own invention. Thanks to his association with workingmen, on the one hand, and his dislike of alchemists, on the other, he was an empiricist, stating as clearly as he could the knowledge available to contemporary miners, metallurgists, and smiths, describing their methods and their tricks. He once remarked, "Those things which we see with our eyes and understand by means of our senses are more clearly to be demonstrated than if learned by means of reasoning."[175] The quality of his scientific mind is shown by his account of the "forked twig"[176] or divining rod, which is critical and skeptical, yet moderate and sensible.

It is paradoxical that the first treatise on mining and metallurgy, next to Biringuccio's in date but wider in scope, was composed by a man who was neither a miner nor a metal-worker, but a physician and burgomaster; Agricola had been a teacher of Greek and Latin, not of science. He was a servant of Aesculapius, not of Pluto or Vulcan, but the classics had awakened and fortified his scientific curiosity and the circumstances of his life and directed it toward geology and metallurgy. He realized the need for a treatise on these subjects and filled it as well as could be done in his time. He was not an inventor, but he was a good recorder, and his *De re metallica* was a standard work for two centuries.[177] It went through many editions in Latin, German, and Italian. The English edition, issued in 1912, was translated and edited by Herbert Clark Hoover and his wife. Mr. Hoover is no doubt the only chief of state who ever translated one of the great scientific classics.

It is worth while to compare Agricola with Paracelsus, two Germans who lived at almost the same time[178] in mining districts and were deeply interested in mining and chemistry. The fame of Paracelsus was incomparably greater, but it was ambiguous and controversial; one cannot help asking oneself whether he was a genuine man of science or a mountebank, a self-deluded enthusiast. No such question will ever be asked about the cautious and critical

Agricola, who was less inspired and less inspiring, but was an honest man of science. Agricola did far more than Paracelsus to increase our knowledge and, what matters even more, to establish sound methods of investigation. While Paracelsus often risked leading us astray, Agricola helped to clear the scientific path.

LAZARUS ERCKER

The third metallurgical author of the sixteenth century is far less important than his two predecessors, but he completed their task. He belonged to the same country as Agricola, for he called himself Lazarus Ercker von Sant Annen Bergk, that is, Annaberg in the Saxon Erzegebirge, close to the Bohemian border, one of the places where Agricola had gathered his own knowledge. Ercker obtained such a reputation as a mining expert that he was employed by Rudolf II to inspect the Bohemian mines and suggest improvements. Some time after 1574 the title of his appointment read "chief superintendent of mines and comptroller of the Holy Roman Empire and the Kingdom of Bohemia." In spite of this high position, very little is known regarding his life and personality.

His great treatise on ores and assaying[179] was written in German and first published in Prague in 1574. It is divided into five books: I. Silver. II. Gold. III. Copper. IV. Lead, tin and other metals. V. Saltpeter.

Ercker was a professional like Biringuccio, not an outsider and distinguished amateur like Agricola. His function as the highest mining officer of the empire had caused him to become very conservative and distrustful of innovations. For example, the Spaniards had introduced amalgamation in Mexico and Peru in order to separate silver from its ores, and in 1588 they offered the secret to the empire. The offer was naturally submitted to Ercker, who reported against it! This seems almost unbelievable, for he had enough chemical skill to test the practical value of amalgamation in his laboratory. Perhaps he was getting old and his mind was unreceptive.

The main characteristics of Ercker's work are its matter-of-factness and soberness; it contains no mystical nonsense and no frills of style. He was a technician and administrator who never lost sight of economic considerations. An industrial process is no good unless it pays, and its ability to pay depends on many factors, which are not simply technical but also political. It may astonish modern readers to learn that his attention was focused primarily on gold and silver, secondarily on copper and lead, but hardly at all upon iron! Iron ore was left to the blacksmiths; it did not concern the assayers or the minters.[180] In spite of its many uses and its economic importance, iron was a base metal, and the chemists, alchemists, financiers, and governors were hypnotized by the precious metals. It is the most complete example of perverted fascination in economic history.

The publication of the three books of Biringuccio, Agricola, and Ercker, not to mention many others of a humbler kind, shows the Renaissance interest in mining and metallurgy. That interest was increased by the Spanish discoveries in the New World and the enormous importation of gold and silver that followed; it was increased also by the vigorous growth of mining in many districts of Europe, by the making of arms and armor, and more generally by the fear of the Turks, the growing need of military and naval preparations. The technical fermentation of the sixteenth century was almost as great as its artistic and religious fermentation.

Fourth Wing

NATURAL HISTORY

AN ASPECT of the Renaissance that has often been emphasized is the rediscovery of the Greek and Latin classics. It
is true that there was a revival of interest in the classics,
and many new ones were discovered or rediscovered, but
many qualifications are needed. To begin with, some
classics were never lost; in the second place, other classical revivals
had occurred during the Carolingian period (in and around the
ninth century), in the twelfth century, and later. It has often been
said that the revival of Greek studies in the West followed the fall of
Constantinople in 1453; as a matter of fact, it began a century earlier,
but it was greatly intensified in the fifteenth and sixteenth centuries.[1]

The art of printing added zest to classical studies. To discover a
new manuscript of Cicero or Celsus was enormously more stimulat-
ing if one could print the new text and spread it triumphantly
throughout the republic of letters. To prepare a critical edition of
an old text seemed futile and hopeless in the manuscript age, but as
soon as it was possible to print the critical edition, it became worth
while to take endless pains: to try to unearth manuscripts, to compare and study them, to collate them, and finally to publish the
results. This was not done as elaborately during the Renaissance as
it is today, but critical editions became gradually more critical and
more elaborate. Scholars were encouraged to compile glossaries, to
add notes and paraphernalia. It was rewarding to take all these pains
to elucidate familiar texts, but think of the excitement when an
entirely new text was found! That was as thrilling as the discovery
today of papyri and clay tablets, with this difference, however, that

if the new text was written in Latin, every educated man could read it; if it was in Greek, it was naturally more esoteric, yet many more scholars could read it than can read hieroglyphics or cuneiform today.

The chief books of natural history that have come down from antiquity were fully available to the learned public before the end of the fifteenth century, notably Aristotle, Theophrastos, Dioscorides, and Pliny.

Latin texts of Aristotle began to appear in 1472, the *De animalibus* in 1476; many of these texts were accompanied by Averroës' commentaries. The Latin edition of Theophrastos' *De historia et causis plantarum* was printed as early as 1483. All these editions were Italian; the Latin translator was Theodoros Gaza (c.1400-75) of Thessalonica, one of the collaborators of Vittorino da Feltre in Mantua, a scholar who knew both Greek and Latin so well that he was able to translate from either one into the other. The Greek texts of both Aristotle and Theophrastos were printed by Aldus Manutius in Venice (5 folio volumes, 1495-98); volumes 3 and 4, which include the zoology of Aristotle and the botany of Theophrastos, appeared in 1497.

As to Dioscorides, the Latin text was printed in Colle di Val d'Elsa (Siena province) in 1478, and the Greek text by Manutius in Venice in 1499. There was such a demand for his *Materia medica* that four more editions of the Greek text were published before the middle of the sixteenth century; the sixth edition, prepared by Janus Antonius Saracenus, appeared at the end of that century (Frankfurt: heirs of And. Wechel, 1598). Six Greek editions in one century! The Latin edition of 1478 was followed by at least seven more, and there were at least three Italian translations, one German, one Spanish, and three French, all before 1600.

It was easier to deal with Pliny the Elder, who wrote in Latin. The first edition of his *Historia naturalis* was printed by J. Spira in Venice as early as 1469, that is, many years ahead of any printed text of Aristotle, Theophrastos, or Dioscorides. Fifteen Latin editions appeared before the end of the fifteenth century, and sixteenth-century editions are very numerous.[2]

Thus by the beginning of the sixteenth century the classics of ancient biology were readily available, not only in Latin but also in Greek, and copies of them could be found in many medical libraries and in the bookshops of every university town in Europe. These texts brought forth a good many commentaries and animadversions, for scholars indulging in such recondite studies were too often of a jealous and cantankerous disposition. It was not enough for them to do their best; they often were anxious to shoot the work of their rivals full of holes. This is especially shocking in the case of editors of second and later editions. It was exceedingly difficult, and meritorious in proportion, to edit an unknown text for the first time. It was relatively easy for epigoni having access to newly discovered manuscripts to correct errors in the first edition, and they did so triumphantly and without mercy. Alternative interpretations of a text caused disputes that often degenerated into quarrels; the contestants were frequently malicious, cross-grained, unfair, and dishonest. The reading of Renaissance polemics gives one a poor idea of the urbanity and humanity of the quarreling scholars. There is still plenty of jealousy and rancor in the academic world today, but the behavior of scholars is on a much higher level.

At first most of the criticism was purely philological. One might claim that the manuscript had been badly read, or that words had been lost, and the detectors of such errors often made mountains out of molehills. Later, as the classical texts were used by people who were less bookish and more truly interested in plants and animals, the incidence of criticism passed gradually from words to things, from *verba* to *realia*. This healthy process was slow at first but increased in speed and intensity when the books were illustrated from nature. The first illustrated herbals followed manuscript traditions and copied the ancient pictures as slavishly as the ancient words, but after a while people became tired of these stereotyped pictures. One had to read the text and digest it in order to realize its inaccuracy, but a picture that did not tally with its legend could be spotted immediately.

THE "GERMAN FATHERS" OF BOTANY

This leads us to one of the most exhilarating chapters in the history of science, which is generally entitled "The German fathers of botany."[3] Any such phrase as "the fathers" invites discussion, but we shall not waste our time on controversy. What really happened—and I consider this as one of the truly great events of the Renaissance— was that as some naturalists realized the need of illustrations made directly from nature, there grew up a class of draftsmen and wood-

HIERONYMUS BOCK (or Tragus) (1498-1554), aet. 46. Portrait at the beginning of his *De stirpium . . . usitatis nomenclaturis,* etc. (Strasbourg, 1552). *Courtesy of Harvard Library.*

cut makers who learned to do this and did it well. Art and science
came together and great was the result. Botanists realized the need
of accurate drawings made straight from nature, but were also aware
of their own artistic limitations; hence they were obliged to enlist
the cooperation of artists, who with their different temperament
brought with them new illumination. Of course the artist was told
what to do, and did his best to satisfy his employer as to completeness and accuracy, but he also had to satisfy his own conscience. If
he was a real artist, the drawing had to be not only accurate but also
beautiful.

This new kind of collaboration was so difficult and complex that
it did not succeed immediately. The first herbal with illustrations
made from nature was the one by Otto Brunfels of Mainz (d. 1534),
the *Herbarum vitae eicones* (Strasbourg: Schott, 1530), including
beautiful drawings of plants by Hans Weiditz. The pictures were
made from nature, but the text itself was still Dioscoridean. Fearful
discrepancies were the result, for Dioscorides described plants of the
Near East, while Weiditz represented those of Germany. In some
cases Weiditz drew plants that were not known to Dioscorides and
hence had no names; Brunfels called them *herbae nudae* (nameless
waifs!). These discrepancies must have been noticed, for a better
collaboration was achieved in the second herbal, the *New Kreütter
Buch* by Jerome Bock, alias Hieronymus Tragus (1498-1554), printed
by Wendel Rihel (Strasbourg, 1539); the artist was David Kandel.
Tragus described plants from nature and made use of German folklore, even to the point of testing local superstitions.

The third "German father" was the physician, Leonhard Fuchs[4]
(1501-66) of Wemding in Swabia. Brunfels and Bock were school-
teachers and preachers, studying plants in their own gardens and in
neighboring fields; Fuchs was a learned physician and a humanist.
His herbal, *De historia stirpium* (Basel: Isingrin, 1542), was far more
elaborate than the preceding ones, describing 400 German plants
and 100 foreign ones; also it was better documented and better written. It may be considered the best herbal of the first half of the sixteenth century, as to both text and illustrations. Fuchs' book contains not only his own portrait but also those of his collaborators,
the *pictores operis*, Heinrich Füllmaurer and Albrecht Meyer, and
the "sculptor" (woodcut maker), Veit Rodolph Speckle. It is a great
pleasure to contemplate the honest faces of these four men who did
such good work together.

LEONHARD FUCHS (1501-66), aet. 41. Portrait in frontispiece to *De historia stirpium* (folio, Basel: Officina isingrininana, 1542). *Courtesy of Harvard Library.*

PICTORES OPERIS,
Heinricus Füllmaurer.   Albertus Meyer.

SCVLPTOR
Vitus Rodolph. Speckle.

HEINRICH FÜLLMAURER and ALBRECHT MEYER, the two artists who drew the plants for Fuchs' *De historia stirpium* (Basel, 1542) and the engraver, RODOLPH SPECKLE. These are the earliest portraits of scientific illustrators. *Courtesy of Harvard Library.*

The fourth "father," Valerius Cordus (1515-44) of Simmtshausen, Oberhessen, was even greater from a purely botanical point of view. He was not satisfied with the plants of his own country but wanted to see the plants that the ancients had described. He traveled widely not only in Germany but also in Italy, and died of a fever, perhaps the result of fatigue, in Rome at the age of 29. He seems to have led botanical excursions, for he was generally accompanied by a few students. Though he is one of the earliest botanists of the Renaissance, his untimely death delayed the publication of his work, which we owe to the piety of Conrad Gesner (Strasbourg: Josias Rihel, 1561). Cordus was not only a botanist but a pharmacist, discoverer of ether and author of the earliest official pharmacopeia, the *Pharmacorum dispensatorium* (Nuremberg: Joh. Petreius, 1546).[5]

There is no doubt that the illustrations contributed very much to the popularity of these early herbals. Some readers in that age, as in our own, preferred looking at pictures to reading the text; this was especially true when the herbals were written in Latin, which put them out of reach of all but the learned doctors. Love of plants and interest in herbs and roots was not by any means confined to scholars; even women might want to know more about them and to be able to recognize them in the fields. Hence the pictures were very welcome. This is shown by the publication of books with a minimum of text and a maximum of pictures. Such was the *Kreutterbuch von allem Erdtgewächs* by Eucharius Rösslin, alias Rhodion (Frankfurt: Christian Egenolph, 1533). A later German botanist, Jacob Dietrich of Bergzabern (1520-90), alias Theodorus Tabernaemontanus, physician, wrote a *Neuw Kreuterbuch* (Frankfurt: Nicolas Basse, 1588-91). In 1590 Basse found it expedient to publish the abundant illustrations separately under a new title, *Eicones plantarum* (a quarto volume of 1128 pp. with 2,255 woodcuts).[6] This is easier to understand when we realize that the making of woodcuts[7] must have cost much time and money. It became a common practice among Renaissance printers to use the same blocks over and over again. The blocks might even be bought or rented by one publisher from another. For example, the woodcuts collected for Tabernaemontanus' book were bought by the English printer, John Norton, who used them to illustrate the first edition (London, 1597) of *The Herball or Generall Historie of Plantes* of John Gerard (1545-1612).

One more German botanist may be mentioned here, Joachim

Camerarius the Younger (1534-98), son of the great classical scholar and reformer, Joachim Camerarius the Elder (1500-74) of Bamberg. The younger Camerarius is far less illustrious than his father, yet he did good service to botany with his *Hortus medicus et philosophicus* printed by Feyerabend (Frankfurt, 1588). In this case also the illustrations were published separately. The publisher had thought of a new trick: one could buy either the text or the *Icones*, or both bound together. Camerarius had been educated in Wittenberg, the Lutheran citadel, but had traveled extensively in Germany, Hungary, and Italy and he had accumulated a good knowledge of plants and of botanists. He died in his birthplace, Nuremberg.

This list is sufficient to give an idea of the leading role of the Germans in the botanical renaissance of the first half of the sixteenth century. It is curious that this revival was not only German but Lutheran. The first two "fathers" had been educated for the cloister. Brunfels was a Carthusian monk but abandoned his monastery after his conversion to Lutheranism; he became a preacher and schoolteacher as well as a botanist. Bock was for a time a Lutheran pastor. Fuchs was a faithful Catholic until his arrival in Ingolstadt, where he turned Lutheran. Tabernaemontanus and Camerarius were born Protestants; Camerarius' father had been an associate of Melanchthon and wrote his biography.

There was also a steady progression in the early "fathers," Brunfels (1530), Bock (1539), Fuchs (1542), Cordus (d. 1544). Each was somewhat greater than his predecessor, though in the last case we can only guess, for Cordus died before having given his full measure.

While the Germans were undoubtedly the first in the field and gave the earliest examples of modern illustrated herbals, they soon had imitators in Italy, the Low Countries, Spain and Portugal, Switzerland, France, and England. Not only were the European fields, forests, and mountains explored but botanical surveys were undertaken in Mexico, India, and other countries.

The early Germans had been of necessity provincial, but the age of geographical discovery soon had repercussions upon the study of natural history. The earliest navigators and conquistadores had had no time and no wish for such things, but the returning crews and soldiers brought news of many strange sights that could be seen in Asia or America. Sometimes they brought the objects themselves:

fruits, seeds, birds, and men. The "naturalists" of Europe were allured and stimulated by the possibilities opened to them by little knowledge and much imagination. By the middle of the sixteenth century botanists were vying with one another to obtain novelties from India, from the New World, from frozen countries, marshes, and deserts—from anywhere and everywhere. The plants and animals of distant and exotic countries were either radically new or sufficiently different from those already known to be startling, to cause perplexities, and to invite further investigation. There emerged a new kind of scientist, the traveling naturalist, the scientific explorer. The greedy adventurers of early days were now replaced by men in search of knowledge. The quest for truth inspired the new men with a missionary zeal, and they were prepared to suffer many hardships for the sake of science.

The discoveries made in foreign lands excited the naturalists who were obliged to stay at home, such as physicians, professors, and keepers of botanical gardens and greenhouses, and forced them to describe more accurately and more completely the faunas and floras of their own countries. Thus exploration abroad led to deeper investigations and thus to better knowledge of the forms of life that could be observed nearer home. So much new knowledge was amassed that it tended to create confusion, and there was an increasing need for new surveys and richer herbals.

One of the leading botanists of the mid-century was the Italian Pier Andrea Mattioli of Siena (1500-77), who won fame for his commentaries on Dioscorides, first published in 1554[8] and reprinted in many editions, periodically revised and corrected, not only in Latin but also in many vernaculars. Mattioli's commentary on Dioscorides became a treatise on botany, just as a "Ptolemy" was actually a new treatise on geography. Mattioli's publications were immensely popular; some 32,000 copies of them were sold.[9] His authority was so great that discoverers of new plants who did not want to write books communicated their information to Mattioli to be included in his next edition (there were no scientific periodicals in those days). A good example is the publication by Willem Quackelbeen of Courtrai (d. 1561) of the plants that he and his patron, Ogier Ghiselin de Busbecq, had discovered in Turkish lands. This news, dated Constantinople, 1557, first appeared in Mattioli in 1581;[10] it was of no small importance. We are indebted to these two Flemings for the

PIER ANDREA MATTIOLI (1500-77), aet. c.65. Portrait first published in the *Commentarii in sex libros Dioscoridis* (folio, Venice: Valgrisius, 1565). It did not appear in the editions of 1554 and 1558, but was many times reprinted in later editions of Mattioli's works. *Courtesy of Harvard Library.* For other portraits see Günther-Schmid, *Archiv für Geschichte der Medizin,* 30: 133-51 **(1937).**

introduction into Europe of the horse-chestnut, the lilac, and the tulip. The popularity achieved by tulips in the following century is fascinating, but that is another story.

CHRISTOPHER PLANTIN

The success of books dealing with voyages and natural history was largely due to the general interest in exotic countries, which was especially keen in those regions of Europe whose trade was international and in the great harbors that attracted ships from everywhere. The cities of Flanders were exceptionally prosperous. Bruges had been its main harbor for centuries, but by the end of the fifteenth century it was displaced by Antwerp, which then became one of the leading commercial and financial centers of Europe.[11] Among the printers who were attracted by Antwerp's prosperity was one Christopher Plantin (c.1520-1589) of Touraine, who learned his profession in Caen and became one of the outstanding printers of his time. The house founded by Plantin is of special concern to us not only because of its Biblical and classical publications but chiefly because so many scientific books issued from its presses, many of them in illustrated editions. The Plantin imprint was such a good trademark that the editions were relatively large, and Plantin books could be bought in the best bookshops all over Europe. Among the men of science whose books Plantin helped to distribute were Belon and Rondelet, Cornelius Gemma, G. B. della Porta, Dodonaeus, Clusius and Lobelius, Vesalius, Charles Estienne, Christoval Acosta, Garcia da Orta, Monardes, and Valerius Cordus. Plantin was a learned printer in a polyglot city. Not to mention Greek and Hebrew books and the Polyglot Bible (8 vols., 1572), which established his reputation, he published books not only in Latin but also in French, Dutch, German, and Spanish. As the Belgian provinces were under Spanish rule, many books were issued in Spanish not only by Plantin but by other printers in Antwerp, Ghent, Bruges, Brussels, Louvain, etc.[12] The international orientation of Flemish printers is illustrated by the fact that the earliest books printed in English were not printed in England but at Bruges in Flanders.[13]

The Plantin press under Christopher's guidance became the largest in northern Europe. In his peak year, 1575, just before the Spanish Fury, he printed no less than 83 editions, varying in size from 800 to 2,500 copies. He used up to 22 presses; at the time of his death he

CHRISTOPHORI·S PLANTINVS *Ar. hitypographus Regius.*
vixit annos LXXV· *obntque Antuerpiæ* CIƆ·IƆ·LXXXIX·

CHRISTOPHER PLANTIN (1520-89), aet. 69. Portrait at the end of his life by
Henri Goltzius (1558-1617). Published by Jan Moretus (Plantin's son-in-
law and successor) in Joannes Bochius, *Epigrammata funebria at Christ.
Plantini manes* (Antwerp, 1590). Plantin holds a pair of compasses and
his typographical motto, "Labore et constantia," can be read on the
table. The Plantin Museum owns a copy of this portrait "avant la
lettre" on which Plantin's full monogram has been traced by hand.

was still running 10 presses in Antwerp and 4 in Leiden. About 1565
he was employing 21 printers, 18 compositors, 3 apprentices, 2 type-
founders, and 5 proofreaders.[14] He published many herbals in Latin
and vernaculars, all beautifully illustrated by artists and woodcut
makers permanently attached to his establishment. The building that
he erected near the Grand Place in Antwerp in 1576 still exists. It
was used by his son-in-law, Jan Moretus, and by eight generations
of printers during three centuries, down to Edouard Moretus; it is

now a museum of typography called the Musée Plantin-Moretus. This is the most interesting museum of its kind in the world, for it helps us to visualize the shop of a sixteenth-century printer with all its appurtenances.

DODONAEUS, CLUSIUS, AND LOBELIUS

The leading botanists whose works were published by Christopher Plantin were Rembert Dodoens, Charles de l'Ecluse, and Matthias de Lobel, two of them Flemings and one from Artois, a little *"pays"* squeezed between Flanders and Picardy.[15] Plantin accumulated a large number of woodcuts that could be used repeatedly in different books, which could thus be illustrated at a relatively low cost. Thanks to this and to the prosperity of Flanders, it is not surprising that many of the outstanding herbals of the second half of the sixteenth century bore the Plantin imprint. The team of Flemish botanists in the second half of the sixteenth century is as remarkable as the German Lutheran team in the first half.

These three men are better known under their Latin names, Dodonaeus,[16] Clusius, and Lobelius. Dodonaeus was born in Mechelen (Malines), near Antwerp, in 1516. He must have been a man of means, for after obtaining a medical degree in Louvain he visited various universities and medical schools in France, Italy, and Germany. He was appointed town physician in his native city, and gradually won so much distinction that when Vesalius left Spain (1564) for his pilgrimage to the Holy Land, Philip II wanted Dodonaeus to replace him. Dodonaeus declined the royal offer. He may have regretted it a few years later (1572), when Mechelen was pillaged by Spanish troops; his own house was destroyed and he was ruined. In 1574 he was called to the imperial court at Vienna and appointed physician to Maximilian II (until 1576), then to Rudolph II. Ten years later he received his greatest opportunity, a professorship of medicine at the University of Leiden,[17] but unfortunately he did not hold it very long, for he died in March 1585.

His main work is a herbal first published in Flemish (Antwerp, 1554); later editions, gradually revised, were published in French, English, and Latin. His French translator was Clusius (1557). The best known edition is the fifth (first Latin), the *Stirpium historiae pemptades sex sive libri XXX*, printed by Plantin in 1583 and reprinted by the same firm in 1616.[18]

REMBERT DODONAEUS (1516-85), aet. 35. Reproduced from *A niewe herball . . .* , English version of Dodoens' Herbal by Henry Lyte (folio, London: Gerard Dewes, 1578).

The *Pemptades* (fives) were so called because the book had been published in instalments from 1565 on. It presented first-hand descriptions of many plants, most of which belonged to the Low Countries. The *Pemptades* was a kind of national flora, explaining where plants grow, when they flower, etc. The order was not alphabetical, as in Fuchs; an attempt was made to classify plants according to their main characteristics. The publication of Dodonaeus' book in Latin and three vernaculars, with excellent illustrations, ensured its diffusion all over the republic of letters, not only in Europe but also in Asia and America.[19]

Clusius (1526-1609), nine years younger than Dodonaeus, was born at Arras (Atrecht). He studied in Ghent and at the Collège des Trois Langues in Louvain; read law in Marburg, where he became a Lutheran; and completed his education in Montpellier, where he was Rondelet's[20] disciple and collaborator. It is said that he helped Rondelet write his masterpiece *De piscibus marinis* (on marine fishes) (Lyon: M. Bonhomme, 1554-55) in good Latin. He never became a physician like Dodonaeus, but he was a full-fledged humanist, a man of letters and a student not only of botany but of many other sciences. In spite of his complex genius, or perhaps because of it, his life was a long struggle against poverty. He managed to support himself by his own writings and by translating into French (in Plantin's service) the Dutch herbal of Dodonaeus, and into Latin the Portuguese herbal of Garcia da Orta, the Spanish writings of Christoval Acosta and Nicolas Monardes, and the French works of Pierre Belon. He was called to the imperial court at Vienna and was a "familiar"[21] of Maximilian II and Rudolph II; his position was not well defined, but it would seem that he was prefect of the medical garden (1573-76) and probably in charge of the other imperial gardens. After losing credit at the Viennese court because of his religious opinions, he traveled in England and the Netherlands, established himself for a time in Frankfurt, and found his final harbor in Leiden. He was not Dodonaeus' successor (as he was not a physician), but was appointed prefect of the *Hortus medicus* (1592). He died in Leiden in 1609.

Besides botanical books, his abundant writings include various historical works and many translations into French and Latin. I shall mention only two of his humanistic publications, his edition of letters of Nicolas Clenard[22] (Antwerp: Plantin, 1566) which he had discovered in Salamanca, and his translation from Latin into French of two Plutarchian biographies, Hannibal and Scipio Africanus (Paris, 1567).

His fame is based upon his botanical publications, of which the most important are his flora of Spain, *Rariorum aliquot stirpium per Hispanias observatarum historia* (Antwerp: Plantin, 1576) and the flora of Austria and Hungary, *Rariorum aliquot stirpium, per Pannoniam, Austriam et vicinas quasdam provincias observatarum historia* (Antwerp: Plantin, 1583). It is hardly possible to exaggerate the importance of these books, largely based upon personal observation, which introduced a great deal of material not available in the early German herbals. During his stay in Leiden Clusius prepared a complete edition of his works. The first volume, entitled *Rariorum plantarum historia,* was beautifully published by Plantin's son-in-law Moretus (Antwerp: Plantin, 1601); it includes revised editions of the floras of Spain and Austria. The second volume, *Exoticorum libri decem,* published by another son-in-law, François Raphelengien (Antwerp: Plantin, 1605), contains his translation of the Indian floras of Garcia da Orta and Christoval Acosta and of the American flora of Nicolas Monardes, that is, descriptions of the floras of the East and West Indies.

According to Cuvier, Clusius described about 600 new plants. He was not a botanical theorist but a good observer and some, at least, of his drawings were made by himself. He was one of the first to observe, describe, and delineate mushrooms and his original drawings and water-colors have been preserved.[23] On the basis of these studies he might be called the father of mycology.[24] The Plantin editions of his works were admirably published and illustrated.

Thanks to Clusius, the botanical horizon was enormously enlarged before the end of the Renaissance. His reputation was such that, like Mattioli, he received much botanical information from distant correspondents; this was eventually published in one or another of his books, full credit being given to his informants.

After the completion of his *opera omnia* he published many more books, e.g. his Latin translations of Pierre Belon. During his life he had often been plagued by illness, but in the quiet atmosphere of Leiden, so congenial to his religion, he spent what were probably his happiest years, sixteen in all. He died there in 1609 at the age of 84.[25] His illustrious colleague, the philologist Joseph Justus Scaliger (1540-1609), died in the same year.

The third Fleming, Lobelius[26] (1538-1616), was born in Rijssel (French Lille, Départment du Nord). After some traveling in Germany and Italy he proceeded to Montpellier, where he was Rondelet's pupil. When the latter died in 1566 he bequeathed his botanical manuscripts to Lobelius, then 38, who was his favorite disciple. This recognition from his old master was like the dubbing of a knight. Unfortunately, this was also the time when Philip II sent the Duke of Alva to the Netherlands; the latter's Blood Council inaugurated a period of terror. Many Flemings had already taken refuge across the water in England, and Lobelius joined them. His first book was published in London (1570-71). He was appointed physician to William the Silent and resided in Delft until William's assassination in 1584. He then stayed for a while in Antwerp, probably in order to be in touch with the Plantin firm, but soon returned to England, where he supervised the medical herb garden of Edward Zouche[27] at Hackney (London), herborized in Middlesex, was eventually appointed botanist to James I, and died at Highgate on March 3, 1616.

His book was first published under the title *Stirpium adversaria nova perfacilis vestigatio* (460 pp., London: Thomas Purfoot, 1570-71). It was a joint production of Lobelius and Pierre Pena, who had been his fellow-student at Montpellier, lived in England with him, and was very familiar with the Languedoc and Pyrenees floras.[28] A book published in Antwerp in 1576, *Plantarum seu stirpium historia . . . cui annexum est Adversariorum volumen* (folio, Plantin), contains under a new cover the unsold leaves of the London book. Either Thomas Purfoot was not a good publisher or the English public was singularly indifferent, for in 1605 there still remained enough unsold leaves of the 1571 volume to issue them again together with Lobelius' *In Rondeleti methodicum pharmaceuticum officinam animadversiones* (156 pp., folio, London: Thomas Purfoot, 1605).

The Plantin edition of 1576 was richly illustrated with almost 1,500 large woodcuts. There were even more pictures—some 2,181, many of large size—in his Dutch *Kruydtboek* (Antwerp, 1581). These were published separately in an album, *Icones stirpium seu plantarum . . . cum septem linguarum indicibus* (2 vols., obl. quarto, Antwerp: Plantin, 1591).

The novelties of Lobelius' herbal were derived mainly from the floras of southern France, the Low Countries, and England (more

than eighty "first records" of English plants are ascribed to him).
His main title to fame, however, lies in his much improved classification, which he explained in the preface of his first book (1570-71).
He defended the idea of an *ordo universalis* to which all plants were
subject. His classification was based upon the characteristics of
leaves, and he was able to adumbrate the distinction between di-
cotyledons and monocotyledons. Moreover, he printed a synoptic
table of species at the beginning of each of his groups. Crude as it
appears to be, his effort is the most important of the Renaissance in
that fundamental field, the classification of plants. His album was
often referred to by Linnaeus, while the illustrations were frequently reproduced in later works; his large collections of them
invited plunder and made it almost unavoidable.

It is almost impossible to compare the scientific merits of these
three men, Dodonaeus, Clusius, and Lobelius. Irrespective of personal merit, each herbal was bound to be a little better than its
predecessors. Progress was tangible in the matter of theory, and one
sees the gradual improvement in the classification of plants from
Fuchs' alphabetic disorder (1542) to Lobelius' rudimentary classification (1571).

Lobelius' interest in botanical theory was evidenced also in his
remarks (in the same preface) on the existence of plants in higher
latitudes that could also be observed on high mountains further
south. He was apparently the first to make this observation, which
was generalized later by the Pyrenean botanist, Louis Ramond,[29]
and finally introduced into botanical geography by Alexander von
Humboldt.

Lobelius seems to have been a less amiable character than the
two other Flemings, and his Latin was rude compared with that
of Clusius. He was full of pride and vanity, rough, disparaging, and
even spiteful.[30] It must be added, however, that he was willing to
recognize the great efforts of some of his predecessors and especially
of the Flemish botanists and gardeners, above all Clusius.

In spite of many vicissitudes, the life span of these three men was
reasonably long; Dodonaeus died youngest, at 68, Lobelius lived
until he was 78, and Clusius, though poor in health and money,
until 84. The worst miseries of their lives were due to religious persecutions or the fear of them. The Spanish terror and the Inquisition made life hard and terrible in the Low Countries. Lobelius
managed to keep out of this more than the others, but Dodonaeus

and Clusius witnessed many atrocities. This suggests the question, what was their religion? It is tempting at first to contrast the three Flemings, as Catholics, with their Lutheran predecessors. But Clusius was a Lutheran early in life, while Dodonaeus and Lobelius grew up in the Roman faith, but became Protestants, probably from disgust with Spanish intolerance. This is confirmed by the fact that Dodonaeus spent the last sixteen years of his life at the University of Leiden; Lobelius was in the service of William of Orange, and after the latter's murder (1584) he preferred to reside in England under Elizabeth and James I.

THE EARLY BOTANIC GARDENS

Popular as well as scientific interest in plants was enormously increased by the herbals, especially those that were illustrated. This was shown in the many gardens of the period, which in turn stimulated interest in botany. Such gardens were not novelties; gardens of many kinds had existed in Egypt and other parts of the ancient world, and continued to ornament and enrich the human scene, but they became more important during the Renaissance. *"Jardins d'agrément"* became as numerous as kitchen gardens and were one of the means of artistic consciousness and creation. The love of beautiful gardens was often expressed by poets, such as Ronsard; remember also his famous poem, "Contre les bûcherons de la forêt de Gastyne," lamenting the destruction of a beloved forest.

The study of "simples," or medicinal plants (or rather of all plants, for none lacked "virtues" of one kind or another), was one of the scientific branches of medicine. Professors of *materia medica* began to feel that illustrations were not enough; it would be better if students could be shown the actual plants. These could be found in the fields or woods, but it was much more convenient to have them ready at hand near the classrooms and to be able to view them in all seasons in order to study their life cycles. Medical gardens had probably been planted in antiquity, and they had become a regular feature of monastic life.[31] A well-ordered monastery would have such a garden and the brother in charge of it was entitled *hortulanus* or *herbolarius;* there was also in the cloister a room or an outhouse where the roots and herbs were dried and preserved, or their juices squeezed out and distilled.

The medical schools needed something more, however. It was not enough to collect the standard herbs, it was necessary to explore the whole vegetable kingdom. The teaching of botany required more elaborate and systematic gardens.

It is impossible to say when the first "botanic gardens," in the new sense, were established, for the first attempts were unsystematic and unpublicized. The first gardens recorded were the final results of a long evolution. Even then the story is by no means plain, for there are disputes over places and dates. Among the earliest known botanic gardens was that of Luca Ghini di Croara d'Imola (c.1490-1556), established in Pisa about 1544. The garden of Padua was founded a little later and its first prefect (1546 to 1561) was Luigi Anguillara. There was a botanic garden in Florence about 1550. The first examples are thus found in northern Italy, where there were at least three botanic gardens before the middle of the sixteenth century.[32] Many more gardens were created in the following centuries, as it was realized more widely that a faculty of medicine was essentially incomplete without one.[33]

There was great rivalry between the early gardens, for the keepers, stimulated by the latest herbal, wanted to have as many novelties as they could get hold of. This was easy when the keeper or prefect was a man of Clusius' international reputation, and the Leiden garden became under his direction one of the most famous in Europe.

Botanists visiting the gardens of other universities than their own would make discoveries. For example, Lobelius saw papyrus for the first time in Pisa. It is probable that many Egyptian plants were cultivated in Padua, for Alpino was appointed prefect of the Padua garden in 1603. Prospero Alpino da Marostica had spent five years in Egypt (1580-84) and is immortalized by his book De plantis Aegypti (Venice: Franciscus Senensis, 1592), the first flora of that country or of any country in the Near East, outside of Dioscorides.

Though the purpose of the botanic gardens was ancillary to that of the medical schools, we may be sure that their keepers took pains to acclimatize favorite flowers. For example, Clusius was the originator of bulb culture, and prepared the way for the tulip craze that swept Holland in the seventeenth century.[34] His friend and patron, Marie de Brimeu,[35] princess of Chimay, called him "Le père de tous les beaux jardins de ce pays."

Gardens of acclimatization were not yet born, however, though Pierre Belon tried unsuccessfully to persuade the king of France to organize one and to create a kind of arboretum. He succeeded in introducing certain trees (the cedar of Lebanon), and wrote a treatise on cone-bearing trees, *De arboribus coniferis* (Paris: B. Prévost, 1553),[36] (the first monograph on a plant group in Western literature), also another treatise explaining the needs of forestry and the means of acclimatizing "wild trees"—*Les Remonstrances* . . . (Paris: Corrozet, 1558).[37]

HERBARIA

The plants growing in botanic gardens were not always easily available; moreover, one might wish to identify them in winter, when the northern gardens were covered with snow. It is very strange that the idea of drying plants and preserving them for reference did not occur to anyone before the sixteenth century.[38] Yet there is no information *ad hoc* before that time. It is not so surprising after all if we bear in mind that the scientific study of plants (not only herbs and drugs) had hardly begun. The sixteenth century was the century of herbaria[39] as well as the century of herbals.

The history of botanic gardens may be said to begin with Luca Ghini, who established one at Pisa in 1544; he was also the initiator of the art of preserving plants by pressing them between sheets of paper. He sent such plants to Mattioli in 1551. His own herbarium is lost, but the oldest extant was prepared by one of his disciples, Gherardo Cibo, in 1532 and following years. It is kept in the Biblioteca Angelica in Rome.[40] Other herbaria were gathered by Andrea Cesalpino for the grand duke of Tuscany, Cosimo I de' Medici (d. 1574) and for the Tornabona family,[41] and by Ulisse Aldrovandi for his own needs. This herbarium, including more than 4,000 plants, can still be seen at the University of Bologna.

An Englishman, John Falconer,[42] who had traveled in Italy, had also collected an herbarium, which we know because of references to it made by Luigi Anguillara, William Turner, and Amatus Lusitanus.

The oldest extant herbaria of Germany were collected by Caspar Ratzenberger about 1559 and by Hieronymus Harder in 1574-76. The Harder herbarium is in the Deutsches Museum in Munich. One of Ratzenberger's herbaria, including 746 plants, is in the Cassel Museum; it was completed by order of Moriz der Gelehrte (landgrave of Hesse-Cassel, 1592-1627); another is the *Herbarius vivus* of the grand ducal library of Gotha.

To pass to Switzerland, it is probable that plants were dried and kept by Conrad Gesner (1516-65) in Zurich. Another of Rondelet's disciples, Felix Platter (1536-1614), physician in Basel, had collected a herbarium which was examined and praised by Montaigne when he passed through Basel in 1580.[43] It is now in the University of Bern. It contains 813 species, including specimens obtained by Platter not only in Switzerland and Germany but also in France, Italy, and Egypt. The outstanding French herbarium of this period is the one collected by Jehan Girault dated 1558 and still extant in Paris.[44]

According to Mrs. Arber[45] there are in different cities of Europe more than twenty herbaria that were formed, or at least begun, in the sixteenth century. The most impressive document, however, is the admirable portrait of the apothecary, Pierre Quthe, painted in 1562, aet. 43, by François Clouet (Louvre). He is seated near a table upon which an open herbarium can be clearly seen.

The oldest literary reference to herbaria is in Spigelii,[46] *Isagoges in rem herbariam libri II* (1606), where they are called *horti hiemales* (winter gardens); the most usual term, however, was *herbarium vivum* (*herbarius* meant botanist). The word *herbarium* was ambiguous, for it served to designate both our herbal and our herbarium.[47]

Did any Renaissance botanists think of "Naturselbstdrucke," that is, self-impressions made by plants upon a sheet of paper? One man did at least, Leonardo da Vinci. His interest in plants was great and he left us exquisite drawings of them; he not only suggested the method of self-impression but applied it to a sage leaf.[48] It is strange that this idea did not occur earlier, for nature had given many examples of it. Some fish fossils are hardly more than "Naturselbstdrucke," but they are very detailed and extremely instructive. Not to speak of the ancients, such fossil fishes were shown to Saint Louis in Sidon (Lebanon) in 1253 and referred to by Joinville (XIV-1).[49]

BOTANICAL TEACHING

Under the combined influence of beautifully illustrated herbals, other paintings and drawings, lovely gardens, and medical needs, one would expect botanical teaching to achieve greater importance and vitality. This occurred, but only to a limited extent. Botanical teaching improved very slowly because it remained subordinated to medicine, as completely as trigonometry was to astronomy. The main scientific bases of the medical art were anatomy, botany, and astronomy (more exactly astrology). Botany meant Dioscorides or *materia medica,*[50] and Renaissance botany was to a large extent a commentary on Dioscorides. The leading botanists, however, including Mattioli, were dragged from their libraries to the fields and the mountains. They learned to depend upon the botanic gardens and obliged their students to examine the plants in these gardens or in the course of special excursions. The initiator of botanical excursions for students was Valerius Cordus, and we may safely assume that field work of various kinds increased considerably during the second half of the sixteenth century.

As for the teachers of *materia medica,* some old fogies continued to read Dioscorides to their classes almost in the same spirit as they might have read Cicero or Virgil, but the younger men became more aware of botanical realities; indeed, some of the youngsters had completely fallen under the spell of plants. The transition took probably the same form as in anatomy; the lectures (or readings) were completed by demonstrations, and the demonstrator (the anatomical prosector, the chemical experimenter, and the botanical ostensor) was a low-paid and unrespected assistant. If the professor was a good man, I imagine that he was anxious to handle the demonstrations himself and did so. The lecture on *materia medica* was followed by the exhibition of plants in the classroom and later more fully in the medical garden.[51] When did botanical teaching become sufficiently rich to emancipate itself from *materica medica?* It is impossible to say, for the emancipation was generally determined by local conditions and above all by the genius of individuals.

In the case of botany, the ostensor was often the same man as the prefect of the botanical garden,[52] and if he were really able he might obtain considerable prestige (e.g. Clusius). In some faculties the professor of *materia medica* might defend his subject, while the director of the garden defended botany. Most of the professors of botany were entitled professor of medicine; they held one of the chairs devoted to *materia medica.*

It is highly probable that the great herbalists, if they were invited to teach *materia medica,* took advantage of their opportunity to teach a good deal of straight botany and to fire their students' enthusiasm for plants. A born botanist could not do otherwise.

GUILLAUME RONDELET (1507-66), aet. 47. Portrait printed in frontispiece to his *Libri de piscibus marinis* (Lyon: Matthias Bonhomme,
1554). *Courtesy of Harvard Library.*

Judging by the activities of his disciples even more than by his own,
Guillaume Rondelet was a great botanical teacher (whatever his
title was), and thanks to him the school of Montpellier became one
of the great nurseries of botanists. It is said of one of Rondelet's
successors in Montpellier, Richer de Belleval,[53] that he was the first
to teach botany independently of medicine. This does not tally with
another statement, according to which the oldest chair of botany
was the one founded at Padua in 1533.[54] It would be more prudent

to say that Richer de Belleval was one of the first; his main interest was his garden, where he tried to grow all the plants of Languedoc.

Botany was very slow in establishing itself as an independent subject; the time and conditions varied from university to university, the main factors being personalities. Until the end of the last century most academic botanists were doctors of medicine.

PHYSIOLOGY

The only way to emancipate botany from medicine was to develop it in non-medical directions. One of the ways was through horticulture, of which there was no formal teaching until later. Another was physiology, the study of plant life, but the minds of Renaissance men of science were not yet prepared for that. Andrea Cesalpino sidetracked them when he tried to compare the life of plants too closely with that of animals.

Nicholas of Cusa had given a good example in the fourth book of the *Idiota, De staticis experimentis,* where he suggested experiments on growing plants to prove that a part of their weight was derived from the earth, a part from the water, and a part from the air. Nicholas (who died in 1464) was too much ahead of his time; he was a forerunner of the Renaissance whose visions did not begin to be realized until the seventeenth century, by such men as the Fleming, Jan Baptista Van Helmont (1577-1644).

GESNER AND ALDROVANDI

The time of experiment in biology had not yet come. In spite of a growing interest in living plants and living animals, attention was still focused on books, especially on ancient books and the innumerable commentaries devoted to them. Some of the commentators might investigate nature apropos of a text, but they had not yet learned that nature must come first. Thus the greatest heroes were encyclopaedic compilers like Conrad Gesner (1516-65) of Zurich and Ulisse Aldrovandi (1522-1605) of Bologna.

While both of them were primarily botanists, their encyclopaedias were devoted chiefly to zoology. They may have thought that the botanical field was overworked by the herbalists, and that it was time to put the animal kingdom in order. The best work in zoology was not done by them, however, but by such men as the two French-

AN.   AET.36.

PIERRE BELON (1517-64), aet. 36. First published in *Les observations de plusieurs singularitez* (Paris: G. Corrozet, 1553) and in the identical editions of the same book (Paris: Guillaume Cavallet, 1554 and 1555). The portrait faces page 1 in the 1554 edition. The same portrait was reprinted thrice in other books of Belon's during his lifetime (1555, 1557, 1558). There is no other contemporary portrait. *Courtesy of Harvard Library.*

men, Guillaume Rondelet (1507-66), Pierre Belon (1517-64), and their followers.

Nevertheless, the syntheses that Gesner and Aldrovandi managed to complete were exceedingly useful. Gesner's *Historia animalium* was published by Froschauer in Zurich in five folios (vols. I-IV, 1551-58; vol. V, posthumous, 1587)—a total of some 4,000 pages with hundreds of illustrations. Aldrovandi's encyclopaedia was even larger; its publication was begun by Bellagamba in Bologna almost half a century later. The first folio volume appeared in 1599, when Aldrovandi was 77. Only four volumes appeared within his lifetime, nine more between 1616 and 1668. Except for the first volume (on birds), Aldrovandi's encyclopaedia belongs to the seventeenth century.

Gesner's five volumes and Aldrovandi's first are a summary of Renaissance zoology. The influence of their abundant illustrations was even stronger than that of the texts, for the latter reached only the humanists, while the pictures could reach every thinking person. Even before 1600 there was a large and rapidly growing public that was intelligent and anxious to obtain more knowledge, yet knew little or no Latin. Self-made men in business, or even in science, who had not learned Latin in their youth, could never overcome that initial handicap. But they could learn a good deal of zoology by examining the pictures in Gesner and Aldrovandi and spelling out the legends and a minimum of text.[55]

These books are still useful today; Gesner and Aldrovandi make it as easy for us to assess the state of knowledge on definite subjects by the end of the sixteenth century as the *Naturalis Historia* of Pliny the Elder to measure its state by the middle of the first.

Much of the information given by Gesner and Aldrovandi was ancient, mediaeval, or fabulous; much had been obtained by contemporary naturalists; much more came from travelers, sailors, whalers, and hunters, who could not help noticing the birds,[56] fishes, insects, and animals of newly discovered or rediscovered worlds. The parrots and other striking birds in the islands on the way to America and in America itself astonished the European invaders.[57] Many other creatures were noticed: turkeys, peccaries, llamas, alpacas, tapirs, armadillos, vampires, etc.

One of the greatest economic events of the Renaissance was the mysterious disappearance of herring from the Baltic, about 1500, which deprived large populations of one of their cheapest foods.[58] This led to the search for new fishing grounds and to the exploitation of the Iceland, Greenland, and Newfoundland fisheries.

Settlers of what is now Canada became acquainted with elk, and what was more important, with a number of fur-bearing animals, such as the deer, marten, fox, and above all the beaver. Similar discoveries were made in Russia, and the Muscovite Company of of London obtained in 1553 a monopoly of the exchange of Russian furs (foxes, martens, sables) for other goods. The exploitation of Siberia began later, for it was not until 1580 that Ermak Timofeev crossed the Urals.

All these events are fairly well known because of their economic and political repercussions, which were considerable; they also had an impact on the writers of zoological books. There was unfortunately another side to this. The novelties of the New World were so many and so strange that the returning soldiers and sailors could not resist the temptation to embellish and exaggerate them. The bookish scholars were very credulous, and did not hesitate to identify the marvels of the New World with the mythical monsters with which they were so familiar. Morus explains the psychological situation so well that I shall quote his own words: [59]

> On the whole the Renaissance was not a rationalistic age. Men like Leonardo da Vinci and Pomponazzi,[60] the philosopher, were exceptions to the rule. On the other hand the men of the Renaissance were not really mystics who got lost in the supernatural. Rather they were surrealists, who projected the antique tradition and the products of their own imagination into reality and by so doing increased their range of vision without ever quite leaving the plane of the real. The fabulous animals of antiquity now took on a reality they had never had in the middle ages. All forms of them were admitted into zoology, where they were counted just as real in every attribute as animals that had actually been seen. The basilisk, the Egyptian phoenix, the gryphon, the salamander, again came into their own during the Renaissance. The three sirens mentioned in Columbus's log fall into this surrealist category, rather than into the class of primitive superstition exemplified by the *homens marinhos*. Columbus assures us that he himself had seen them leaping about in the sea.

In spite of their prodigious learning some of these scholars were easily bamboozled, because they had no notion of the experimental method, often lacked common sense, and unconsciously hoped to justify their fantastic dreams. Thus a man like Julius Caesar Scaliger (1484-1558), Erasmus' enemy, found it equally simple to accept the dogma of Cicero's perfection and the tale of the basilisk. In 1555 Olaus Magnus[61] wrote a description of the sea-serpent. Magnus was the authority on the northern regions, and as good a man as Conrad Gesner accepted his tale and reproduced his illustration. Even the naturalists, soaked in the Renaissance atmosphere of learning and credulity, were not immune. We must not be too severe on them, however, because the sea-serpent still reappears from time to time.

MINERALOGY AND GEOLOGY

As to stones, the knowledge available at the beginning of the sixteenth century is represented by various little books, of which the most characteristic is probably the *Speculum lapidum* (mirror of stones) put together by Camillo Leonardi of Pesaro, who was physician to Cardinal Cesare Borgia (1475-1507). It was first published by Joan. Bap. Sessa (Venice, 1502), and often reprinted. It was translated into Italian (1565), and an English translation was published in London as late as 1750.[62] It is divided into three parts dealing respectively with (1) generalities, (2) description of 279 minerals, (3) figures engraved upon gems and their astrological meanings. The most interesting part is the second, a summary of ancient and mediaeval knowledge. The author had no understanding of the relationships between minerals (chemical analysis was as yet nonexistent); hence he arranged them in alphabetical order according to their Latin names. Like the mediaeval herbals, the mediaeval lapidaries (and this is one, in spite of its late appearance) were anthologies of magic and medical folklore.

We need not speak of other sixteenth-century books on stones, for they simply continued the ancient and mediaeval literary traditions. Considerable knowledge was gained from mining, but it was mixed up with folklore and fantastic myths. Yet there was in it a nucleus of sound experience that was steadily growing. In the Saxon Erzgebirge and neighboring districts mines had been exploited for centuries; the knowledge of miners and prospectors remained traditional and empirical, but by the end of the fifteenth century, under the combined pressure of science, business, and banking it tended to become more rational. Examples have been given in Wing Three when we spoke of the *Bergbüchlein* (c.1505-1510) and the *Probierbüchlein* (c.1524); they dealt not only with metallurgy but also with mineralogy and geology, and Agricola made good use of them. At the turn of the century Leonardo da Vinci made excursions in the Italian Alps, observed their structure, and asked himself pertinent questions. He had no interest in mining but a deep interest in nature, and his reflections were those of a geologist. He speculated on what had created the mountains and on the erosion that was chiseling them.

GEORGIUS AGRICOLA

In the meantime Agricola had begun his work. The book of his discussed in Wing Three, *De re metallica,* was his last work, published posthumously by Froben in 1556. But before that he had written and Froben had printed a whole series of other books that were geological.[63]

Bermannus (1530) is a conversation between Bermann the "miner, mineralogist, student of mathematics and poetry" and his two learned friends, both physicians: Nicolaus Ancon, a philosopher acquainted with Avicenna, and Johannes Naevius, who practiced in Annaberg and was more familiar with Dioscorides, Pliny, Galen, etc. It begins with a history of mining in the Erzgebirge. Various problems of mineralogy, mining, and geology are discussed. The main purpose is to correlate ancient knowledge with Saxon mining lore. Many mineralogical terms appear in printed form for the first time. The first description of bismuth is significant because, as Bermannus points out, this means that there are more than seven metals (as was commonly believed). Bismuth is somewhat confused with cobalt, but that could hardly be helped.[64] The preface to this book was written by no less a person than Erasmus, who praised Agricola's Latin; he must have enjoyed it, for *Bermannus* was a well written introduction to a subject that was new to him.

De natura fossilium (1546) is a deeper study that shows how much Agricola had learned in sixteen years; it is his most important mineralogical work. He continued to revise it after publication and his corrections and additions were included in the second (posthumous) edition published by Froben in 1558. It is a review of the various classifications of fossils[65] that had been suggested by men of science beginning with Aristotle; Agricola ends with his own classification, based upon physical properties (color, weight, luster, shape, texture, solubility, fusibility, etc.) That was the best that could be done before the birth of modern chemistry. He mentioned a few medical properties but left out most of those listed in the lapidaries.[66] His classification was the first scientific one. The minerals were divided into five main groups: (1) earths, (2) "stones properly so-called" (as distinguished from rocks; precious and semiprecious stones), (3) "solidified juices" (salt, vitriol, alum, etc.), (4) metals, (5) compounds (galene, pyrite, etc.). A great many minerals were identified in this book for the first time. The *De natura fossilium* extends to ten books, as follows: I. Physical characteristics and classification of "fossils." II to VII. Descriptions of the minerals. IX. Furnace operations. X. Compounds.

The *De ortu et causis subterraneorum* (1546) is a treatise on geology rather than mineralogy. Much of it is a refutation of the views of the ancient philosophers, alchemists, and astrologers. It discusses the origin of ores and metals, the origin of underground heat and underground vapors (believed to be the cause of volcanic explosions and earthquakes), the growth of mountains and their decadence due to water and wind erosion, and the creation of ore channels.

The *De animantibus subterraneis* (1549) is a small book dealing with creatures that live in the mines and caverns or spend a part of their life underground. It was a pioneer work of its kind but meager.

None of these books enjoyed the fame of the *De re metallica*. Its popularity was due partly to the need for it (technical books have often been best-sellers) and partly to its abundant illustrations.[67] Agricola was not the father of metallurgy (Biringuccio had preceded him), but he may be called the father of mineralogy.

A FEW PROBLEMS

Mineralogical and geological problems were discussed not only in books like Agricola's but also in general philosophical treatises or in monographs. For example, one of the perennial problems that exercised the mind of every natural philosopher was the saltness of sea water.[68] Why is the sea salt? Or in reverse, if the sea waters percolate underground into the springs (as was generally believed), why are most springs sweet? An ingenious answer was suggested by Juan de Jarava[69] in 1546. Sea water, he suggested, is distilled up through the mountains in caverns that act like gigantic alembics: an interesting example of chemical experience wrongly applied to geology.

Not many years after Agricola's death the Academia Veneta[70] published a booklet by the Dominican father Valerius Faventies (Valerio of Faenza?), a dialogue entitled *De montium origine* (Venice: Aldus, 1561). According to Adams[71] this was the first book dealing exclusively with the origin of mountains. It described the ten theories that had been put forward from the Holy Bible and Aristotle down to his time, without drawing any conclusion. This was wise, for the origin of mountains is a problem of extreme complexity. At present all the old explanations have been rejected and many new ones have been offered, but none has been completely accepted.

The last volume of Conrad Gesner's encyclopaedia of natural history to appear within his lifetime was the *De rerum fossilium, lapidum et gemmarum maxime figuris et similitudinibus liber* (Zürich: apud Gesnerum, 1565).[72] The items dealt with—"fossils," stones, and gems—were classified in fifteen groups; each group was very heterogeneous. Almost every class includes organic fossils as well as inorganic. The book gives one a poor idea of the compiler's intelligence, and even of his honesty, for his borrowings were not always acknowledged. Perhaps he compiled it too hastily in the shadow of death.

A friend of Gesner's, Johann Kentmann, physician in Torgau, compiled a list of 1,600 mineralogical specimens in his collection, *Nomenclaturae rerum fossilium quae in Misnia praecipue et in aliis regionibus inveniuntur,* which was issued together with Gesner's *De rerum fossilium* (Zurich, 1565).

One more book of this period must be mentioned, namely, the *Sarepta*[73] (folio, Nuremberg: D. Gerlatz, 1571), written by a Lutheran minister in St. Joachimsthal, Johann Matthesius, whose geological interest had been awakened by Agricola's *Bermannus.* It was a collection of sermons for miners, all the geological and mineralogical statements of the Holy Writ being explained, illuminated, and moralized. It shows that the good pastor was very familiar with the mining lore and customs of his parishioners.

Gesner's book, published in 1565, was a typical Renaissance production, in both its strength and its weakness, but Aldrovandi's came too late to be so considered. It was the fruit of Aldrovandi's long life of brooding on natural questions of every kind. In his will he referred to a package of notes labeled *geologia ovvero de fossilibus,* but the book based upon them did not see the light until 1648. Aldrovandi, by the way, seems to have been the first to use the word geology in its modern sense.[74]

Another *fin de siècle* book was the one prepared by the Fleming Simon Stevin.[75] The second book of his geography, printed in his

Hypomnemata mathematica[76] and entitled *De hylocinesi*[77] *terrestris globi,* is a summary of physical geology, discussing the changes in the crust of the earth and the forces that produce them. Stevin's background was that of an engineer, not a naturalist, and he tried to explain the earth's changes in mechanical terms. Thanks to his robust common sense he was able to anticipate modern views, for example, that such changes are not necessarily due to catastrophic convulsions but to continuous physical agencies whose working can be witnessed by living persons. He explained various forms of erosion, noticed the difference in the profiles of the two banks of a river and the gradual development of its meanders, and observed the dissolution of earths and minerals in water, the destruction and "growth" of rocks and metals, etc. As his knowledge of "mountains" was restricted to the dunes of Holland, his account of them was very imperfect. Yet his total achievement is remarkable.

At the beginning of this book I referred to *Das Antlitz der Erde* by Eduard Suess and remarked on the vast difference between knowledge of the earth in 1450 and 1900. By 1600 the difference was still very great but had been narrowed a little by the investigations and meditations of such men as Agricola and Stevin. They could not analyze the "face of the earth" as well as we can, but they were already sure that its lineaments and wrinkles and the vessels and nerves underneath were not arbitrary. They could not give complete explanations (nor can we always), but they were aware of the possibility of finding such explanations and had started to search for them. This in itself was great progress.

Some of the riddles to be solved were of immediate concern to miners, who could not escape them. Why were some metals or some ores associated to the extent that the presence of one could be inferred from that of another? How did it happen that ores appeared in the form of veins or stringers, lodes or seams? Mechanical explanations were not sufficient; they might account for the channels but not for the particular ores. The topic is very difficult and complex and a good treatment of it would be a cross-section of the whole of geological thought.[78] Let us just peep at it.

Mediaeval fancies are well symbolized by the golden tree growing up from the center of the earth whose branches and foliage brought gold near the surface. It was described by Peter Martyr[79] to account for the presence of gold in the New World, and the beautiful legend was kept alive by many earnest writers. The golden tree was one of the fixtures and ornaments of alchemical literature in the seventeenth century and later. The concept of the unity of nature had traversed the ages; in particular, minerals were not conceived as essentially different from plants, or plants from animals; there were transitions from one group to another and the three kingdoms of nature were not sharply separated.[80] Plants and animals grow and can reproduce themselves, so why not minerals? Even learned men like Geronimo Cardano and men of genius like Bernard Palissy (1580) spoke of the "seeds of metals" and of their propagation. A few writers, like Jacques Aubert (1575) dared to contradict these theories, but they were promptly rebuked, as Aubert was by Quercetanus.[81] Not only did metals grow, each in its own way, but they might "mature" and change into higher metals. This idea, set forth in the *Bergbüchlein,* was one that readers could readily accept, for it was part and parcel of mining lore. In 1575 Gabriel Frascata[82] explained the gradual maturation of baser metals into nobler ones. There were some fundamentalists, it is true, who rejected any concept of change; the world was now as God had created it; but their position was indefensible. By way of compromise, Franciscus Rueus[83] claimed, as St. Augustine (V-1) had done eleven centuries before him, that Creation was not final but potential; it implied evolution. It was a little risky, however, to apply that theory to rocks and metals.

The main source of progress was the existence in the Erzgebirge and other mining or mountainous districts of an increasing group of trained observers, who did not accept the myths but tried earnestly to understand nature. "Field geology" was developing at the same time as "field botany" and "field zoology." The new spirit was well expressed by the Danish humanist, Petrus Severinus (1571).[84]

FOSSILS AND MINERAL COLLECTIONS

It has been remarked above that the word fossil was ambiguous, for it might refer to any object dug out of the earth, either a stone or the remains of a living creature. One cannot make a list of the men who understood the true nature of organic fossils and another of those who did not; it is not so simple. The true nature of fossils had been realized a long time ago by such men of genius as Ibn Sīnā (Avicenna, XI-1) and well expressed by Leonardo da Vinci. As the latter's views were hidden in his own notes, they could hardly influence his contemporaries. Before Leonardo's death, the world of organic fossils was brought to public attention by an accident. The task of repairing the citadel of San Felice at Verona in 1517[85] necessitated the quarrying of blocks of stone that included a great variety of organic remains, many of which were immediately recognizable. Was it possible to dismiss all of them as *lusus naturae* (sports of nature)? One of the most intelligent men of the age, Girolamo Fracastoro (1483-1553), himself of Verona,[86] showed that they were truly organic remains, and furthermore could not be the relics of the biblical deluge, for the latter had been a local event and had lasted only one hundred and fifty days. Such fossils were found not only in Verona but in many other places, and occurred at many different levels.

The reality of organic fossils was recognized by other men such as Cardano (1550), Palissy (1580), and Andrea Cesalpino (1596),[87] but rejected by others, such as the anatomist, Gabriele Falloppio (1557), Michele Mercati (1574), and Giov. Batt. Olivi (1584). Agricola and Conrad Gesner (1565) recognized the true nature of some fossils but not of others. The confusion persisted long after the end of the sixteenth century, and was not completely cleared up by the discoveries of the Dane Nicolas Steno (1638-87) and the Italian Antonio Vallisnieri (1661-1730).

Mineralogical knowledge was much increased by the collectors, who made it possible to compare easily specimens of many kinds from different places. The first on record was one of Gesner's friends, Johann Kentmann, physician in Torgau (Saxony), who published a catalogue of his collection, the *Nomenclaturae rerum fossilium* already mentioned (Zurich, 1565). It lists some 1,600 specimens with their names in Latin and German, and includes a plate showing his cabinet.

There must have been many other collections, such as those made by Palissy and Aldrovandi, for museums of natural curiosities became fashionable before the end of the century, and "fossils" (whether of organic origin or not) were often striking objects, the very things to please a dilettante and excite the admiration of visitors. Moreover, they were very easy to preserve and exhibit.

A remarkable collection of minerals was obtained for the Vatican by Sixtus Quintus (Pope 1585-90). It was described and beautifully illustrated by Mercati (1574).[88] Another collection, made in Verona, was described by Olivi (1584).[89] These two excellent men, who had so many fossils in their care, persisted in considering them as sports of nature.

BERNARD PALISSY

All things considered, the two outstanding figures of Renaissance geology were the German Agricola and the Frenchman Palissy. I have spoken often of the first, but as yet have said little of the second. Palissy is so much *sui generis* that it is better to consider him apart. Next to Leonardo, he is the best representative of the man of science who was not a scholar, whose knowledge was found not in books but in the very bosom of nature.

About the middle of France's Atlantic coast, between Poitou in the north and Guyenne in the south, are squeezed two small provinces, Aunis and Saintonge, whose capitals are La Rochelle and Saintes on the Charente. We do not know exactly where and when Bernard Palissy was born, for he was a peasant. The date was about 1510, and the place was in the diocese of either Agen or Saintes. At any rate, his early life was so closely connected with Saintes that we may call him a Saintongeais. His education was rudimentary and certainly did not include Latin, but he was intelligent and eager for knowledge. He decided to become a *vitrier*, which was not so much a glazier as a maker of stained glass for churches; this was traditionally a noble art.[90]

As soon as his apprenticeship was completed he undertook his *tour de France*.[91] It was customary for young craftsmen, before establishing themselves, to travel from town to town, working here and there as opportunity arose, observing anything new or noteworthy, and gaining experience and maturity. If the young man was earnest, intelligent, and ambitious, and if he loved his craft, he was bound to learn a great deal and to develop his personality. We know that Palissy traveled across Guyenne, Gascony, the Pyrenees, Béarn and Bigorre, Languedoc and Provence, and Burgundy, then back to the west and home via Anjou, Brittany, and Poitou. Such an education was different from that of the schools but at least as rich, and much closer to life. It was as though he visited many countries, each with its own arts and usages, but all speaking kindred dialects. Palissy observed not only the city artisans in their shops but also the farmers in the open country. Every aspect of nature drew his attention, fields and forests, mountains and valleys, springs and rivers. He was saddened by the ignorance of the farmers and the contempt in which they were held. Were they not doing the most useful kind of work?

After his return Palissy married and established himself in Saintes, but general insecurity caused the art of stained glass to die out. He was able to earn some money surveying and even received a royal commission to survey the salt marshes of Saintonge when the introduction of the *gabelle* made that necessary.[92] The practice of surveying enabled him to make many observations, for example, of fossil shells, of which he found large accumulations.[93] A piece of Chinese porcelain or of Italian *faenza* fell into his hands and kindled in him a new vocation: he would become a potter. But first he must obtain the secret of the marvelous white enamel that had struck his fancy. This aspect of Palissy's life is well known by his own account of his endless trials and continual failures, which almost ended in tragedy. The story has been embellished and become legendary, how he reduced his family to poverty, burning his furniture and the very floor of his house in order to feed his insatiable furnaces. He succeeded at last in producing not anything comparable to the best Chinese or Italian wares but a kind of rustic pottery. He made enamels of many colors, but the originality of his work lay more in the form than in the substance of his wares. He did not work with a potter's wheel but made large plates to which he applied molded figures of plants and shells, reptiles and fish. Some of his plates are perhaps of greater scientific than artistic interest. His art appealed to Renaissance imagination, and in 1548 he obtained the patronage of a great lord, the constable of Montmorency,[94] and through him, somewhat later, that of the Queen Mother.

The Calvinists had made great progress in the western provinces and by 1554 were strongly established in La Rochelle, and more generally in Aunis and Saintonge. An independent man like Palissy, who had received no scholastic indoctrination and had perhaps suffered from clerical superciliousness, was very susceptible to the new preaching. He witnessed the burning alive of heretics in Saintes, his workshop and kilns were destroyed, he was imprisoned but was finally released, thanks to Montmorency's protection, and appointed "inventor of rustic pottery to the King."[95] He was also working in various castles as a landscape architect in the Renaissance style, which implied the construction of artificial grottoes and the mixing of art objects with the trees and flowers. He was permitted to establish a pottery near the Louvre, in the gardens of the Tuileries;[96] his pottery replaced the old tile works. At the time of the Saint Bartholomew massacre (night of August 23, 1572), Palissy was saved. Catherine de' Medici, an Italian princess and a patron of the arts, was a very practical woman, who did not want to be deprived of her best servants, such as Palissy and Paré. Palissy remained in her service and that of her sons almost twenty-five years, but during a new outburst[97] against the Huguenots in 1588, in spite of his long service and his old age, he was thrown into the Bastille, where he died in 1589.[98]

The sixteenth century was a time of agricultural progress in France and other countries. Many men knew and loved the land as husbandmen, vine-growers, and foresters do, but Palissy's knowledge and love were deeper because he was a potter. He had examined all the kinds of sand, clay, and marl that he might need for his pots, and rocks that might be used in making glazes and enamels.

His first book, *La Recepte véritable par laquelle tous les hommes de la France pourront apprendre à multiplier et à augmenter leurs thrésors* . . . (La Rochelle: Barthélemy Berton, 1563) was dedicated to his royal patron—"A ma très chère et honorée dame, Madame la Royne mère"—and his gratitude to her was beautifully expressed in his preface. The book is a medley of facts and ideas about agriculture and geology, mineralogy and chemistry, philosophy, theology, etc., which reveals his vast experience as well as his lack of formal education. It includes a history of the reformed church in Saintes and of the local disorders; his account inspires confidence, since he was a witness, a gentle one.

This book was published about the time he moved to Paris and began his work at the Tuileries (1563/64). Its publication gave him some prestige, and he made friends at the court and in town, chancellors and councillors, surgeons, doctors, and learned men. He was enjoying his work as an artist and a man of science when the peace was broken again by the Saint Bartholomew purge, and though he escaped the ordeal, it was better for him to disappear. He went for a time to Sedan,[99] then traveled in the Ardennes, Germany, and Flanders, rounding out the information he had obtained in his youth in southern France. He was now better disciplined and knew more definitely what he wanted.

After the peace of La Rochelle (June 1573) he returned to Paris, and in 1575, during Lent,[100] he offered to give public lessons on natural history, particularly physical geography, geology, chemistry, and mineralogy. His lectures were the first of their kind in Paris and perhaps in the world. They were advertised on placards in various parts of the city, and the admission charge was on *escu* for each lecture. Palissy did not appeal to university students, who had their own courses of lectures, but rather to physicians, dilettanti, and *gens du monde*. His lectures were original in that their substance was derived from nature and from his own observations and experiments. We may assume that he had read a great deal, but his ignorance of Latin made it impossible for him to drink from the usual sources of learning. He did not know half so much as the learned naturalists, but much of his own knowledge was new to them, and his emphasis was often different from theirs. Another original feature of his lectures was the fact that he had accumulated a collection of "fossils" of every kind and used them as specimens. His collection was probably the first to be used for demonstration purposes by a lecturer. For example, he may have shown organic fossils and explained that they were the remains of living creatures that had died and had been gradually mineralized; he may have shown also living specimens of the same creatures. We have no means of knowing how complete his demonstrations were. At any rate, however imperfect and tentative, his lectures were a welcome novelty and were well attended; he has left a list of thirty-four distinguished members of his audience, most of them physicians, some of whom were attached to the royal court or to princely families.[101] Palissy seems to have repeated the course every year for at least ten years.

The substance of the lectures is well known to us, for it was printed under the title *Discours admirables* . . . (Paris: Martin le Jeune, 1580). This book is almost three times as long as his earlier one, but less diffuse and discursive (Palissy had learned much in seventeen years). It is a collection of eleven treatises dealing with (1) waters, fountains, etc., (2) alchemy, (3) potable gold, (4) mithridate (an electuary), (5) ice, (6) various kinds of salts (origin and growth of minerals), (7) common salt and how to extract it from salty marshes, (8) origin and physical qualities of common and precious stones, (9) various kinds of clay, (10) earthenware, enamels, and firing, (11) marl,[102] its utility, how to recognize and where to find it. The whole was written in the form of a dialogue between Theory (one of the learned doctors) and Practice (Palissy). It was a defense of experience against book learning.

At the end of his "Epistle to Readers" he referred to his audience as his "little academy." One of its members was the nobleman, Jacques de la Primaudaye of the Vendômois, whose son Pierre wrote a book entitled *L'Académie françoise* (Paris, 1575),[103] which had an immense success. It was a treatise on virtues and vices, religious offices and other duties. Did the title suggest to Palissy his reference to his little academy?

The *Discours admirables* are not admirable as a scientific treatise, and I fear that the original lectures were not well organized, but they were full of good ideas, the opinions of a practical man who had spent a lifetime observing and interrogating nature without prejudices and almost without superstitions.

Palissy was the first to recognize that the water of springs and rivers derives from rain and snow. He observed the petrification of wood and recognized the true nature of other fossils (shells, fishes, etc.); he was thus one of the ancestors of palaeontology. From the presence of fossils in rocks he deduced the former existence of seas and lakes in which they were deposited. He was the first to do so in France, where little further progress was made on this subject until the time of Etienne Guettard (1715-86), two centuries later. His physical and chemical ideas were not very clear or very new, but he rejected the transmutation of metals and did not hesitate to denounce the alchemists. His own chemical knowledge was based on the many experiments he had made when trying to find the perfect enamel; he had tried some 300 mixtures, combining various clays and sands with tin, lead, iron, steel, antimony, copper sulfate, ashes of tartar, litharge, stone of Périgord (manganese), etc. The art of pottery required physical experiment; he had to find out how much heat was needed in his furnaces and how to regulate the speed of firing his materials and the speed of cooling them. He was aware of the existence of a multitude of salts, and knew that salts in solution were very different from those in solid form. It was impossible for him (or for anybody else) to express his results in scientific terms, but he had obtained without outside help a good deal of empirical knowledge. When he started his research in ceramics all clays were very much alike to him, but he learned to differentiate them and to find out the possibilities of each kind. He had some intuition of what we call "affinity."

Applying his ideas to the earth, he understood that changes are taking place all the time. "The earth is never idle." Various kinds of soils are stratified under great pressure, and water is always percolating from one level to a lower one. Just as different clays, sands, and rocks reacted differently in his furnaces, they behaved differently in the earth itself.

His general views on the formation of rocks and metals were comparable to those of Agricola in that he exaggerated the importance of water and minimized that of fire; they were both potential Neptunians (it is instructive to observe the slow incubation of Werner's theories). He made a few experiments on crystallization and believed that the growth of ores was a phenomenon of the same nature. He loved the soil like a true peasant, understood its pregnancy in a more scientific way, and tried to analyze its different properties. While he lacked chemical knowledge, his experience as a ceramist had taught him the great difference between one lump of earth and another; an intelligent farmer had some inkling of this, but Palissy added to it a new kind of experience, not agricultural but technical.

The blindness of the farmers shocked him. They knew the value of manure but wasted much of it. It was full of "salts" that were washed away by the rain when muck heaps were allowed to stand too long in the courtyard. Though he had no knowledge of chemistry, his interest in agriculture was chemical and he was an incipient agricultural chemist. At any rate, he was asking himself sensible questions. The mismanagement of forests shocked him almost as much;[104] carelessness in wood-cutting was a useless "murder of trees."

Having learned what he knew in the hardest way, he wanted to mark out easier ways for his followers. Hence his deep concern with teaching. Those who know should make their experience available to others. His two books, the *Recepte véritable* written at 54 (1563) and the *Discours admirables,* seventeen years later, were his testament to posterity. Educated people often write too early, directly they are out of school and before they have obtained any real knowledge; they mix up their meager experience with their ill-digested book learning and tend to overvalue the mixture. Self-taught men like Palissy write late in life under the combined pressure of geniune experience and social duty.

He was an actively kind man, pious and generous, tolerant and prudent, but very naïve. He loved God and nature, and in spite of the many cruelties he had witnessed he loved his fellowmen. He is different from the many naturalists of his time, except Agricola, in that his interest was largely restricted to the earth, to land and soil, to what we would call geology, mineralogy, and to some extent physics and chemistry. His books are not scientific in the same sense as those of Agricola and other naturalists; they are unique examples of pre-scientific literature.

He had read all the books available to him in French, and by the middle of the sixteenth century many had been translated: the Bible, Vitruvius, Pliny, various alchemical books, and the contemporary writings of Cardano, G. B. della Porta, Belon, and Rondelet. Much could be read in French, but some of the best could not. Scientific literature in French was a heterogeneous body, incomplete and capricious. Palissy's own books were a very original addition to it.

He is one of the creators of the French language. His lack of Latin was a help as well as an impediment, for he was obliged to find new ways of expressing his new ideas. His style was as naïve, honest, and as rich as his own personality, and he has obtained an honorable place in French literature.

The value of Palissy's ideas was not recognized as promptly as that of Agricola's because they were not published in scholarly books. Even in France his scientific fame was not established until much later. Father Marin Mersenne was the only man of the seventeenth century who appreciated his rustic genius. A fuller appreciation was obtained later thanks to Antoine de Jussieu (1718), Fontenelle (1720), Réaumur (1720), and Guettard (1770).[105]

Like other men of his age, Palissy lived under the shadow of the religious wars of the sixteenth century (actually dynastic as well as religious), which devastated many parts of France, ruined its commerce, and demoralized its people.[106] Montaigne's immortal essays were in large part a reaction to the political dissensions of his time. Palissy was a much simpler man than Montaigne. He had become a Protestant in early youth and remained one throughout his life.

He was, however, quiet and unaggressive, and his mind was occupied with artistic and scientific problems. Yet this gentle and kindly man spent his last years in prison. We cannot admire too much the peaceful men who minded their own business and did their best in their several pursuits, men like Palissy and Montaigne, Michel de l'Hospital,[107] Jean Bodin, Jacques Auguste de Thou,[108] and the majority of men of science.

Fifth Wing

ANATOMY AND MEDICINE

I. The New Anatomy

IT IS NOT an uncommon mistake to believe that anatomical research ceased during the Middle Ages because of ecclesiastical intolerance. Actually, anatomical dissection in one form or another was never completely abandoned. To be sure, dissections of human bodies were sometimes forbidden, and always rare. This was due not only to religious interdiction but chiefly to popular superstitions and civil policy. There has always been deep in men's hearts (even to this day) a superstitious fear of dead bodies and a strong repugnance to necropsy. Such repugnance might have been assuaged by belief in the immortal soul, but it was not, and most people continued to attach an irrational sacredness to inanimate corpses. As to civil policy, it is clear that the disposition of human bodies had to be very strictly controlled. Even today, we are not allowed to dissect any body, except under very special conditions in the anatomical laboratories of accredited medical schools. In the fourteenth century the number of licensed dissections increased; this made possible the work of such men as Mondino de' Luzzi (XIV-1) and Guido da Vigevano (XIV-1).

There is another aspect of the matter that is generally overlooked. One of the greatest anatomists of antiquity, Galen of Pergamon (II-2), dissected monkeys, and his very important anatomical treatises are based chiefly, if not exclusively, on monkey material. During the early Middle Ages an anatomical school flourished in Salerno, where most of the work was based on pigs.[1] The Salerno anatomists were not permitted to dissect men, or at least their opportunities of doing so were exceedingly rare; they had no monkeys, but plenty of pigs. Galen was not especially interested in

172

monkeys, nor were the Salerno clerks interested in pigs; they dissected these animals because they wanted to understand the structure of the human body.

You remember the scandal caused by Darwin's theory of evolution. Many theologians took up arms against him (and they continue to do so in backward countries), because his implication that man was a lateral descendant or a cousin of the apes seemed to them a religious outrage, an intolerable blasphemy. Their anger was foolish, because Darwin and his followers were concerned only with bodies. The relationship of human to animal bodies was obvious; it had been taken for granted not only by pagans but also by Christians. These learned theologians should have known that from the religious point of view the difference between men and, say, pigs or monkeys is not so much a matter of anatomy as one of psychology. The essential difference between men and animals lies in the fact that the body of the former, and his only, is informed by an immortal soul.

When we say that men are the children of God, we do not think of their perishable and corruptible bodies but of their eternal souls, of the divine light that is in them. What does it matter then that the bodies of men and animals resemble each other? Galen and the Salernitans were fully aware of that many centuries before the modern anatomists. All the bodies of the higher mammals have the same organs, the same general structure, as if they had all been built, more or less well, from the same kind of blueprints.

As new medical schools were created during the Renaissance in many countries and there was some rivalry between them, it was realized more keenly that anatomy could not be taught without public dissections; hence such dissections became more numerous. Whatever resistance there was came less from the Church than from superstition and from the scholastic frame of mind. The average professor had never done any dissection of his own and despised that kind of work. He refused to soil his hands and preferred to study the books of Galen or Avicenna. The first public dissections were organized in the following way (we know the pattern from published texts and also from contemporary woodcuts).[2] The professor of anatomy sat in a very high cathedra and read aloud slowly the text of, say, Galen. Much below the professorial chair, on the level of the lower seats of the hall, stood an assistant dissecting a body laid out on a table. If the reader and the prosector were well synchronized, the students could see the dissection of the parts described in the text. The bodies needed for such demonstrations were provided by the city; they were generally the bodies of criminals who had just been executed. This had two consequences; first, the dissection of women or children was much rarer than that of men; second, public dissections could take place only at irregular intervals when material was available. We know that at Padua, in Vesalius' time, when many criminals were condemned to death at the same time, the medical school would arrange with the city to have the executions spaced out in order better to satisfy the needs of anatomical teaching.

Such public dissections were very insufficient, however, for research purposes. The professor reading his book could hardly see what was going on below his feet; the students did not see very much or very well; the only person who had a good chance of learning something was the prosector. It must be added that if the professor was of the true scholastic type (and he often was), he would have more confidence in his text than in the dissected body. The story is told of a professor who, being confronted with a discrepancy between the text and the dissection, preferred to throw the blame upon the miserable body rather than upon Galen.

There were, of course, real anatomists, born anatomists, who were not satisfied with such a routine and wanted to see reality with their own eyes and in their own way. I shall speak only of two of them, the greatest of all, the Italian Leonardo da Vinci and the Fleming Andreas Vesalius. Leonardo was the real pioneer, for his anatomical investigations were already begun before the end of the fifteenth century, while those of Vesalius culminated in 1543.[3]

As the Sixth Wing will be entirely devoted to Leonardo, it will suffice to say here that although he was an artist, not a physician, he managed (I wonder how?) to obtain human bodies, dissected them with extreme care, and, what is equally important, made admirable drawings. These drawings exist to this day, the richest collection of them being in Windsor Castle. Anatomical drawings of the soft internal parts of the body are extremely difficult, and some of those made by Leonardo more than 450 years ago have never been equaled (photographs, however good, cannot always replace them). Unfortunately, as they were not published until our own times, they could hardly influence the progress of anatomy. Leonardo was the greatest

forerunner of modern anatomy,[4] but the real creator thereof was
Vesalius.

ANDREAS VESALIUS

Andreas Vesalius, son of a doctor, was born in Brussels in 1514.
He was a born anatomist and as a boy he was already eager to dissect whatever was available to him. He studied at Louvain (not far
from Brussels), then at Paris, where his teachers were Jacques Dubois
(Jacobus Sylvius, 1478-1555) and Johann Günther of Andernach
(Jean Gonthier, Guinterius, 1505-1574). Both men were distinguished
anatomists of the old Galenic school, and Vesalius' first publication
was an edition of Günther's "anatomical institutions according to
Galen" (*Institutiones Anatomicae secundum . . . Galeni sententiam
ad candidatos Medicinae* [Venice: D. Bernardinus, 1538]). Later, in
the same year, he published his *Tabulae anatomicae* (Venice: D.
Bernardinus, April 1538). These books were still essentially Galenic
and mediaeval. He had been appointed, at the age of 23, professor
at the University of Padua, where he was free to continue his anatomical investigations as he pleased. He was perhaps the first university professor to do away with the prosector or ostensor and do
the dissecting himself. It would have been impossible, impatient and
impulsive as he was, to watch a prosector doing badly what he could
do himself much better.

In June 1543 he published the masterpiece that immortalized him,
The Fabric of the Human Body (*De humani corporis fabrica,* folio,
Basel: Oporinus, 1543). The same *annus mirabilis* had witnessed a
few weeks before the publication of Copernicus' treatise *De revolutionibus orbium coelestium*.[5] Thus modern anatomy and modern
astronomy were born in the same year within a few weeks. Vesalius
published a second edition of his *Fabrica* in 1555 (same printer);
this included a few changes (for example, concerning the cardiovas-
cular system),[6] but the *magnum opus* remained essentially the same.

If he had died in his year of victory, 1543, as Copernicus did, his
fame would hardly have been less than it was. It is thus unnecessary
to describe at length his later years, though they numbered more
than twenty. At the time of publication of the *Fabrica,* Vesalius was
only 29 (while Copernicus was 70). He seems to have been a bit difficult to deal with; he got impatient with academic jealousies and
accepted the post of physician to Charles V, and later to the latter's

ANDREAS VESALIUS (1514-64), aet. 28. Made in 1542 by John Stephen of Calcar and published in the first edition of the *De humani corporis fabrica* (Basel: Joannes Oporinus, 1543). M. H. Spielman, *The Iconography of Vesalius* (London: Bale, 1925).

son and successor, Philip II. The position of a royal physician was not always pleasant for a man as independent and cantankerous as Vesalius, and he got into serious trouble. According to one story, he started a dissection a bit too early, when the body was still alive (this was not impossible) and was in danger for his own security. Happily, in those days, when a man had got himself for any reason in too tight a corner, he could escape by undertaking a long pilgrimage; instead of blaming him, everybody would be obliged to commend his piety, and by the time he came back (if he came back), the situation might be cleared up in one way or another. In 1564 Vesalius undertook a pilgrimage to Jerusalem. On his way to the Holy Land or on his way back he stopped in Cyprus, where he received an offer from the Venetian senate to resume his professorship in Padua. He sailed back, but the ship that was carrying him was shipwrecked near the island of Zacynthos (Zante) and Vesalius died there before October 15, 1564; he had not yet completed his fiftieth year.[7]

Vesalius' work was facilitated by many circumstances. Not only did printing make possible the publication of such a book, a richly illustrated folio, but it had made available in Greek and Latin the anatomical works of Galen. Vesalius himself was one of the contributors to the Latin edition of Galen published by the Juntine press in Venice in 1541. It was he who edited or reedited Galen's books on the dissection of nerves, on the dissection of veins and arteries, and also the great treatise on anatomical procedure.[8] Vesalius had a deep knowledge of Galen, as is proved repeatedly in the *Fabrica*.

Another stimulant to Vesalius' mind was the development of the graphic arts that was occurring with singular intensity in his own time. The artists of Florence had created the art of perspective, Leonardo had explained the "science of painting," men of science had been gradually trained not to be satisfied with words; they wanted to see things, to see them clearly and in the round, in their wholeness and in their surroundings. The magnificent drawings in the *Fabrica* were not made by Vesalius but obviously were done under his direction. The artist was John Stephen of Calcar,[9] a Fleming, a pupil of Titian; he held the brush or pen in a masterly way but Vesalius' was the directing mind. These drawings, as well as the text or even more so, constituted a revolution in scientific method.[10]

The *Fabrica* reveals also Vesalius' learning; he was a real humanist, conversant not only with Latin and Greek, but also with Arabic
and Hebrew. His great success, however, was not due to his learning,
Galenic and otherwise, or to his artistic feeling, or to the opportunities opened to him by the graphic arts, but to his immense experience as a dissecter. The authority of Galen was so great, however,
that in most cases he was not able to emancipate himself from it.

This is not the place to speak of Vesalius' many followers in various countries. Nevertheless it is well to say a few words about his
Italian contemporary, Bartolomeo Eustachio (c.1520-74), whose anatomical achievements were considerable but remained (like Leonardo's) largely unknown.[11] His main work remained unpublished,
except that the plates discovered by Giovanni Maria Lancisi (1654-
1720), physician to Clement IX, were published in Rome in 1714
with Lancisi's commentary.

The Belgians are justly proud of their illustrious countryman,
Vesalius. They tried to celebrate on an international scale the fourth
centenary of his birth (1514) and of the *Fabrica* (1543), but their purpose was twice frustrated, because of the German invasions of Belgium in 1914 and 1943.[12]

II. The New Medicine

THE NUMBER OF Renaissance physicians was enormous.[13] There was
one or more in every town of Europe, and they clustered, then as
now, around the many medical schools, around the civil and ecclesiastical courts, and in the prosperous cities. The best way to give a
general view of the new tendencies is to introduce half a dozen of
these men: the German Swiss Paracelsus; three Italians, Ficino,
Cardano, and Cornaro; the Spaniard Servetus; and two Frenchmen,
Jean Fernel and Ambroise Paré. Many other physicians have already
made an appearance in other parts of this book.

PARACELSUS

The most original and erratic of these physicians was Paracelsus,
whose life has been outlined in the Third Wing, when we spoke of
him as a chemist, *"princeps chemicorum."* He is such an important

figure, however, that it is worth while to come back to him and discuss his medical ideas. If we may believe him, he was not simply an M.D., but a double doctor, "beyder Artzenei doctor" (*utriusque medicinae doctor*). Whether he was a double doctor, a single one, or none, matters very little today, but what kind of man was he—a genius or a charlatan?

In my opinion, he was both to a high degree.[14] His unsociability and the deformities of his wounded personality may possibly be traced back to his childhood. He lost his mother when he was nine and had no stepmother. He was left alone to grow up as well as he could and his growth was erratic and loveless. In the course of time he acquired a good deal of experience, but his learning was meager. He had enough theoretical knowledge for guidance of a sort but not enough to be smothered by it as was the case with many of his over-learned colleagues. He was very intelligent, but being a self-made man and badly educated, he was immoderately proud and full of conceit. It is probable that the professors and successful practitioners snubbed him whenever they had an opportunity, for his vanity and bad manners were obvious enough, while his genius was not.

Galenism was then the mark of medical respectability. His main targets were naturally Galen and Avicenna, the second Galen, but these two masters were out of his reach and his poisoned arrows fell upon their defenders, the pompous and complacent professors of medicine. His bitterness against those "ignorant fools" who did not appreciate him is understandable to us, but it was not to them, and they did not like him.

We can form a pretty good idea of his character from the apology that he wrote while he was living in Carinthia in 1537-38. After his expulsion from Basel ten years before he had traveled far, learned much, and quarreled often. He had written many books but most of them remained unprinted. This was for him a period of rest and stocktaking but not of peace. He composed a new book against the physicians (*Labyrinthus medicorum errantium*) and the apology entitled *Reply to certain calumnies of his enemies* or *Sieben Defensiones*.[15] It is a passionate defense of his character, activities, and medical philosophy. He felt misunderstood and ill used and his defense turned easily, as was his wont, into an attack against the conventional and selfish doctors who paid no heed to him. He explained his own astrological and religious beliefs. God can cure every disease; the good doctor will be able to do so, with God's help, if he be a good Christian and if his heart be full of love and mercy. The good doctor must also be a chemist, however, and be able to use the chemical tools that God had made available to him. He himself had obtained (he went on to explain) much experience in travel[16] and his main source of knowledge was not any book written by man but the book of nature (*Codex Naturae*). Such views were not original with him; we find them expressed over and over again by other men, especially self-made men such as Bernard Palissy; but they were undoubtedly sincere. Paracelsus and Palissy expressed similar opinions because their experience in very different fields (pottery and medicine) had been of much the same kind.

Medical teaching before Paracelsus was based upon anatomy and botany; it was his main achievement to add to these two legs a third one, chemistry. He was not the first to use chemical drugs (as opposed to herbs);[17] some such drugs, e.g. mercury, had been used from time immemorial, if not in the West, at least in eastern Europe and Asia. Many mineral drugs were listed in Dioscorides,[18] and in almost every herbal. Some alchemists had probably increased their number, men like Ramon Lull, Arnold of Villanova, and John of Rupescissa,[19] but Paracelsus was the first to declare boldly that the aim of alchemy was not to make gold but to prepare medicines. He had forerunners as everybody has, but he was the real originator of iatrochemistry. This was recognized by the great Dutch physician, Hermann Boerhaave (1668-1738), who was the leading physician of Europe two centuries after Paracelsus. Boerhaave was still far away from Lavoisier (though the latter was born five years after his death), but he was half way between Paracelsus and ourselves. In the historical introduction to his *Institutiones et experimenta chemiae* (Leiden, 1724),[20] he states very clearly Paracelsus' merit as a chemist who applied his chemical knowledge to medicine. That was the core of Paracelsus' medical doctrine and the main cause of his opposition to Galen and Avicenna, who did not pay sufficient attention to chemistry.

The Galenic drugs[21] were almost exclusively of vegetable origin; many were infusions or decoctions which were generally so diluted that they could do no harm. Galenic medicine was a kind of homeopathy. Mineral drugs were more concentrated, powerful, and violent. They were more active than most of the herbs, but more dangerous in proportion, and one can readily understand why the average physician was afraid of using them. The methods that Paracelsus defended with the abusive eloquence of a quack might cause healings which could not have been obtained with gentler means; it is highly probable that they also caused accidents and deaths, which he might forget but which his adversaries would not. He was extolled as a savior by his disciples, but despised and insulted by his enemies. His charlatanism, coarseness, and overweening self-confidence might influence some people in his favor, but increased the distrust and condemnation of others.

Among the drugs that he was among the first to use were *lapis infernalis* (silver nitrate, lunar caustic), copper vitriol, corrosive sublimate (mercury chloride), sugar of lead (lead acetate), arsenic and antimony compounds, dilute sulphuric acid, sweetened oil of vitriol, tinctures of iron and iron saffron (colcothar), etc. Whether or not he was the first to use *lapis infernalis* does not matter very much; what matters is his general belief in the efficacy of chemical agents. It is interesting, however, to say a few words about a drug that has been generally ascribed to him because of a curious misunderstanding—laudanum.[22] It is true that Paracelsus referred to it many times, but his laudanum was not very different from the Greek *ladanon;*[23] it was definitely not an opiate. Paracelsus was not shy of using opium; he used it openly, but he did not include it in his laudanum. In contrast, the laudanum that was so popular one or two generations ago was essentially an alcoholic tincture of opium to which various other drugs might be added. The introducer of our laudanum was not Paracelsus but the "modern Hippocrates," Thomas Sydenham (1624-89), whose prescription of it remained in the pharmacopoeia until recently.

Opium deserves a short digression. Its use as a drug is immemorial in the East, and it is still the main resource of many doctors in such countries as India and China. It does not cure but soothes the pain, lulls the patient, and gives nature a better chance to effect her own cure. We often think of opium smoking as a terrible and degrading vice and it often is just that, but for many Orientals it is hardly more dangerous than alcohol with us, and as far as its medical use is concerned, most of them, doctors included, would call it one of the blessings of life. Men and women are bound to suffer and life may be bitter, but opium is a means of relaxation, comfort, and consolation.

To return to Paracelsus, it is no wonder that his age was also the age of the earliest pharmacopoeias as opposed to herbals and of new apothecary shops differing from the herbalist shops.[24] This suggests again that Paracelsus was not by any means the only or the first of his kind, though he was the most significant. Iatrochemistry is a fruit of the sixteenth century, and Paracelsus was not so much its creator as its main expounder. The quarrel between his followers, the iatro-chemists, and the Galenists increased in heat and ill will during the sixteenth century but reached its climax only in the following century, especially in Paris. The Faculty of Medicine of that city fought the rear-guard battles against the new drugs, especially against the use of antimony,[25] in the second half of the seventeenth century. The leaders of the opposition were successively Jean Riolan, father and son (1538-1605, 1580-1657), and the silly dean Guy Patin (1601-72), who fought the chemists with as much virulence and wit as he fought the "circulators" (Harvey's disciples).[26]

Paracelsus had the intuition, based upon false analogies, that the physiological processes were chemical processes governed by *archaei* or spirits, vital forces. A disease occurred when one of the *archaei* did not govern properly; chemical agents made it possible to awaken the delinquent *archaeus* and restore the equilibrium. The general concept went back to Galen and beyond; the novelty was in the emphasis on chemistry. It would perhaps be clearer to say on alchemy; the alchemists had tried innumerable reactions and had accumulated a vast amount of empirical knowledge but had not yet been able to emerge from empiricism. Chemistry, therefore, did not yet exist. Iatrochemistry preceded it, even as iatrophysics anticipated physics; it was less a result of chemical knowledge than a stimulant to chemical research. Paracelsus anticipated chemical biology (or biological chemistry) at a time when the principles of biology and the principles of chemistry were equally unknown. It is thus as irrelevant to discuss his prophetic ideas from any technical point of view as it would be to criticize Isaiah from the point of view of modern sociology.

Having spent a good part of his life in the vicinity of mines, Paracelsus was called upon to treat miners and metal workers and he did not fail to observe their peculiar ailments. This led him to the composition of one of his most original books, *Von der Bergsucht und anderen Bergkrankheiten* (on the miners' sickness and other miners' diseases).[27] It may have been written as early as 1538 or even 1534, but was not published until many years after his death (by Dillingen in Schwaben, Bavaria, 1567). This was the first treatise devoted to an occupational disease and was almost the only work of its kind until the publication of Ramazzini's in 1700.[28]

Von der Bergsucht is divided into three books dealing with (1) pulmonary diseases, the miner's phthisis and the effects of choke damp (mainly CO_2), (2) the diseases of smelter workers and metallurgists, (3) those induced by mercurial vapors.

According to the author these diseases were caused by local and tangible conditions, which he described, but also by more general ones, meteorological and astronomical (astrological), the effects of the "chaos" (gas) in which the workmen lived, for that chaos was partly ruled by astral influences. He was on safer ground when he discussed chemical factors, chiefly the poisonous effects of metallic dusts that penetrated the workmen's mucous membranes, lungs, and skin. Diseases were caused by coagulations, precipitations, and deposits of complex sediments[29] which he called *tartarus* or *tartarum*.[30] The idea and the term were not new; they had been used already by Albert the Great (XIII-2), but Paracelsus inserted them in his medical theory. His *tartarus* was not a single substance but a vague combination of the three principles (mercury, sulphur, salt). These views are far from clear, but the situation was hopelessly beyond the analytical methods of his age. Miners worked hard and sweated profusely in a dusty and ill-smelling atmosphere; they caught colds which weakened them, were often the victims of a kind of consumption, and died miserably. He realized that they were slowly contaminated and described the symptoms of chronic arsenic poisoning (pallor, thirst, gastro-intestinal disturbances, skin eruptions, and general debility). He distinguished between other kinds of poisoning caused by alkalis, antimony, and mercury. The last he had good opportunities of observing in the localities of Tirol, Carinthia, and Carniola, where mercury was mined and refined.

This treatise would hardly satisfy the medical reader of today, for it dealt with problems which it was as yet impossible to formulate clearly, let alone solve, but it was the first achievement of its kind and is enough to establish his fame.

Another achievement was his recognition of endemic goiter and his observations connecting it with cretinism.[31] In a lecture on goiter (which he called *struma* or *Kröpf*) delivered in Basel in 1525 he ascribed it partly to the minerals dissolved in drinking water. He was not the first to deal with goiter and even to recognize its endemic nature, but his observations were the most significant of his century.[32]

From Roman times on, and even from earlier times, the healing properties of various mineral waters had been recognized and some physicians had taken full advantage of them. Many treatises were written on balneology and gathered in the *Collectio de balneis* (Juntae, Venice, 1533). Paracelsus is not included in that collection,[33] and this may explain why his own contributions were not so well known. He devoted a booklet to mineral waters, recommending those of Gastein (Salzburg province), Toplicza (Transylvania), Göppingen (Donau circle, Württemberg), Plombières (Vosges), etc.

The Platonic concept[34] of microcosm vs. macrocosm was a commonplace of Renaissance thought. Like Leonardo, Cardano, Palissy, and others, Paracelsus accepted it implicitly. The contrast and symmetry of the body and the universe obliged one to consider the body as a whole, even as one considered the universe in its totality. It might be expedient to envisage parts of either but one should never lose sight of the wholeness. To the individual soul corresponded the soul of the world, God. The soul of man was as closely tied to a living body as God was tied to the eternal universe. In addition to the divine soul, there was also in man a *spiritus vitae* (vital spirit) or chemical *archaeus*. A disease did not concern the body alone but also the whole spirit, partly divine and partly animal. To use a modern term, Paracelsus' medical philosophy was psychosomatic.[35]

Epilepsy had been discussed by Hippocrates, and Arabic physicians such as Avicenna had paid considerable attention to mental diseases, but toward the end of the Middle Ages those diseases were of greater concern to theologians than to medical men. Paracelsus reacted strongly against this, and wrote a treatise *Von den Krankheiten so die Vernunft berauben . . .* , the whole title of which reads in English "The diseases that deprive man of his reason, such as St. Vitus' dance,[36] falling sickness, melancholia, and insanity and their correct treatment." It was written in his thirties (c.1521) but was not printed within his lifetime; it was edited by Adam von Bodenstein (Basel, 1567).[37]

Paracelsus rejected the common notion that mental troubles were caused by ghosts or demons; their origin, he claimed, was neither more nor less spiritual than that of the bodily diseases. He made a distinction between feeble-mindedness and various forms of mania, such as could be observed in *lunatici, insani, vesani, melancholici*. A sickness of the mind might dominate the body, the worst sickness being that of the will. What is perhaps most unexpected is his belief that the ravings of maniacs might be instructive (this was an astounding anticipation of modern psychopathology, but it was ill defined). He was one of the first to separate the sexual components from other factors in the development of hysteria (which he called *chorea lasciva*) and to realize that unreasonable behavior might be the result not of a real disease but of a grave emotional disturbance. He was profoundly convinced of the individuality and personality of each and every man, in health or illness.

It is typical of his iatrochemical enthusiasm that the therapeutical part of his treatise on mental diseases includes the use of a good many chemical drugs as well as of abominable concoctions. He mentions such drugs as *aurum potabile, oleum auri*, vitriols, salts of sulphur, mercury, arsenic, and ammonia. Though magnetic knowledge was still rudimentary, he recommended the use of a magnet for therapeutic purposes; he was thus in a vague way a forerunner of Franz Anton Mesmer (1734-1815) and other "magnetizers." Though he recommended other irrational treatments, he also believed in psychotherapy which was highly rational. The good physician must use persuasion and prayer and do everything he can to encourage the self-healing of a man's soul; he must be gentle and compassionate. This is perhaps the best part of a treatise that is full of incongruities and of ideas not fully realized until our own day.

To complete our portrait of Paracelsus, we must examine also his mythological views. This is facilitated by Sigerist's study of his treatise *De nymphis sylvanis pygmaeis salamandris et gigantibus* (on nymphs, sylphs, pygmies, salamanders, and other spirits) (Nissae Silesiorum [or Neysse, modern Neisse]: Joannes Cruciger, 1566).[38] This treatise was very different from that on miners' diseases, but it was a product of the same environment. The miners' folklore was rich in myths that had grown up naturally to account for all the mysteries and fatalities of mountains, caverns, mines, and smithies. The ignorant and superstitious men obliged to spend a good part of their lives underground, to endure fatigue, accidents, diseases, and premature death in such a forbidding environment, compensated for these miseries with fables. An inquisitive and sympathetic observer, such as Paracelsus, could not help absorbing the mythology as well as the pathology of the German mines.

This folklore was a combination of Biblical stories with classical mythology and local invention. The miners, and Paracelsus with them, believed in the existence and ubiquity of various creatures that were neither men nor angels nor devils. These creatures suggest comparison with the *jinn* of Islamic folklore, whose fanciful deeds are told in the *Thousand and One Nights*. Paracelsus classified them according to the elements; each element has its own chaos (atmosphere or environment). The chaos of men and sylphs is air, water is the chaos of nymphs, earth that of pygmies (gnomes), fire that of salamanders. Each of these groups has its own aberrations or monsters. Thus sirens are monsters of the water people, giants are those of the sylphs, dwarfs those of the pygmies, and will-o'-the-wisps those of the salamanders. Other aberrations, such as earthquakes and comets, may concern large regions of the earth or the whole of it. Each of these monsters or aberrations is an omen and a warning.

Those fantasies were part of the texture of Paracelsus' science; they were also woven into his religion. Though he was a faithful Catholic at peace with the Church, his orthodoxy was as questionable in religion as in medicine, and he was very lucky to escape the curiosity of the Inquisitors. Man, he would have said, must walk in the light of God, as interpreted by the Holy Church, and in the light of science (or philosophy), as interpreted by the student of nature, the faithful reader of the *Naturae codex*.

To sum up, he was an extraordinary individual, full of ambiguities and contradictions: he was a reckless experimentalist, his sounder views were crudely mixed with metaphysical and magical ideas, and his rational cures could not always be separated from miraculous ones. He was original to the point of extravagance, indiscreet and bombastic, generous and foolish, a kind of medical gypsy, restless and dogmatic, a man of genius *and* a charlatan. His quackish appearance was partly due to his own weaknesses but partly—it is fair to remember—to the weakness and imbecility of contemporary knowledge. We may be disgusted by the presumption, vagueness, and irresponsibility of his statements, but in most cases there was no possible way in his time to express his intuitions with any clearness and precision. A man writing in his style today would be promptly dismissed as no good, but Paracelsus was writing about 1525, more than four centuries ago, and he did his best.

No wonder that his books were received with enthusiasm by a few kindred spirits but with distrust by the majority of sensible people. A generation after his death (c.1569), Duke Albrecht V ordered the monasteries of Bavaria to read and study the works of Hippocrates and Galen rather than the new ones. He did not name Paracelsus, but the latter was perhaps in his mind the main offender.

Paracelsus was neither a genuine discoverer nor a great teacher, but he was an exciter, a catalyzer, the outstanding medical prophet of the Renaissance. The scholarly physicians who edited, translated, or explained the Greek classics may have despised him, but in some respects he was standing head and shoulders above them.

GERONIMO CARDANO

Vesalius is remembered as an anatomist, Paracelsus as a chemist or iatrochemist, Geronimo[39] Cardano as a mathematician. We have already spoken of Cardano's achievements in algebra, but his contemporary fame was very largely medical and philosophical. He studied medicine in Pavia and Padua and obtained his doctorate in 1526, but was not admitted into the College of Physicians of Milan because of his illegitimate birth. He settled down as a country doctor in Sacco (near Padua) and married; according to his own recollections, the years he spent there (1526-32) were the happiest of his life. In 1532 he was able to return to Milan as a lecturer in mathematics; but his first published book was medical, a booklet on the bad practices of the contemporary physicians (*De malo recentiorum medicorum medendi usu libellus,* Venice: Ottaviano Scotto, 1536). A few years later he was finally permitted to practice medicine in Milan, and he did so well that by the middle of the century he was spoken of as one of the leading physicians not only of Milan but of Europe. His fame was based not only on medical but on mathematical and philosophical accomplishments. His treatise *De subtilitate rerum* (Nuremberg: J. Petreius, 1550) was considered by many readers as the climax of his wisdom, or, indeed, of wisdom in general.

In 1552 he was summoned to attend the Most Reverend John

Hamilton, archbishop of Saint Andrews, one of the most eminent personalities in Scotland, who was suffering intolerably from
asthma. Cardano obeyed the flattering summons and traveled to
London via Lyon, Paris, and Calais. He spent more than a month
observing his illustrious patient, surveyed critically every detail of
his diet and habits, and made various recommendations.[40] To put
it in modern terms, he seems to have discovered that His Eminence
was allergic to various things (such as feathers) and ordered their
removal. It would be foolish to say that Cardano discovered the
mysteries of allergy, but he was aware of the mysteries of health
and disease, was ready to experiment, and had sound intuitions.
The asthma was cured or alleviated and the grateful archbishop
rewarded him generously.

Cardano returned home via Antwerp, Cologne, Strasbourg, and
Basel. From then on his medical fame continued to increase in spite
of the vicissitudes of his life. His name was bracketed with that of
Vesalius. As far as I can see, his main merits as a doctor were common sense, open-mindedness, and readiness to attach more weight to
the results of experiment than to the sayings of Hippocrates, Galen,
and Avicenna. Like the best physicians of all times, he had great
faith in spiritual factors. Said he, "A man is nothing but his mind;
if that be out of order, all is amiss, and if that be well, all the rest
is at ease."[41]

His first medical book had been a clever way of establishing himself. To denounce the errors of physicians was a way of suggesting
that one knew better. This was not a novelty in medical literature.
It will suffice to recall the treatise *De erroribus medicorum* composed
by Roger Bacon (XIII-2).[42] In the course of his life Cardano composed other medical works, many of which remained unpublished,
and there were plenty of medical items in his "philosophical" works.
The *Opera omnia* edited by Charles Spon extended to ten folio
volumes (Lyon, 1663) out of which four are medical (vols. VI-IX),
while the tenth contains many medical articles. His most valuable
contributions, however, occurred in a philosophical treatise, the
De subtilitate rerum (1550); we may find there the first suggestions

To read the whole mass of his medical effusions would require
courage and perseverance. At any rate, his medical fame was hardly

for the teaching of the blind and for the teaching of the dumb and
deaf. That is enough to redeem his memory.

based upon them, inasmuch as many remained unknown until 1663;
it was based upon his cure of John of St. Andrews and upon his
other writings. Naïve people were led to believe that the author of
the *Ars magna*, the *Consolatio*, the *Subtilitas rerum*, and the *Rerum
varietas* must be a great physician; such absurd conclusions are not
uncommon today. Cardano is one of the best examples of the spe-
cialization of genius. He was certainly not great as a physician, but
the Renaissance believed him to be great, even supreme, and we
must take that fact into account in order better to understand his
time and himself.

MICHAEL SERVET

There is an immense contrast between Servetus and Cardano. The
latter was a devil of a man, a rascal of genius, a man who might
worry about cubic equations or physical subtleties but did not
bother about moral issues; Servet's mind, on the contrary, was tortured by religious perplexities, and he died at the stake in Geneva,
in 1553, a martyr of his own conscience. I sometimes wonder whether
Cardano, who was then at the top of his fame, ever heard of
Servetus' fate and, if so, what he thought of it. The whole tragedy
was beyond his understanding. He may have said, as many people
say about martyrs, "Why did he not stay quiet and keep his doubts
to himself? What a fool he was!"

Michael Servet was born in 1511 in Navarre, was educated in
Aragon and called himself Hispanus, a Spaniard. There is no need
of recalling in detail the vicissitudes of his ardent pilgrimage.[43] He
lived in various countries and spent the best part of his adult years
in Lyon, Paris, and Vienne. He was primarily a classical scholar,
something of a Hebraist, and he investigated the geography of
Ptolemy, the works of Galen, and above all the Holy Scriptures.
Though his education in Aragon and Toulouse was Catholic, the
study of the Bible and of the early Fathers had led him away from
Trinitarianism. He reached the extraordinary conclusion that the
First Council of Nicaea (325), which had condemned Arianism, had
switched the Church to the wrong track. Such a conclusion was exceedingly bold and dangerous, for it was heretical not only from the
Catholic point of view but also from that of Lutherans and Calvinists. By his defense of this doctrine Servet made himself obnoxious
to almost every one, yet he persisted; he could not help it; he was

driven by his conscience. His first books (1531-32) were devoted to Unitarianism, as was his last one, the *Christianismi Restitutio* (1553), which caused his execution within the same year.

His religious ideas were central to all his thinking. For example, he was an experienced physician who had studied Symphorien Champier, Fernel, Vesalius, Sylvius, and Gunterius, but his anatomical ideas were soon mixed up with theology. He believed that blood was the vehicle of the divine spirit or the soul; hence if one wished to understand the soul, one must understand the motion of the blood through the body. Now the blood could not pass from the right ventricle of the heart to the left, because the septum separating them is watertight. He rejected the Galenic fancy that the septum was pierced with invisible holes through which the blood could percolate,[44] and convinced himself, on the strength of his own dissections, that the blood was diverted to the lungs, where it was mixed with air, cleaned and reddened, and then returned to the auricle. In other words, Servet had discovered what is misleadingly called the lesser or pulmonary circulation.[45] This discovery was explained in his *Christianismi Restitutio*, where theologians coming across it would be unable to understand it, while the anatomists would never find it.

The fourth centenary of Servet's martyrdom was celebrated in 1953 in many universities all over the world, and the speakers paying tribute to his memory often spoke of him as a martyr of science. That was misleading. He was a martyr not of science but of the freedom of thought. His book was destroyed not because of the scientific discovery it contained (the Inquisition paid no attention to that) but because of its heretical purpose. Servet had the unusual distinction of being condemned to death twice, in June 1533 by the Catholics of Vienne and four months later by the Calvinists of Geneva. It was the latter who actually executed him, but the moral responsibility of the judges was the same in both cases.

Servet was burned at the stake in Champel (a suburb of Geneva) on October 27, 1553. There is a story in this connection to which I attach great importance. On the 350th anniversary of the execution (October 27, 1903), the Calvinist congregation of Geneva erected a monument to his memory. It bears a moving inscription stating their repentance: We love and respect our great teacher Calvin but regret that he was the victim of an intolerant age and ordered Servet's death because of the latter's nonconformity. Though generally over-looked by tourists, this unique monument is more impressive than the great Wall of the Reformation.

The churches have always preached that if we be wrong and sin, we must repent. If our contrition is sincere, we may be forgiven and improved; if we do not repent, there is no chance of improvement or pardon. That is very true, but the churches themselves have never admitted the possibility of their being wrong. Like other insti-tutions (governments, political parties, sects, labor unions), the churches have often sinned and committed crimes, but they have never repented. They felt that they could not repent without jeop-ardizing their prestige and their authority. No peace will ever be possible without the expression of collective guilt and collective repentance. The Calvinists of Geneva have given the world a mag-nificent example, which most people are not yet able to appreciate.

JEAN FERNEL

The three doctors of whom I have spoken were complex and elusive personalities. Cardano was a mathematician and gambler as well as a physician in the ordinary sense; Paracelsus was a chemist and prophet; Servet a religious rebel. The three of them had conned the medical books that were standard in their time, the books that served as textbooks in the medical schools, but in addition, Cardano was deeply interested in arithmetic, geometry, and mechanics, Para-celsus in alchemy, while Servet was scrutinizing the Bible and the early Fathers. Hence each of them had in him conflicting ideals; their personalities were split; they were rebels. In contrast, Fernel, the founder of physiology, and Paré, founder of the new surgery, were highly conservative; both were in the service of the kings of France.

Jean Fernel[46] (1497-1558) is generally called of Amiens (Ambi-anus), although he was not born in that city but in Montdidier, a small town in the same diocese. His parents soon moved to Clermont en Beauvoisis, and it was in that town, not far from Paris, that he received his education. A little later he was sent to Sainte Barbe, one of the colleges of the University of Paris. The date of his birth was 1497, and he obtained his M.A. in 1519; he had done well, yet was dissatisfied. The University was out-of-date, mediaeval, and it resisted the new tendencies that had grown with such exuberance in

JEAN FERNEL (1497-1558), aet. 57. Portrait in his *Medicina* (Paris: Andreas Wechel, 1554). This is the only contemporary portrait. For a discussion of this and other portraits see Sir Charles Sherrington, *The Endeavour of Jean Fernel* (Cambridge University Press, 1946), pp. 55, 180-82.

Italy and were now invading France. The clerks of the Sorbonne were not even as advanced as many Brothers of Common Life who tried to harmonize classical literature with Scripture.

Happily François I and his court were more open-minded. It was in those years (before May 1519) that he was giving hospitality to Leonardo da Vinci in Amboise; he welcomed many artists in Fontainebleau, where Guillaume Budé[47] was the keeper of his rich library of Greek and Latin manuscripts. Eleven years later the king began to appoint royal professors, who together constituted the Collège Royal, independent of the Sorbonne and more often than not antagonistic to it. The French Renaissance developed because of royal and princely patronage in spite of the University's hostility or inertia.

Young Fernel, sensitive to the new tendencies, was ambitious to become a master of Latin. He must be able to write the noble language as elegantly as Erasmus and Budé, Lefèvre d'Etaples and Josse van Clichthove;[48] these four men were a generation older than himself, his teachers rather than his own friends. The main conflict for him, in his formative years, was not between Catholicism and Protestantism, for his attitude was probably similar to that of Lefèvre (orthodox but liberal, if anything more conservative than the older man), but rather the conflict, fostered by the Renaissance, between scholasticism and the humanities. In the meantime he was studying mathematics and astronomy, but he had to choose a profession, and he hesitated for a while between the Church, the law, and medicine. His scientific predilections may have been the determining factor in the choice of the latter, for medicine was almost the only scientific profession and the safest. He obtained his M.D. in Paris in October 1530, and henceforth his interest was almost exclusively medical.

His modernism was well illustrated in his *Dialogi,* written at 45 in 1542.

This age of ours sees art and science gloriously re-risen, after twelve centuries of swoon. Art and science now equal their ancient splendour, or surpass it. This age need not, in any respect, despise itself, and sigh for the knowledge of the ancients. The orator to-day attains the height of oratory. Philosophy excels in every branch. Once again music, geometry, the handicrafts, painting, architecture, sculpture, and many other kinds of skill display themselves in such measure as in no wise to fall short of the achievements of antiquity, which won universal praise. . . . Our age to-day is doing things of which antiquity did not dream. Antiquity held Demetrius high for his engines of war, but to-day we have petards which hurl a flaming bomb. Good God, how destructive and swift compared with the old catapult! How efficient to-day the printing-press for the diffusion of all kinds of learning. To-day we have paper, once called Fabriano, supplanting wax, bark and skin. Hence "letters" to-day reach their high-water mark. The ocean has been crossed by the prowess of our navigators, and new islands found. The far recesses of India lie revealed. The continent of the West, the so-called New World, unknown to our forefathers, has in great part become known. In all this, and in what pertains to astronomy, Plato, Aristotle, and the old philosophers made progress, and Ptolemy added a great deal more. Yet, were one of them to return to-day, he would find geography changed past recognition. A new globe given us by the navigators of our time. Over and above that a method of ascertaining what geographers term "longitude," in whatever quarter of the globe.[49]

This sounds already like the battle of the ancients and the moderns which was to break out in the seventeenth century.[50] That

Fernel was keenly aware of the progress of medicine, which he was helping to create, was natural enough, but it is more interesting to note in his statement references to progress in other fields: the "flaming bomb," paper and printing, the New World, the new geography and the new globe.

After obtaining his M.D. Fernel settled in Paris and married. In 1536 he was teaching medicine at the Collège de Cornouailles,[51] and he gradually became a very successful practitioner. He was in attendance upon Catherine de' Medici, her husband, the dauphin Henri, and his mistress, Diane de Poitiers; when François I died in 1547 Henri succeeded him (as Henri II) and Fernel continued in his service, becoming chief court physician in 1556. From the middle of the century his practice took so much of his time that he was obliged to abandon his lectures. He was in the king's service during the English campaign and the taking of Calais, then returned to Fontainebleau, where he died of a fever on April 26, 1558. He was buried in Saint Jacques de la Boucherie (of which the Tour Saint Jacques is a relic).

His first books were mathematical, the *Monalosphaerium* (1527), the *Cosmotheoria* (1528), and the *De proportionibus* (1528). These three books were handsomely published in folio editions by Simon de Colines, who was then the best Parisian printer. The first was the description of an astrolabe of his own invention and the third dealt with fractions. The second, *Cosmotheoria*, on the shape and size of the earth, is more significant. It contains Fernel's measurement of a meridian based upon the distance of two places, Paris and Amiens, which have almost the same longitude.[52] This gives him a modest place in the history of geodesy, but his medical influence was much greater.

His fourth book, and his first on medicine, was the *De naturali parte medicinae* (Paris: S. de Colines, 1542). The title, "on the natural part of medicine," was an awkward way of referring to the body and its functioning; it suggested Galen's treatise on the use of parts. Galen's treatise might be called the first treatise on physiology; Fernel's was also physiological. He began writing it in 1538. Its publication met a real need, as was proved by its success in Italy and England as well as in France; it remained a standard work until Harvey's publication of the *De motu cordis* (1628), and even until later for the physicians who refused to accept Harvey's views.

He then published a treatise on pathology under the title *De vacuandi ratione* (Paris: Christian Wechel, 1545). The book which Fernel himself always called *Dialogi*, the *De abditis rerum causis* (Paris: Christian Wechel, 1548), was already written or drafted in 1542. Dedicated to Henri II, it was a discussion in the form of dialogues of many physical and physiological questions which perplexed him and which he could not solve. Since his perplexities were those of his age, the book sold very well; it was reprinted almost thirty times within a century. His last work, the *Medicina* (Paris: Christian Wechel, 1554), contained the sum of his knowledge.[53]

There were altogether thirty-four editions of Fernel's *Opera* before 1681. Every doctor of the late Renaissance and the seventeenth century had the opportunity of using one of them; he could hardly escape them.

Fernel was the first man to use the word "physiology" roughly as we use it, to mean the study of the body's normal functioning.[54] His treatment of the subject is very different, however, from that followed in our own textbooks, where it is divided according to the main functions, circulation, respiration, digestion, muscular motion, etc. In Fernel's time these functions were imperfectly understood and, in some cases, not even recognized. Circulation was not understood until Harvey (1628), respiration not until Lavoisier (1777), the nervous function not until much later. Fernel discussed such mysteries as innate, or life-preserving, heat versus elemental heat; he could conceive of nutrition and growth only in alchemical terms. But he was doing his best, clearing the ground, denouncing some obvious errors, such as the abuses of uroscopy (physicians sometimes based their diagnostic on the urine of a patient without bothering to see him), Aristotelian dogmatism, Arabic subtleties,[55] and astrological fantasies.

His attitude to astrology is particularly instructive, for it changed gradually from subservience to skepticism and withdrawal. He was not an experimentalist, but he was a good observer, and it finally dawned upon him that astrological prognostications were untrustworthy and irrelevant. He was, we should remember, a practical physician who had many aristocratic and exacting patients to satisfy, plus a good many others. One wonders how he could find time to write his books, because he was often engaged in bedside work from daybreak to far into the night. It was because of his authority as a clinician that he was taken into the royal service; it was said that he had saved the life of Diane de Poitiers in 1543, and in the following year he attended Catherine de' Medici when she was giving birth to her first child.[56] He attended Henri II until the end of his own life in 1558; when the king was killed at a tourney held in Paris in the following year (July 1559), Ambroise Paré and Vesalius were at his bedside.[57]

Fernel was as good a physician and physiologist as it was possible to be in his time, for he had considerable experience, was a careful and prudent observer, and was able to disentangle himself from astrological and other superstitions. At the beginning he had some trouble with the ultra-conservative Faculty of Medicine of Paris because of his objections to excessive bloodletting and to other old-fashioned procedures, but the Faculty's inertia was gradually overcome—not before his death, but before the end of the century. By that time, forty years after his death, he had become an authority, a new Galen, not only in France but in Europe, and the Faculty of Paris canonized him. Harvey's discovery diminished his authority with the "circulators," but increased it with the "anti-circulators," for example, such die-hards as Guy Patin. Hence his later fame was of a somewhat dubious kind.

Nevertheless he played a not unimportant part in making the new physiology possible; he made no discovery himself, but cleared the ground for further advances.[58] In a summary of physiological progress his name might almost be omitted, but it would be unfair to leave him out altogether. A similar case is that of Boyle's *Sceptical chymist* (London, 1661), which contains no chemical discovery, yet is one of the great books in the history of chemistry. If Fernel had been an experimentalist as well as an observer he might have done what Harvey did; on the other hand, much in physiology could not be discovered without microscopy, physics, and chemistry. Fernel was a Renaissance physician, while Harvey belonged to the age of Bacon and Galileo.[59]

RENAISSANCE SURGEONS

Before introducing Paré, who was a surgeon, it is necessary to say a few words about Renaissance surgery. Surgeons are now at the top of the professional scale, and it is hard to remember that for a long time they were at the bottom or very near it. The main difference between them and physicians was that the latter, legitimate ones at least, were M.D.s, a degree that could be obtained only in medical schools, where everything was taught in Latin. Surgeons, on the contrary, regardless of their skill, were generally ignorant, or were supposed to be ignorant, because they knew only the vernacular. Yet there had been a fine surgical tradition in the Middle Ages, illustrated by such men as the Fleming Jan Yperman (XIV-1), the Frenchman Gui de Chauliac (XIV-2), and the Englishman John Arderne (XIV-2).[60]

As we have already pointed out apropos of anatomy, Renaissance physicians were gentlemen and scholars who preferred to read books and discuss words and ideas rather than to soil their hands with menial work—and surgery in all its forms was held to be menial and undignified. Thus manipulations were generally left to underlings. The surgeons were charged with clystering, cupping, bleeding, applying leeches, washing wounds and anointing them, curing skin troubles, excising or amputating limbs, cutting for stones or hernias, etc. These occupations were so varied, some easy, others delicate and difficult, that a professional distinction shaped itself which was more clearly established, in Paris at least, by the creation of the College or Guild of Saint Côme (St. Cosmas) at the end of the thirteenth century and the beginning of the fourteenth.[61] Similar colleges were established in other cities, e.g. in Marseille. In the Paris college clinical teaching was better organized than in the medical school. From 1419 on the surgeons of France constituted a disciplined body, of which the king's first barber was the head. The graduates of the Collège de Saint Côme were high-class surgeons (*chirurgiens de longue robe*)[62] as distinguished from their lower brethren, the barber-surgeons. A similar distinction occurred in other countries.

The cleavage between physicians and surgeons did not begin before the thirteenth century. Up to that time most medical practitioners were clerks in holy orders (the educated class). In 1215 the Fourth Lateran Council forbade clerks to practice surgery (because the spilling of blood was horrible); the practice of medicine was completely forbidden to priests and monks by Honorius IV (Pope 1285-87). The separation of physicians from surgeons was completed during that interval (1215-1286).

The medical schools were too few and too small to supply a sufficient number of doctors, and the M.D.s, then as now, flocked to the cities and the most populated regions. Yet some kind of medical service had to be provided for the country; the vacuum was filled by surgeons, barbers, and all kinds of irregulars, bone-setters,[63] *"inciseurs"* (that is, men who performed incisions or amputations; they dealt with hernias and the cutting of stones), eye surgeons (chiefly for cataracts), and tooth drawers. We must not forget midwives, who had a virtual monopoly of obstetrics, except in the highest spheres.[64]

There developed in France and other countries triangular rivalries between physicians (M.D.s), surgeons,[65] and barber-surgeons, not to mention the irregulars, who were sometimes tolerated and sometimes persecuted and driven out. This three-cornered tension began in the fourteenth century, if not earlier, and continued through the Renaissance and into the seventeenth century and even the eighteenth. Its development varied from country to country, and it ended in each country at a different time.[66]

There was still another class of surgeons, the military surgeons. It was not a new class; Homer was already familiar with it, and war has been throughout the ages a school of surgery. As the use of guns and other firearms increased, more soldiers were wounded and crippled. The wounds caused by firearms had a special appearance and for some time it was believed that such wounds were poisoned. This belief was shared by all the early Renaissance surgeons, such as Brunschwig (1497), Vigo (1514), and Gersdorff (1517).

Hieronymus Brunschwig was the first important German writer on surgery. His *Buch der Cirurgia* (Strasbourg: Johann Grüninger, 1497) is the best description of the surgical art at the beginning of the Renaissance. It is a splendid volume, illustrated with forty-eight woodcuts, which helped the reader to know the instruments and how best to use them. It is easily accessible in the facsimile reprint edited by Henry E. Sigerist (Milan, 1923).[67] This book contains the first detailed account of gunshot wounds; he regarded them as poisoned, and advised on how to get the poison out by profuse suppuration.

Brunschwig's follower, Hans von Gersdorff, alias Schylhans, who was also an Alsatian, published a well illustrated book more specifically devoted to army surgery, the *Feldbuch der Wundtartznei* (Strasbourg: Schott, 1517), in which the discussion of gunshot wounds was more elaborate; Gersdorff did not regard them as poisonous, but his treatment of them was very brutal. The indefatigable Paracelsus wrote books on the same topic.

The main surgical authority (before Paré, i.e., before 1545) was the Italian Giovanni da Vigo (1460-1525) of Rapallo (Genoa) who was primarily a surgeon, but was physician to Pope Julius II.[68] His *Practica in arte chirurgica* (Rome, 1514) was extremely popular. It was unusual for a surgical book to be written in Latin, though perhaps less so in Papal Rome; the *Practica* was often reprinted not only in Latin, but also in French, English, Italian, German, Dutch, Spanish, and Portuguese.[69]

The military surgeon was usually employed by the prince or general leading the army, and his first duty was to them or to high officers, but he would also attend common soldiers if he had time.

AMBROISE PARE

The greatest of the military surgeons was undoubtedly Ambroise Paré (1510-90). He was born, not in 1517, but more probably in 1510 near Laval in Maine (just east of Brittany). He started his career at the bottom of the scale, for he was trained as a barber-surgeon, the kind of fellow to whom the meanest medical jobs were left. He distinguished himself so well, however, that he became a regular prosector at the Hôtel Dieu[70] in Paris. He thus had excellent opportunities of learning anatomy. By 1537 he was already commissioned as a military surgeon to one of the armies. He held other similar jobs and took part in many campaigns; the fact that many generals competed for his services is sufficient proof of his ability.

It is hardly possible to ascribe definite innovations to him, but his experience was considerable and varied. He studied all the books that were available to him in French[71] and was well acquainted with ancient and mediaeval surgery. What matters perhaps more was that he was intelligent and was a born surgeon. Among many procedures, he managed to resurrect and to popularize three of great value. These concerned the treatment of gunshot wounds, stopping hemorrhage after amputations or incisions, and the delivery of babies in cases of abnormal presentation (podalic version).

As gunshot wounds were believed to be poisonous, the common practice was to cauterize them or to treat them with boiling oil, which caused great suffering and feverish complications. It so happened that one day the supply of hot oil ran out and Paré was obliged to do without it; after much anxiety, he discovered that the patients who had not been tortured with boiling oil were recuperating much faster. After this he used that method less and less and finally abandoned it altogether. A problem of every surgeon was to find suitable ointments; the recipes were sometimes fantastic, but the kind of man who had it in him to make experiments and to learn from them was perhaps able to reject the more obnoxious recipes and to select the more soothing ones, which facilitated the healing of wounds.[72]

When limbs had to be amputated because of incipient gangrene, the main difficulty was to stop the bleeding fast enough. This was done by cautery; Paré realized that ligaturing the blood vessels was far less painful and far more effective, and that was his method.

The common run of military surgeons were illiterate brutes; Paré was more literate and, moreover, he was merciful. He always did his very best but even then was never sanguine of success, for he knew the difficulties to be overcome; he was aware of the mysteries of human reactions and could appreciate the gravity of each case. Hence his familiar, oft quoted, saying, "Je le pansay, Dieu le guarist" (I dressed him but God healed him). That saying was not very original but it caught the popular fancy, and many people know Paré only because of it.

His merit was recognized not only by the military men who needed his skill but also by the doctors and anatomists who employed him as prosector between wars. Thus the famous Sylvius,[73] Vesalius' teacher and later his enemy, encouraged Paré to publish his first book, *La methode de traicter les playes* (Paris: Gaulterot, 1545), dealing with the treatment of gunshot wounds. Leaving out of account revised editions and translations, he published eight different works.[74]

On his first books Paré was entitled *Maitre barbier et chirurgien de Paris*. In 1552 he was appointed surgeon to Henri II; when the latter was fatally wounded at a joust in 1559, Paré and Vesalius were both called to his bedside. After that, he was *"chirurgien ordinaire"* to François I and Charles IX, *"premier chirurgien"* to the latter and to Henri III, and finally king's councillor. In spite of royal favor he had many difficulties with the faculty and the College of St. Cosmas. The latter institution recognized his exceptional merit, however, and permitted him to graduate without Latin. His success created jealousies and learned doctors tried to make fun of his ignorance. This may explain his tendency to add more learning to his last and least important book, on the mummy (1582). Whether he had obtained that learning by himself or with the help of secretaries, it is second-hand and spurious.

There has been much discussion concerning Paré's religion.[75] He had leanings toward Protestantism, and all the printers whom he employed had Huguenot connections, but he was a prudent man and conformed in every rite to the Catholic tradition. He escaped the St. Bartholomew purge and served the kings of France, which would have been impossible if he had compromised himself.

Jealousies and malice could not dampen his fame, which began long before his death and increased afterward, as is shown by the many collected editions of his works. The first of these appeared as early as 1575 (Paris: Gabriel Buon). By the time of his death in 1590 three editions of his complete works had been issued by the same printer (1575, 1579, 1585), and one in Latin in 1582 (Paris: Jacques Du Puys). Later editions were published in French, Latin, German, and Dutch, and an abridged edition was translated from the Dutch into Japanese (c.1706).[76]

Frenchmen call Paré the father of modern surgery, and the title seems to be as well deserved as such a title can be. The Germans reserve it, however, for another man, Wilhelm Fabry von Hilden (near Düsseldorf) or Fabricius Hildanus (1560-1634). Without discussing Fabry's merit, he was born half a century after Paré and, except for his treatise on gangrene, *De gangraena et sphacelo* (Cologne, 1593), his work belongs to the seventeenth century. Paré was definitely a man of the Renaissance, while Fabry was not.

TWO HYGIENISTS: FICINO AND CORNARO

Let us now speak of two men who did not practice medicine but were deeply concerned with health and longevity. The first, Marsilio Ficino of Florence (1433-99), we have already met in Wing Three. He was the translator of Plato and Plotin into Latin, but he also wrote books of his own, the most popular of which was *De triplici vita* (Florence: Misconini, 1489). The first of its three parts is a *regimen sanitatis*. Many *regimina* were composed in the Middle Ages,[77] but this was the first devoted to scholars. What should sedentary and learned people do to preserve their health? Ficino was not the very first to tackle that subject; he had been preceded by no less a man than Plutarch (I-2) and he was followed in the course of time by such men as Bernardo Ramazzini of Modena in 1700[78] and by Simon André Tissot of Lausanne in 1766. The second part of his book, *De vita producenda,* shows that Ficino was a pioneer also in macrobiotics,[79] the art of lengthening life, but his contribution was not significant.

The most original book on longevity was published in 1588 by a Venetian gentleman, Luigi Cornaro,[80] who not only wrote a book but proved its argument by his own example. He was born at Venice in 1475, the scion of an illustrious family, and was puny and irritable in childhood. As he grew up in a restless period,[81] he indulged in so many dissipations that he found himself, at the age of 35, so riddled with ailments of every kind that he longed to die. He pulled himself together and became very temperate. He reduced his diet until he found that the optimal amount was 12 ounces of food a day plus 14 ounces of wine. Instead of dying, he extended his life by sixty years and almost became a centenarian. Moreover, his health and happiness improved until he could say, "I never knew the world was beautiful until I reached old age." He married a distant cousin who gave him but one daughter, Chiara (or Clara), but she married and had eight sons and three daughters; there were thus eleven grandchildren to brighten his old age.

After the foolishness of youth he had gradually conquered himself and proved to be very sensible and a man of taste. He loved agriculture (*la santa agricoltora*), hydraulics, and architecture; he built a beautiful house in Padua and villas in the hills, and busied himself reclaiming marshes and suggesting ways of improving the Venetian lagoon.[82] He was a member of a small academy meeting in the rooms of Cardinal Pietro Bembo, and thus became acquainted with other virtuosi, such as Girolamo Fracastoro. He enjoyed the beauty of nature and took exercise in town or in the hills, of course with due moderation. On one occasion, when he was the victim of a carriage accident, he refused to be bled or to take physic yet recovered completely. When he was growing old his family feared that he was starving himself. He answered that the older a man is, the less food he needs, but they would not believe him. As he was very considerate of their feelings, he increased his diet from 12 to 14 ounces for food, and from 14 to 16 ounces for wine, but soon was so uncomfortable that he was obliged to resume his previous ration. He claimed that "a man cannot be a perfect physician of anyone save of himself alone." That was true of a sensible man in reasonably good health; it was certainly true when it came to determining the best diet. What was good for one man would not be good for another.

His regimen was largely psychological, for he was trying to preserve his peace of mind; apparently he was able to avoid controversies or to temper them. For example, at one time he was the victim of lawsuits, but he managed to get out of them without losing his equanimity.

At the age of 83 he published the treatise that has immortalized his name, *Trattato de la vita sobria* (Padua: G. Perchacino, 1558) and he composed three shorter essays to complete it at the age of 86, 88, and 90. The four items were eventually published together under the common title *Discorsi della vita sobria*. They were often reprinted and translated, but his fame rests primarily upon the *Trattato*, which was often published separately. He died in Padua on May 8, 1566, at the age of 91.[83] Though he did not live quite as long as some people have believed, few people reach the age of 91 in good health, and even fewer have written pieces at the age of four score and three.[84]

The book is well written and delightful to read, sometimes rhetorical, as was the fashion of the day, but with moderation. It is indeed a defense of moderation in everything, not simply in diet and exercise. The only disagreeable feature of it is that the author was much too pleased with himself. It obtained the success it deserved, being frequently reprinted in Italian and translated into many languages.[85] The book is one of the perennials of the world's literature.

Many authors had spoken of moderation in diet or otherwise before Cornaro. His distinction lies in having replaced vague advice with precise details and in having proved the value of his recipe by his own life. He had proved that temperance in drink and food is one of the guarantees of health and perhaps of long life. Did he suspect the role of heredity? How old were his parents and ancestors when they died? We seem to have reached the conclusion at present that everybody is like a clock set to run for so long and no longer; it is easy enough to shorten the duration but hardly possible to lengthen it. Cornaro's account is impressive, however, because of its simplicity and inner conviction. It is scientific in its relative brevity and matter-of-factness. The alchemists talked a great deal about longevity and claimed to insure it by miraculous and secret means. Cornaro did not allow any alchemical or astrological nonsense to spoil his book, and in this respect he was a wiser man than Ficino.

The great age reached by Cornaro is astonishing because the expectation of life was much smaller in his time than in ours. Montaigne complained of old age when he was 45; it is true that he suffered from the stone. We must remember, however, that although fewer people reached the age of 70 in the sixteenth century than now, the few who did had perhaps as good a chance as our septuagenarians have of becoming centenarians. Moreover, the correlation between longevity and health is much smaller than most people think; one may be healthy and short-lived or sickly and long-lived. Many centenarians have reached that extreme age because they were born that way and no accident stopped their career.

The best way to end this section is to quote from Edmund, the bastard son of the Earl of Gloucester:

This is the excellent foppery of the world, that, when we are sick in fortune, often the surfeits of our own behaviour, we make guilty of our disasters the sun, the moon, and stars; as if we were villains on necessity; fools by heavenly compulsion; knaves, thieves, and treachers, by spherical predominance; drunkards, liars, and adulterers, by an enforc'd obedience of planetary influence; and all that we are evil in, by a divine thrusting on —an admirable evasion of whoremaster man, to lay his goatish disposition on the charge of a star! My father compounded with my mother under the Dragon's tail, and my nativity was under Ursa Major, so that it follows I am rough and lecherous. Fut, I should have been that I am, had the maidenliest star in the firmament twinkled on my bastardizing.[86]

Thus did Shakespeare, who symbolized the climax and the close of the Renaissance, express his contempt for astrology. This was one of the main diseases of the period, a disease which is still with us, though with less intensity, and which will last as long as human folly.

III. New Diseases

IT IS NATURAL that the age of exploration and discovery should reveal new diseases or throw new light upon old ones. For example, the long sea voyages, during which the diet of seamen was very restricted and miserable, caused the appearance of scurvy (scorbutus). It was not a complete novelty, for besieged populations had sometimes suffered from it. The earliest description, written by Jean de Joinville (XIV-1), refers to the members of the Sixth Crusade besieged in Damietta (1250).[87] The sufferings of Vasco da Gama's crews in their voyage to India (1498) were described by Camões in the fifth canto of Os Lusiadas (Lisbon: 1572). A better description of the disease was given by Antonio Pigafetta of Vicenza in his account of Magellan's voyage round the world; the observation of scurvy decimating the sailors was made on November 28, 1520.[88] Similar agonies were suffered by the crews of the French explorer, Jacques Cartier, sailing to Canada and up the St. Lawrence River in 1534-36.[89] Many sailors did not have to go so far to suffer the loathsome disease, for they were stricken by it in the North and Baltic Seas.

Boudewijn Ronsse of Ghent (d. Gouda 1596) is said to have been the first, in 1564, to recommend the use of lime juice as a preventive;[90] lime juice was recommended also by two English seamen, Sir Richard Hawkins in 1593 and Sir James Lancaster in 1600. Yet navies were very slow in following their advice, and not much was done before the publication of Lind's Treatise on the Scurvy (Edinburgh, 1753).[91]

A disease of the same kind, pellagra, was introduced into northern Italy from America; we are told that it was called "Columbus' sickness," and was caused by a diet based too exclusively on corn.[92]

It is only in our century that we have become aware of vitamins. We now know that scurvy and pellagra are deficiency diseases caused by the lack respectively of vitamin C and vitamin B in the diet; hence both diseases can be avoided by using food containing these vitamins. People of the Renaissance could not even imagine such notions, and scurvy was a regular scourge afflicting the seamen of many countries.

Many other diseases caused considerable distress during the Renaissance. The following list may suffice for a brief account.[93]

Smallpox and measles appeared in Germany (1493) and in Sweden (1578). Paré described such fevers.

In 1572 there was an epidemic of lead poisoning *(colica pictonum)* in southern France, probably due to the use of lead in wine presses.

Yellow fever decimated the population of Ysabella, San Domingo, in 1493.

Typhus fever was epidemic in Italy in 1505 and 1524-30, and was first described under the name of *febres lenticulae* by Girolamo Fracastoro in his *De contagione* (1546), book II, ch. 6. It was the "gaol fever" which decimated the courtrooms of the Black Assizes of Cambridge (1522), Oxford (1577), and Exeter (1589), the fever being transmitted from the prisoners to the audience by lice. After the siege of Granada (1489) the same affliction had appeared in Andalusia, where it was called *tabardillo,* a term no longer used in Spain but still common in Spanish America. The Hungarian disease *(morbus hungaricus),* endemic in various parts of Europe during the sixteenth century, was probably a form of typhus.

Diphtheria, described by Hartmann Schedel in 1492, was epidemic in Spain during the last two decades of the sixteenth century; the Spaniards named it *garrotillo* (a reference to *garrote,* capital punishment by strangulation).

Whooping-cough was first described by Guillaume Baillou (Ballonius) in 1578. The *coqueluche* described by Paré was very different from ours.

Ergotism was endemic in Spain in 1581 and 1590, and also in Germany in 1581, 1587, 1592, and 1595-96. The Spanish and German forms of that disease were very different.[94] The Faculty of Medicine of Marburg discussed in 1597 the latest epidemic of it, concluding that it was caused by bread made from spurred rye. They were right, for ergotism is caused by fungi attached to cereals, especially rye, and having the appearance of a spur.[95] As spurred rye occurred in earlier times, ergotism must have occurred also, but more attention was paid to it during the sixteenth century.[96]

The sweating sickness *(sudor anglicus)* described by John Caius was not specifically English.[97] An epidemic of it afflicted England in 1528-29. It was probably a kind of influenza; it may be that the French *coqueluche* and *trousse galant,* the German *Hauptweh,* and the Italian *mal mazzuco* and *mal del castrone* were other forms of the same disease.

The acute fevers *(epidémies aiguës)* described by Julian Le Paulmier in his *De morbis contagiosis* (Paris: D. Du-Val, 1578) were perhaps also some kind of influenza. The versatility of that disease had already been observed by Rabelais (1542): "Les catarrhes descendront ceste année du cerveau ès membres inférieurs."

As to tropical diseases or diseases affecting sailors, a book was published at the end of the century by an anonymous author (George Wateson or Whetstone?): *The cures of the diseases in forraine attempts of the English nation* (London: Lownes, 1598).[98] Its contents are given in verse:

> The burning fever, calde the Calenture,
> The aking Tabardilla pestilent,
> The Espintas prickings which men do endure.
> Cameras de sangre, Fluxes violent,
> Th' Erizipila, swelling the Pacient,
> Th' Tiñoso, which we Scurvey call,
> Are truly here described and cured all.

This incomplete survey is sufficient to show that new diseases appeared or old diseases reappeared in new forms or with greater virulence, or became endemic. This illustrates the great difficulties inherent in the study of many diseases. For us who are familiar with the idea that some diseases are caused by specific organisms, the discovery of such organisms in foreign countries or their importation into our own is not more astonishing than the discovery and importation of, say, plants or animals. Just as plants or birds were not quite the same in the New World as in the Old, we are not astonished to find similar variations in microorganisms. Organisms vary not only in space but also in time, and therefore diseases also may vary. But men of the Renaissance could hardly imagine microorganisms; at best they conceived of them vaguely, as Girolamo Fracastoro did in his *De contagione* (1546). Let us keep in mind that new diseases may appear in a definite environment which were not there before, or that old diseases may suddenly take on a new complexion and become more aggressive, more dangerous, or more abundant (endemic or epidemic). This will help us to understand the problem of syphilis.

We shall now consider the two diseases which may be called the Renaissance diseases *par excellence;* both date from the end of the fifteenth century. The first is a physical disease, syphilis; the second is a mental one, the fear of witchcraft.

SYPHILIS

A new and frightful disease appeared at the time of the capture of Naples in 1495 by Charles VIII.[99] Its appearance was so sudden and dramatic that one can hardly resist the conclusion that it was a new disease which had been brought by Spanish sailors returning from Haiti at the end of Columbus' first voyage in March 1493. Spaniards had brought the disease to Naples, where it was transmitted to the French conquerors. It spread like wildfire when the French returned from Naples; they brought it to Rome, to northern Italy, and to France. Hence it was often called the French sickness or the French pox; when it spread to other parts of Europe the new victims called it after their nearest neighbors, from whom it had come to them.[100]

The hypothesis that the sickness came from America was formed very early, say as early as 1510. It has been vigorously attacked by the great historian, Karl Sudhoff (1853-1938), and his school. Sudhoff claimed that the disease was endemic in Europe throughout the fifteenth century, if not before, and that from the twelfth century on physicians were using mercury recipes to fight skin troubles which may have been related to the new disease.

It seems to me that the theory of American origin is more probable, though it cannot be completely proved.[101] Its plausibility is strengthened by two sets of considerations. In the first place, syphilis has definite symptoms, and it is hard to believe that all the great physicians of the past would have overlooked them if they had been present. There is no mention of these symptoms and no description of any disease suggesting this one in the abundant literature anterior to 1495 in Greek, Arabic, Latin, or Hebrew. Moreover, if the disease had prevailed in earlier times, would not Boccaccio, Chaucer, or other poets have referred to it? In the second place, the explosive development of syphilis at the end of the fifteenth and in the early sixteenth century suggests that it was a new disease for which Europeans were utterly unprepared.[102] If literature on syphilis was lacking before 1495, it was abundant afterward; every year from 1495 on has witnessed the publication of at least one book or paper on the subject.

In the early accounts syphilis was occasionally confused with other diseases, such as leprosy and yaws.[103] Such confusion could not be completely avoided until not only the symptoms but the aetiology and the pathogenic microbes of each disease were known. This knowledge was not available until our own day. The bacterium of leprosy was discovered by the Norwegian, Armauer Hansen, in 1871, the *spirochaeta* of yaws by the Italian, Aldo Castellani, in 1905, the *spirochaeta pallida* of syphilis by the German, Fritz Schaudinn, in May 1905.

To return to the fifteenth century, whether or not syphilis flourished in Europe before 1495 is an academic question. It may have been latent before that year, but from 1495 on it was endemic or epidemic; it soon became a widespread social disease affecting people of all kinds and conditions. For example, one of the earliest treatises[104] on syphilis was written by Caspare Torella of Valencia, who was physician to Alexander VI (Rodrigo Lanzol y Borgia, Pope 1492-1503). Within two months (September-October 1497) Torella had the opportunity of treating and observing seventeen cases of syphilis in the Pope's family and court; he described five typical cases. What luck it was for him to discover seventeen cases of the new disease in the first family of Rome; could any of his colleagues do better? There was no squeamishness in his report.

At first the favorite treatment was by means of mercurial ointments, and various scholars have argued the antiquity of syphilis because of the ancient use of mercury. But mercury was used immemorially and is still used today for various skin troubles that have nothing to do with syphilis.

Among many sixteenth-century publications on the subject the most original is the Latin poem published by Girolamo Fracastoro, *Syphilis sive Morbus gallicus* (Verona: Stefano Nicolini da Sabbio, 1530).[105] The poem describes the misfortune of a handsome shepherd, Syphilus, who, having outraged Apollon, is punished with a new and frightful disease. From this poem the disease got its name syphilis; it is the only disease having a poetic name. Note that Fracastoro, like many of his predecessors, assumed that it originated in the West Indies. His main intention was to sing the praise of a new remedy, *guaiacan,* to which he devotes the third and last canto of his poem.

The discovery of that wonderful drug (as it was first thought to be) seemed to confirm the American origin of the disease. According to a mediaeval conceit God had placed remedies close to the ailments they would cure. If syphilis came from the West Indies it was natural to hunt for a remedy in that region. This was done and the herb was duly found; it was called by the Haitians *guaiacan*.[106] As the story goes, the herb was discovered by a man named Consalvo[107] who had contracted the disease at Naples and sailed to America to find the remedy and cure himself; he not only found it, but brought back a large amount of it and sold it at a good price.

The first treatise on guaiac was written by Nicolas Pol[108] in 1517, *De modo curandi corpora Alemanorum a morbo gallico infecta cum ligno indico guaicanun appellato* (first known edition, Venice: Ioannes Patavinus and Venturinus de Ruffinellis, 1535). A couple of years later the German humanist, Ulrich von Hutten (1488-1523), who had cured his syphilis with guaiac (or had that illusion),[109] wrote another treatise, *De guaiaci medicina* (Mainz: Johann Schoeffer, 1519) which he dedicated to the archbishop of Mainz. At the end of it he did not scruple to write something like this, "I hope that Your Eminence has escaped the pox but should you catch it (Heaven forbid but one can never tell) I would be glad to treat and heal you." This was a typical Renaissance trait. The good archbishop realized that no offense was meant and took none; the knight Ulrich simply wanted to ingratiate himself with his benefactor. Syphilis was a terrible disease, far more than it is now,[110] but it was not considered more disgraceful than other diseases and did not cause the hypocrisy that it does today.

Another anti-syphilitic drug was found in the East Indies; the people of the Renaissance did not see much difference between the East and the West Indies. This was *China smilax* (China-root), whose virtues were defended by no less a person than Vesalius in his China-root epistle (the original Latin title is too long to be quoted), printed by Joannes Oporinus (Basel, 1546).

An American herb of the same family,[111] sarsaparilla, was discovered at about the same time. All these drugs—guaiac, China-root, and sarsaparilla—raised great hopes, and "cured" many people for a while, until the hopes were frustrated and the sick people disillusioned, but soon new hopes were kindled and a new cycle begun.[112]

From the humanistic point of view the hero of this story was

Fracastoro, whose poem on *Syphilis* appeared in 1530. He was an
extraordinary man. *Syphilis* was his most popular composition and
most people know him only because of it, but he has other titles to
fame, for he was one of the most versatile doctors of a versatile age.
Girolamo Fracastoro was born in Verona about 1478 (not 1483), educated in Padua, and lived until 1553. His most important medical
work was not the poem *Syphilis* but a prose treatise on contagion
published sixteen years later, *De contagione et contagiosis morbis et
eorum curatione* (Verona, 1546).[113] This contains the first description of typhus fever (chapter 6, Book II, *De febre quam lenticulas
vel puncticulas vocant*). People had known from time immemorial
that some diseases were contagious; it is only in the light of such
awareness that some Biblical verses can be understood (*Leviticus*
XIII-XV). Mediaeval nations were painfully acquainted with epi-
demics, such as the Black Death, which decimated them from time
to time. There are a great many mediaeval and Renaissance treatises
that attempt to explain the spreading of such diseases like floods or
forest fires.[114] The most popular explanations of these calamities
were astrological, and the authors of prognostications were always
foretelling new plagues on the basis of ominous conjunctions of
planets. Fracastoro was the first to justify the Hebraic rules of
prophylaxis by the assumption that the infections are carried from
one individual to another by minute bodies *(seminaria contagio-
num)* capable of self-multiplication. This was an adumbration of
modern theories; it was not very clear but it was impossible to do
more before the invention of the microscope and other discoveries.

Fracastoro was not only a physician, poet, and prophet; he was
also one of the first to understand the true nature of fossils and to
refer to the existence of a magnetic pole.

His poetical work is a typical example of a Renaissance illusion.
Many humanists were so deeply interested in Latin poetry, especially in Virgil, that if they had scientific tendencies they were
tempted to express them in poetical form. Fracastoro's poem is asserted to be the best poem of this kind written in the sixteenth
century; I find it unreadable. Such a mixture of two opposites,
poetry and scientific teaching, was not a novelty, however.[115] Didactic poetry is one of the oldest forms of literature. At the beginning,
poetry was less a state of mind than a convenient form of expression.
At a time when writing was not yet invented or was not generally

used, rhythms and metrical devices were the best aids to memory, and therefore things to be remembered were composed in verse. Hesiod and the didactic poets of the Hellenistic age had the best of reasons for doing what they did; such excuses had lost their validity in the age of printing.

The Renaissance was even more famous for its arts and letters than for its knowledge, yet poems like Fracastoro's reveal a fundamental misunderstanding of both poetry and science.

WITCHCRAFT

We do not know how old syphilis is; *spirochaeta pallida* may have existed almost from the dawn of life, but it did not become the cause of a social disease until 1495. The story of witchcraft is similar. Belief in witchcraft is extremely ancient and is found everywhere. Not to go back to prehistoric times, remember the warning in Exodus (22:18): "Thou shalt not suffer a witch to live;" yet except in primitive communities the fear of witchcraft remained sporadic and relatively rare until the late Middle Ages.[116] It flared up like a forest fire whenever there was a menace of heresy, for theologians, consciously or not, confused heresy with witchcraft. It is easy to jump to the conclusion that people who disagree with us are bad people. Witches were men or women who had sold their soul to the Devil. It was easy to punish heretics and dissenters by assuming that they too were in league with the Devil, and the orthodox would mutter, "Those troublemakers are witches and should be treated as such; they deserve neither good faith nor mercy."

It is thus natural that fear of witchcraft became more virulent at the end of the fifteenth century, when the Church felt itself jeopardized by increasing criticism and disaffection. A large amount of combustible material had already been gathered when Innocent VIII (Pope 1484-92) put the torch to it with his bull of December 5, 1484, *Summis desiderantes affectibus*, and especially when two Dominicans, complying with Innocent's wishes, produced soon afterward the *Malleus maleficarum*, the "witchhammer" (Speyer: Peter Drach, c.1484), one of the most benevolent and maleficent books ever issued.[117]

Everything was now ready for the witch mania, which broke out with increasing vigor and cruelty. The *Malleus* was a code of procedure for the guidance of inquisitors; it explained in great detail how to detect, expose, convict, and punish witches. From one point of view it might be considered a textbook of sexual psychopathology, but nobody was yet able to see it in that light. The fear of witches was the main cause of their persecution, and the persecutions increased the fears. There appeared and spread everywhere a mass psychosis the like of which was not experienced again until our own enlightened day. The procedure followed in many witch trials was scrupulously recorded. When torture was used we are given the details. The inquisitors were not bad people; at least, they fancied themselves to be far better than the average; were they not working unceasingly for the greater glory of God?

Nicolas Remy, inquisitor of Lorraine, caused nearly 900 witches and sorcerers to be burned to death within fifteen years (1575-90). He was a very conscientious man, and toward the end of his life he had a guilty feeling because he had spared a few children. Is it right to spare baby vipers? The good bishop of Treves, Peter Binsfeld, ordered the death of some 6,500 people.[118]

There is no need to describe the very complex and pedantically elaborate procedure; it must suffice to indicate the guiding principles. When the inquisitors entered a new district they issued a proclamation calling on all people to give intelligence against suspected witches; if any persons withheld such intelligence they were liable to be excommunicated and to suffer temporal penalties. To inform was a sacred duty. The names of the informers were not divulged. Suspected persons, including those who might have been denounced by private enemies, were kept in ignorance of the charges against them and of the evidence upon which these charges were based; they were presumed to be guilty and it was up to them to prove that they were not. The judges used every means, mental and physical, to force them to confess and to name their accomplices. Promises of remission or leniency were made to them in order to encourage their confessions, but it was understood (by the judges) that there was no moral obligation to keep faith with sorcerers or heretics, except perhaps for a short while (just as long as confidence was expedient). Each knavery used against them was justified by the holy purpose. The more torture was practiced the more necessary it became. These statements can easily be confirmed and amplified by reference to the *Malleus* and other books and also more concretely by the records of actual trials, which are fairly numerous.

Many witches confessed their horrible crimes and described their association with the Devil; their descriptions of the latter tally so often and in so many standardized features that one might take them as an objective proof of his reality.[119] Each recorded confession was a new proof of the reality of witchcraft. The victims were not so much the victims of a particular court as of a pernicious system which became more and more pernicious as it grew.

The witchcraft delusion could not be cured by theologians, who tended, on the contrary, to aggravate it. The poor women (the majority of witches were female) who were burned at the stake were neurotics whom we would send to hospitals or asylums. Most of the trouble was not a matter of sin and heresy to be scrutinized by theologians, but a matter of psychopathology to be dealt with by doctors of medicine. The first physician to make the attempt (in 1563) is one of the least known heroes of the Renaissance but one of the greatest, the Dutchman Jan Wier.[120]

This illustrious man was born in Grave, in the Dutch province of Brabant,[121] in 1515/16; his father was a prosperous dealer in hops. He himself grew up, like all his contemporaries, in a world the sinister realities of which were obscured by supernatural and magical fancies. At the age of 17 he became the apprentice of Henricus Cornelius Agrippa;[122] he obtained his M.D. in Orléans in 1537, was city physician in Arnhem (on the Rhine) and finally (1550) private doctor to William, duke of Cleves.[123] His principal work was written under the patronage of Duke William, who deserves our gratitude. It was published under the title *De praestigis daemonum et incantationitus ac veneficiis* (Basel: Joannes Oporinus, 1563), and was many times reprinted before the end of the century in Latin, French, and German. A Dutch translation was prepared by himself (1567). He died at the age of 72 on February 24, 1588 at Tecklenburg near Osnabrück (southwest Hanover province), where he had been called for a consultation.

He explained many of the aberrations of "witches" in medical terms, though not, of course, as clearly as would be done today. It was he, however, who introduced the medical point of view, which, during the climax of the witchcraft obsession, required a very high and clear vision and unusual courage. Thanks to him and his followers,[124] "witches" are now considered mental cases and treated as such. We try to heal them with loving care. In the "good old days" they were terrorized, persecuted, and treated like criminals or worse. Those who were a little unbalanced before the trial were completely unbalanced at the end of it; they had no chance of recovery but were driven unyieldingly to rebellion, madness, and final execution. The judges, however inhuman, should not be judged too severely; they were ignorant, stupid, and fanatical and did their best according to their own lights. There were probably a few sadists among them (that is another mental disease) but the majority were conventional "good Christians." That is the final tragedy; the judges and executioners were the main victims.

Such a situation may reappear under different forms. It is always the same kind of mass psychosis, but its appearance varies because the mentally sick (the prosecutors and their victims) center their delusions upon the outstanding cause of fear or anxiety of their environment. During the Renaissance the main cause of trouble was witchcraft (or was it heresy?); often it was pestilence[125] or war; today it is Communism. In every case the original issue was confused with other issues, which aggravated the evil and intensified the repression. Thus, in the sixteenth century, the main danger was heresy, and it was found expedient to involve the Devil. This was done by the people in good faith and by their leaders, more often than not, in bad faith. When we judge these criminal aberrations, we should be indulgent, because similar delusions, betrayals, "procedures" and "confessions" disgrace our own times. All things considered, it is not quite so disgraceful to hate and kill in Stalin's name as to do so in the name of Christ or of God.

Wier's merit will be seen more clearly if we compare him with his contemporaries. One of the most famous was the Frenchman, Jean Bodin, who was born in 1520 at Angers, where he was educated by Carmelite brothers and received his first legal training; he then spent ten years studying law at Toulouse. He became a courtier, magistrate, and diplomat, and devoted most of his attention to political matters. He has received considerable praise for his writings on economic problems, education, and philosophy, and above all for his original analysis of sovereignty and government, *Les six livres de la République* (Paris: Jacques Du Puys, 1576),[126] which has sometimes been compared with the *Esprit des lois* (1748) of Montesquieu. Under the stress of the religious wars that were desolating France, he composed, in 1588, a curious dialogue, the *Colloquium heptaplomeres de rerum sublimium arcanis abditis,* the seven inter-locutors being a Jew, a Muslim, a Lutheran, a Zwinglian, a Roman Catholic, an Epicurean, and a Theist![127]

Jacques Cujas (1522-90) and Jean Bodin, contemporary alumni of the law school of Toulouse, were the main authorities in law and government of their country; moreover, the latter was also the leading economist, and a philosopher who tried to be unprejudiced. Yet the same man wrote another famous (or infamous) book entitled *La démonomanie des sorciers* (1580), an unabashed and truculent defense of the witchcraft mania and all the injustices and cruelties that stemmed from it. This shows how deeply entrenched that evil was, for, I repeat, Bodin was one of the best informed[128] and wisest men of his age. His *Démonomanie* was a mediaeval manifesto in the face of incipient liberalism. He proved the existence of witches on the basis of Holy Writ, the ancient theologians, and the decisions of the Faculty of Theology of Paris. Not to believe in witchcraft was as impious in his opinion as not to believe in God. He claimed the necessity of punishing not only witches but also ill-advised people who refused to believe in the possibility of witchcraft. He died at Laon (Aisne) in 1596.

The *Démonomanie des sorciers* was not an original book; on the contrary, it owed its success to the fact that Bodin's prejudices were shared by the majority of French thinkers.[129] It was aptly dedicated to Monseigneur Christofle de Thou,[130] "premier président en la Cour de Parlement" (that is, the highest magistrate of France), and published by J. Du Puys (Paris, 1580). As Bodin was reading the proofs he received a copy of Wier's book and added a refutation of it, "in order to defend God's honor against the sorcerers."[131] Need-less to say, the *Démonomanie* was very popular, more so than Wier's *Prestigiae;* at least a dozen editions of it appeared before 1601, 8 in French, 2 in Latin, and 2 in Italian. Thus was the poison of witch-craft scattered anew all over Europe with the blessings of an honor-able man.

Fortunately Montaigne was more enlightened than the learned Bodin and more humane. He declared himself a skeptic as to the reality of witches and suggested that it would be better to torture corpses than living people.

Belief in witchcraft was really a disease, a mental disease, which was even more terrible than syphilis and caused the cruel death of thousands of innocent men and women. Moreover, this illustrates some aspects of the Renaissance less glamorous than those that are generally featured, yet essential for a correct understanding of the period. The Renaissance was a golden age of letters and arts, but it was also an age of intolerance and cruelty; it was sometimes inhuman to a degree hardly surpassed at any later time except our own.

Of many examples that might be cited, the Saint Bartholomew massacre of 1572 is perhaps the worst; but the joy that it caused is more shocking than the crime itself. Gregory XIII (who was then beginning his papacy, 1572-85) was so pleased that he declared that the massacre was better than fifty victories like that of Lepanto (1571). By way of celebration he ordered a Te Deum, fireworks, and the striking of a medal.

In 1578 Juan de Escovedo was murdered in Madrid by order of Philip II.

In 1580 the Cardinal Secretary of State declared that the Pope would consider it a blessing if Queen Elizabeth, who was excommunicated, were killed—a gentle invitation to murder.

In 1584 William the Silent, founder of the Dutch Republic and first Stadholder, was assassinated in Delft.

In 1587 Mary Stuart, Queen of Scots, was beheaded at Fotheringhay.

In 1588 Henri, duke of Guise, and his brother, the cardinal, were murdered at Blois.

This list, which is incomplete, covers only sixteen years.

All these crimes were the fruits of intolerance; they proved nothing except the stupidity and baseness of the people who ordered or encouraged them.

Montaigne's skepticism extended to medicine,[132] and rightly so, for medical science was still rudimentary. The fundamental ignorance of physicians was equaled only by their presumption. This explains the popularity of medical writers of the type of Cardano, Della Porta, and Paracelsus. Many mediaeval superstitions were amplified and given a new currency in pseudo-medical books. The fact is that there was little that a sixteenth-century physician could do to alleviate the pains of his fellow-men that could not have been done as well by Galen or even by Hippocrates. Medical ignorance was hidden in learned treatises that seemed more profound than they were because they were written in Latin, and physicians themselves preferred to speak in Latin rather than in the vernacular; this situation continued well into the seventeenth century, as is shown by Molière's comedies. Medicine was as yet hardly a science, yet it was the main scientific focus and market; most men of science were M.D.s and their scientific status was established by that degree. The Latin trappings delayed the revolt of common sense and made it more difficult for original minds to assert and defend themselves. It took at least two more centuries to make the people, and even the men of science themselves, realize that the progress of science is made possible by good experiments and responsible theories rather than by learned arguments and eloquence.

In the meantime learning was supreme, learning plus superstition plus extraneous humanities, for ideas were not improved by being expressed in Latin, not even by being put in Latin verse. Irrelevant learning is no longer a danger today, but the fight against superstition, intolerance, and endemic irrationalism must be continued. We must be ready to fight them even as we fight the weeds in our gardens; there is no end to it. We cannot relax. And we must continue also to fight against lying and hypocrisy. Even now there are too many people, good citizens, pillars of society, who are afraid of science because they are afraid of truth; they will not face the facts of life. In order to cure a disease we must first understand it; the same is true of social diseases. In order to heal them we must first know them as well as possible.

The Renaissance was an age of superstition, but so is our own, under the surface; science has made gigantic progress in certain fields, but in others, e.g., in politics, national and international, we are still fooling ourselves.

The history of science is not simply the history of discoveries and new ideas that are closer to reality; it is also the history of the defense of these ideas against recurrent errors, illusions, and lies. We must replace darkness with light; that is the main function of science.

Art reveals beauty; it is the joy of life. Religion means love; it is the music of life. Science means truth and reason; it is the conscience of mankind. We need all of them—art and religion as well as science. Science is absolutely necessary but it is never sufficient.

Sixth Wing

LEONARDO DA VINCI:
ART AND SCIENCE

 LEONARDO DA VINCI beautifully illustrates the best aspects of the Renaissance.[1] In earlier chapters I was obliged to deal with some of its less attractive features, and it is pleasant to end with one of the immortals. Leonardo is as alive today as he ever was.

Since the growth of knowledge is the core of progress, the history of science ought to be the core of general history. Yet the main problems of life cannot be solved by men of science alone, or by artists and humanists; we need the cooperation of them all. Science is always indispensable but never sufficient. We are hungry for beauty, and where charity is lacking nothing else is of any avail.

Two illustrious figures who typify the Renaissance man's feeling for both art and science are the Florentine Leonardo da Vinci and his younger contemporary, Albrecht Dürer of Nuremberg. They never met, nor did they influence each other, but they were children of the same age, and the scientific problems they encountered were similar. Dürer devoted more time to art, Leonardo to science. Leonardo was the better scientist and the deeper philosopher.

Since most of the people who have studied Leonardo's work are men of letters or art critics, it is necessary to explain that the historian of science cannot use their methods without danger. An eloquent sentence, of which there are so many in his manuscripts, may testify to his literary genius. A single incomplete sketch may reveal the great artist. But we cannot draw large conclusions from a single remark on a scientific topic, unless the idea is developed and confirmed. For example, we cannot call Leonardo a predecessor of

Copernicus merely on the ground that he once wrote, "The sun does not move."[2] What exactly did he mean? There is no way of knowing. A man of science must prove, or at least explain clearly, what he has in mind. The illustrious Sigmund Freud has ventured to reconstruct Leonardo's secret psychology on the basis of a single fragment in which Leonardo alludes to a dream of his childhood.[3] Such reasoning is completely unscientific, but Freud's fame has given his book on Leonardo an undeserved prestige.

On the other hand, Leonardo's scientific genius is far more difficult to evaluate than that of other men of science whose works were published in their own lifetimes. There are three reasons for this. First, it is not always possible to know what he meant, and his notes were never revised for publication. Second, Leonardo was a child of the Renaissance, and almost every one of his ideas has mediaeval roots.[4] Moreover, the tradition that he gathered was not a literary tradition but rather an oral and manual one.

Leonardo was born on April 24, 1452 (New Style)[5] at Borgo di Vinci, in the foothills above Florence; he belonged on the paternal side to a well-known family but was born out of wedlock. His parents married soon after his birth, but they did not marry each other. His father founded a new family in which Leonardo was not wanted. If he had been well born, his father would probably have provided for his education and sent him eventually to the University of Florence, where he would have been crammed with Latin and scholastic learning. Instead, it was thought in the family circle that apprenticeship to a skilled craft would be good enough for him, and he was sent to the *bottega* (or studio) of Andrea del Verrocchio (1435-88). This was a blessing in disguise, for instead of an academic education that lacked contact with reality, he received the best kind of training for a boy of his temperament and genius. His father's choice of Verrocchio was an extremely happy one, and we cannot help being grateful to him for having entrusted the upbringing of young Leonardo to a man who was then one of the leading artists and craftsmen of Florence.

In Verrocchio's studio Leonardo was given a chance of learning many crafts, of discussing every question of the day, and of solving real and tangible problems such as life and art suggest at every turn. Verrocchio was not only a very great artist; he was a thinker, an ingenious craftsman—in a word, Leonardo's prototype. Leonardo

was about 12 or 13 years of age when he was apprenticed to Verrocchio and he spent about twelve years in the studio of the Via
del Agnolo; these were the formative years of his life. We may say
that Leonardo received his whole education from Verrocchio and
the many other artists[6] who came every day to the studio. We may
even assume that without Verrocchio the miracle of Leonardo would
not have occurred. Verrocchio was Leonardo's St. John the Baptist.

It is not my purpose to speak of Leonardo as a man of letters. His
literary works consist of an enormous mass of fragments (notes and
drawings) that has come to us in the greatest disorder. Some of his
thoughts are so deep that one is reminded of Pascal's *Pensées,* but
Leonardo's notes are fragments from many very different books, all
mixed together; and to this hodgepodge are added incongruous and
capricious notes, dreams, and hallucinations.

Another curiosity that has puzzled the critics and will always continue to puzzle them is the fact that the notes are written in mirror
writing: in order to read them one must hold them up to a mirror.
Why is this? My guess is that Leonardo was left-handed[7] and that
when he began to write without anybody's supervision, he wrote
naturally in reverse as left-handed children often do. Then he
realized the advantage of such writing for the sake of secrecy and
continued to use it. There is no doubt that his mirror writing was
fluent and easy; it is sometimes very hard to decipher it even with
the help of a mirror.

Very few of the fragments are dated or datable. One of our greatest difficulties is that Leonardo often contradicted himself on fundamental issues and it is impossible to know which was his final
opinion.

The most pathetic document concerning him is the draft of a
letter that he wrote in 1482-83 to the duke of Milan, Lodovico
Sforza, to offer his services. He enumerates all his merits as inventor and military engineer; it is only at the very end that he mentions his artistic abilities. At this time he was 30 years old, and some
of his less gifted friends were already established and famous.[8] All
his life he was the victim of his ambiguous genius. As André Gide
put it: "Avec du talent on fait ce qu'on veut, quand on a du génie
on fait ce qu'on peut."

The "duce" of Milan accepted his services and, what is better, he
seems to have left Leonardo plenty of freedom, for this first Milanese

period (1483-99) was fertile in every one of his chosen fields (painting, anatomy, mathematics, technology). After the duke's defeat[9] and the capture of Milan Leonardo's life became that of an exile, a refugee, passing restlessly from one city to another. The best of these errant years (*il tempo della vita errante,* 1499-1512) were again spent in Milan, this time under French rule. In this, his second Milanese period, he continued his efforts to canalize streams, studied geometry with Luca Pacioli[10] and anatomy with Marc Antonio della Torre.[11] In 1512, however, Milan was reconquered by the Italians and Leonardo was obliged to move out (I imagine he was compromised as a collaborator). He obtained the patronage of Giuliano de' Medici[12] and went to Rome in 1513, accompanied by his young friend, Francesco Melzi. They spent two years at the Belvedere in the Vatican, but the proximity of Michelangelo, whom he disliked,[13] and of the German Giovanni degli Specchi,[14] who was a deceiver, irritated him and drove him away. He finally accepted the hospitality of François I in Cloux, near Amboise.[15] Leonardo and Francesco traveled to Cloux in 1515; they brought with them three paintings, St. Anne with the Holy Virgin and Child, St. John the Baptist, and the portrait of a woman (probably Mona Lisa, La Gioconda),[16] also all his notes and anatomical drawings, which he bequeathed to Francesco Melzi.[17] He died in Cloux on May 2, 1519.

To return to his scientific work, two aspects of it began very early, in Verrocchio's *bottega*: the "science of painting" and mechanics. Leonardo's idea that there can be a "science of painting" may be an illusion, but after all, why should one not speak of painting science just as one does of medical science? In both cases scientific facts or theories are applied to an art, the art of painting or of healing. The science of painting included, in the first place, linear perspective, which was exciting Florentine artists, Filippo Brunelleschi, Leon Battista Alberti, Paolo Uccello, Piero delle Francesca, Andrea del Verrocchio, and Leonardo; and second, the far subtler matter of aerial perspective, which for centuries had been mixed up with optics, meteorology, the theory of colors and shades, and many other things. The Chinese had made penetrating observations on this subject at least as early as the sixth century,[18] and Leonardo was the first to rediscover some of them in the West.

Leonardo was a born mechanician as well as a painter; his mechanical tendencies were fostered in Verrocchio's studio. Verrocchio was a sculptor, a painter, and a goldsmith; his best known work is the equestrian statue of Bartolommeo Colleoni in Venice, perhaps the greatest monument of its kind in the world.[19] The erection of such a monument involved the solution of many mechanical problems. During the years of his adolescence Leonardo was constantly speculating about various machines that would make it easier to satisfy the needs of peace and of war. The only available source of continuous power was hydraulic; it was necessary to dig canals, which were the best means of moving heavy materials, and to build water-mills on running rivers.

Leonardo's quaderni are full of mechanical projects, drawn in such complete and precise detail that they sometimes look like blueprints; in fact, it has been possible to reconstruct some of the machines that he invented. But had he invented them? That is not certain; there were many inventors in the fifteenth century, and even in the fourteenth.[20] Most of them were illiterate, and in many cases secrecy was their only protection.

From hydraulics Leonardo passed to aerodynamics, and he made a good many observations, detailed and accurate, concerning the flight of birds. His projects were comparable not to those of Daedalus and Icarus, but rather to those of engineers of the last century who tried to solve the problem of human flight before motors had been invented. Leonardo asked himself very reasonably, "Why should man not be able to do what the birds do?" and reasoned that to imitate them we should, first of all, find out exactly how they do it. The observations he made on that subject were not equaled until the nineteenth century.[21] How do birds soar, how do they fly with or against the wind, how do they direct their flight and reach their goal? He observed the adjustment of wings and their flexing, the various kinds of feathers, the movement of the tails, and how these means are used for going up and down, gliding, soaring, balancing, and alighting without breaking their legs. In short, Leonardo did everything that could be done in his time. It would be wrong to call him a forerunner of Copernicus or Harvey, but he fully deserves to be considered one of the pioneers of aviation.

It would be very misleading to imagine that Leonardo resembled a present-day inventor, whose aim is more often than not to make money. He was a practical man, but he was also a philosopher, so much in love with his ideas that he lost interest in their realization.

As we all know, when an inventor suddenly has a great idea, that is not the end of the matter but the beginning; the most difficult task is still to come. He has to work out innumerable details, ascertain industrial and commercial possibilities, and adjust his plans to reality. Leonardo, having no patience and no talent for that sort of thing, could not be a successful inventor. He was a little like those men who love to flirt with women, but withdraw if their advances are too welcome. They do not want to be involved. He was a philosopher rather than an engineer, more interested in principles than in their application. Unfortunately the principles of mechanics were as yet by no means clear. Leonardo continued old traditions that can be traced back to Aristotle and Archimedes, but were extremely irregular, capricious, and secret. Did he know the ancient and mediaeval writings on mechanics? It is very improbable. He mentions Archimedes half a dozen times, and he mentions also Biagio Pelacani (XIV-2) and Albert of Saxony (XIV-2). This does not prove much. All these writings were in Latin, and Leonardo's knowledge of Latin was empirical and rudimentary. Being an Italian, he could get the gist of a Latin sentence, but he could not have read a Latin book. He was almost illiterate, read very little and quoted less.

In spite of what has been claimed to the contrary, he was not a mathematician; he loved mathematics in the Platonic style but knew only the elements, and those not too well. He was a mechanician by instinct and tried all his life to understand the phenomena of statics and dynamics; he even tried to understand the rules of hydraulics and aerodynamics, but in vain. He could write: "Mechanics is the paradise of mathematics because it gives us the fruits of that science."[22] That was a poetic saying, an admirable intuition, but the fruits were still very far from maturity. It was impossible to solve the fundamental problems, because they could not yet be formulated. Leonardo continued bravely the mediaeval incubation; the birth could not take place until the time of Simon Stevin and Galileo, and mechanics began to mature only toward the end of the seventeenth century with Huygens and Newton.

In the marvelous field of mechanics Leonardo, genius though he was, could only grope his way like a blind man. In another field, however, it was possible to obtain valuable results at once. This was anatomy. Here again he was continuing mediaeval traditions, for it is wrong to believe that dissections were forbidden throughout the Middle Ages. There were distinguished anatomists like Mondino de' Luzzi (XIV-1) and Guido da Vigevano (XIV-1). Human dissections, however, were rare and badly organized; the obstacles came from scholasticism rather than from religion. The experimental spirit was hardly awakened, and what is worse, the art of observing with precision and without prejudices was almost unknown. Physicians were dominated by Galen and Avicenna to such an unbelievable extent that they were unable to see with their own eyes. It was here that Leonardo's genius revealed itself, though even in this case the revelation was incomplete and miscarried.

One can say that modern anatomy was founded by two men, Italian and Flemish: Leonardo and, a little later, Andreas Vesalius of Brussels. There is an essential difference between them, however; Leonardo dissected some thirty bodies and left an abundance of notes and drawings, but he never composed an anatomical treatise. Vesalius, however, published in 1543 a great work, *De humani corporis fabrica,* which is truly the basis of modern anatomy. Leonardo's notes and drawings remained almost unknown until our century; Vesalius' book deeply influenced all the anatomists who followed him. One must conclude that Vesalius alone is the founder.

Nevertheless, although Leonardo's immediate influence was negligible, his anatomical work was astounding. Vesalius was a physician and a professor of anatomy, who might have been expected to perform dissections. Yet Leonardo, an artist and a mechanician, performed many and did them as well as Vesalius, though not as methodically.

The dissections that students perform today in the anatomical laboratories of our medical schools are very easy; running water, refrigeration, and antiseptics have greatly lessened the unpleasantness of such work. None of these conveniences was available to Leonardo, and the fulfillment of his self-imposed task required tremendous will power.[23] Moreover, while Vesalius was assisted by a professional artist, John Stephen of Calcar, Leonardo was obliged at various stages of his horrible task to interrupt it and begin immediately another kind of work of extreme delicacy, drawing as accurately as possible what he saw. Some of his anatomical drawings have never been equaled.

Leonardo's curiosity went far beyond that of other painters and sculptors, who were obliged to have some knowledge of artistic anatomy, that is to say, the layout of superficial muscles. The Florentine artists, who were draftsmen rather than colorists, studied that kind of anatomy with enthusiasm. That tradition, begun by Donatello, was carried to extremes by Antonio Pollaiuolo and brought back to moderation by Verrocchio and Leonardo. The sculptor's model or the painter's sketch must be sufficiently precise and sensitive to indicate the presence of muscles. The spectator must be able to divine their presence without being too conscious of them.

Artistic anatomy has been dominated from the beginnings of art by mathematical and mystical considerations. The love of symmetry and of numbers has led artists of all times to discover arithmetical relations between the sizes of different parts of the body and to establish a canon of human beauty. Such preoccupations existed in ancient Egypt, India, and Greece.[24] Leonardo and his younger contemporary, Albrecht Dürer, were no strangers to them.

Leonardo was interested not only in the beauty of the human body; he was searching for beauty in the three kingdoms of nature. He left behind many sketches of animals, plants, shells, and rocks. Some of his investigations would be classified today in the fields of physical geography, mineralogy, and geology. His drawings make us think of those of Ruskin, whose curiosity in both art and science was equally keen and complex. He was one of the first to give a rational explanation of fossils; the shells found imbedded in mountain rocks were the remains of creatures that had lived in the seas or on beaches and had been lifted up later on. He was one of the first men in the West to explore the high Alps not only as an artist but also as a man of science. The peoples of Europe were generally afraid of mountains, which they fancied were inhabited by goblins, gnomes, and devils. Christianity had not succeeded in dissipating or even in diminishing those superstitions, while Buddhism had encouraged opposite ones. The Buddhists of China and Japan have always associated high peaks with divine power and their most popular temples have been built upon the slopes or the tops of mountains. From this point of view, Leonardo was an Oriental. His thoughts on art and nature would ravish Indian, Chinese, or Japanese readers. His instinctive Orientalism was caused to a large extent by his lack of Western superstitions and inhibitions. His nonconformism was that of a truly great man; it was not deliberate, but spontaneous and natural.

His thought was much more scientific, more rational, than that of the great majority of his contemporaries, but he was not completely free from prejudice. Such freedom is hardly possible in our own time; it was absolutely impossible in his. Men of genius have a freer mind and a clearer vision than other men, but there is a limit to their clear-sightedness and to their emancipation. Leonardo's mind was shackled by two kinds of prejudice, which may be named Platonic and Galenic.

The first was represented mainly by the idea of microcosm and macrocosm, first explained in the *Timaios* of Plato and widely transmitted by the Neoplatonists and the Qabbalists. The microcosm of our body is a much reduced copy of the macrocosm of the universe: our bones are like the rocky skeleton of the earth; there is in us a lake of blood comparable to the seas; the rhythm of our breathing and of the pulse is like that of the tides, the "circulation" of blood is like that of water; the fur of animals, our hair, and the feathers of birds are like grass and leaves; rumbling in the bowels is like an earthquake, and so on. Those comparisons, which could be extended indefinitely, were commonplace in his time, at least among intellectuals.

It is not necessary to assume that Leonardo read either the *Timaios* or any one of the many books derived from it, for such ideas were in the air; he had heard them referred to or discussed in Verrocchio's *bottega* and elsewhere. Analogies as vague and grandiose as those of the microcosm and macrocosm would easily seduce the imagination of poets and artists.

During the Renaissance Platonic prejudices colored every thought; the prejudice that I call Galenic was less common. The motion of the blood, revealed by the pulse, was explained by Galen[25] not as a real circulation (possible only in a closed trajectory) but as a rhythmical back-and-forth movement. Even so, in order to justify his explanation, he was obliged to assume that the blood penetrating the right ventricle passes through the wall *(septum cordis)* and thus reaches the left part of the heart. How did it pass through the *septum,* which seems watertight? Through invisible holes. Leonardo was so hopelessly obfuscated by this Galenic invention that he was able not only to see these invisible holes but to draw them.[26] It would be hard to find a better example of the limitations even of genius. Leonardo's was a free mind and a great genius, yet he had been bamboozled by Plato's magic and Galen's authority to the extent of seeing things that did not exist and even of showing them to other people.

One ends by asking oneself—and I must do so at the risk of vexing my readers—whether Leonardo was really one of the great scientific creators.

His love of science and his zeal need not be argued; it is certain that his activities were those of a man of science as well as those of an artist, but is it possible to ascribe to him a single discovery, except such as are contained implicitly in his drawings?

In order to receive credit for a discovery it is not enough to make it. One must explain it; one must prove very clearly that one has understood it; one must be ready to defend it. One might say that a discovery is not completed until it has been justified in public.[27] An original idea that crosses a man's brain like lightning is as necessary as the seed of a plant, and just as insufficient if the seed does not germinate.

Leonardo's ideas were like seeds that failed to mature. They remained buried in his notes and drawings. He sometimes thought of writing books on anatomy, painting, and perhaps other subjects, but he never did so. Fra Luca Pacioli wrote to Duke Lodovico Sforza on February 9, 1498 that Leonardo had completed "a treatise on painting and on the motions of the human body," and Giorgio Vasari declared in 1550 that a Milanese painter had shown him a manuscript of Leonardo's which he intended to publish in Rome.[28] It is improbable that these manuscripts ever existed, at least in a form ready for publication, but it is possible that Leonardo's disciple, Francesco Melzi, who inherited his archives, may have composed an anthology of extracts (or commissioned someone else to compose it). There is in the Vatican Library a collection of 944 extracts from Leonardo's notes (*Codex Urbinas 1270*, XVIth century) which is the indirect source of the *Trattato della Pittura* dedicated to Queen Christina of Sweden and published in Paris in 1651, two centuries after Leonardo's birth. As to the anatomical treatise, it did not even achieve such indirect, tardy, and posthumous publication.

In short, Leonardo never published his ideas; he did not even take the trouble to put them in order for publication. This failure may have been partly due to his lack of literary education, for which his genius was never able to compensate. His defects were very different

from those of the majority of his contemporaries. Their books are
chock full of quotations to the point of incomprehensibility. Leonardo's notes contain hardly any quotations, and his references to
"authorities" are rare and vague; for example, he refers nine times
to Aristotle, six times to Vitruvius, five times to Archimedes, as many
times to Ptolemy and Pliny, twice to Avicenna's anatomy.[29]

The most elaborate part of Leonardo's scientific work is that on
anatomy, yet this exerted little, if any, influence. The only anatomist
with whom he worked and consulted was Marc Antonio della Torre
(1481-1511), who was thirty years younger than he, died very young,
and left no traces.[30]

As long as Leonardo was alive, few people had a chance of seeing
his anatomical drawings. I can name only Antonio de Beatis, secretary to Louis, cardinal of Aragon, who admired them in Cloux.
Vasari and Gian Paolo Lomazzo saw them later in Melzi's hands,
but they were not competent to appreciate their scientific value.
One might say that the evolution of anatomy would have been the
same if Leonardo had not existed.

Leonardo was one of the greatest men of science in history, but
the world which admired him as an artist did not discover the man
of science until many centuries after his death. He remained unknown by his own fault, for he did nothing to publish his discoveries; in most cases, indeed, he did not even bother to complete
them.

This lack of perseverance has hurt the artist almost as much as
the man of science. He has left us only a few paintings (less than ten)
and some of them are not quite finished. The equestrian statue
which would have rivaled Verrocchio's Colleoni was not cast.[31] The
Last Supper which he painted in the refectory of Santa Maria delle
Grazie in Milan has faded until it is but a pale image of what it was.
He spoiled other paintings by technical experiments or capriciously
abandoned them. Nevertheless, he influenced many younger painters,[32] while he failed to influence contemporary scientists.

Nothing is more curious and perplexing, however, than the
caprices of the mechanical inventor. Leonardo invented or reinvented a whole series of machines, yet he overlooked two of the
greatest inventions not only of his time but of all time: printing and
engraving. He could not have been unaware of their existence, for
printed books, woodcuts, and copper engravings had become fairly

common before the end of his life;[33] one could buy them in many shops in Florence, Milan, and elsewhere. Leonardo must have handled printed books, but he did not refer to them.[34] He made drawings for the *Divina proportione* of Luca Paccioli (Venice: Paganinus, 1509), and it may be that he engraved them himself. He must have seen woodcuts and engravings, but I found only a single phrase in his abundant writings which may possibly refer to them, "il modo di ristemparlo."[35] Did he despise such inventions, as did some Florentine snobs?

A man as intelligent as he was should have understood at once that these two inventions were of incalculable value, not only because they permitted the indefinite multiplication of copies with little effort, but chiefly because they made possible the production of copies that were identical and standard. This was important in every field, but especially in science. It made possible, for example, the publication of mathematical books and astronomical tables that could be used with confidence (errors could be definitely corrected in a later edition). Engraving permitted the addition to the text of accurate illustrations that enormously increased its practical value. How did it happen that Leonardo ignored and rejected all this? Evidently he had some blind spots, in spite of his genius.

We are always reminded of his two weaknesses, lack of formal instruction in his youth, and lack of material ambition. He was and remained all his life *un uomo senza lettere*. Some of our greatest men were illiterate; genius can exist without education and the best education in the world will not give genius to the man who lacks it. It is probable that Leonardo paid but little attention to books, and if so, why should he have bothered about printing?

The abundance of his notes should not mislead us; they were not those of a man of letters but rather those of a man of science and a philosopher. He sometimes wrote brilliant sentences, but this was due to his power of thought rather than to power of expression. Besides, he never went beyond the composition of sentences or paragraphs; he may have thought of writing books, but he never made the necessary effort. Such repugnance to writing is not rare among real artists, technicians, and even men of science. The latter are ready to take infinite pains in their investigations, but they often have trouble in writing up their reports and sometimes they postpone that unwelcome task indefinitely.

Leonardo could have written a book if he had wanted to, but he never wanted to badly enough. It is the same with his paintings; he could easily have painted many more, but he never had enough energy. Yet the very few paintings that he managed to complete suffice to immortalize him.

He is the best example of a rare and precious type: the man who does not give the full measure of his genius. Most talented people do the opposite. They try to give us more than their measure, that is, they bluff us. They begin to write a book before they know their subject, and learn as they go along. On the other hand, there are men of science and learning who never cease to accumulate notes and never find time to organize them and put them in good form. Leonardo belonged to the second group, but not because of defects in his nature. This was noticed by that devil of Aretino, Pietro,[36] in a spark of decency: "I tell you that Leonardo was equal to the very greatest, but his genius was of such a high quality that he could never be pleased with what he had done."

We should not forget that he lived in an age that was as revolutionary as ours but far more cruel. It was the age of despotic rulers like Lodovico Sforza and Cesare Borgia (the "Prince" of Machiavelli) and of violent enthusiasts, like Savonarola. Leonardo preserved his equanimity and his wisdom. He was an artist, a poet, a contemplator, a dreamer. On account of such "weaknesses" he became greater, closer to perfection, than if he had been more capable and "efficient." If a man is good and wise, why should he be efficient into the bargain?

The best way to explain this, the deepest and most moving aspect of his personality, is to compare him with another artist of his own time, Albrecht Dürer[37] of Nuremberg. As artists they were both supreme, each in his own way, but it is certain (to me at least) that Leonardo was the greater man. While Leonardo was a dreamer, paralyzed by his genius, Dürer was a practical, capable, and "efficient" man. If a man made a contract with Dürer for a portrait, he would be sure to get it at the agreed time together with the bill; if he made such a contract with Leonardo, he might get it or he might not. Administrators generally prefer the more docile and dependable type, and from their point of view they are right. It is not surprising that Dürer achieved material success and that Leonardo did not.

The comparison between these two men is valid because they were interested, roughly speaking, in the same things; the difference between them was that Leonardo accumulated notes and perplexities, while Dürer's thoughts, though less deep, were more fertile. Dürer would not bother much about a subject unless he had a practical purpose, such as the writing of a book. He not only prepared his books as any bookmaker would, but he printed them. We have three treatises written and illustrated by him. The first, *Unterweysung der Messung mit dem Zirckel und Richtscheyt*, contains instructions for measuring with compass and ruler (1525); the second, *Etliche Underricht zu Befestigung*, is devoted to fortifications (1527); the third, *Vier Bücher von menschlicher Proportion*, to the proportions of the human body (posthumously published in the year of his death, 1528).[38]

The fact that Dürer was concerned with artistic anatomy and not with deeper anatomy is significant. Dürer was always practical and earthbound; Leonardo was the opposite. While Leonardo disdained typography and engraving, Dürer understood immediately the commercial possibilities of both arts. Instead of producing a single drawing, a woodcut or copperplate enabled him to publish at once a hundred copies or more. Moreover, he was quick to realize that it was no more difficult, but far more profitable, to publish whole albums of engravings, such as the Passion of Our Lord or the Life of Our Lady. He established himself as printer, engraver, and bookseller. Each of his three books bears the note (in German), "Printed in Nuremberg by Albrecht Dürer, the Painter." At the commercial fairs of Frankfurt and Nuremberg Dürer had his own shop and display. When he traveled in the Low Countries in 1520-21 he brought with him a large number of his engravings, which were easy to pack and profitable to sell; he distributed free copies to important people, princes, bishops, or governors, whose good will he wished to capture, and he sold many more. We are well informed about his business dealings, because he kept careful accounts of all his receipts and expenditures. Another typical trait: Dürer signed all his works and often added the date.

Leonardo did not bother about such matters. He was as indifferent to chronology as the Hindus and for the same reason, for he considered all things *sub specie aeternitatis*.

Dürer was a businessman,[39] a man of substance living in his own comfortable house; he was capable of taking some interest in scientific questions, but he was not a man of science. Leonardo, on the contrary, was a pure artist, a disinterested inventor, a man of science, a cogitator, a Bohemian; he was decidedly not a businessman or an administrator. He was anxious to obtain not money, or power, or comfort, but beauty and truth. He wanted to understand God, nature, art, himself, and other men. I admire them both but I love Leonardo.

Few people are able to understand this, because their ideals are confused and upside down. They like to speak of spiritual values but they always give top priority to material values. They speak of beauty and art but comfort comes first. They speak of peace but make war almost unavoidable. They pray on Sunday but their motto is: Business first, business and power, conformity to social conventions, etc. Most men are social hypocrites. Leonardo was not.

Leonardo was a rebel, one of the worst or the best kind, one who does not even bother to state his disagreement and disapproval but pursues his own mission.

Leonardo's self-portrait, made by him toward the end of his life,[40] shows a tired face. Leonardo was then less than 67 years old, but he had suffered much because of the world's cruelties and his own anxieties. His outstanding merit is to have shown by his own example that the pursuit of beauty and the pursuit of truth are not incompatible. He is the patron of all those men, few in number, who love art and science with equal fervor.

Leonardo was a defender of reason, an enemy of superstition, but an idealist. There was in him an original and deep conviction that the only things that really matter are spiritual. The supreme discipline is that of love. As he put it, "The love of anything is the fruit of our knowledge of it, and grows as our knowledge becomes more certain."[41]

One might add, and no doubt he did so, that without love there can be no real knowledge.

APPENDIX TO SIXTH WING

Leonardo Chronology

THE SCIENTIFIC achievements of Leonardo can hardly be dated because they stretch over long periods of time. The following chronology will enable readers to locate his artistic creations within the frame of his life. Very few of his innumerable notes are dated, and these few are more often than not insignificant. The paintings and some drawings can be dated more or less; critics do not always agree as to their authenticity or their exact date. Sometimes we know the date of beginning but not that of completion.

My main authorities are Sir Kenneth Clark, *Leonardo da Vinci. An account of his development as an artist* (222 pp., 68 pls., Cambridge University Press, 1939) and Germain Bazin, editor, *Hommage à Léonard de Vinci* (142 pp., ill., Paris: Musée du Louvre, 1952).

I. YOUTH IN FLORENCE, 1452-82

1452. April 24 (N.S.) Leonardo's birth in Vinci, the son of a Florentine notary, Ser Piero, and a country woman, Catarina (*Isis*, 43: 125).

1466. Leonardo enters the *bottega* of Verrocchio, Via del Agnolo in Florence, and remains there about twelve years. He may have entered the *bottega* a little later.

1472. Leonardo is admitted as a master painter in the Guild of St. Luke, in Florence.

1472-73. He paints the angel in Verrocchio's *Baptism of Christ* (Uffizi).

1472-73. *The Annunciation* (Uffizi).

1473. August 5. First dated drawing, landscape of Val d'Arno (Uffizi).

c.1474. Portrait of *Ginevra de' Benci*, a Florentine lady married in January 1474 (Liechtenstein Gallery, Vienna). Its ascription to Leonardo is doubted by some critics.

1476. April 8. Leonardo and other painters are accused of homosexuality; he is exonerated. Later, the accusation and exoneration were repeated.

1478-80. The *Benois Madonna* (Hermitage). Authorship uncertain. Drawings for it are unquestionably by Leonardo (e.g., *La Vierge aux fruits,* Louvre).

c.1480. The *Madonna Litta,* in profile (Hermitage). Difficult to appreciate because it was badly repainted at least twice. Study for it in the Louvre.

1481. The Monastery of San Donato orders a painting for its high altar, *The Adoration of the Magi.* Two incomplete studies (Uffizi, Louvre). Leonardo is now working in his own studio.

c.1482. Letter to Lodovico Sforza il Moro offering his services (Richter no. 1340). His services are accepted and he moves to Milan.

II. FIRST MILANESE PERIOD (1483-99) DURING THE RULE OF LODOVICO IL MORO

1483. April 25. The Confraternity of the Immaculate Conception, Milan, orders a painting which became *The Virgin of the Rocks* (Louvre). The order was given to Leonardo and the brothers Evangelisto and Ambrogio da Predis.

c.1483. *St. Jerome* doing penance in the desert with lion, drawing (Vatican).

c.1483. Portrait of *Cecilia Gallerani,* one of Lodovico's mistresses (Czartoryski Gallery, Cracow). Is this by Leonardo, Boltraffio, or some other? This "lady with a weasel" in her arms looks very much like the *Belle Ferronnière* in the Louvre (see 1495-96).

1485. March 16.[1] Leonardo observes a total eclipse of the sun.

c.1485+. *Portrait of a musician,* head finished, body not (Ambrosiana, Milan).

1488. Verrocchio's death.

1488-90. Studies for the Sforza equestrian monument (Windsor).

1491. January 26. Drawings for a tournament in honor of Ludovico il Moro and his wife, Beatrice d'Este.

1493. November 30. Model of a horse of gigantic size, exhibited in Milan to celebrate the wedding of Bianca Maria Sforza with the Emperor Maximilian I. The marriage took place at Innsbruck on March 16, 1494.

1495-96? Portrait traditionally called *"La belle ferronnière"* (Louvre). If not by Leonardo, it is a work of his school. It is probably a portrait of Beatrice d'Este (she died on January 2, 1497). Surprising likeness to the "lady with a weasel" (see c.1483).

1497. *Last Supper (Cenácolo)* in Santa Maria delle Grazie (Milan).

---

[1] The date March 16 is Julian; the extrapolated Gregorian date would be March 25. This eclipse was conspicuous in western and central Europe (it ended in Russia); the track of totality passed through France into Bavaria and Austria (A. Pogo).

1498. February 9. Luca Pacioli praises Leonardo in his dedication of *Divina Proportione* to Lodovico Sforza. Leonardo provides geometric drawings for that book, which was not published until eleven years later (Venice: Paganinus, 1509). Leonardo must have drawn these figures without instruments, for they are inaccurate.

c.1498. Cartoon of the *Virgin and Child with St. Anne and St. John the Baptist* (Burlington House, London).

1499. October 6. The armies of Louis XII enter Milan.

1499. December. Leonardo goes to Mantua at the invitation of Isabella d'Este. It was probably then that he drew her portrait (cartoon in the Louvre). She was then 25. Isabella (1474-1539) and Beatrice (1475-97) were two sisters, daughters of Ercole I d'Este.

III. VARIOUS PLACES, CHIEFLY FLORENCE, 1500-1505

1500. April. Back in Florence.

1502. In the service of Cesare Borgia, Leonardo inspects the fortifications of Romagna.

1503-1506. Portrait of *Mona Lisa*. Born in 1479 in Florence, she married, in 1495, Francesco di Bartolommeo di Zanobi del Giocondo of Florence (la Gioconda, la Joconde). She was 24 in 1503. It was one of the three paintings which the cardinal of Aragon saw in Cloux in 1517. There are at least 61 old copies of it.

1504. January 24. Leonardo gives his advice about the best location for Michelangelo's David.

1504. May 4. Contract between the Signoria and Leonardo for the wall painting, *The Battle of Anghiari*,[2] to decorate the Salone del Cinquecento (*gran consiglio*) in the Palazzo Vecchio (P. della Signoria) in Florence. Leonardo did his work in 1504-1505, then abandoned it; the unfinished painting was eventually destroyed but is known from ancient copies.

1504. July 9, Wednesday. Death of Leonardo's father, Ser Piero, notary at the Palazzo del Podestà, Florence. He was 80 years old and left behind him ten sons and two daughters (Richter nos. 1372, 1373A, 1373).

IV. SECOND MILANESE PERIOD (1506-13), UNDER FRENCH RULE

1506. May. Leonardo returns to Milan at the request of the French governor, Charles d'Amboise, count of Chaumont (d. 1511).

1506-1508? *Virgin of the Rocks* (National Gallery, London). A copy of the

---

[2] Victory of Florentines over Milanese in 1440 at Anghiari, eastern Tuscany, northeast of Arezzo.

Louvre painting by Leonardo, or a member of his school. See 1483.

1506-1509. *Bacchus,* first known under the name *St. John in the Desert* (Louvre).

1507. May 24. Louis XII visits Milan; Leonardo helps to organize festivities at the Castello Sforzesco.

1507. July 24. Louis XII appoints Leonardo as his painter and engineer. Leonardo spends six months in Florence for the legal defence of his patrimony.

1508-10. *St. Anne, Virgin and Child* (Louvre). Leonardo was thinking of such a composition since 1498. There are 27 known copies.

1509+. *St. John the Baptist* (Louvre). See 1515?

1510. Leonardo expects to complete his "anatomy" in the winter (Richter no. 1376).

1511-12. Studies for the Trivulzio monument (Windsor).

1513. September 24. Leonardo leaves Milan for Rome with Francesco Melzi and others.

V. ROME, 1513-16

1513. December 1. Arrives in Rome, the guest of Giuliano de' Medici, elder brother of Giovanni (Leo X), at the Belvedere, Vatican. He remained there until 1516 (Richter no. 1376B).

1515. January 9. Giuliano de' Medici leaves Rome to be married in Savoy. On the same day Louis XII dies. Leonardo's own note *ad hoc* (Richter no. 1377).

1515? *St. John the Baptist* (Louvre). See 1509+.

1516. Autumn. Poorly treated by the Pope, who preferred his rivals, Michelangelo and Raphael, Leonardo leaves with Francesco Melzi on his way to France, via Milan.

1516. Self-portrait, drawn with red chalk (Torino). As Leonardo looks like a very old man, this can hardly have been made before 1516, when he was 64.

VI. AMBOISE, 1517-19

1517. Leonardo and Francesco Melzi are the guests of François I at the little chateau of Cloux, in the royal domain of Amboise. Leonardo receives a pension of a thousand "écus soleil" and Francesco one of four hundred. "Ascension Day at Amboise 1517 in May at Cloux" (Richter no. 1377B).

1517. October 10. Cardinal Luis d'Aragon and his secretary, Antonio de Beatis, visit Leonardo at Cloux (Antonio's account of the interview is extant).

1518. June 24. "St. John's Day at Amboise in the palace of Cloux" (Richter no. 1378).

1519. May 2. Leonardo dies at Cloux at the age of 67. According to Vasari, François I was at his bedside. This is not true; the king was not in Amboise at that time.

1519. August 12. Leonardo is buried at Amboise.

Notes

In these notes works frequently cited are abbreviated as follows:

Appreciation. George Sarton, *The Appreciation of Ancient and Medieval Science during the Renaissance, 1450-1600.* University of Pennsylvania Press, 1955.

History of Science. George Sarton, *History of Science* (to the time of Christ). Vol. 1, Harvard University Press, 1952. Vol. 2 to be published in 1957.

Horus. *Horus,* a guide to the history of science (Waltham, Mass.: Chronica Botanica, 1952).

Introduction. George Sarton, *Introduction to the History of Science* (to the end of the fourteenth century). 3 vols. in 5, Baltimore: Carnegie Institution of Washington, 1927-48.

Isis. *Isis: International review devoted to the history of science and civilization.* Founded by George Sarton, who edited it from 1913 to 1952. Since 1941 it has been published by The History of Science Society, Cambridge, Mass.

Klebs. Arnold Carl Klebs, "Incunabula scientifica et medica," *Osiris,* 4: 1-359 (Bruges, 1938).

Osiris. *Osiris: Commentationes de scientiarum et eruditionis historia rationeque.* Edidit Georgius Sarton Gandavensis. 11 vols., Bruges: St. Catherine's Press, 1936-54.

NOTES TO PREFACE

1. James Westfall Thompson and others, *The Civilization of the Renaissance* (University of Chicago Press, 1929). *The Renaissance, a Symposium* (93 pp., 20 figs., New York: Metropolitan Museum, 1953). Sarton, *Appreciation.*

2. For more details see *Horus,* pp. 42-43.

3. For more information about him see *Introduction,* 3: 1517-20). Immanuel Bonfils was a very distinguished mathematician, one of the pioneers of the decimal and exponential calculus, but he is still unknown to the majority of historians of mathematics.

NOTES TO FIRST WING

1. The coincidence is great but not as great as some people claim. It has been said that they died on the same day, April 23, 1616, but that is a quibble. Cervantes died on April 23 by the Gregorian calendar, Shakespeare on April 23 by the Julian calendar, that is, ten days later. Cervantes was 69 and Shakespeare only 52 at the time of death. Cervantes did his best work late in life (Don Quixote 1605, 1615).

2. This statement can be easily verified, because two English translations of the *Dialogo* appeared in 1953: the first by Giorgio de Santillana, being a revision of the one by Thomas Salusbury (1661), which had long ceased to be available; the second a modern version by Stillman Drake. The first was published by the University of Chicago Press, the second by the University of California Press (reviewed in *Isis*, 45: 213-15).

3. The Eastern philosopher and physician, Ibn Sīnā (XI-1), and the Hispanic one, Ibn Rushd (XII-2). Here and elsewhere, XI-1 means first half of eleventh century, XII-2 means second half of twelfth century, etc.

4. That fear was reflected in the language; for example, the Arabic word *bid'a* means novelty, but it also means heresy. The Spanish word *novedad* had similar overtones, but not the old Latin *novitas*.

5. For mediaeval examples see *Introduction*, 3: 1256.

6. 3 vols., Prague: Tempsky, 1883-1919. The book is known to most geologists in the French translation directed by Emmanuel de Margerie, a revised edition of the original prepared with the help of some twenty French geologists (4 vols., Paris: Colin, 1897-1918) or in the English translation, directed by William Johnson Sollas (5 vols., Oxford: Clarendon Press, 1904-24). Sarton, "La synthèse géologique de 1775 à 1918," *Isis*, 2: 357-94 (1918).

7. Cardano gloats over this in his autobiography, at the beginning of chapter 41. He was born with the sixteenth century, in 1501. Quoth he, "I was born in this century in which the whole world became known whereas the ancients were familiar with but little more than a third part of it. . . . The conviction grows that as a result of these discoveries the fine arts will be neglected and but lightly esteemed, and certainties exchanged for uncertainties." A wrong prophecy.

8. The words "literary efforts" refer to belles-lettres. Historical books were composed in Spanish by González Fernández de Oviedo y Valdés (1478-1557), Bartolomé de las Casas (1474-1566), Hernán Cortés (1485-1554), Francisco Lopez de Gómara (1510?-60), Bernal Diaz del Castillo (fl. 1568), etc. In his *Essais*, Montaigne often referred to American facts, most of which he had obtained from the French translations of López de Gómara and of Las Casas. The studies of natural history in Nueva España by Francisco Hernandez (1514-87) were not published until much later (Mexico, 1615; Rome, 1628, 1651).

A good example of indirect American influence is Thomas More's *Utopia* (Louvain, 1516). The island Utopia was located in the realms that Amerigo Vespucci had visited (Vespucci is named at the beginning of the book).

9. The first complete edition (Reggio, 1481) was followed by many others. Their bibliography is complex (*Introduction*, 3: 1806, 1809).

10. The impact of humanism upon the study and teaching of geography was

investigated by François de Dainville: *Les Jésuites et l'éducation de la société française. La géographie des humanistes* (564 pp., Paris: Beauchesne, 1940; reviewed in *Isis*, 40: 296).

11. For example, the "five mountains" *(wu shan)* of China. Reginald Fleming Johnston, *Buddhist China* (420 pp., London: Murray, 1913). W. E. Soothill and Lewis Hodous, *Dictionary of Chinese Buddhist Terms* (530 pp., London: Kegan Paul, 1937), p. 117. Mountains are often referred to in Greek mythology, but there is no evidence of mountain cults or of pilgrimages to the summits in the Buddhist manner.

12. The initiators were two German-Swiss: first the illustrious naturalist and encyclopaedist, Conrad Gesner (1516-65), who wrote a letter on the admiration of mountains, *De montium admiratione* (Zürich, 1541); and second, his pupil and biographer, Josias Simler (1530-76), author of the first treatise on the Valais and the Alps, *Vallesiae descriptio et commentarius de Alpibus* (Zürich, 1574). The Latin texts of both treatises and their French translations are given by W. A. B. Coolidge, *Josias Simler et les origines de l'alpinisme jusqu'en 1600* (947 pp., Grenoble: Allier, 1904). For the few mountain ascensions in mediaeval times and those of Petrarch in 1336 and Rotario d'Asti in 1358 (?), see *Introduction*, 3: 510, 1163, 1171, 1628.

13. The main restorer of Alpinism and Alpine studies was a French Swiss, Horace Bénédict de Saussure (1740-99). Douglas W. Freshfield, *The Life of H. B. de Saussure* (491 pp., London: Arnold, 1920; reviewed in *Isis*, 6: 64-71).

14. John Colet (1467?-1519), dean of St. Paul's, founder of St. Paul's school, lectured in Oxford on New Testament. William Grocyn (1446?-1519), one of the first teachers of Greek in Oxford. Thomas Linacre (1460?-1524), Greek and Latin scholar, medical humanist.

15. Martin Van Dorp (1485-1525), humanist and theologian, studied and taught at the University of Louvain. In his *Epistola de moriae encomio* (Louvain, 1515) he advised Erasmus to write in praise of wisdom, as if Erasmus did not know very well what he was doing when he praised folly.

16. First English translation of *Utopia* by Ralphe Robynson (1551), often reprinted. Convenient edition in Everyman's Library (1910).

17. Elizabeth Frances Rogers, *The Correspondence of Sir Thomas More* (608 pp., Princeton University Press, 1947; reviewed in *Isis*, 39: 83). Contains 218 letters, that is, all of them, Latin and English, except those to and from Erasmus edited by P. S. Allen. It includes (pp. 28-74) a new edition of the letter to Martin Dorp in Erasmus' defense.

18. Ascham's views on English are discussed by Richard Foster Jones in his excellent book, *The Triumph of the English Language. A survey of opinions concerning the vernacular from the introduction of printing to the Restoration, 1476-1660* (354 pp., Stanford University Press, 1953).

19. Ascham's English works edited by William Aldis Wright (324 pp., Cambridge University Press, 1904).

20. For the Arabic tradition, see Nabih Amin Faris and Robert Potter Elmer, *Arab Archery. A book on the excellence of the bow and arrow and the description thereof* (194 pp., Princeton University Press, 1945; reviewed in *Isis*, 36: 219); annotated English version of the Arabic text. One of its curiosities is the ex-

planation of finger reckoning (*Introduction*, 3: 1865). For the Japanese tradition, see Eugen Herrigel, *Zen in the Art of Archery* (108 pp., London: Routledge and Kegan Paul, 1953).

21. His baptismal names (given as always in Latin) were Joannes Lodovicus, but Spaniards always call him Luis Vives (not Juan Luis). His mother was of the March family, made illustrious by Ausias March (1379-1459) of Valencia, the "Catalan Petrarch" (*Introduction*, 3: 511).

22. An objective proof of Vives' cosmopolitanism is given by the curious fact that biographies of him are found not only in the Spanish collections but also in the *Dictionary of National Biography* (58: 377-79 [1899]) and in the Belgian *Dictionnaire de Biographie Nationale* (26: 789-800 [1938]). He was at home in Flanders, Brabant, and England as well as in Aragon. Said he, "Patriam Flandriam et Brabantiam nomino in quam voluntate propria ascitus sum" ("I call Flanders and Brabant fatherland, having adopted them of my own accord"). His cosmopolitanism is equally clear in the distribution of the first editions of his works. Out of 53 items spaced over thirty years (1514-43), 21 first appeared in Louvain, 19 in Bruges, 6 in Paris, 5 in Oxford, and 2 in Breda. All of these editions but one were prepared by Vives himself and presumably published where he was living at the time. The only exception is the *De veritate fidei Christianae*, issued posthumously in Bruges in 1543 by his widow, Margarita Valldaura, a Spanish woman whom he had married in Bruges in 1524. See *Catálogo de la Exposición bibliográfica celebrada con motivo del IV Centenario de la muerte de Luis Vives* (114 pp., Barcelona, 1940), by Felipe Mateu i Llopis; Juan Estelrich, *Vives. Exposition organisée à la Bibliothèque Nationale* (Paris, 1941).

23. Erasmus was the first of the triumvirate to die, in 1536, and the English antiquary, John Leland (1506?-52), addressed to Vives a letter of consolation, *Ad Lud. Vivem graviter Erasmi morte perturbatum consolatio* (1536). Guillaume Budé (1468-1540) and Luis Vives died four years later. Budé was a very learned man but much less interested in education than Erasmus or Vives.

24. *De Europae statu ac tumultibus* (Louvain, 1522). *De pace inter Caesarem et Franciscum Galliarum Regem* (Oxford, 1525). *De Europae disidiis et bello Turcico* (Bruges, 1526). *De concordia et discordia in humano genere* (Bruges, 1529). *Liber de pacificatione* (Bruges, 1529).

25. Foster Watson, *Vives and the Renascence Education of Women* (New York: Longmans Green, 1912), English version, with commentary, of many texts by Vives and others.

26. A part of it was put into English by Foster Watson: *Vives on Education, a translation of the* De tradendis disciplinis, *with introduction* (Cambridge University Press, 1913).

27. English translation, *Concerning the Relief of the Poor, addressed to the Senate of Bruges, January 6, 1526* (New York: New York School of Philanthropy, 1917).

28. His *Opera omnia* (less the commentary on *Civitas Dei*) were first published fifteen years after his death (2 vols., folio, Basel, 1555). More complete edition (8 vols., folio, Valencia, 1782-90). Very convenient Latin-Spanish edition, *Obras completas* (2 vols., Madrid: Aguilar, 1947-48). There is a large collection of Vives items at Columbia University.

29. *Op. cit.*

30. Jan Amos Komenský, born in Moravia 1592, died in Amsterdam 1670. See Sarton, "Comenius redivivus," *Isis*, 30: 425-51 (1939); Robert Fitzgibbon Young, *Comenius in England* (99 pp., Oxford University Press, 1932). Comenius was strongly influenced by Vives (*Isis*, 30: 435).

31. For more details on the *Devotio moderna*, the Brothers of Common Life, and the *Imitation of Christ*, see *Introduction*, 3: 1356-62, 1408, and index.

32. Cusanus and Erasmus will be dealt with presently. Rudolph Agricola (1443-85) was a classical scholar of Dutch origin, who wrote many books, taught in Worms and Heidelberg, and died in the latter city. Adrian VI was another Dutchman, who was tutor of Charles V, and during the latter's minority governed Spain with Cardinal Ximenes. He was Pope for less than two years (1522-23), the "Dutch Pope," and tried in vain to reform the Church.

33. Martin Luther (1483-1546) of Eisleben and St. Ignatius (1491-1556) of Loyola, Guipúzcoa, the German protagonist of the Reformation and the Basque founder of the Counter-Reformation, were almost exact contemporaries, and died at about the same ages, 63 and 65 years.

34. Constantinople (Istanbul) was taken by Muhammad the Conqueror on May 29, 1543, and the last Byzantine emperor, Constantinos XI Palaiologos, died in the final struggle near one of the gates of the city. The date 1453 has often been chosen as the boundary between the Middle Ages and the Renaissance. My date, 1450, is practically the same, but emphasizes the invention of printing rather than the end of the Byzantine Empire, which did not cause a real discontinuity in western Europe.

35. Erasmus' letters were soon collected and Erasmus (like Cicero) was fully aware of it. Earlier printed editions of them are superseded by the *Opus epistolarium Des. Erasmi Roterodami, denuo recognitum et auctum per P. S. Allen* (11 vols., Oxford: Clarendon Press, 1906-47). This monumental work brought fame to its editor, Percy Stafford Allen (1869-1933), whose biography may be read in vol. 8 (pp. v-xx, portrait); after Allen's death, it was continued by Helen Mary Allen and Heathcote William Garrod. It contains 3,141 letters from and to Erasmus and other documents dating from 1484 to 1537.

36. The *Adagia*, a collection of Latin anecdotes and proverbs illustrated with caustic and witty remarks, was one of the most successful books of the Renaissance. Such a collection invited additions and it was frequently revised and augmented. There were a great many editions in many countries under various titles, *Adagiorum collectanea, Adagiorum chiliades, Adagiorum epitome;* also translations, excerpts, etc. Many of the selections were restricted to war and peace (Basel, 1517, etc.) First English edition, *Prouerbes or adagies* (1539), often reprinted.

37. Translated into French and German in 1520 and later into English as *The Praise of Folie* (London, 1549). Modern English translation by Hoyt Hopewell Hudson (Princeton University Press, 1941).

38. The Greek part of the Complutensian edition had been printed before, at Alcalá de Henares (Complutum) in 1514, but it was not published until 1522. It is the date of publication, not of printing, that counts; the first is tangible, the other is not.

39. The most convenient survey of Erasmus' life is the album by Daniel Van Damme, *Ephéméride illustrée de la vie d'Erasme* (64 pp., Brussels: Musée d'Anderlecht, 1936). See also Sarton, "Communion with Erasmus," *Isis*, 27: 416-29, 4 figs. (1937).

40. *Divi Hieronymi omnia opera* (9 vols., folio, Basel: Johann Froben, 1516). The letters referred to were written to Jacob Batt (Orléans, December 11, 1500) and to one Greverade (Paris, December 13, 1500). *Opus epistolarum Des. Erasmi*, edited by P. S. Allen, (Oxford, 1906), 1: 320-24, 331-33.

41. As quoted by Lucien Febvre in *Un destin, Martin Luther* (Paris: Rieder, 1928), p. 90. Erasmus was not hostile to Augustine, however, and edited his works (10 vols., folio, Basel: Johann Froben, 1528-29).

42. Quentin Metsijs (1466?-1530) was an almost exact contemporary of Erasmus (1466?-1536), but he was a native of Antwerp, while Erasmus came from Rotterdam.

43. Leonardo's Jerome (c.1483, Vatican) represents another tradition, St. Jerome in the desert with his lion. For the Metsijs' tradition, see Georges Marlier, *Erasme et la peinture flamande de son temps* (Damme: Musée van Maerlant, 1954), especially chap. 6, "Saint Jérôme, patron des humanistes chrétiens" (pp. 169-216).

44. On October 31, 1517 Martin Luther nailed his ninety-five theses to the door of the Wittenberg church.

45. See *Introduction, passim*, e.g. 3: 50-52, 1046-48.

46. Melanchthon was a professor of Greek and theology in Wittenberg, and wrote the first Protestant treatise on dogmatic theology, *Theologicae hypotyposes* (Wittenberg, 1521?; Basel, 1522), better known under the title of the third and later editions, *Loci communes seu Hypotyposes* (Augsburg, 1524). The French version was entitled *La Somme de théologie, ou Lieux communs* (1546; Geneva, 1551). Though he was Luther's main assistant, he was tolerant enough to be faithful to Erasmus and to encourage Sébastien Chateillon.

47. More details in *Introduction*, 3: 330.

48. My examples have been taken from the French language, which is more familiar to me, but similar stories could be told about the other vernaculars of western Europe. As to English, it has been very well expounded by Richard Foster Jones, *The Triumph of the English Language* (*op. cit.*); the book deals with the triumph of English over Latin, not over other vernaculars, except French in the law courts. In 1650 English was established as the only language to be used in legal practice.

49. He spoke French in France, let us say, as an English officer spoke Arabic in Egypt. It is significant of the hold of his native language upon him that when Erasmus died in Basel in July 1536, his last words were in Dutch, "Lieve God" (Dear God), and yet he had had very few opportunities of speaking Dutch after 1495.

50. For oblates, see *Introduction*, 3: 327, 477. *Oblatus*, past participle of *offero*, means "offered" (offered to the Church).

51. Montaigne had in his library Greek and Latin editions of Plutarch's *Parallel Lives*. Amyot's translation of the *Lives* appeared in 1559 and of the *Oeuvres morales et meslées* in 1572 (both works published in Paris by Michel de Vascovan).

Montaigne's *Essais* contain 258 quotations from the *Oeuvres morales* and 140 from the *Vies*. Read his tribute to Amyot in *Essai* II, IV.

52. *Triumph of the English Language,* cited, p. 32.

53. Yet Latin continued to be the language of learning for at least another century. As late as 1645 the French booksellers were still making a larger profit on books published in Latin than on those in French. W. H. Lewis, *The Splendid Century* (London: Eyre, 1953), p. 290. This statement is not buttressed with references but it is plausible. One must remember that the truly educated people knew Latin, while the less educated people did not buy books.

NOTES TO SECOND WING

1. I have dealt with many of these in my Rosenbach lectures on *The Appreciation of Ancient and Medieval Science during the Renaissance.*

2. The best survey of the very rich arithmetical literature was given by David Eugene Smith (1860-1944) in *Rara arithmetica* (524 pp., 246 figs., Boston: Ginn, 1905) and *Addenda* (62 pp., 1939; reviewed in *Isis,* 32: 468). For such matters I cannot do more than refer the reader to Smith's book, his masterpiece. Yet no such bibliography, international in scope, can ever be complete, however diligent its author. Two additions to it deserve mention here, if only to encourage further research, especially in the vernaculars of lesser currency. Louis C. Karpinski, "The first printed arithmetic of Spain: Francesch Sanct Climent, *Suma de la Art de Arismetica,* Barcelona, 1482," *Osiris,* 1: 411-20 (1936), in Catalan. Bertha M. Frick, "The first Portuguese arithmetic" (Lisbon, 1559), *Scripta Mathematica,* 11: 327-39 (1945).

3. 2nd ed., Leipzig: Teubner, 1900, vol. 2, pp. 213-648.

4. The next in importance is that by Gino Loria, *Storia delle matematiche* (3 vols., Torino, 1929-33; 2nd ed., Padua, 1937). The Renaissance is covered in pp. 249-388 of the second edition. This work is valuable chiefly for its account of the Italian mathematicians.

5. His mechanical genius was analyzed by Frank D. Prager, "Brunelleschi's invention and the renewal of Roman masonry work," *Osiris,* 9: 457-554 (1950).

6. Aerial perspective is art, but linear perspective is geometry. It is the conical projection of objects upon a plane, the center of projection being the artist's eye. The perpendicular (or distance) of the eye to the plane is the line of direction or line of sight (direct radial); the intersection of that line with the plane is the center of vision (or principal point). All lines coming from infinite parts are naturally parallel to the direct radial; they seem to meet at the center of vision, which is called the vanishing point. In this chapter I ought to speak only of linear perspective, but for the artist linear and aerial perspective were inseparable.

7. Leonardo's *Trattato della Pittura* was published only in 1651, in Paris, in an edition dedicated to Queen Christina of Sweden. Its tone is distinctly Leonardian and it tallies with fragments in Leonardo's Mss. There is no reason for doubting its authenticity *grosso modo.*

8. Nuremberg: J. Petreius, 1533. It speaks well for Arabic mathematics that the *Shakl al-qattā'* was almost on the same level as the *De triangulis omnimodis,* although Naṣīr al-dīn al-Ṭūsī died in 1274, Regiomontanus in 1476, two centuries later.

9. These tables of 1596 were abbreviated by the German, Johann Adam Schall (1591-1666), Jesuit missionary to China from 1622 on, and introduced by him to the Chinese in 1631 (*Isis*, 33: 389).

10. For a summary of Sumerian or Babylonian mathematics see *History of Science*, 1: 68-74.

11. But not fractional ones, which had been understood by a contemporary of Immanuel Bonfils, Nicole Oresme (XIV-2). The idea of exponential calculus and indirectly that of logarithms were in the air from the fourteenth century on, but did not come to fruition until three centuries later.

12. For example, if we represent roots by the letter R with an exponent indicating whether the root is one, square, cubic, etc.,

$$R^1\,12 = 12$$
$$R^2\,9 = 3$$
$$R^3\,27 = 3$$

Chuquet remarked that

$$R^{12} = R^6 \cdot R^2 \text{ or } R^4 \cdot R^3$$

13. By Aristide Marre in Boncompagni's *Bullettino* (vols. 13-14, 1880-81). The *Triparty* remained unknown to most historians until its explanation by Paul Tannery in *Bibliothece Mathematica* (1887), pp. 17-21, and in his *Mémoires*, 5: 1-7 (1922); and by Moritz Cantor, *Vorlesungen*, vol. 2, pp. 347-64 (1899).

14. I pointed this out in my study of scientific incunabula, in the chapter entitled "Their retrogressive character," *Osiris*, 5: 62-66 (1938). Note that printing was introduced in Lyon in 1473, and that by 1484 at least seven printers were flourishing in that city. Another example was quoted above. As Regiomontanus' life was cut short early, in 1476, his great treatise on trigonometry was not published until 1533. It is probable that the same misfortune, untimely death, befell Chuquet. He was not able to push through the printing of his *Triparty* and there were no competent friends to publish it after his death.

15. Lyon: Huguetan, 1520; revised edition, 1538. Fine copies of both editions are in the Harvard Library. Its splendid copy of the first belonged formerly to Michel Chasles. Both editions are described in *Rara Arithmetica*, pp. 128-31 (1908).

16. Venice: Paganinis, November 1494. The title page (*Osiris*, 5: 161 [1938]) is a table of contents, too long to be reproduced.

17. For example, a section on weights, measures, and coins, taken from Giorgio Chiarini (Florence, 1481). Commercial accounts were very complicated in those days, because measures and moneys were different in each country, and might even vary from one city to another, say from Venice to Milan or Florence.

18. D. E. Smith in *Isis*, 6: 311 (1924).

19. In the public debates each contestant deposited a sum of money which was forfeited to the winner; in addition, it is highly probable that other forms of gambling were involved.

20. The insults and obscenities which the "humanists" did not hesitate to exchange are beyond belief. The example given in my *Introduction* (3: 1294) illustrates the abusive language of Jean de Montreuil (d. 1418), but the same habits continued throughout the fifteenth and sixteenth centuries. Many of the humanists lacked urbanity. Humanism and humanity were two very different things.

21. The main challenger, Tartaglia, published the whole story and all the documents ad hoc for his own vindication. The documents have been published anew and discussed by Ettore Bortolotti, "I cartelli di matematica disfida e la personalità psichica e morale di Cardano," *Studi e memorie per la storia dell' Università di Bologna*, 12: 3-79 (1933); summarized in Oystein Ore, *Cardano the Gambling Scholar* (264 pp., Princeton University Press, 1953), pp. 53-107.

22. Pascal, having discovered the areas, volumes, and centers of gravity of the cycloid and the volumes engendered by it, issued in 1658 a challenge concerning them which attracted much attention but in a quiet way; there was no public debate. Cajori, *History of Mathematics* (New York: Macmillan, 1919), p. 165.

23. Was a time when a champion algebraist attracted public attention less civilized than one in which the main hero is the champion boxer or basketball player?

24. *Artis Magnae sive de regulis algebraicis liber unus* (Nuremberg: Petr. Joh. Petreius, 1545), one of the outstanding mathematical books of all time. It was not sufficiently advanced, however, to be considered as the foundation of modern algebra. This would imply a deeper knowledge of the theory of equations than could be reached in the sixteenth century. Hence it is misleading to compare it with the books of Copernicus and Vesalius (1543).

25. Cardano's results and 'Umar's were independent, but their common features were not due to accidental coincidence. They were bound to find similar results, because they were analyzing correctly the same situation. Both of them classified equations not as we do, according to the top power of the unknown, but according to the number of different terms which they included. For example, if in the general equation

$$ax^3 + bx^2 + cx + d = 0$$

we assume that one or more of the coefficients b, c, d are negative or null, we obtain what 'Umar and Cardano considered to be different forms of cubics.

26. When the cubic has three real roots they are yielded in a form involving imaginaries. Imaginary roots were first recognized by Bombelli (1572), but imperfectly; a better recognition by Albert Girard (1629) is definitely post-Renaissance. We may say that imaginaries as well as logarithms escaped Renaissance mathematicians.

27. A transcendental number is one that cannot be defined by any combination of a finite number of equations with rational integral coefficients.

28. His father, Fazio Cardano, was a lawyer in Milan, who prepared the first edition of the *Prospectiva communis* of the archbishop of Canterbury, John Peckham (XIII-2), printed in Pavia in 1482 (Klebs 738.1).

29. The only book of his translated into English during the Renaissance. Cardanus' *Comforte* was translated by Thomas Bedingfield (London: Marshe, 1573; revised 1576).

30. Was this edition of 1544 the first? I wonder, because it was published together with the *De libris propriis* and a new edition of the *Consolatio*.

31. To complete the history of Cardano's family, his wife, Lucia, died in 1546 at the age of 31, leaving three children: Giambattista (executed in 1560, aet. 26); Chiara, who was eventually married; and Aldo. At the time of their mother's death, the children were 12, 10, and 3 years of age and Cardano was constitu-

tionally unable to watch over them. During the last years of his life, Cardano was left alone with Giambattista's son (born 1543), who was called Fazio (after the boy's great-grandfather) and seems to have been faithful and kind to the old man. Cardano bequeathed to him his estate, except the books and papers.

32. His cantankerousness had created many enmities and his international fame many jealousies. This may explain the accusation. It is true that he had written a book in praise of Nero, and his *De subtilitate* contained an inconclusive dialogue between a Christian, a Jew, a Muslim, and a pagan, but generally speaking, he had been much more prudent in such matters than in others.

33. The first edition of *De vita propria* was published only sixty-seven years after his death by Gabriel Naudé (Paris, 1643); it was reprinted in Amsterdam in 1654 and again in the first volume of the *Opera omnia* (Lyon, 1663). English translation by Jean Stoner (New York: Dutton, 1930).

As to his autobibliography, Cardano had published it in middle life, at least as early as 1544. It contains many biographical details. A later edition which I have examined bears the significant title *Liber de libris propriis eorumque ordine et usu, ac de mirabilibus operibus in arte medica per ipsum factis* (Lyon, 1557).

His autobiography (*De vita propria*) is divided into fifty-four chapters; chapter 45 is a long list of the books he has written with various remarks ("Libri a me conscripti. Quo tempore, cur, quid acciderit").

34. Chapter 35 of his *Vita propria* is entitled "Alumni atque discipuli" (wards and disciples); he enumerated fourteen pupils who were also his familiars. In those days, pupils or apprentices generally lived with their master. The three most important of his pupils were Lodovico Ferrari, whose death, in 1565, he did not mention; Gasparo Cardano, a cousin twice removed; and Rodolfo Silvestri (or Selvatico), who was very generous to Cardano at the time of the latter's arrest in 1570 and traveled with him from Bologna to Rome. Selvatico practiced medicine in that city.

35. *De vita propria* (caput XLI). First edited by Gabriel Naudé (Paris, 1643). Reprinted in the *Opera omnia*, vol. 1, pp. 1-54 (Lyon, 1563), p. 34.

Cardano was not alone in his century in realizing the astonishing achievements of his contemporaries. See the quotation from Jean Fernel, page 193. We owe an admirable graphic testimony of the same kind to the Flemish artist, Jan Van der Straet (Giovanni della Strada, Joannes Stradanus; Bruges, 1523; Florence, 1605), in his series of drawings published under the title *Nova reperta* (20 pl., Antwerp: Ioannes Galleus, 1638).

A splendid facsimile edition of these plates was issued by Bern Dibner (Burndy Library, No. 8; Norwalk, Connecticut, 1953). The Dibner series covers the following topics: Title, *Nova reperta*, synoptic composition. 1. America (Amerigo Vespucci, 1497). 2. Magnet (Flavio Biondo of Forli, 1451; *Introduction*, 3: 510, 715). 3. Gunpowder ("Berthold der Schwarze;" *Introduction*, 3: 1581). 4. Printing. 5. Clocks without pendulums. 6. Guaiacum. 7. Distillation. 8. Silk (Justinian the Great, VI-1). 9. Stirrups. 10. Watermills. 11. Windmills. 12. Olive oil. 13. Sugar. 14. Oil colors (Jan Van Eyck, c.1390-1441); *Introduction*, 3: 111, 1834). 15. Spectacles. 16. Determination of longitudes by magnetic declination (Petrus Plancius, 1552-1622; reviewed in *Isis*, 41: 213). 17. Polished armor. 18. Amerigo Vespucci dis-

covers the Southern Star (as in Dante's *Purgatory*, 1: 22-27; *Introduction*, 3: 487).
19. Copper engraving. This is followed by four plates of another series: 1. America
rediscovered; 2. Columbus; 3. Vespucci; 4. Magellan.

The names mentioned are those included in the legends. The selection is
curious; many of the items were not new inventions but old techniques to which
the new age had given a new currency; for example, the weaving of silk had
become so important that Stradanus devoted another series of six plates to it,
Vermis sericus. It is remarkable that three of the plates in the Dibner series
honored Vespucci.

36. *Opera omnia*, edited by Charles Spon, with biography by Gabriel Naudé
(10 vols., folio, Lyon, 1663). Vol. 1, Philologica, Logica, Moralia. Vol. 2, Moralia
quaedam et Physica. Vol. 3, Physica. Vol. 4, Arithmetica, Geometrica, Musica.
Vol. 5, Astronomica, Astrologica, Onirocritica. Vols. 6-7, Medicinalia. Vol. 10,
Opuscula miscellanea.

37. As quoted by Ore, *op. cit.*, p. 52, no source given. The most elaborate
studies on Cardano in recent years are those of Angelo Bellini (1872-1949), especially his *Gerolamo Cardano e il suo tempo* (338 pp., ill., Milan: Moepli, 1947;
reviewed in *Isis*, 40: 131). Yet the writing of a well documented biography and
bibliography remains to be done.

38. 6 vols., usually bound in 3, Venice, 1556-60.

39. Franz Woepcke, *L'algébre d'Omar al-Khayyam* (Paris, 1851), p. 13. David
S. Kasir, *The Algebra of Omar Khayyam* (New York: Columbia University Press,
1931), p. 54. Kasir's book is reviewed in *Isis*, 19: 529.

40. Chu Shih-chieh, *Ssŭ-yüan yü-chien* (Precious mirror of the four elements),
written in 1303. *Introduction*, 3: 701-703. Jottings on the science of the Chinese.
Arithmetic, *Shanghae Almanac for 1853 and Miscellany*, Shanghai, Herald Office,
1852. Karl L. Biernatzki, "Die Arithmetik der Chinese," *Crelle's Journal*, 52: 59-94
(1856). Yoshio Mikami, *Development of Mathematics in China and Japan* (Leipzig, 1913), p. 90. At the beginning of the Precious Mirror Chu gives, according to
an old model, not his own, what he calls the diagram for the eight lower powers:

41. This *Traité* was already printed at the time of Pascal's death in 1662, but it was not published until 1665. Pascal's discovery was anterior to 1654.

42. It would be better to say the first treatise on mathematical probability. The word *probabilitas* is Ciceronian; it might be translated "likelihood." The common non-mathematical idea was discussed by Luis Vives in vol. 3 of his *De disciplinis* (Antwerp, 1531).

43. It was discussed in *Introduction*, 3: 1813. The word *zara* was derived from the Arabic *zahr*, pl. *azhār*, meaning dice, hence the word *azár* in Spanish, our own word *hazard*, and its equivalents in other European languages. A very curious semantic deviation: dice, chance or risk, accident. Benventuno's commentary was first printed at Speyer, Bavaria, in 1477.

44. We owe this to Oystein Ore, *op. cit.* This book includes an English translation of the *Liber de ludo aleae* by Sydney Henry Gould plus mathematical commentary by Ore and a very readable introduction. The *Ludus aleae* was first published in Cardano's *Opera omnia*, edited by Charles Spon (Lyon, 1663).

45. Florian Cajori. *History of Mathematical Notations* (2 vols., Chicago: Open Court, 1928-29; reviewed in *Isis*, 12: 332-36, 13: 129-30). The history covers 851 pages with 126 figures and, needless to say, it is incomplete.

46. The first example of the creation of a system of symbols and notations for newer and older mathematical ideas was given by Leibniz (1646-1716). Dietrich Mahnke, "Leibniz als Begründer der symbolischen Mathematik," *Isis*, 9: 279-93 (1927). Even so, the symbolism of new theories (vectorial and tensorial geometry, potential, etc.) was marred as late as the nineteenth century by many irregularities and duplications. *Isis*, 1: 491-92 (1913).

47. Even in French. I have before me (in the Harvard Library) a pamphlet entitled "Sentence Donnée par le Roy contre maistre Pierre Ramus & les Livres Composez par icelluy contre Aristote. Pronuncée à Paris Le XXVI de mars 1543. Avant Pasques" (Paris, Benoist de Gourmont).

48. College founded in Paris by François I in 1530, outside of the University as a complement to it. It is the Collège de France of today. For its history, see *Le Collège de France (1530-1930), livre jubilaire* (Paris, 1932).

49. For example, he picked a quarrel with the Sorbonne on the pronunciation of Latin, insisting that the u after a q should be sounded *quisquis, quamquam* (not kiskis, kamkam) and that the h in *mihi* should be pronounced gutturally like a Spanish j. Note that the pronunciation of Latin was then as delicate a subject as that of French, and nobody likes to be told that he speaks ill.

50. The same is true of every political massacre; private vengeances can be and are easily hidden under the veil of patriotism or orthodoxy.

51. Especially in Calvinist ones. The Lutherans preferred Melanchthon's logic and leadership to "Ramism."

52. Many books have been devoted to Ramus. It will suffice to quote an ancient one by Charles Waddington: *Ramus* (480 pp., Paris, 1855), a more modern one by Frank Pierrepont Graves: *Ramus and the Educational Reformation of the Sixteenth Century* (236 pp., New York: Macmillan, 1912), and a very elaborate one by Walter J. Ong, S.J.: *Ramus* (to be published by Harvard University Press).

53. "Regina, mater regis." Catherine (1519-89), daughter of Lorenzo II de'

Medici, the wife of Henri II and the mother of three kings, François II, Charles IX, and Henri III. She was the actual ruler of France during the reign of Charles IX (1560-74) and as such was responsible for the Massacre of St. Bartholomew (1572). She died in 1589. She was full of superstitions, clever but stupid, faithless, and fond of intrigues to the point of crime. She was a true Medici in her love of magnificence and her patronage of artists.

54. Ramus had used the title *Scholae* before for his *Scholae grammaticae* (1559) and the *Scholae physicae* (1565). The *Scholae mathematicae* (1569) was his last use but his disciples, chiefly Joannes Piscator (1546-1625), used it repeatedly in new editions of his other books published after his death. *Scholae in liberales artes* (1578). *Scholae dialecticae* (1581). *Scholae rhetoricae* (1581). *Scholae metaphysicae* (1583). This emphasized the unity of his books, as if each were but a part of a great encyclopaedia, and it probably helped to increase and unify his influence.

55. For which see *History of Science*, 1: 278, 440, 503. It is significant that Ramus brought together mathematical problems of his time and of the fifth century B.C.

56. Florian Cajori, *History of Mathematics* (2d ed., New York: Macmillan, 1919), p. 142.

57. Even today, the majority of students remember not so much their teachers as the textbooks which they were obliged to con in college. Men of science who are the authors of popular textbooks are far better known to their students than those who only wrote monographs. It is true that the latter may have a far greater reputation with their colleagues and true rivals and their expectation of enduring fame is much greater.

58. *Introduction*, 3: 315, 480. The Ghibellines were feudal and county people, imperialists; their opponents, the Guelfs, were tradesmen and bankers, city people, Papists. Italian politics had been dominated by their rivalry.

59. A second edition was issued by the same printer, G. Rossi (654 pp. and tables, quarto, Bologna, 1579).

60. Carl Immanuel Gerhardt, *Der Briefwechsel von Leibniz mit Mathematikern* (Berlin, 1899), pp. 559, 565.

61. Rafael Bombelli, *L'algebra. Libri IV e V compredenti "La parte geometrica" inedita* . . . pubblicata a cura di Ettore Bortolotti (306 pp., Bologna: Zanichelli, 1929; reviewed in *Isis*, 14: 425-26). As this part of Bombelli's work was practically unknown until 1929, it could not exert any influence.

62. Cantor's account of Bombelli is naturally incomplete, because it was anterior to Bortolotti. For a general account see Gino Loria, *Storia delle matematiche*, 2: 68-83 (1931) or 2nd ed., pp. 314-23 (1950). Many special papers on Bombelli have been published by Bortolotti, Amedeo Agostini, Loria, and Heinrich Wieleitner.

63. The greatest political historian of that age, Jacques Auguste de Thou (Thuanus, 1553-1617) wrote an immense history of his own times, *Historia sui temporis*, extending from 1543 to 1617. His account of Viète begins with the statement that the latter died in his climacteric year. The climacteric (or great climacteric) year was the 63rd (9 x 7) or sometimes the 81st (9 x 9). There were other critical years in a man's life, but the 63rd was supposed to be especially critical. De Thou's very interesting notice of Viète was read by me in the French

standard translation (London, 1734, vol. 14, pp. 162-66). The Latin text was originally published in four folio volumes (Paris, 1604-1608). De Thou tried to be impartial between Catholics and Protestants and was criticized from both sides.

64. The *"parlements"* of Paris and of many French provinces were not parliaments in the English sense. They were primarily courts of justice, yet they had some deliberative functions and could oppose royal absolutism to some extent. Therefore the members of such *parlements* were something more than judges, for they acted as magistrates and royal councilors, and they had considerable prestige. Viète was connected later with the Parlement of Paris sitting in Tours. The details of his parliamentary career do not concern us, but only the fact that he was a high magistrate of that special kind.

65. One thinks at once of another mathematical amateur, Pierre de Fermat (1601-65), who was councilor for the *parlement* of Toulouse. Viète and Fermat were men of the same background, but Viète was a man of the Renaissance and Fermat one of the Cartesian and Pascalian age. Neither Viète nor Fermat is dealt with by Julian Coolidge in *The Mathematics of Great Amateurs* (Oxford: Clarendon Press, 1949; reviewed in *Isis*, 41: 234-36).

66. The full-fledged humanist was obliged to demonstrate his familiarity with Greek. Latin was so much used in scientific circles that it was hardly considered as a learned language. The true learned language was Greek.

67. In 1948 I investigated the existing original prints of Viète and of his early commentators in the Harvard Library, Bibliothèque Nationale, British Museum, etc. and collected many notes and photostats, but was forced to abandon that work when I realized that it would take me years to carry it through.

68. The original *Canon* is followed by a trigonometrical treatise *Universalium inspectionum ad canonem mathematicum liber singularis* (Paris: Mettayer, 1579).

69. G. Sarton, "First explanation of decimal fractions, 1585," *Isis*, 23: 173 (1935).

70. They included, besides those mentioned in the text, *In artem analyticam isagoge seorsim excussa ab opere restitutae mathematicae analyseos, seu Algebra nova* (Tours: Mettayer, 1591); and *De aequationum recognitione et emendatione* (1591, known through Anderson's reprint of 1615).

71. Not libri VIII! Book VIII is the only known book of that series. Were the others not printed? Or were they lost? Considering Viète's method of publication, the second alternative is plausible. It is as if we knew of our colleagues' publications only those of which they were kind enough to send us offprints.

72. Joseph Justus Scaliger (1540-1609). almost a complete contemporary of Viète, was the son of the equally famous Julius Caesar Scaliger (1484-1588). Joseph was an illustrious classical scholar and chronologist but a poor mathematician, at least as compared with Viète. He became a Protestant in 1562 and found himself more than once under Jesuit fire; his last years were embittered by controversies in which he was the loser. His most important works are *De emendatione temporum* (1583) and *Thesaurus temporum* (1605), the first a treatise on chronology, the second a treasury of dates.

73. Adrianus Romanus (1561-1615) of Louvain was one of the greatest mathematicians of his time. It is hard to resist the temptation of writing about him at

greater length; this is the main difficulty in a book like this one, to resist endless opportunities, for every great man had rivals, and each of them would drag in many others. Romanus was a good algebraist and geometer and he simplified spherical trigonometry. The best account of his life and work was given by Father Henri Bosmans in the *Biographie nationale de Belgique,* 19: 844-88 (1907).

74. *Francisci Vietae ad Problema, quod omnibus mathematicis totius orbis construendum proposuit Adrianus Romanus responsum* (Paris, 1595; *Vietae opera,* 305-24, 1646).

75. *Problema Apolloniacum quo datis tribus circulis, quaeritur quartus eos contigens ab illustri vivo D. Francisco Vieta . . . propositum jam vero per Belgam Adrianum Romanum constructum* (20 pp., Würzburg, 1596). *Francisci Vietae Apollonius Gallus, seu, exsuscitata Apollonii Pergaei peri epaphon geometria ad V. C. Adrianum Romanum Belgam* (Paris: David Le Clerc, 1600; *Vietae opera,* pp. 325 ff., 1646). The *Peri epaphōn* is a treatise on contacts or tangencies (*epaphai*) which is known through Pappos' summary (III-2). The *Apollonius Gallus* was followed seven years later (Venice, 1607) by the *Apollonius Redivivus* of Marino Ghetaldi of Ragusa, but that is another story.

76. The story is told by De Thou in his *Historia sui temporis,* cited above. From the same source comes the story about Viète's cryptography, below. De Thou, of course, was not a mathematician. The equation of the 45th degree submitted by Adrianus, including all the odd powers of *x*, seemed hopeless, but Viète recognized immediately that this equation was the general formula determining the 45th part of the arc subtended by a given chord. In the equation set by Adrianus the given chord was the side of a regular pentadecagonal polygon, that is, a chord of 24°. The answer was provided by the chord of the arc of 32′; it then sufficed to consult a table of sines. De Thou says that Viète solved the problem immediately; that is incredible, but his trigonometrical experience enabled him to find the solution with astonishing ease.

77. Philip II was king of Spain from 1556 to 1598; Henri III, king of France from 1574 to 1589.

78. Charles J. Mendelsohn, "Bibliographical note on the *De cifris* of Leone Battista Alberti," *Isis,* 32: 48-51 (1940/47). For information on Trithemius, Vigenère, Viète as cryptographer, and others see Joseph S. Galland, *Historical and Analytical Bibliography of the Literature of Cryptology* (210 pp., Evanston, Ill., Northwestern University, 1945).

79. Catherine de Parthenay (1554-1631). In 1575 she was married again, to René II, viscount of Rohan, and had five children by him, the eldest one being the famous Duc Henri de Rohan (1579-1638), general and chief of the Calvinists under Louis XIII. Hence she is catalogued by the Bibliothèque Nationale under the name Rohan-Soubise. Her letters were edited by Hugues Imbert (Niort, 1874).

80. The dedication of one of them reads: *Inclvtae principi Melusinidi Catharinae Parthenaeensi piissimae procerum Rohaniorum matri. . . .* Melusinides is a reference to one of the most popular mediaeval fables. Melusina was a fairy, daughter of another fairy and of the king of Albany; she married Count Raymond and built for him the castle of Lusignan (near Poitiers, in Poitou), cradle of the illustrious family of Lusignan. Members of that family took part in the First Cru-

sade, and Guy de Lusignan became king of Jerusalem (1186) and Cyprus. He founded the dynasty of Lusignan d'Outremer, which ruled Cyprus until 1489. The Parthenay were another illustrious family of Poitou, mixed up in the Melusina fable. The tale was first told in prose by Jean d'Arras in 1387-94. As it included all kinds of feudal traditions and mediaeval fancies, it was extremely popular not only in French but in many other languages, English, Flemish, German, Spanish, Bohemian, Danish, Swedish, and Slavonic. The first printed edition was probably the French one of Geneva, 1478, revised by Ch. Brunet (Paris, 1854).

Jean d'Arras' novel was put into verse, c.1401, by La Coudrette, chaplain to Guillaume VII Larchevêque, seigneur de Parthenay. La Coudrette's poem was translated into English verse before 1500. Edition by Walter W. Skeat, *The Roman of Partenay or of Lusignan, otherwise known as the tale of Melusine* (287 pp., London: Early English Text Society, 1866; 2nd revised ed., 1899). This is the most useful edition because of abundant notes and an excellent index. The English poem is 6,615 lines long.

In line 1,135 of the English poem it is said that Melusine called the castle which she built Lusignan after the second part of her own name. (Mère des Lusignan, Mère Lusigne, Merlusine, Mélusine).

81. The polar triangle of a spherical triangle is another spherical triangle whose vertices are the poles of the sides of the given one. Viète's theory of polar triangles was elaborated by Willebrord Snel (1627).

82. He tried to introduce new technical terms, most of which are now forgotten, but it is amusing to recall that he also tried to reject *algebra* and replace it by *analysis*, as in the title *In artem analyticam isagoge* (1591). His objection to *algebra* was that the word was nonsensical; it was nonsensical to him because it was of Arabic, not Greek, origin.

83. It should be noted, however, that their treatises appeared many years before the final edition of Viète's works by Frans Van Schooten (Leiden, 1646). By 1645 Girard and Harriot had long been dead.

84. Joseph Bertrand (1822-1900), *Eloges académiques* (2e série, 143-96, 1902), p. 176.

85. For Jean Trenchant, see D. E. Smith, *Rara arithmetica*, p. 320 (1908). *Isis,* 21: 207-209 (1934); 24: 113 (1935).

86. Stevin was not an absolute innovator in such matters. Double-entry bookkeeping had been used by the stewards of Genoa in 1340 and in the Medici accounts, Florence, 1395; the earliest printed account was that of Luca Pacioli in his *Summa de Arithmetica*, Venice, 1494 (*Introduction,* 3: 124, 126, 1111). As to the separation of state from private accounts, there were also precedents (*Isis,* 21: 272 [1934]), but Stevin's explanation was more complete and forceful. It was published in his *Livre de compte de prince à la manière d'Italie* . . . Leiden, 1608). The duke of Sully's *Economies royales* was printed in his château of Sully in 1638; his reminiscences refer to the time of his ministry under Henri IV (king 1589-1610).

87. This story has been told by me with considerable detail in "The first explanation of decimal fractions and measures (1585) together with a history of the decimal and a complete facsimile of Stevin's *Disme,*" *Isis,* 23: 153-244 (1935). Many adumbrations of the decimal calculus are mentioned, including Viète's, but I did

not speak of one which had not yet been discovered, that of Immanuel Bonfils (XIV-2).

Solomon Gandz, "The invention of the decimal fractions and the application of the exponential calculus by Immanuel Bonfils of Tarascon," *Isis,* 25: 16-45 (1936). *Introduction,* 3: 1518.

88. For details, see *History of Science,* 1: 68-74.

89. "The end of the Renaissance" is correct, in spite of the fact that Stevin published his discovery clearly and completely in 1585, for it was too revolutionary and too simple to be understood at once. The popularity of decimal fractions was much increased by the invention of common logarithms by Napier and Henry Briggs; the first table of common logarithms of trigonometric ratios was published by Edmund Gunter (London, 1620), the first table of common logarithms of numbers by Henry Briggs (London, 1624). Even that did not suffice to introduce decimal fractions into common use, because the logarithms were unknown to the great majority of people. It took a century or two to put them over.

90. Fractions of the type $1/n$ were privileged (as in ancient Egypt), e.g., $\frac{1}{2}$ *dimidia pars,* $\frac{1}{4}$ *quarta pars* . . . (the word *pars* might be left out except with *dimidia*); as were also those of the type $(n-1)/n$, e.g., $2/3$ *duae partes,* $4/5$ *quattuor partes.* The Egyptian name for $2/3$ was *sewy,* meaning two parts, just as in Latin. That expression has remained in English; we speak of a pitcher "two parts full" meaning two-thirds full; a curious vestige.

91. Throughout the Middle Ages and the Renaissance, sexagesimal fractions were called astronomical or physical, vs. the common fractions. They were the highbrow fractions reserved for scientific purposes.

92. One might object that some of these names express a fraction, but one did not think of $5/12$ when saying *quincunx* any more than we think of five when we say Fifth Avenue. The strangest of these names is *bes;* it meant $8/12$ or $2/3$, a very privileged fraction since early Egyptian days. The word *as* was sometimes used to mean totality, and Vitruvius used it to designate unity and also 6. If *as* was 6, then *bes* was 4.

93. An objector might say that fractions could be canceled also in the case of complex numbers, e.g., £2 5s. 7d. may be reduced to 547 pence and no fractions are left. True, but this requires a careful computation, which with larger numbers might become risky. On the decimal basis, no computations are needed; merely move the decimal point.

94. Stevin did not use parentheses but circles. His convention was that n in a circle means $(1/10)^n$.

95. *Isis,* 21: 251 (1934).

96. This is explained in great detail in my *Introduction,* 2: 16-19; 3: 110-37, 1105-21.

97. Cusanus *seems* to have conceived that both the earth and the stars rotate around a polar axis, and that the earth rotates also around an equatorial axis (to account for the precession of the equinoxes).

98. The old German biography, *Copernicus,* by Leopold Prowe (2 vols., Berlin, 1883-84) has been corrected and completed in many memoirs, most of them in German and Polish. The foremost Polish investigator is Ludwik A. Birkenmajer:

Nikolaj Kopernik (in Polish, 722 pp., Cracow, 1900; French summary, Cracow, 1902; reviewed in *Isis*, 7: 204); *Stromata Copernica* (in Polish, 410 pp., Cracow: Academy of Sciences, 1924; reviewed in *Isis*, 16: 136-38). Brief but well informed biography by Angus Armitage (184 pp., London: Allen, 1938; American edition, 220 pp., New York: Schuman, 1947; reviewed in *Isis*, 39: 175).

99. The diocese of Ermeland (Latin, Varmia) was a large territory corresponding roughly to East Prussia. It was ceded to Poland by the Teutonic Knights in the Treaty of Thorn, 1466, and passed to Prussia only in 1772. Thus in Copernicus' time it was undoubtedly Polish, which does not mean of course that all its inhabitants were of Polish race or language. It was reassigned to Poland by the Potsdam Conference in 1945. The see of the diocese was Heilsberg.

100. The word canon (*canonicus*) has many meanings, and an account of its semantic development would involve a good deal of ecclesiastical history and canon law. In Copernicus' time the canons of a cathedral were in charge of its economic administration and, to some extent, of the administration of the diocese. Copernicus may have been in minor orders but was never ordained a priest.

101. The prince bishop was the temporal as well as the spiritual head of his diocese. Thus Copernicus was concerned with financial and monetary problems and also with medical and military matters. In 1520 he was appointed as commander-in-chief of Allenstein (Olsztyn), which was beleaguered by the Teutonic Knights. His concern with monetary questions is shown in a little tract, *Monetae cudendae ratio*, written in German in 1522, rewritten in Latin in 1528. Similar ideas had been expounded by two Frenchmen, Jean Buridan (XIV-1) and Nicole Oresme (XIV-2). *Introduction*, 3: 1283, 1495, 544. Copernicus emphasized how dangerous it was to debase the coinage. This, he claimed, was one of the four main disasters which could befall a nation, the others being discord, high mortality, and poor harvests.

102. I have just received (February 1955) from Poland a beautiful volume, *Teofilakt Symokatta: Listy* (Panstwowe wydawnictwo naukowe, Warsaw, 1953), which illustrates Copernicus' devotion to his uncle Lucas, as well as his own humanism. Copernicus translated into Latin a very curious work of Theophylactos Simocattes (VII-1), *Epistolae morales rurales amatoriae*, and added a preface dedicated *ad reverendissimum dominum Lucam* (Krakow: Joh. Haller, 1509). The volume includes a Polish introduction by Ryszard Gansiniec, a facsimile of the Latin translation of 1509, a critical edition of it, the original Greek text, and a Polish version. This is a very remarkable and unexpected addition to Copernican literature.

103. The territory is disputed to this day, so that the geographical names mentioned above may not be equally clear to every reader. Here are a few equivalent names:

Thorn: Latin Torunum, Polish Torún.
Vistula is the Latin form, German Weichsel, Polish Wisla, Russian Visla.
Danzig: Latin Gedanum, Polish Gdańsk.
Warsaw: Latin Varsavia, German Warschau, Polish Warszawa.
Cracow: Latin Cracovia, German Krakau, Polish Kraków.
Frauenburg: Latin Fravenburgum, Polish Frombork.
Heilsberg: Latin Heilsberga, Polish Lidzbark Warmiński.

Frauenburg is on the Frisches Haff, a lagoon 56 miles long in the Gulf of Danzig, called in Polish Mierzeja Wiślana and in Russian Frishes Gaf. At the eastern end of the Frisches Haff lies Königsberg, now in Soviet Russia (Latin Regiomontanum, Russian Kaliningrad). Heilsberg is inland, about 40 miles southeast of Frauenburg.

104. *Introduction*, 3: 1398. The University of Cracow will soon celebrate its sixth centenary.

105. Regiomontanus (1436-76), who died soon after Copernicus' birth, was the main German astronomer of his time. His name refers to Königsberg, not the old city (the Kaliningrad of today), but a little place in the duchy of Coburg (Upper Franconia, Bavaria). Copernicus was probably acquainted with every publication written, edited, or printed by Regiomontanus, including, of course, his posthumous trigonometrical treatise, *De triangulis* (Nuremberg, 1533).

106. *Isis*, 36: 256. Rhaeticus gave him a copy of it not in 1538 but some time later; Copernicus could not use it, but for his purpose the books published in Venice (1496, 1515) were sufficient.

107. Copernicus was not a practical astronomer; perhaps his many duties had left him no time for that. Only twenty-seven observations can be credited to him.

108. In the same way biologists often speak of Nature as if she were a person wishing or doing this or that; it is a manner of speech for the sake of brevity.

109. As all the stars move together, the Ptolemaic belief implied the existence of a starry sphere. This sphere became unnecessary as soon as it was realized that it is the earth and not the stars that rotate.

110. The date of its composition is difficult to ascertain. Birkenmajer would place it in 1512 or earlier; others place it much later. Assuming it was the tract that was brought to Clement VII's attention, it cannot be later than 1534.

111. Three copies of it exist today in the libraries of Vienna, Stockholm, and Leningrad. The Vienna copy was published by Maximilian Curtze (Thorn, 1878), the Stockholm copy by Arvid Lindhagen (Stockholm, 1881). Leopold Prowe's text is based upon both (*op. cit.*, 2: 184-202). English translation by Edward Rosen (*Osiris*, 3: 123-41 [1937]), reprinted in his *Three Copernican Treatises* (Columbia University Press, 1939; reviewed in *Isis*, 32: 358).

112. Wittenberg was the cradle of Lutheranism (1517). The University of Wittenberg, founded in 1502, became after 1517 the first Protestant university; it was made famous by the teaching of Luther and Melanchthon. Rhaeticus was a protégé of the latter. The first complete Lutheran Bible was printed at Wittenberg in 1534.

113. An English translation of the *Narratio prima* appeared in Edward Rosen's book already mentioned (New York, 1939). The same book includes also the translation of a letter which Copernicus addressed from Frauenburg, on June 3, 1524, to the Rev. Bernard Wapowski, Canon of Cracow and secretary to the king of Poland. The purpose was to criticize some astronomical views of Johannes Werner of Nuremberg (1468-1528). One of Werner's books (Nuremberg, 1522) contained a *Libellus super viginti duobus elementis conicis*, the first treatise on conics in Christian Europe. Copernicus must have known it, yet he never thought of using conics instead of combinations of circles; the time was not ripe.

114. *De lateris et angulis triangulorum tum planorum retilineorum tum*

sphaericorum libellus (Wittenberg, 1542). This was printed under Copernicus' name, as was the *Narratio prima* in 1540. Rhaeticus' name does not even appear; this proves his devotion to his master.

115. Culm or Kulm on the Vistula, Chelmno in Polish. It was under Polish control from the fifteenth century to 1772, and again after 1919.

116. It is now easily available in the *Kopernikus gesamtausgabe* (Munich: Oldenbourg, 1944-49). This edition, supervised by Fritz Kubach, is in two quarto volumes, of which the first contains the facsimile of the Nostitz Library Ms., and the second a critical edition of the text printed in 1543 (reviewed in *Isis*, 41: 343).

117. Andreas Osiander (1498-1552) was a Lutheran theologian, professor of Hebrew, and preacher in Nuremberg. He and his followers (the Osiandrists) disagreed with Melanchthon.

118. Alessandro Farnese, Pope under the name of Paul III from 1534 to 1549.

119. Erasmus Reinhold (Rheinholt), *Prutenicae Tabulae coelestium motuum* (Tübingen, 1551) in three parts, each with a separate title.

120. Now in Czechoslovakia. Kaschau is the German name; Kassa in Hungarian, Košice in Czech.

121. It was called *Opus palatinum* in honor of the Elector of Palatine, Frederick IV, who paid the printer's bills. Like all the old tables (e.g., Viète's *Canon* of 1579), it contained a good many errors, for which see R. C. Archibald in *Mathematical Tables and Aids to Computation* (vol. 1, no. 1, p. 30, 1943).

122. According to his own statement in his dedication to the Pope, Copernicus kept his ideas hidden in him "not only nine years but almost four times nine years." The exact interpretation of this statement is difficult, but it is clear that he devoted almost thirty-six years to the elaboration of his ideas; he had passed his seventieth anniversary when he died.

123. The statement was made in a letter by Melanchthon, written on October 16, 1541, during the Copernicus-Rhaeticus collaboration.

124. *Tischreden* (no. 4638, vol. 4, Weimar, 1916), p. 412. This is the only reference to Copernicus in the *Tischreden;* he is not named ("de novo quodam astrologo fiebat mentio qui probaret terram moveri et non coelum . . .").

125. Pierre Gassendi (1592-1655) was one of the first moderns to defend atomism openly. He wrote a Latin biography of Brahe (Paris, 1654; The Hague, 1655; reviewed in *Isis*, 43: 140).

126. Essai XII, in vol. 2 of Pierre Villey's edition (Paris, 1930-31), p. 473.

127. We owe a monumental edition of Brahe's work to John Louis Emil Dreyer (1852-1926): *Tychonis Brahe Opera omnia* (15 vols., Copenhagen, 1913-29); reviewed in *Isis*, 5: 149-51). Vol. 15 contains a general index. We owe him also an excellent biography, *Tycho Brahe* (Edinburgh, 1890); it is a pity that he did not prepare an improved edition of it toward the end of his life. John Allyne Gade's biography, *Life and Times of Tycho Brahe* (Princeton University Press, 1947; reviewed in *Isis*, 39: 176-79), is a more modest book for the general reader; it gives a good account of Brahe's background and of his character but contains many scientific and other errors.

128. The nova of November 1572 was described by Brahe in his *De nova et nullius aevi memoria prius visa stella* (Copenhagen, 1573), facsimile reprint, Copenhagen, 1901; critical edition in Dreyer's *Opera* (vol. 1, 1913).

129. One wonders what Brahe would have thought of the "space wasted" between the galaxies observed by twentieth-century astronomers!

130. Copernicus needed 7 for Mercury, 5 each for Venus, Mars, Jupiter, and Saturn, 4 for the moon, and 3 for the earth.

131. His intellectual training in Copenhagen, Wittenberg, and Rostock was inferior to Copernicus' in Cracow and Italy, and probably his intellectual capacity was much less than that of Copernicus.

132. Hveen (or Hven) in the Öresund separating Denmark from Sweden; it is now in Swedish territory. I did not visit Hveen (where there is little to see) but observed it from the Danish coast, north of Copenhagen.

133. Though nothing remains of the observatory, its organization and equipment are very well known from Brahe's own descriptions in *Astronomiae instauratae mechanica* (Wandsbek in Schleswig-Holstein, 1598). See also Francis Beckett, *Tycho Brahe's Uraniborg and Stjerneborg* (44 pp., folio, pl., Copenhagen, 1921; reviewed in *Isis*, 6: 156), description of Uraniborg in Danish with English summary. A study on the printing-press and its output was written in Danish by Lauritz Nielsen (80 pp., pl., Copenhagen: Pedersen, 1946; reviewed in *Isis*, 41: 112.
Brahe built two observatories, the main one, Uraniborg, in the center of the island and later Stjerneborg (castle of stars) in the southeast angle. For the sake of stability, the latter was underground except for the emerging cupolas.

134. Brahe's observatories, instruments, and methods were described in detail, whereas little is known of the methods of earlier astronomers.

135. He fully recognized their importance and himself published his correspondence with them: *Epistolae astronomicae* (176 pp., Uraniborg, 1596). When the Cassel observatory was neglected after the landgrave's death, Brahe hoped to obtain Rothmann's collaboration but failed.

136. *Nicolai Raymari Ursi Dithmarsi Fundamentum astronomicum* (Strasbourg, 1588). "Ursus" died in 1600.

137. His account of it appeared in his *De mundi aetherii recentioribus phaenomenis, liber secundus qui est de illustri stella caudata* (Uraniborg, 1588). It is reprinted in Dreyer's *Opera* (vol. 4, 1918) together with Brahe's other writings on that comet. The comet was observed in many parts of the world. Western literature ad hoc was surveyed by C. Doris Hellman: *The Comet of 1577* (488 pp., Columbia University Press, 1944; reviewed in *Isis*, 36: 266-70). A study of Arabic, Persian, and Turkish Mss. is being made by Professor Süheyl Ünver of Istanbul, Professor Aydin Sayili of Ankara, and Madame Sevim Tekeli of Ankara.

138. Brahe wanted to investigate each subject as deeply as possible. One subject—say the nova of 1572—would lead to another, and so the work remained unfinished.

139. *Historia coelestis britannica* (folio, vol. 3, prolegomena, pp. 88-90, London, 1725). This was compiled by John Flamsteed (1646-1719), the first astronomer royal. The first edition of 1712, does not include the third volume. Flamsteed lists his own coordinates together with those listed in the *Alphonsine Tables* and those of Copernicus, Brahe, and the landgrave of Hesse.

140. The history of that false concept, trepidation of the equinoxes (i.e., periodic oscillation of the precession around its main value) is very complicated.

See *History of Science,* 1: 445-46. Some mediaeval astronomers rejected it, such as al-Farghānī (IX-1), al-Battānī (IX-2), Ibn Yūnus (XI-1), John of Sicily (XIII-2), Bernard of Verdun (XIII-2), Pietro d'Abano (XIV-1), and Levi ben Gerson (XIV-1). The majority, including Regiomontanus and Copernicus, accepted it. Brahe's rejection, confirmed by Kepler, was final.

141. Brahe was also an astrologer, we should remember, and so was Kepler. Henrik Rantzau (pseudonym Christianus Cilicius Cimber) wrote various astrological books and historical books slanted toward astrology. In 1576 he published a book on hygiene similarly slanted (reprinted five times in the sixteenth century); in 1593, a *Diarium sive Calendarium* giving dates in Julian and Gregorian style 415 pp., Wittenberg, 1593), many times reprinted.

142. *Astronomiae instauratae mechanica* (Wandesburgi-Wandsbeck, 1598). It was translated into English by Hans Raeder, Elis Strömgren, and Bengt Strömgren, except the long dedication to Rudolf II and various poems (144 pp., quarto, ill., Copenhagen: Munksgaard, 1946; reviewed in *Isis,* 41: 109).

143. Maurice, prince of Orange, was the son of Willem the Silent, founder of the Dutch Republic and its first Stadholder (1579-84), and he was Stevin's patron. Brahe could not appeal to Wilhelm IV, Landgrave of Hesse, than whom no one could have helped him more, because Wilhelm died in 1592; his son and successor, Maurice of Hesse, was not interested in astronomy.

144. Styria (Steiermark) was then a province of Austria, under Hapsburg control since 1246. Rudolf II was the upper lord. How then could Kepler find a refuge in Prague? There was more freedom in Prague than in the provinces, and Rudolf II was so fond of astronomers, astrologers, and alchemists that he was willing to overlook their Protestantism. He almost drove the Carthusians out of Prague, because an alchemist had complained that their prayers and services disturbed him!

145. It is interesting to compare the collaboration of Kepler and Brahe with that of Rhaeticus and Copernicus. In both cases the younger man was Protestant, the older Catholic; the collaboration lasted about two years, and the younger man lived to complete the work of the elder. Kepler, however, used Brahe's data for a new and higher purpose. In the field of science this is not treason but justification.

146. It has often been claimed that Newton was the first scientist to be so honored (in 1727), and the French say that Victor Hugo was the first poet to receive national obsequies (in 1885), but Tycho Brahe was much ahead of both.

147. *De vita et morte D. Tychonis Brahe oratio funebris D. Johannis Jessenii* (Prague, 1601; Hamburg, 1610); reprinted by Gassendi in his own biography of Brahe (Paris, 1654), pp. 252-72. It is true that Jessen's praise was part of a funeral oration, yet we may accept it in the same spirit that we accept the criticisms of others.

148. The Latin reads "Nulla in ipso, praeterquam temporis, animadversa avaritia."

149. Drever, *ob. cit.,* pp. 124-25.

150. I use the words "heliocentric theory" because the phrase "Copernican system," which, strictly speaking, means the planetary theory set forth by Coperni-

cus in 1543, may lead to ambiguity. In common language the "Copernican," or heliocentric, system is often opposed to the "Ptolemaic," or geocentric, system. In this sense "the Copernican system" is the one expounded by Kepler in 1609 and 1619.

151. The word is a combination of prosthesis (addition) and aphairesis (subtraction); it is not a very good term to designate the operation made possible by such a formula as

$$2 \sin a \sin b = \cos (a - b) - \cos (a + b).$$

152. Ibn Yūnus had established an observatory in Cairo which lasted from 1005 to the end of Fāṭimī regime in 1171 (Introduction, 1: 716).

153. See Bradley's paper ad hoc in Philosophical Transactions no. 406, vol. 35, pp. 637-61 (1729). Facsimile reproduction in Isis, 16: 233-65 (1931).

154. Ludwig Darmstaedter, Handbuch zur Geschichte der Naturwissenschaften (2te Auflage, Berlin, 1908).

155. A star of annual parallax of 1″ is one from which the radius of the earth's orbit would appear under an angle of 1″. Its distance would be one parsec $=$ 3.258 light years $=$ 3.083 x 10^{13} km.

156. For calendar reform see Introduction, 2: 19-20; 3: 45, 951.

157. It is called Paulina de recta Paschae celebratione (Fossombrone, 1513).

158. Biem's project was first edited by Ludovicus Birkenmajer: Martini Biem de Ilkusz Poloni Nova calendarii romani reformatio, 1516 (Cracow, 1918; reviewed in Isis, 7: 204). Ilkusz (now Olkusz) is near Cracow.

159. Aloysius Lilius, Compendium novae rationis restituendi Kalendarium (Rome, 1577). This was a posthumous publication; Lilius died in 1576.

160. Henri Bernard [Maitre], Matteo Ricci's Scientific Contribution to China (Peiping: Vetch, 1935; reviewed in Isis, 26: 164-67).

161. Clavius, Romani calendarii a Gregorio XIII P. M. restituti explicatio (680 pp., folio, Rome: Zannettus, 1603). Lilio's calendar is inserted in the tables for epacts (numbers denoting the excess of the solar year over 12 lunar months, about 11 days). The most difficult problems to be solved concerned the adaptation of the calendar to the computation of Easter.

162. Clavius was already famous before the pontificate of Gregory XIII, and was called extravagantly "the Euclid of his time." After the promulgation of the new calendar his fame increased considerably. Sixtus V (Pope 1585-90) remarked, "Had the Jesuit order produced nothing else than this Clavius, on this account alone should it be praised" (another extravagance). A more solid proof of his contemporary fame was the publication of his Opera omnia (5 vols., folio, Mainz, 1612), begun before his death. Best bibliography in the Bibliothèque de la Compagnie de Jésus (Brussels, 1891), 2: 1212-24; this includes the Chinese translations.

163. The term "leap year" probably originated as follows. As the ordinary year of 365 days is one day longer than 52 weeks, every date moves one day every year, but leaps two in a leap year. For example, July 4 was a Saturday in 1942, a Sunday in 1943, a Tuesday in 1944 (leap year), a Wednesday in 1945, etc.

164. The morrow of September 2, 1752 was declared to be September 14. The

New Style (as the new calendar was called) implied the beginning of the year on January 1 instead of March 25.

165. *Isis*, 16: 237 (1931).

166. Dreyer, *op. cit.*, pp. 132, 280. I assume that Brahe used it in his astronomical records, not in his correspondence, for that would have been very inconvenient. Such a reform cannot be carried through by an individual but only by a nation.

167. In Van Schooten's edition of Viète's *Opera mathematica* the last three items (vol. 3, pp. 449-544) are devoted to the calendar, *Ratio kalendarij vere Gregoriani, Kalendarium Gregorianum perpetuum, Adversus Christophorum Clavium expostulatio.*

168. Essais III, X, and XI. In Villey's edition (vol. 3, pp. 452, 482): "L'éclipsement nouveau des dix jours du Pape m'ont prins si bas que je ne m'en puis bonnement accoustrer."

169. For *Regimen IV* see *History of Science*, 1: 371; for *Epinomis ibid.*, 1: 453.

170. Simon de Phares, *Recueil des plus célèbres astrologues et quelques hommes doctes*, edited by Ernest Wickersheimer (320 pp., Paris: Champion, 1929; reviewed in *Isis*, 13: 167).

171. Nostradamus (Michel de Nostredame) is perhaps the best known to modern lovers of astrology. Of Jewish origin, he was born in Saint Remy (Bouches du Rhône) in 1503 and died in 1566. He studied medicine in Montpellier, wandered for many years in the south of France, and established himself in 1544 as a physician. He was a devoted doctor, but in 1550 he began to prophesy. He published seven centuries (hundreds) of prognostications (Lyon, 1555) and three centuries more (Lyon, 1558), very often reprinted. When one makes so many prophecies, some of them are bound to be verified, and the others are soon forgotten. He enjoyed the protection of Catherine de' Medici, and his popular reputation was immense.

172. Son of the more justly famous Gemma Frisius (1508-55), whose main scientific contributions were reproduced in facsimile by A. Pogo (*Isis*, 22: 469-506 [1935]).

173. This list, taken at random, could be extended indefinitely.

174. On the comet of 1577 see C. Doris Hellman, *op. cit.* On mediaeval comets see Lynn Thorndike, *Latin Treatises on Comets between 1238 and 1368* (Chicago University Press, 1950; reviewed in *Isis*, 42: 162).

175. (Regiomontanus) *Joannis de Monteregio de Cometae magnitudine longitudineque ac de loco ejus vero problemata XVI* (Nuremberg, 1531), with a preface by Johann Schoner.

176. The story was embellished in later writings, for example in Andrew Dickson White, *History of the Warfare of Science and Theology* (2 vols., New York, 1896, reprinted in 1923). White's story contains many errors, but the central facts are correct: the superstitious fears caused by the comet of 1456 were combined with the fear of Turkish invasions. J. Stein, S.J., "Calixte III et la comète de Halley," *Pubblicazioni della Specola astronomica vaticana*, vol. 2, pp. 5-39, Rome, 1909.

Calixtus had good reason to be frightened, for he witnessed many calamities:

the fall of Constantinople and the Turkish menace—the Turks were then as threatening as were, later, the Germans under Hitler or the Russians under Stalin—a pestilence in Rome, and earthquakes in Naples. The comet was like a symbol of evil done and a presage of more to come.

177. The intervals between successive appearances are unequal because of perturbations induced by Jupiter. The intervals amount to (77 ± 2.5) years. Every passage of the comet since 240 B.C. has been observed, either in Europe or in China, except the one of c.163 B.C.

178. Pierre Bayle, however, must be credited with a generous pre-Halley attack on such superstitions: *Pensées diverses sur la comète de 1680* (Rotterdam, 1683). G. Sarton, "Boyle and Bayle," *Chymia,* vol. 3, 1950, pp. 185, 172.

179. Chiefly but not exclusively Shī'a (*Introduction,* 3: 1068, 1460). For a general introduction to gematria see *ibid.,* 3: 363.

180. Giovanni II Pico della Mirandola (1463-94) began his study of Hebrew in 1485/86. Being helped by three Jewish scholars he obtained a very good knowledge of it and accumulated a collection of 107 Hebrew manuscripts. Pearl Kibre, *The Library of Pico della Mirandola* (344 pp., Columbia University Press, 1936), pp. 37-48.

181. Postel's translation was the first printed publication of the *Sefer yezirah.* The Hebrew original appeared later (Mantua, 1562). For other information on cabalistic treatises see *Introduction,* 2: 366-68, 878-80.

182. Eugene Defrance, "Catherine de Médicis, ses astrologues et ses magiciens envoûteurs," *Documents sur la diplomatie et les sciences occultes au XVIᵉ siècle* (Paris: Mercure de France, 1911).

183. Henry Carrington Bolton, *The Follies of Science at the Court of Rudolph II* (222 pp., Milwaukee, 1904).

184. Lynn Thorndike, "The court of Paul III," in his *History of Magic and Experimental Science* (6 vols., Columbia University Press, 1923-41), vol. 5, pp. 252-74.

185. The best source of information is Lynn Thorndike's work cited above, reviewed in *Isis,* 6: 74-89, 23: 471-75, 33: 691-712. Volumes 4 to 6 deal with the Renaissance, and contain a rich profusion of facts and bibliographical references.

NOTES TO THIRD WING

1. The *Opera omnia* of Cusanus were published once in the fifteenth century and three times in the sixteenth. The first edition, by Martin Flach, in Strasbourg, appeared in two folio volumes after Cusanus' death, perhaps after 1486 and certainly before 1501, without indication of place or date. Volume 1 (102 leaves) contains six treatises including the *De docta ignorantia,* the *Apologia doctae ignorantiae,* and the *Idiotae libri quatuor.* Volume 2 (170 leaves) contains sixteen treatises, *De visione Dei, De pace fidei, Reparatio Kalendarij, De mathematicis complementis, De mathematica perfectione,* etc. The second edition is simply a reprint of the first (Milan: Stefano, Dolcino, 1502). The third edition, more critical and with new items, was prepared by Jacques Lefèvre, Faber Stapulensis (3 vols., Paris: Josse Badius, 1514). Fourth edition, 3 vols. (Basel: Henri Petri, 1565). There are many early editions of separate treatises.

A new edition of the *Opera* is being prepared by the Academy of Heidelberg. Vol. 1, *De docta ignorantia*, edited by Ernest Hoffman and Raymond Klibansky (202 pp., Leipzig: Meiner, 1932; reviewed in *Isis*, 21: 211-13). Vol. 2, *Apologia doctae ignorantiae*, edited by R. Klibansky (61 pp., 1932; reviewed in *Isis*, 20: 457-64). Vol. 5, *Idiota*, edited by L. Bauer (1937). The entire stock of these volumes was destroyed during one of the air attacks on Leipzig, December 4, 1943. The only volume published after the war is Vol. 15, *De non aliud*, post mortem L. Bauer, ed. Paul Wilpert. Vol. 7, *De pace fidei*, edited by R. Klibansky and Dom Hildebrand Bascour, will appear in 1955 (also in Supplement 3 to *Mediaeval and Renaissance Studies of the Warburg Institute*, London). In preparation, Vol. 12, *De venatione sapientiae* and *De apica theoriae*, edited by Klibansky; Vol. 3, *De coniecturis*. Information kindly supplied by Dr. Klibansky, Montreal, December 9, 1954.

The first Cusanus text in English was *The Idiot in four books. The first and second of Wisdome, the third of the Minde, the fourth of statick Experiments or experiments of the Ballance* (232 pp., very small size, London: Will Leak, 1650). The fourth book covers pp. 170 to 231.

Cusanus' library and instruments were bequeathed by him to the hospital (or asylum) that he had founded in Cues, where they still are. His four astronomical instruments, bought in 1444, are the oldest German instruments of their kind in existence. J. Hartmann, "Die astronomischen Instrumente des Kardinals Nikolaus Cusanus," *Abhandlungen der Gesellschaft der Wissenschaften zu Göttingen, math. Kl.*, 10, 56 pp., 12 pls., Berlin, 1919); "Die ältesten deutschen astronomischen Instrumente," *Zeitschrift für Instrumentenkunde*, 40: 221-35, 7 figs., Berlin, 1920; reviewed in *Isis*, 4: 139.

2. Sir William Thomson's presidential address at the British Association for the Advancement of Science, Edinburgh, 1871. See his *Life* by Silvanus P. Thompson (2 vols., London: Macmillan, 1910), vol. 2, p. 600.

3. Hygrometric and sounding instruments were also described by his close contemporary, the Italian Leon Battista Alberti (1401-72). Nicholas' dates are 1401-64.

4. The precision needed for astronomical work was great, because four seconds of time equal one minute of arc. For Brahe's chronometry see J. L. E. Dreyer, *Tycho Brahe* (Edinburgh, 1890), pp. 159, 258, 322-25.

5. The clockmakers must have increased in numbers throughout the sixteenth century, especially in Nuremberg, for they constituted a guild. Until 1568, however, their guild was combined with that of the locksmiths.

6. For details see Abbot Payson Usher, *History of Mechanical Inventions* (rev. ed., Harvard University Press, 1954), pp. 187-210, 304-31. For the pre-Renaissance mechanical clocks see also *Introduction*, 3: 143-44, 716-22, 1124, 1540-47.

7. For the mediaeval incubation see *Introduction*, 3: 145-48, 736-40, 1126-27, 1564-67; *Isis*, 40: 120; 41: 207-10.

8. The principal figures were Giovanni Battista Capuano of Manfredonia (fl. 1475), Alessandro Achillini of Bologna (1463-1512), Leonardo da Vinci (1452-1519), Agostino Nifo (1473-1538), Niccolò Tartaglia of Brescia (1506-59), Girolamo Cardano of Pavia (1501-76), Alessandro Piccolomini of Siena (1508-78), Giovanni Battista Benedetti of Venice (1530-90), Guido Ubaldo del Monte of Pasaro (1545-

1607), and Bernardino Baldi of Urbino (1533-1617). All these men transmitted, corrected, and clarified mediaeval ideas and prepared Galileo's revolution. It would be worth while to investigate in detail their individual contributions and the filiation of their ideas. I am familiar with this Italian chain, but it is possible that similar chains, or links, existed in other countries.

9. *Discorzi e dimostrazione matematiche intomo a due nuove scienze* (Leiden, 1638).

10. For an account of the Archimedian tradition see *Appreciation*, pp. 140-42.

11. More details in my first Stevin memoir (*Isis*, 21: 241-303, 30 figs., [1934]), pp. 250-52, 274-78. Facsimiles of three title pages, pp. 292-93.

12. They were reprinted together under a common title, *Weeghconst* (statics) in his *Hypomnemata mathematica*, which were published in Leiden, 1605-1608, by order of Prince Maurice of Orange, in three editions, Dutch, Latin, and French (the French edition was not completed). The statical writings are collected in the fourth volume of the Latin edition.

13. Examples are given in *Appreciation*, p. 214, note 19.

14. For the invention of gunpowder see *Introduction*, 2: 1036-38; for firearms 3: 722-26, 1547-50; for armor 3: 1555-61; for early treatises on military technology 3: 1550-55. Bernhard Rathgen, *Das Geschütz im Mittelalter* (quarto, Berlin: Verein deutscher Ingenieure, 1928; reviewed in *Isis*, 13: 125-27).

15. To be more precise, "external ballistics" as opposed to "internal ballistics," dealing with the motion of the projectile within the gun.

16. After Prosper Elie Charbonnier, *Essais sur l'histoire de la balistique* (334 pp., Paris, 1928; reviewed in *Isis*, 15: 376-80). Many sixteenth-century and later treatises are enumerated on pp. 273-94. Thomas M. Spaulding and Charles Karpinski, *Early Military Books in the University of Michigan Libraries* (Ann Arbor, 1941; reviewed in *Isis*, 34: 77). According to them, Blondel's book was written in 1675 but Louis XIV forbade its publication at that time lest his enemies profit by it.

17. The parabolic motion of projectiles was discussed by Galileo in his *Discorsi e dimostrazioni matematiche* (Leiden, 1638), Fourth Day, pp. 244 ff. in Crew's translation (New York, 1914). Galileo was not aware of the fact that the parabolic trajectory would occur only in a vacuum.

18. The caliber is the diameter of the bore, which is larger than the diameter of the bullet. The word is derived from the Arabic *qālib* (pl. *qawālīb*) meaning mold or form.

19. Published in his *New Principles of Gunnery* (London, 1742), translated into German by Leonhard Euler (Berlin, 1745), and retranslated into English 1784-1805.

20. For other examples see *Appreciation*.

21. Edited by Fazio Cardano (father of the more famous Geronimo Cardano) and published by Corneno in Pavia in 1482 and in Paris after 1500 (Klebs 738.1-2). It was frequently reprinted until as late as 1627.

22. 288 pp., folio, Basel: Episcopii, 1572. For a longer account of the pre-Renaissance tradition of Ibn al-Haitham see *Introduction*, 1: 721; 2: 22; 3: 141, 1123; also *Isis*, 34: 217-18 (1943). My reference (*Introduction*, 1: 721) to an

earlier edition of Alhazen is misleading. That was not Alhazen's main treatise but a short tract of his, *Petri Nonii de crepusculis . . . Allacen de causis crepusculorum* (Lisbon: Ludovicus Rodericus, 1542). Nonius is the Portuguese mathematician, Pedro Nuñez (1492-1577), inventor of a means of increasing the accuracy of graduated instruments, the *nonius* (later, *vernier*).

23. *Opticae libri quatuor ex voto Petri Rami novissimo per Fridericum Risnerum ejusdem in mathematicis adjutorem olim conscripti* (Cassel: Wilhelm Wessel, 1606). This book was annotated by Willebrord Snel: Johan Adriaan Vollgraff, *Risneri Opticem cum annotationibus Willebrordi Snellii. Pars prima, librum primum continens* (312 pp., Ghent: Plantin, 1918; reviewed in *Isis*, 29: 491), no more published. Willebrord Snel (1596-1626) discovered the law of refraction ten years before Descartes' publication of it in 1637. Vollgraff is best known as the final editor of Huygens' *Opera* (22 vols., The Hague, 1888-1950; reviewed in *Isis*, 29: 431-33; 42: 56-57).

24. There was also a vigorous tradition in Arabic (*Isis*, 34: 217-18) and even one in Hebrew, represented mainly by Levi ben Gerson (XIV-1).

25. *Introduction*, 3: 142, 602, 607. Daniello Barbaro, *La pratica della perspettiva* (Venice: Borgominieri, 1568), p. 192. For G. B. della Porta see below.

26. Henry Crew, *The Rise of Modern Physics* (370 pp., Baltimore, 1928; reviewed in *Isis*, 11: 530), p. 95. The Aristotelian reference is to *Problems*, section XV, chapter 10. The *camera obscura* belongs to the Middle Ages, the telescope to the seventeenth century.

27. Quṭb al-dīn al-Shīrazī (XII-2), al-Qarāfī (XIII-2), Kamāl al-dīn al-Farisi (XIV-1); Witelo (XIII-2), Dietrich von Freiberg (XIV-1).

28. For mediaeval explanations see *Introduction, passim*, 2: 23, 761, 1018; 3: 141, 704, 707. Though al-Qarāfī belongs to the thirteenth century, he was dealt with in *Introduction*, 3: 708. R. E. Ockenden, "M. A. de Dominis and his explanation of the rainbow," *Isis*, 26: 40-49, 2 figs. (1936).

29. He showed his merit in other fields, such as the history of numbers. For example, he argued that every perfect number is hexagonal and hence triangular. This appeared in his *Arithmeticorum libri duo*, at the end of his *Opuscula mathematica* (Venice: Franciscus Senensis, 1575). Leonard Eugene Dickson, *History of the Theory of Numbers* (Cornegie Institution of Washington, 1919), vol. 1, p. 9; reviewed in *Isis*, 3: 446-48.

30. It was published many years after the author's death by the care and with the annotations of his friend, Christopher Clavius (Naples: Tarquinius Longus, 1611). In the dedication by the printer there is a reference to the admirable invention of the optic tube (*optica fistula*), meaning telescope or microscope. The discovery of the telescope had been announced in March 1610 by Galileo in his *Nuncius sidereus*.

31. The book is available to English readers through Henry Crew's translation (New York: Macmillan, 1940; reviewed in *Isis*, 33: 251-53).

32. Many of Della Porta's plays were published separately. First collection of them (Venice, 1597). Complete set (4 vols., Naples, 1726). Modern edition (2 vols., Bari, 1910-11). Many plays were published in English during the eighteenth century.

33. The first edition, in four books, was printed by Matthias Cancer (Naples, 1558), when the author was at least 18, and perhaps 23; then again by Christopher Plantin (135 f., Antwerp, 1561). Later editions are increased to 20 books (Naples, 1589). There are so many editions that the bibliography is difficult. The difficulty is increased because one must consider at least two kinds, the *Magia* in IV books (1558) and the *Magia* in XX (1589). Some of these editions appeared as late as the end of the seventeenth century. The French translation of the *Magia* in IV books printed in Lyon in 1650 has a second part entitled *Introduction à la belle magie, surnaturelle, naturelle et artificielle,* by Lazare Meyssonier.

34. This has been pointed out many times in my *Introduction*, e.g., 3: 45. Lynn Thorndike, "The Catholic Reaction, Index, Inquisition and Papal bulls," *History of Magic,* vol. 6, pp. 145-78 (1941).

35. One of the most successful works of scientific vulgarization of the last century was Louis Figuier's *Les merveilles de la science* (4 vols., plus 2, Paris, 1867-91). Similar titles have been used in our century; there is no harm in them if the word *"merveilles"* is properly understood.

36. *De furtivis literarum notis vulgo de ziferis libri IV* (228 pp., Naples: J. M. Scotus, 1563). This book was reprinted in London by J. Wolph (228 pp., London, 1591); see Joseph S. Galland, *Bibliography of Cryptology* (Northwestern University, 1945), pp. 146-48.

37. *Suae villae pomarium* (323 pp., quarto, Naples: H. Salvienus et C. Caesaris, 1583) and *Suae villae olivatum, sive liber sextus* (78 pp., Naples: M. Cancer's heirs, 1584). These are elaborate descriptions of the orchards and olive groves of his estate, and discussion of the care of fruit trees.

38. *Villae libri XII* (Frankfurt: Wechel's heirs, 1592); architecture of a country house and description of its gardens and arbors. The twelve books of the *Villa* are devoted to (1) the house, (2) trees for cutting, (3) trees producing acorns, (4) cultivation and graftage, (5) orchard, (6) olive yards, (7) vineyards, (8) trees of the vineyard (*arbustum*), (9) flower garden, (10) kitchen garden, (11) cultivated fields, such as corn fields, (12) meadows. Books 5 and 6 were probably reprints or revisions of his earlier books *Pomarium* (1583) and *Olivetum* (1584). This is a treatise on husbandry derived from Della Porta's experience as a country squire but also from many earlier books, chiefly the *Ruralia commoda* of Pietro de' Crescenzi (XIII-2) and the *Praedium rusticum* of his older contemporary, Charles Estienne (1501-64). Pietro de' Crescenzi was a Bolognese, not a Neapolitan like Della Porta. His treatise was printed as early as 1471 (by Schüssler, in Augsburg). There are no less than 13 incunabula, 6 in Latin, 3 in Italian, 2 in French, 2 in German (Klebs, 310-13); also many sixteenth-century editions in Latin, Italian, French, German, and Polish. *Introduction,* 3: 811-15. As to Charles Estienne's *Praedium rusticum,* it was first printed by himself (648 pp., Paris, 1554). It was translated into French, German, Dutch, English (1600), and Italian, and is perhaps best known in its French form, *L'agriculture et maison rustique* (155 f., Paris: J. Du Puis, 1564), often reprinted, commonly called *Maison rustique.*

39. *De humana physiognomonia* (Sorrento, 1586), with his portrait. The purely descriptive part is so rich that Della Porta has been called the founder of physiognomy or Lavater's forerunner. Both designations are wrong. The Swiss

poet, Johann Kaspar Lavater (1741-1801) had many forerunners; the earliest
treatise on the subject, ascribed to Aristotle, was followed by many others in
Greek Arabic, Latin, etc. *Introduction*, 1: 136 and *passim*. For the Arabic physiognomy, Youssef Mourad, *La physiognomie arabe* (162 pp. in French, 90 pp. in
Arabic; Paris: Geuthner, 1939; reviewed in *Isis*, 33: 248-49). Della Porta compared men with various animals, but such comparisons had already occurred in
Aristotle's *Historia animalium*. In short, this was far from being a novelty but was
rather the revival of immemorial and traditional fancies.

40. *Phytognomonica* (Naples: H. Salvianus, 1588), a study of the "physiognomy"
of plants and comparison of plants with animals; also a kind of herbal or a
medley of botany, medicine, and much else.

41. *Pneumatica* (Naples: A. Pace, 1601). Added to it is a mathematical treatise,
Curvilineorum elementorum libri II.

42. *Ars reminiscendi* (42 pp., Naples: J. B. Subtilis, 1602).

43. *Coelestis physiognomoniae libri VI unde quis facile ex humani vultus
extima inspectione poterit ex conjectura futura praesagire, in quibus etiam
astrologia refellitur et in anis . . . demonstratus* (191 pp., quarto, Naples: J.
Subtilis, 1603). A "celestial physiognomy" without astrology!

44. *De distillatione libri IX quibus certa methodo cujuslibet mixti in propria
elementa resolutio perfecte docetur* (154 pp., quarto, Rome, 1608, ex typ.
Camerae apostolicae) with his portrait. Another edition (149 pp., Strasbourg:
Zetzner, 1609) was entitled *De distillationibus*. Della Porta was an alchemist and
believed in the transmutation of metals, but he was also a chemical experimenter, and it is significant that his book was published by the papal press,
perhaps as an antidote against wilder alchemical compositions.

45. *De aëris transmutationibus* (Naples, 1609?; Rome, 1614), on the strength of
which Della Porta was called the first modern meteorologist. This claim, as well
as others made on his behalf with no more justification, is evidence of the prestige that he enjoyed.

46. Nicolas Claude Fabri de Peiresc (1580-1637). Biography in Latin by Gassendi
(Paris, 1641); in French by Pierre Humbert (325 pp., 8 pls., Paris: Desclée, De
Brouwer, 1933; reviewed in *Isis*, 22: 348). Seven volumes of Peiresc's correspondence were published from 1888 to 1898; they cover only the correspondents
whose names begin with A, B, and C.

47. Compare the old Tradescant museum in Oxford described by Robert
Theodore Gunther, *Early Science in Oxford* (vol. 3, 576 pp., ill., Oxford, 1925;
reviewed in *Isis*, 8: 375-77). There were few museums of curiosities in the sixteenth
century, many more in the seventeenth and eighteenth. Modern museology was
very slow in developing.

48. For the early history, which is full of difficulties, see *Introduction*, 2: 1024-
27; 3: 242. The Chinese invention seems to have been contemporary; in any case,
it did not influence the Western one. Marco Polo (XIII-2) does not refer to
spectacles.

49. Richard Greeff. *Die Erfindung der Augengläser* (120 pp.. Berlin: Alexander
Ehrlich, 1921), p. 102. Wills dated from 1372 to 1524. accounts from 1473.

50. E.g., the posthumous *De morbis internis* (Paris: C. Macaeus, 1571) of

Jacques Houlier, or the *Ophalmoduleia, das ist Augendienst* (Dresden: Mathes Stöckel, 1583) of Georg Bartisch.

51. The earliest scientific book on spectacles was written in Spanish by Benito Daza de Valdes: *Uso de los antojos para todo genero de vistas en que se enseña a conocer los grados que á cada uno le faltan de su vista* (Seville, 1623), but that takes us out of the Renaissance.

52. The Virgin and Child, of the Milanese school, plate 2 in Greeff's book, cited. No source given and no date, but presumably sixteenth century.

53. *Introduction*, 2: 761.

54. Frédéric Marguet, *Histoire générale de la navigation du XV° au XX° siècle* (307 pp., Paris, 1931; reviewed in *Isis*, 19: 235-37). In spite of its title, this book does not contain much information on Renaissance navigation. For ancient coastal navigation, see Richard Lefèbvre des Noëttes, *De la marine antique à la marine moderne. La révolution du gouvernail, contribution à l'histoire de l'esclavage* (Paris: Masson, 1935; reviewed in *Isis*, 26: 484-86). There is an excellent discussion of fifteenth-century navigation in Samuel Eliot Morison, *Admiral of the Ocean Sea: A Life of Christopher Columbus* (2 vols., 894 pp., ill., Boston: Little Brown, 1942; reviewed in *Isis*, 34: 169-172); the author is not only a great historian, but also a sailor and an admiral.

55. There are many studies of Renaissance meteorology, but none comparable in amplitude and accuracy to those of Gustav Hellmann (1854-1939), whose work deserves high tribute. I have in my files a complete bibliography of Hellmann's writings prepared by the Reichsamt für Wetterdienst in Berlin (May 1937) and corrected by the U. S. Weather Bureau. I had planned to publish it in *Osiris* but have not yet been able to do so (March 1956). His most important works are listed below.

From 1893 to 1904 Hellmann edited the *Neudrucke von Schriften und Karten über Meteorologie und Erdmagnetismus* (Berlin: Asher), in fifteen parts, the last of which contains addenda and errata to the whole series (reviewed in *Isis*, 1: 706; 2: 139; etc.)

Neudrucke no. 1 (1863) contains Leonard Reynman's *Wetterbüchlein von wahrer Erkenntnis des Wetters*, first published by Hans Schobosser in Munich in 1510. This was one of the first books of its kind in German.

Another book (*Neudrucke* no. 5, 1896), *Die Bauern-Praktik*, meant for the peasantry, was exceedingly popular. The first edition was issued in 1508; there were 40 editions in the sixteenth century, but only 19 in the next three centuries. The *Bauern-Praktik* was translated into French, English, Czech, Dutch, Danish, Norwegian, Swedish, and Finnish.

Rara Magnetica, 1269-1599 (Neudrucke no. 10, 1898).

Wetterprognosen und Wetterberichte des XV. und XVI. Jahrhunderts (Neudrucke no. 12, 1899).

Meteorologische Optik, 1000-1836 (Neudrucke no. 14, 1902).

Beiträge zur Geschichte der Meteorologie, Veröffentlichungen des K. Preussischen Meteorologischen Instituts, nos. 1-15, Berlin: Behren, 1914-22. This contains many monographs on Renaissance meteorology, such as no. 1, *Aus der Blütezeit der Astrometeorologie*, and no. 6, *J. Stöflers Prognose für das Jahr 1524*

(1914). *Entwicklungsgeschichte des meteorologischen Lehrbuches* (1917), no. 8. *Die Wettervorhersage im ausgehenden Mittelalter, XII. bis XV. Jahrhundert* (1917), no. 14. *Die Meteorologie in ausserdeutschen Flugschriften und Flugblättern* (1922).

Die Meteorologie in den deutschen Flugschriften und Flugblättern des XVI. Jahrhunderts (*Abhandlungen der preussischen Akademie der Wissenschaften, physische Klasse*, 96 pp., Berlin, 1921; reviewed in *Isis*, 5: 224).

Many of Hellmann's investigations were centered upon German writings, but these were not essentially different from those of other countries.

For *computi, calendaria*, etc., which often contained weather forecasts, see the note on Anianus (XIII-2) in my *Introduction* (2: 992), my review of *Le grant Kalendrier* (*Isis*, 8: 354-55), and Klebs (1937) under the headings *Calendarium, Compost et calendrier des bergers, Computi, Kalender deutsch*.

56. The *Ephemerides* of Regiomontanus (Nuremberg: Regiomontanus, 1474, etc.; Klebs 839.1-14); the *Tabulae astronomicae* of Alfonso X el Sabio (Venice: Ratdolt, 1483; Klebs 50.1-2); the *Tabulae celestium motuum et canones* of Giovanni Bianchini (Venice: Bevilaqua, 1495; Klebs 188.1); the *Almanach perpetuum* of Abraham ben Samuel Zacuto (Leira: Samuel d'Ortes, 1496; Venice, 1496; Klebs 1054, 1-4).

57. Abraham ben Samuel Zacuto (b. Salamanca 1450, d. Turkey c.1515) and Martin Behaim (b. Nuremberg 1459?, d. Lisbon 1507) were almost exactly contemporary.

58. All these tables were used much more by astrologers than by navigators; this explains their relative abundance, the former being far more numerous than the latter.

59. Rupert T. Gould, *The Marine Chronometer* (London: J. D. Potter, 1923; reviewed in *Isis*, 6: 122-29). It was only in 1825 that chronometers were generally issued to ships of the British navy.

60. Morison, *Admiral of the Ocean Sea*, cited, vol. 1, p. 243.

61. An excellent account of Columbus' navigation was given by Samuel Eliot Morison in *Admiral of the Ocean Sea*, cited, vol. 1, pp. 240-63. Columbus' navigation was very primitive; many improvements were made during the sixteenth century, yet Renaissance navigation was rudimentary until the end. Columbus was a D.R. (dead reckoning) navigator pure and simple, but one of uncanny genius. Like every other navigator he used sounding leads in the vicinity of land.

62. George Anson (1697-1762), admiral. Quoted from *Isis*, 6: 122. Similar examples are given by F. Marguet, *Histoire générale de la navigation*, cited, pp. 57 ff.

63. For the early history of the compass see *Introduction*, 1: 764; 2: 24, 629; 3: 714-16, 143, 151. Li Shi-hua, "Origine de la boussole," *Isis*, 45: 78-94, 175-96 (1954), elaborate restatement of the Chinese case. According to Li the use of the compass for navigation was already described c.1116 in the Pên-ts'ao-yen-i. See, however, *Introduction*, 1: 764.

64. *Isis*, 37: 178. Facsimile of title page.

65. This text and nine sixteenth-century texts were reprinted with facsimiles by Gustav Hellmann, "Rara magnetica, 1269-1599," *Neudrucke von Schriften und Karten über Meteorologie und Erdmagnetismus*, no. 10 (Berlin: Asher, 1898).

66. For the history of magnetic declination, see *Introduction*, 3: 715, 183, 1124, 1506. A. Crichton Mitchell, "The discovery of the magnetic declination," *Terrestrial Magnetism*, 42: 241-80 (1937); reviewed in *Isis*, 29: 261.

67. Nowhere on his routes was the declination more than half a point (5⅝°), and in the West Indies he was often in places of zero declination. Happily for early navigators, there was no "deviation" (aberration caused by the ship itself) in the time of wooden ships.

68. Facsimile reprint of it (folio, 180 pp., Munich: Obernetter, 1915) in the collection edited by Joaquim Bensaude, *Histoire de la science nautique portugaise à l'époque des grandes découvertes*, vol. 5. On Bensaude's efforts see *Isis*, 1: 716-18; 3: 424-26. H. D. Harradon, "Treatise on the sphere and the art of navigation, Francisco Falero," *Terrestrial Magnetism*, June 1943, pp. 79-91; "The shadow instrument by Pedro Nunes," *ibid.*, December 1943, pp. 197-99.

69. H. D. Harradon, "Extracts on magnetic observations from logbooks of João de Castro, 1538-39 and 1541," *Terrestrial Magnetism*, September 1944, pp. 185-98.

70. Pedro de Medina (c.1493-?), *Arte de Navigar* (folio, s.l., 1545), liber VI, cap. III, VI. Italian translation (Venice, 1555), French (Lyon, 1561, 1569, 1576). Ernst Gerland, *Geschichte der Physik* (Munich, 1913), p. 237.

71. H. D. Harradon, "The letter of Georg Hartmann to Duke Albrecht of Prussia," *Terrestrial Magnetism*, September 1943, pp. 126-30.

72. For Fracastoro and Sanuto see Ludwig Darmstaedter, *Handbuch zur Geschichte der Wissenschaften* (Berlin, 1908), *sub annis* 1530, 1588. Mercator's text is given in English by H. D. Harradon, "Mercator to Antonius Perrenotus, bishop of Arras, 1546," *Terrestrial Magnetism*, December 1943, pp. 200-202. Mercator conceived the magnetic pole as different from the geographical pole, but his location of it was arbitrary.

73. Not published in the *Philosophical Transactions* but separately. Reprinted in G. Hellmann, *Neudrucke* no. 4 (Berlin, 1895), oldest map of isogonic, isoclinic, and isodynamic lines, 1701-1821. We may recall that Halley was also the author of the first meteorological chart, which illustrated his historical account of the trade winds and monsoons (*Philosophical Transactions* no. 183, 1688). Reprinted in Hellmann's *Neudrucke* no. 8 (Berlin, 1897).

74. Variation means declination. The word variation is still used in America with that meaning. This use should be deprecated, because declination varies in space and time and it is awkward to speak of variations of the variation.

75. The Latin translation, *Limeneuretice sive Portuum investigandorum ratio* (Leiden, 1599), was made by no less a personage than Hugo Grotius (1583-1645), author of the *De iure belli ac pacis* (Paris, 1625), sometimes called the founder of international law. G. Sarton, "Science and peace," *Isis*, 42: 3-9 (1951). The English translation was done by Edward Wright, *The haven-finding art* (London, 1599). The French one, *Trouve-port*, was also published in 1599 and reprinted in *Les oeuvres mathématiques de Simon Stevin augmentées par Albert Girard* (Leiden: Elzevir, 1634, vol. 2, pp. 171-76). I denied the existence of the French edition of 1599 (*Isis*, 21: 256 [1934]), but a copy of it was offered for sale by Herbert Reichner (New York) in 1944. There is a copy also in the Bibliothèque Nationale, Paris, *Le Trouve-port traduit d'allemand en françois* (30 pp., fig.,

Leiden: Plantin, 1599). It was translated not from German, as the title says, but from Dutch.

76. For Stevin's *Havenvinding*, see *Isis*, 21: 253-56, 279 (1934). For Petrus Plancius (1552-1622), see his Dutch biography by J. Keuning (187 pp., ill., Amsterdam, 1946; reviewed in *Isis*, 41: 213-14). Petrus Platevoet (Plancius) was a Fleming like Stevin, but he was born near Bailleul (now Département du Nord, France), Busbecq's native country. H. D. Harradon, "The Haven-finding art of Stevinus," *Terrestrial Magnetism*, March 1945, pp. 63-68.

77. See Naples edition of 1589, p. 143.

78. *Mécographie de l'eymant* . . . (Toulouse et Venès, 1603); *Mécométrie de l'eymant, c'est à dire la manière de mesurer les longitudes par le moyen de l'eymant* (folio, 327 pp., Venès, 1603).

79. *A Discourse mathematical on the variation of the magneticall needle. Together with its admirable diminution lately discovered by Henry Gellibrand, professor of astronomie in Gresham College* (22 pp., London: William Jones, 1635). Facsimile reprint in Hellmann's *Neudrucke*, no. 9 (Berlin, 1897).

80. I used the facsimile edition published by Mayer and Müller (Berlin, 1892).

81. Rufus Suter, "A biographical sketch of Dr. William Gilbert," *Osiris*, 10: 368-84 (1952). Includes the Latin text of the epitaph and English translation.

82. Fabricius ab Aquapendente (1537-1619), professor in Padua after 1562. His most famous pupil was William Harvey, who studied in Padua from 1597 to 1601, that is, about thirty years later than Gilbert.

83. The Royal College of Physicians had been founded in 1518, largely because of Linacre's efforts. Thus did Linacre pave the way for Gilbert twice, in Cambridge and in London.

84. The one who influenced him most was probably the mathematician Edward Wright, author of *Certaine errors in navigation* (London: Sims, 1599), who wrote a eulogistic preface to the *De magnete*. Gilbert befriended also another mathematician, Henry Briggs, the inventor of decimal logarithms.

85. This was partly confirmed soon after Gilbert's death by the Arctic explorer, Henry Hudson (d. 1611). Hudson found in 1608 that the dipping needle was almost vertical in lat. 75°.

86. According to Thomas Blundeville's book of 1602, Gilbert had thought of determining the *latitude* at sea by measurement of the inclination.

87. This recalls a superstition that was prevalent until our own day and probably still is, the value of "sleeping along the meridian" (*Isis*, 22: 525-29 [1935]; 25: 449 [1936]; 26: 448-49 [1937]).

88. That fancy was developed by Kepler.

89. This is natural enough. The scholastic methods of dialectic had formed minds for a thousand years and could not be easily abandoned. The power of scholasticism subdued Gilbert as it did Descartes a generation later, not to mention the rank and file.

90. Thomas Blundeville, writer on horsemanship (1565) and other subjects, who flourished at Newton Flotman in Norfolk.

91. Sir William Boswell (d. 1649), ambassador at The Hague (*orator apud Foederatos Belgas*).

92. Many examples are given by Jean Pelseneer: "Gilbert, Bacon, Galilée, Képler, Harvey et Descartes; leurs relations," *Isis*, 17: 171-208 (1932).

93. Among these investigations I should like to single out those carried under the auspices of the Carnegie Institution, of which I had the honor to be a member. A branch of the Institution, the Department of Terrestrial Magnetism, was created in 1904. Its first director was Louis Agricola Bauer (1865-1932), who had earlier obtained recognition by his elaborate study of the secular variations of terrestrial magnetism. "Beiträge zur Kenntniss des Wessens der Säcular-Variation des Erdmagnetismus" (dissertation, Berlin, 1895).

94. For *portolani*, see *Introduction*, 2: 1047-50; 3: 182, 1141, 1144, 1591, 1599. There were ancient, Byzantine and Arabic, probably also Chinese, equivalents of the Western *portolani* but none has yet been discovered. Armand Delatte, *Les portulans grecs* (Liége, 1947; reviewed in *Isis*, 40: 71-72).

95. Nuñez called it *rumbus* after the Greek *rhombos*, meaning a magic wheel; the name *rumbus* (rhumb in English) was given to any point of the compass or wind rose and hence to the line of navigation in any constant direction. The term loxodrome (opposed to orthodrome, great circle) was introduced by Willebrord Snel in his Latin translation of Stevin's *Liber de histiodromia* (Leiden, 1605), in the *Hypomnemata mathematica*. The name loxodrome is used only in mathematical language; English sailors continue to say rhumb (or rhumbline).

96. For references, see G. Sarton, "Simon Stevin," *Isis*, 21: 278 (1934). Mercator's "correction" of 1541 was relative. Globes were far too small for great correction. On a globe of 60 cm. radius (an unusually large one), 1 mm. $=$ 11.5 miles! (Marguet, cited, p. 44).

97. In the Mercator projection the meridians are parallel to each other and the parallels of latitude are straight lines whose distance from each other increases with their distance from the equator, so that the degrees of latitude and longitude always remain in the same ratio as they are on the sphere. It is almost the same as the cylindric projection, where the sphere is projected from its center upon a cylinder tangent along the equator, and the cylinder is then developed upon a plane.

98. For Biondo and Petrarch's map, see *Introduction*, 3: 510.

99. Klosterneuburg is in Lower Austria, on the Danube, seventeen miles northwest of Vienna. Elaborate study of the cartographic work of that school by Dana Bennett Durand, *The Vienna-Klosterneuburg map corpus of the fifteenth century* (510 pp., 23 pls., Leiden: Brill, 1952; reviewed in *Isis*, 44: 384-85).

100. G. de Reparaz, "Les précurseurs de la cartographie terrestre. La première carte topographique a été levée au Portugal au XVIᵉ siècle," *Actes du VIᵉ Congrès international d'histoire des sciences*, 249-60, 2 figs., Amsterdam, 1950; reviewed in *Isis*, 44: 118.

101. F. G. Emmison, *Catalogue of maps in the Essex Record Office 1566-1855* (Chelmsford, 1947; reviewed in *Isis*, 41: 402).

102. Fernand Van Ortroy, "Bibliographie de l'oeuvre de Pierre Apian," *Le bibliographe moderne*, 5: 89-156, 284-333 (1901). Charles Sherrington, *The Endeavour of Jean Fernel with a list of the editions of his writings* (233 pp., Cambridge University Press, 1946; reviewed in *Isis*, 41: 212). Fernel was primarily a

physician and Sir Charles' attention was naturally focused upon physiology, not geodesy. Alexander Pogo, "Gemma Frisius," *Isis*, 22: 469-507 (1935), including complete facsimiles. The memoir of Franz Joh. Müller, *Studien zur Geschichte der theoretischen Geodäsie* (212 pp., Augsburg, 1918; reviewed in *Isis*, 3: 438-39) is not relevant because it begins only in the seventeenth century.

103. The history of topography is an endless subject. To appreciate its scope it will suffice to consult the list of geographical atlases in the Library of Congress, compiled by Philip Lee Phillips (4 vols., Washington, 1909-20; *Introduction*, 3: 1899) or better still the volumes of *Imago Mundi*, an annual publication devoted to the history of cartography, edited by Leo Bagrow (since 1935; *Horus*, 220; for vol. 8, 1951, *Isis*, 44: 181). The subject partakes of science, bibliography (of the most difficult kind), and art, and its devotees require a special and complex training. Their investigations are very tricky, but enjoyable in proportion.

104. History of the Platonic Academy in *History of Science*, 1: 397-400, 1952.

105. Paul Oskar Kristeller, *Il pensiero filosofico di Marsilio Ficino* (512 pp., Florence: Sanson, 1953), pp. 334-37. The same book was translated into English before its publication in Italian (455 pp., Columbia University Press, 1943). I have not seen the English edition; the Italian one contains a list of all the authors mentioned by Ficino (pp. 451-63).

106. Interlaced design in a circle with the inscription in its central part. Reproduction of it in Edward MacCurdy, *The Notebooks of Leonardo* (New York: Reynal and Hitchcock, 1938), vol. 2, p. 588. Jean Paul Richter, *The Literary Works of Leonardo* (Oxford University Press, 1939), vol. 1, p. 393, footnote on page 387. Dürer copied the design without the inscription, or with his own monogram instead.

107. Examples in *Isis*, 16: 143-45 (1931).

108. Bernardino Telesio (1509-88) of Cosenza in Calabria. His main work was the *De rerum natura juxta propria principia* (Rome: Bladus, 1565). Edition by Vincenzo Spampanato (3 vols., Modena, 1910-23; reviewed in *Isis*, 2: 206-208).

109. It was revived in Rimini in 1745 for a short period, reorganized in Rome in 1795, suppressed again in 1840, reestablished in 1847, abolished by Mussolini in 1939, and reestablished in 1944. Thus it was wrong to say in 1950 that the Accademia dei Lincei was then 347 years old; it was first founded in 1603 and by 1950 had been in existence, off and on, for 170 years.

110. *Crusca* means chaff or bran. The Florentine academy took *Crusca* for its name and a sieve for its emblem to show its function of separating good words from bad ones. The idea was excellent, but the name was not felicitous, for their purpose was to keep the good part of the grain and throw out the chaff. Should it not have been called the *Accademia della farina*, rather than *della crusca?*

111. Henri Pirenne, *Histoire de Belgique* (Brussels: Lamartin, 1923), vol. 3, 3rd ed., pp. 324-28. Victor Fris, *Bibliographie de l'histoire de Gand* (Gand: Vyt, 1907), p. 199.

112. Fourteen treatises of the XIV/XV centuries are described in *Introduction*, 3: 1550-54.

113. This final appointment is explained by the fact that Pier Luigi Farnese

was the son of Alessandro Farnese, who was Pope Paul III from 1534 to 1549. It is impossible ever to forget that old rascal, Paul III, if one has seen Titian's portrait of him, painted c.1545-49 (Vienna).

114. Klebs 227.1. G. Sarton, "The scientific literature transmitted through the incunabula," *Osiris*, 5: 41-245 (Bruges, 1938), figs. 44-45.

115. Much earlier in the Islamic East. See the Arab treatise on the distillation of perfumes by al-Kindī (IX-1), edited by Karl Garbers (Leipzig, 1948; reviewed in *Isis*, 41: 103 [1950]).

116. E. O. von Lippmann, "Zur Geschichte der ununterbrochenen Kühlung bei der Destillation," *Lippmann's Beiträge*, pp. 127-36 (1923); reviewed in *Isis*, 5: 507.

117. For orientation on mediaeval glass see *Introduction*, 2: 1040, 30, 219, 767.

118. First edition, Rome, 1857. *Introduction*, 3: 756.

119. The story has been beautifully told by Charles Singer: *The Earliest Chemical Industry. An essay in the historical relations of economics and technology illustrated from the alum trade* (352 pp., folio, many ills., London: Folio Society, 1948; reviewed in *Isis*, 41: 128-31). My account is almost exclusively derived from Singer's.

120. La Tolfa is just east of Civitavecchia, on the Tyrrhenian coast, northwest of Rome.

121. Arthur John Hopkins, "A modern theory of alchemy," *Isis*, 7: 58-76 (1925).

122. These delusions have been described more fully in "Ancient alchemy and abstract art," *Journal of the History of Medicine*, 9: 157-73 (New Haven, 1954).

123. Einsiedeln is in one of the oldest cantons of Switzerland, called Schwyz (incorporated in 1291). There is a Benedictine abbey dating back to the tenth century, with a famous black image of the Holy Virgin, thanks to which it became a great center of pilgrimage. Zwingli was parish priest there from 1516 to 1518.

124. Paracelsus' mother was a *Gotteshausfrau des Gotteshauses unserer lieben Frau zu Einsiedeln*.

125. Family of financiers and industrialists; the Rothschilds of the German Renaissance.

126. In the province of Salzburg (Austria). The deathplace of Paracelsus was to be in 1756 the birthplace of Mozart.

127. As early as 1527, in his Basel program, he called himself "utriusque medicinae Doctor ac Professor," which means doctor and teacher of medicine and surgery. He also called himself later Doctor of Holy Writ. He was certainly not a doctor of theology. Was he ever an M.D.? He obtained his *Strassburger Burgrecht* in the Luzerne, the guild of grain-dealers, millers, and surgeons! As a rule, the surgeons were not M.D.'s. According to him, however, he obtained his M.D. in Ferrara. Ernest Wickersheimer, "Paracelse à Strasbourg," *Centaurus*, 1: 356-65 (Copenhagen, 1951). Owsei Temkin, "The elusiveness of Paracelsus," *Bulletin of the History of Medicine*, 26: 201-17 (Baltimore, 1952).

128. Erasmus consulted Paracelsus and there is a medical letter in Latin from the latter to the former written at the end of 1526 (Paracelsus, *Opera omnia*, Sudhoff's ed., 3: 379 [1930]).

129. The students (at least of German universities) celebrated the night of St.

John the Baptist's Day (June 24) with various revelries and a bonfire. It was a night of good-humored extravagance, but Paracelsus used it for a revolt of a deeper kind.

130. The Swiss German (High Alamannic) of the sixteenth century was so different from the literary language that the Germans (not to mention the non-Germans) had difficulty in understanding it.

131. This point of view, very different from that of today, remained dominant until the end of the last century. The Renaissance doctor would have quoted Matthew 7: 6.

132. He recognized it in the preface to his *Paragranum*, drafted in 1529 (Sudhoff edition, 8: 31-125).

133. Capital of the Tirol from c.1420.

134. For the Latin text see Carl Aberle, *Grabdenkmal, Schädel und Abbildungen des Paracelsus* (Salzburg, 1891).

135. Johan Thölde (or Thölden), a Hessian, flourished in the XVI/XVII centuries. He was an industrial chemist as well as an alchemist and part owner of salt works in Thuringia. John Ferguson, *Bibliotheca chemica*, 2: 445-46 (Glasgow, 1906).

136. "*To chaos*" means space; in Hesiod (Theogony 116) the rude unformed whole. It is somewhat like the *tohu wabohu* of Genesis 1: 2.

137. As quoted in English by John Maxson Stillman, *Paracelsus* (192 pp., Chicago: Open Court, 1920), p. 102.

138. Sudhoff listed 73 authors of Paracelsian writings, 34 of them belonging to the sixteenth century (*Bibliographia Paracelsica*, Berlin, 1894, pp. 698-703). Lynn Thorndike, *History of Magic* (vol. 5, 1941), chap. 29, pp. 617-51; chap. 30, "The Paracelsian revival," pp. 652-70, Thomas Erastus or Lieber.

As I have not been able to examine all the Paracelsian books, I cannot be sure that those I have seen are the most significant. Gerard Dorn of Frankfurt wrote the *Clavius totius philosophiae chymisticae* (302 pp., Lyon: heirs of Jacobus Juncta, 1567). Alexander von Suchten of Danzig was the author of the *Clavis alchemiae* and the *De secretis antimonii* (Strasbourg: Michael Toxites, 1570). This Toxites, né Schütz, edited the *Testamentum Paracelsi* (Strasbourg: Ch. Müller, 1574) and an alchemical dictionary *Onomastica duo, 1. Philosophum medicum, 2. Paracelsi* (490 pp., Strasbourg: Bernhard Jobinus, 1574). Adam von Bodenstein of Basel, son of the early Lutheran reformer, Andreas Rudolph Bodenstein of Karlstadt, edited many of Paracelsus' writings and compiled another *Onomasticon* (Basel: Peter Perna, 1575), which is an index to Paracelsian terminology. Leonard Thurneysser cultivated the quackish fringe of Paracelsism and was himself an adventurer and crook of the first magnitude. At the other end of the scale, Andreas Libau, about whom more will be said presently, was more critical. The most distinguished of Paracelsus' adversaries was Thomas Lieber (1522-83) or Erastus, professor of medicine in Heidelberg and Basel. All these were Germans, but there were early Paracelsists in other countries, for example, the Gascon Joseph Duchesne (1544-1609) or Quercetanus.

139. Only 16 of Paracelsus' books were published within his lifetime, chiefly medical works like his first book on guaiac, *Vom Holtz Guiaco* (1529), his *Practica*

(1529), and his book on syphilis, *Von der Französischen Kranckheit* (1530), all of which were printed by Friedrich Peypus in Nuremberg, and the *Grosse Wundartzney* (Ulm: Hans Varnier, 1536), often reprinted, upon which his medical reputation was based. The 16 titles were represented by 28 editions that appeared between 1527 and 1539. Many of his other works circulated *sub rosa* in manuscript form.

Before 1589, 192 editions of Paracelsian works had appeared, one of them being a Latin edition of 26 titles (2 vols., 1900 pp., Basel: Peter Perna, 1575), yet even then much remained unpublished. A great step forward was taken by Johann Huser of Waldkirch im Breisgau, south Baden. Huser, who was a physician in Gross-Glogau, Silesia (now in southwest Poland), collected many manuscripts at a time when more were available than now, and published the first large edition of *opera omnia* (11 vols., Basel: Conrad Walkirch, 1589-91). This edition was reprinted many times, the last time in three volumes by de Tournes (Geneva, 1658). Huser's edition was not by any means complete, yet it included various apocryphal writings, some of which he himself recognized as such.

A critical edition was prepared under the direction of Karl Sudhoff (1853-1938); the books on medicine, natural sciences, and philosophy cover fourteen volumes (Munich: Otto Wilhelm Barth, 1922-33; reviewed in *Isis*, 6: 56), and those on theology and religion, edited by Wilhelm Matthiesen, one more (1923). Other modern editions have appeared in the original German Swiss text, in German translation, or in other languages. The whole of the scientific books, as edited by Sudhoff, was translated into modern German by Bernard Aschner (4 vols., Jena, 1926).

The first translator of Paracelsus into English was John Hester (d. 1593), distiller of St. Paul's Wharf, who published *A hundred and fourteene experiments and cures* (London: V. Sims, 1596). Of other English translations it will suffice to mention C. Lilian Temkin, George Rosen, Gregory Zilboorg, and Henry E. Sigerist, *Four Treatises in English* (270 pp., Baltimore: Johns Hopkins University Press, 1941; reviewed in *Isis*, 34: 48). *Volumen Medicinae Paramirum*, English translation by Kurt Leidecker, Supplement no. 11 to *Bulletin of the History of Medicine*, Baltimore, 1949.

The main Paracelsus scholar of our time was Karl Sudhoff, who, in addition to the *Opera omnia*, published an elaborate bibliography and many monographs.

Karl Sudhoff, *Versuch einer Kritik der Echtheit der Paracelsischen Schriften. I. Theil. Bibliographica Paracelsica, 1527-1893; II. Theil. Paracelsus-Handschriften* (2 vols., Berlin: Georg Reimer, 1894-99).

Eduard Schubert and Karl Sudhoff, *Parecelsus Forschungen* (2 parts, Frankfurt, 1887-89).

Acta Parcelsica, edited by Ernst Darmstaedter (Munich, 1930-32), with Supplement.

Nova Acta Paracelsica, edited by Linus Birchner (Basel, 1944 ff.).

A few biographies and special studies: Anna M. Stoddart (1880-1911), *The Life of Paracelsus* (324 pp., London: Murray, 1911).

Emanuel Rádl, "Paracelsus," *Isis*, 1: 62-94 (1913), reprinted in his history of biological theories (*Horus*, 172).

John Maxson Stillman, *Paracelsus* (192 pp., Chicago: Open Court, 1920; reviewed in *Isis*, 4: 146).

Ernst Darmstaedter, "Arznei und Alchemie. Paracelsus-Studien" (85 pp., *Studien zur Geschichte der Medizin*, Heft 20, Leipzig, 1931; reviewed in *Isis*, 17: 494).

Karl Sudhoff, *Paracelsus* (156 pp., Leipzig: Bibliographisches Institut, 1936).

Franz Strunz (1875-1953), *Paracelsus* (274 pp., Leipzig, 1937; reviewed in *Isis*, 28: 469-71).

Carl G. Jung, *Paracelsica* (188 pp., Zürich, 1942; reviewed in *Isis*, 39: 44-48).

Henry M. Pachter, *Paracelsus* (375 pp., New York: Schuman, 1951; reviewed in *Isis*, 42: 244-46).

A survey of Paracelsism is very much needed, but so far we have only a Swedish contribution by Sten Lindroth, *Paracelsismen i Sverige till 1600—taletts mitt* (540 pp., Lychnos-Bibliotek, 7, Uppsala, 1943; reviewed in *Isis*, 36: 223). One of the chapters discusses the relationship of Paracelsism and Ramism.

140. These two disputes were connected, for the Paracelsists were, of necessity, anti-Aristotelians.

141. The *spiritus fumans* or fuming liquor of Libavius was the liquor or spirit of mercury sublimate. The glass of antimony was a combination of antimony trioxide and antimony trisulphide having a vitreous appearance.

142. Libavius was a voluminous writer, and his later reputation has suffered from this. All of his works have long titles, and in three cases the title begins with the same word, *Alchemia*. These three volumes, though very different, had the same "quoting titles" and were naturally confused (I was one of the victims). Let us exhibit them together:

(1) The earliest is *Alchemia . . . opera e dispersis passim optimorum autorum, veterum & recentium exemplis potissimum, tum etiam preceptis quibusdam operose collecta, adhibitisque ratione & experientia quanta potuit esse, methodo accurata explicata, & in integrum corpus redacta . . .* (the full title covers two pages). A second volume attached to the first, and probably bound with it, is entitled *Commentationum metallicarum libri quatuor de natura metallorum, mercurio philosophorum, azotho et lapide seu tinctura physicorum conficienda . . .* (2 vols., Frankfurt: Peter Kopff, 1597). Vol. 1, 440 pp. plus 18 pp. index; vol. 2, 400 pp.

(2) *Alchymia recognita, emendata et aucta tum dogmatibus et experimentis nonnullis, tum commentario medico, physico, chymico, qui exornatus est variis instrumentorum chymicorum picturis . . .* (folio, 196 pp. plus index, Frankfurt: Peter Kopff, 1506 [meaning 1606]).

(3) *Alchymia triumphans de injusta in se collegii Galeni spurii in Academia parisiensi censura et Joannis Riolani maniographia falso convicta . . .* (928 pp., octavo, Frankfurt: Peter Kopff, 1607).

In these three books, and others of his, the title proper is preceded by the letters D.O.M.A., which probably mean *Deo optimo maximo aeterno*.

These three enormous volumes, published in 1597, 1606, and 1607, are obviously different in size and contents. I have been able to examine only the first one and hence cannot make any comparison. Another book of his in German entitled

Alchymistische Practic (293 pp., quarto, Frankfurt: Peter Kopff, 1603) is probably the translation of no. 1, the original of no. 2, or a new mixture; I have no means of judging. The third *Alchymia* was directed against Jean Riolan the elder, the first of the two Riolans who abused their great influence to steer the Parisian faculty away from "modern" medicine. Jean Riolan (1538-1605) was an ardent defender of Hippocratic medicine against the new "chemical" medicine. His son, Jean Riolan (1580-1657), better known than the father, was an anatomist and Harvey's main adversary. The elder Riolan answered Libavius' criticism in his *Ad Libavimaniam responsio procensura scholae parisiensis contra alchymiam* (186 pp., octavo, Paris: Plantin, 1606).

143. Hermann Kopp (1817-92), *Geschichte der Chemie* (vol. 1, Braunschweig, 1843), p. 114. Max Speter, "Vater Kopp," *Osiris*, 5: 392-460 (1938).

144. Michelius dedicated to the senate and people of Middelburg an *Apologia chymica adversus invectivas Andreae Libavii calumnias* (365 pp., Middelburg: R. Schilders, 1597). Guibert wrote a treatise against alchemy, *Alchymia ratione et experientia ita demum viriliter impugnata et expugnata* (Strasbourg: Zetzner, 1603); Libavius answered it in his *Defensio et declaratio perspicua alchymiae transmutatoriae* (694 pp., Oberursel: P. Kopf, 1604), and Guibert issued a rejoinder entitled *De interitu Alchymiae metallorum transmutatoriae . . . Adjuncta est Apologia in sophistam Libavium* (2 parts, Toul, 1614. See Lynn Thorndike, *History of Magic*, cited, 5: 648, 6; 238-53.

145. This is probably the Greek word *encheireia,* not in the Greek dictionaries, which would mean manipulation.

146. The *Chymia* groups three treatises: (1) *De magisteriis* (meaning principles or elixirs that have transmutatory powers); (2) *De extractis,* that is, various substances—this fills almost half of the book; (3) *De speciebus chymicis compositis* (*elixyr vitae, laudanum opiatum, clyssus.*)

147. On Chinese printing see *Introduction,* 1: 451, 512, 529, 604, 633; 3: 144, 637, 729, 1125, 1588.

148. See *Introduction,* 1: 723, 756; 3: 144, 733, 830, 1125, 1562.

149. On the Chinese government press see *Introduction,* 2: 807, 981; 3: 138, 386.

150. On Chinese paper money see *Introduction,* 2: 28, 574, 764, 982.

151. On Marco Polo see *Introduction,* 2: 1058.

152. On block printing in the West see *Introduction,* 3: 1126, 1563.

153. In his *Pirotechnia*, Book IX, chapter 7, "Concerning the art of the pewterer."

154. Paper was the only material cheap enough for the printing of many books. For the early history of paper see *Introduction,* 3: 174-77. The first German paper mill was established in 1390 (*Introduction,* 3: 1580). The manufacture of paper was facilitated by the greater use of linen. The *"siècle de la chemise"* (fourteenth century) prepared the century of printing. According to Thomas Francis Carter, *The Invention of Paper in China* (Columbia University Press, 1925; reviewed in *Isis*, 8: 361-73; new ed. 1931, reviewed in *Isis*, 19: 426), the manufacture of paper in England began only in 1494.

In spite of its relative cheapness (as compared with vellum), paper was the major item in book production costs. Florence Edler De Roover, "New Facts on the financing and marketing of early printed books," *Bulletin of the Business Historical Society,* 27: 222-30 (Boston, December 1953).

155. A glaring example was given by the late Maxime Laignel-Lavastine, *Histoire générale de la médicine* (3 quarto volumes richly illustrated, Paris, 1936-49). A more recent one is B. L. Van der Waerden, *Science Awakening* (Groningen: Noordhoff, 1954; reviewed in *Isis,* 46: 368), a history of mathematics. The text is very critical, but the illustrations are uncritical, unexplained in the text, and insufficiently related to the text.

156. This has been proved by me so far as science is concerned in "The scientific literature transmitted through the incunabula," *Osiris,* 5: 41-245 (1938), and in *The Appreciation of Ancient and Medieval Science during the Renaissance.*

157. Richard Foster Jones, *The Triumph of the English Language,* cited, p. 32. Jones is concerned mainly with printing in English, but the argument applies equally well to every vernacular.

158. This is done at present by editors who prepare a "critical edition." They take great pains to examine all the Mss., classify them, and trace their genealogy (the *stemma*). The editor of a mediaeval Ms. could not do this, for he could not have obtained all the Ms. copies of the work. For example, see William M. Green, "Medieval recensions of Augustine," *Speculum,* July 1954, pp. 531-34.

159. The word being used in its classical meaning, as in the phrase *"Jovis incunabula Crete"* (Crete, Jupiter's cradle) by Ovid (Metamorphoses, VIII: 99). It is a neuter plural that is now used exclusively to designate a book or books printed before 1501.

160. Riccobaldo da Ferrara (XIV-1), *Chronica summorum pontificum imperatorumque ac de septem aetatibus mundi,* first ed., Rome: Giov. Phil. de Lignamine, 1474. Riccobaldo's account was not delayed so long as it may appear at first view. Printing began about the middle of the century, but its diffusion was slow. Even where printing presses existed, they were not always utilized. Manuscripts continued to be used until the end of the fifteenth century and even throughout the sixteenth. Printing began in France in 1470, but it was not until ten years later that printed books began to replace manuscripts for everyday use in the Sorbonne library. Jacques Monfrin, "Les lectures de Guillaume Fichet et de Jean Heynlin," *Bibliothèque d'humanisme,* 17: 7-23 (Geneva, 1955), p. 10.

161. See list of early treatises on military technology, *Introduction,* 3: 1550-55.

162. This is well explained in Charles Singer's *History of Technology* (vol. 1, Oxford, 1954; reviewed in *Isis,* 46: 294-96), especially in the chapters on mining and quarrying by C. N. Bromehead, on extracting, smelting, and alloying by R. J. Forbes, and on metal implements and weapons by H. H. Coghlan (pp. 558-622).

163. He meant Vulcan, the Roman god of fire, who was not Venus' son, however.

164. The first complete English version of the *Pirotechnia* is also the best modern edition in any language. We owe it to the combined efforts of the metallurgist, Cyril Stanley Smith, and the Italian scholar, Martha Teach Gnudi,

and to the enlightened generosity of the American Institute of Mining and Metallurgical Engineers (502 pp., ill., New York, 1942; reviewed in *Isis*, 34: 514-16).

165. English readers can easily study both in the translation prepared by Anneliese Grünhaldt Sisco with the technical assistance of Cyril Stanley Smith, *Bergwerk- und Probierbüchlein* (196 pp., New York: American Institute of Mining and Metallurgical Engineers, 1949; reviewed in *Isis*, 42: 54). Our quotations are taken from that volume.

Ernst Darmstaedter, "Berg-, Probir- und Kunstbüchlein," *Münchener Beiträge*, Heft 2-3, 112 pp., Munich, 1926; reviewed in *Isis*, 10: 143.

166. Astrology came in very naturally because the seven metals were traditionally associated with the seven planets. Each metal originated under the influence of its planet. The correspondence is as follows, the planets being named in the order of decreasing distance from the earth: Saturn (lead), Jupiter (tin), Mars (iron), Sun (gold), Venus (copper), Mercury (quicksilver), Moon (silver).

The days of the astrological week are obtained from the preceding list by always dropping two planets, Saturday, Sunday, Monday, Tuesday, Wednesday, Thursday, Friday.

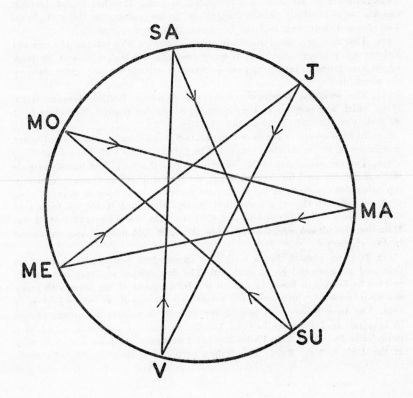

167. Besides four undated editions and the first dated one (Magdeburg, 1524) there are several others: s.l., 1527; Strasbourg, 1530; Augsburg, 1534; 1546, 1565; Nuremberg, 1549, 1564; Frankfurt, 1574, 1580, 1608.

168. Johann Förster (1495-1556), Hebraist who helped Luther to translate the Bible into German (*Allgemeine Deutsche Biographie*, 7, 165). This is notable, for it helps to show that Agricola grew up in a Lutheran atmosphere, yet he remained until the end a faithful Catholic.

169. Sankt Joachimsthal or Jáchymov in northwest Bohemia (now Czechoslovakia), known for its uranium ores.

170. At the end of his dedication he names the following mining towns of Saxony: Freiberg, Annaberg, Marienberg, Schneeberg, Geyer, and Altenberg.

171. Georg Fabricius (1516-71) was a classical scholar and Latin poet (*Allgemeine Deutsche Biographie*, 6: 510-14). It was he who wrote the prefatory ode "in libros metallicos Georgii Agricolae philosophi praestantissimi ad lectorem," a poem of exceptional length (157 lines). In a letter to Melanchthon he announced Agricola's death and described his personality with sympathy. English translation of Agricola's *De re metallica* by Herbert Clark Hoover and his wife (London, 1912; reviewed in *Isis*, 13: 113-16), p. x.

172. The *De re metallica* was dedicated to Duke Maurice, Grand Marshal and Elector of the Holy Roman Empire, and to his brother, the Duke Augustus. The eloquent dedication is dated Chemnitz, December 1, 1550.

173. This is a very good statement of the value of illustrations. His concern with posterity is remarkable. It is quite true that modern editors of his book would have failed to understand some parts of it without the help given them by the woodcuts.

174. The so-called Neptunian theory of Abraham Gottlob Werner (1750-1817), which was popular at the beginning of the last century. According to it all rocks were formed by the agency of water.

175. In his *De ortu et causis subterraneorum*, book 3, as quoted in the Hoover translation of *De re metallica* (p. xii). The *De ortu* deals with physical geology.

176. The *virgula divina* of M. Terentius Varro (I-2 B.C.). The Roman *virgula* was a magic rod used for divination but not for the detection of water or metals. Agricola's description of it for mining purposes occurs in book II (original text, 1556, pp. 26, 28; Hoover's translation, p. 38). He called it *virgula forcata* or simply *virgula* and illustrated its use. Carl von Klinckowstroem and Rudolf von Maltzahn, *Handbuch der Wünschelrute* (Munich: Oldenbourg, 1931; reviewed in *Isis*, 17: 602).

177. It is no wonder that a book that answered so well urgent needs of its time and place should be so successful. The first edition was very handsomely printed by Froben in Basel, in 1556; it is a folio volume of 624 pages with many woodcuts, some of which cover the whole page. It was reprinted by Froben in 1561. The same Froben was enterprising enough to publish a German edition in 1557 and an Italian one in 1563. The German translation was prepared, very imperfectly, by a local man, Philip Bechius, professor of medicine and philosophy at the University of Basel. The Italian version was done by Michel Angelo

Florio, a Protestant refugee who had escaped persecution in the Valtellina and was teaching Italian in London. He should not be confused with his more illustrious son, John Florio (1553?-1625), author of a great Italian-English dictionary, *A worlde of wordes* (1598) and of the English translation of Montaigne's *Essays* (1603). Michel Angelo Florio lived in Soglio (Grisons) from 1557 to 1566. His translation of Agricola was completed there and was dedicated to Queen Elizabeth.

The four editions of Agricola published by Froben were all folios. They had to be, because he used the same blocks in all of them; it was a profitable undertaking. Another German edition was published by Sigmund Feyrabendt in Frankfurt in 1580.

If we compare the sixteenth-century editions of Biringuccio and Agricola, we find 6 of the former against 5 of the latter, but Biringuccio was available in 4 Italian editions and 2 French, while Agricola could be read in 2 Latin editions, 2 German, and one Italian. The distribution of the Agricola text was more nearly complete. Moreover, the Biringuccio volumes were small, while those of Agricola, all of folio size, were more impressive.

The main modern editions, also folios, are the English one by Herbert Clark Hoover and Lou Henry Hoover (672 pp., London: *Mining Magazine*, 1912) and a new German translation by many authors (564 pp., Berlin: Verein deutscher Ingenieure, 1928). (See also Ernst Darmstaedter, "Georg Agricola," *Münchener Beiträge*, 1, 96 pp., 12 figs., Munich, 1926; reviewed in *Isis*, 10: 44). As a mining engineer Mr. Hoover was fully competent to explain all the technical details. Both editions are illustrated in exactly the same way with reproductions of the original woodcuts, and both include all the necessary technical information. To the German translation of the *De re metallica* has been added that of another Agricola treatise, the *De animantibus subterraneis* (Basel, 1549), which is a sort of biological appendix.

178. Paracelsus was born a year before Agricola (1493 vs. 1494) and died fourteen years earlier (1541 vs. 1555).

179. The German title is unmanageable. Printed by Georg Schwartz, the book has 140 leaves 30 cm. high, and is illustrated with woodcuts. All the following editions, seven in number, were printed in Frankfurt and are illustrated in the same way; probably the same blocks were used. These editions appeared in 1580, 1598, 1629, 1672 (with glossary), 1684, 1703, and 1736.

An English translation was made, not too well, by Sir John Pettus (1613-90), deputy governor of the royal mines of England; it was curiously entitled *Fleta Minor. The laws of art and nature in knowing, judging, assaying, fining, refining and inlarging the bodies of confined metals* (London: Thomas Dawks, 1683; reprinted by another publisher, London, 1686). It was called *Fleta Minor* in remembrance of Sir John's stay in the Fleet prison and of the other *Fleta* written c.1290 (a Latin abridgment of the *De legibus et consuetudinibus Angliae* of Henry de Bracton [XIII-2]; *Introduction*, 2: 1130). Another English translation was begun by the mathematician, John Pell (1611-85), known for "Pell's problem" or the "Pellian equation" (*Introduction*, 2: 213; 3: 1535). Pettus and Pell were two strange characters, both of whom knew many vicissitudes and served terms in the debtor's prison. Mining was not a propitious vocation in England. An earlier miner, the mathematician Robert Recorde (1510?-88), died in prison. Frances Marguerite Clark, "New light on Recorde," *Isis*, 8: 50-70 (1925). See also *Isis*, 41: 130.

A Dutch translation was printed in The Hague in 1745. Czech and Latin translations were planned but never materialized.

A new English translation, based upon the second German one (1580) was made by Anneliese Grünhaldt Sisco and Cyril Stanley Smith (393 pp., University of Chicago Press, 1951; reviewed in *Isis*, 43: 271). This is excellent, for it contains all the historical and technical information that the most inquisitive reader might desire. The translators were well prepared for their task by their earlier studies in sixteenth-century metallurgy.

It is remarkable that we owe our knowledge of Renaissance mining and metallurgy largely to American scholars—Mr. and Mrs. Herbert Hoover, Cyril Stanley Smith, Martha Teach Gnudi, and Anneliese Grünhaldt Sisco.

180. The first book devoted exclusively to iron metallurgy was *L'art de convertir le fer forgé en acier et l'art d'adoucir le fer fondu, ou de faire des ouvrages de fer fondu aussi finis que de fer forgé* (588 pp., Paris, 1722) by the illustrious entomologist and physicist, R. A. F. de Réaumur (1683-1757).

NOTES TO FOURTH WING

1. *Introduction*, 3: 355, 1320-22. The statement that Greek studies began during the Renaissance is closer to the truth if the Renaissance itself is made to begin with Petrarch and Boccaccio. This is a matter of definition.

2. For incunabula editions of these four authors see Klebs; also G. Sarton, "Scientific literature transmitted through the incunabula," *Osiris*, 5: 41-245 (1938). For the Renaissance tradition see Sarton, *Appreciation*.

3. There is an abundant literature on the German fathers. The most convenient general account is by Agnes Arber, *Herbals, Their Origin and Evolution, 1470-1670* (Cambridge University Press, 1912; enlarged edition 1938; reviewed in *Isis*, 30: 131-32), with many illustrations. As the pictures are at least as important as the text, I have named the artist whenever it is possible. For example, it is very unfair to remember Brunfels and forget Weiditz. The artist sometimes added portraits of the author and even of himself; thus we are given the earliest portraits of botanists (Bock, Fuchs, and his artists).

The subject of botanical illustration has been covered very pleasantly by Wilfrid Blunt, *The Art of Botanical Illustration* (London: Collins, 1951; New York: Scribner's, 1951), beautifully illustrated, and very learnedly by Claus Nissen, *Die botanische Buchillustration* (2 vols., quarto, Stuttgart: Hiersemann, 1951). Both books cover the subject down to our day. Nissen has elaborate indexes of artists (vol. 2, pp. 239-74), plants, countries, and authors.

4. The beautiful American flower fuchsia is named after him.

5. Chauncey D. Leake, "Valerius Cordus and the discovery of the ether," *Isis*, 7: 14-24, 4 pls. (1925). I call his pharmacopoeia the first official one because it was published after due examination by order of the town council of Nuremberg. The novelty lay not only in the book but in the official sanction given to it. A facsimile reprint was published in Mittenwald, Bavaria, in 1934 (*Isis*, 24: 215).

It has been claimed that the Nuremberg *Dispensatorium* was not the first pharmacopoeia but the second, the first being the *Nuovo receptario composito*, or *Ricettario*, published anonymously by Drago in Florence in 1498 (Klebs 410.1-2). It has even been claimed that the first pharmacopoeia was the *Compendium aromatariorum* by Saladino Ferro d'Ascoli, first printed by Henricus de Harlem (Bologna, 1488) and many times afterwards (five incunabula, Klebs 876.1-2, 680.13-15). It was written about 1430; it may have been composed first in Hebrew. The Hebrew text, *Sefer ha-roqḥim*, was first edited by Suessmann Muntner (Tel Aviv, 1953); see my review of it in *Journal of the History of Medicine* (New Haven, 1955).

6. Other examples could be mentioned, e.g., concerning Dodonaeus, Lobelius, and Camerarius junior.

7. The illustrations of Renaissance herbals were mostly woodcuts. Copper engravings appeared only late in the sixteenth century. According to Mrs. Arber (*Herbals*, cited, 1938 ed., p. 243), the earliest botanical book using copper plates was the *Phytobasanos* of Fabio Colonna (Naples: J. J. Carlinus, 1592), the engravings being ascribed to Colonna himself.

8. He first published an Italian version of Dioscorides (Venice: Nicolo de Bascarini, 1944). The first edition of the commentaries proper was *Commentarii in libros sex Dioscoridis de medica materia* (Venice: Vinc. Valgrisi, 1554), often reprinted and translated, *Compendium de plantis omnibus una cum earum iconibus . . . Accessit ad calcem opusculum de itinere quo e Verona in Baldum montem refertissimum itur . . .* Francisco Calceolario (Venice: Valgrisi, 1571). *De plantis epitome . . . aucta et locupletata a Joachimo Camerario* (Frankfurt, 1586), posthumous. This contains also Francesco Calzolari's booklet, one of the earliest local floras, first published in Italian, *Il viaggio di Monte Baldo* (Venice: Valgrisi, 1566). Calzolari was a son of Verona (1522-1609); his little book is forgotten, but he is immortalized by the lovely American flower calceolaria.

9. According to Mrs. Arber (cited, 1938 ed., p. 94), who does not quote her source or explain how the total was obtained. The number 32,000 is very plausible, however, and I would take it rather as a minimum. By the middle of the sixteenth century the editions of a well-known author could easily reach one or two thousand copies. Mattioli's books were produced in Venice (chiefly by Valgrisi), Padua, Genoa, Lyon, Basel, Frankfurt, and Prague (not in Antwerp, however). He was the botanical best seller of his age.

10. Or before? I have read them in his posthumous *Opera quae exstant omnia* (folio, 1350; Basel, 1598). See my article, "Brave Busbecq, 1522-92," *Isis*, 33: 557-75, 7 figs. (1942). p. 570.

11. At least until 1576, when the city was sacked by its Spanish garrison ("the Spanish Fury"). It was severely crippled in 1585, when Alexander Farnese, duke

of Parma, conquered it, and almost ruined in 1648, when the Treaty of West-phalia closed the Schelde to navigation and favored the growth of Amsterdam.

12. J. Peeters-Fontainas, *Bibliographie des impressions espagnoles des Pays-Bas* (260 pp., Anvers: Musée Plantin-Moretus, 1933).

13. The first English printer, William Caxton (c.1422-91), printed the *Recuyell of the Histories of Troy* and the *Game and Play of the Chesse moralized* in Bruges 1474-75 before establishing a press in England. Between 1477 and 1491 he printed eighty separate books in Westminster.

14. Elizabeth Armstrong, *Robert Estienne* (Cambridge University Press, 1954; reviewed in *Speculum*, 30: 241-46, and in *Isis*, 47: 200 ff.), pp. 27, 47, 57. Robert Estienne, printer in Paris from 1524 and in Geneva from 1551 to his death in 1559, was Plantin's greatest rival outside of Italy, but his publications were almost entirely restricted to the Bible and classics; practically no science.

15. Artois had belonged to the counts of Flanders. During the Renaissance it was, like Flanders, under Austrian, then Spanish rule. We might say, roughly, that these three men belonged to the same country, of which Antwerp was the metropolis. By the way, "artesian wells" are so called because the earliest ones were dug in Artois, c.1750.

16. The name has a curious botanical connotation, for Dodone in Epeiros was the seat of the oldest Greek oracle, a Pelasgic foundation dedicated to Zeus. The oracle was rendered by the rustle of oaks and beeches. In the course of time Dodone was superseded by Delphoi.

17. The University of Leiden was founded in 1575 by William of Orange as a reward for the city's heroic defense against the Spaniards the year before. It soon became one of the leading universities of the world. The oldest university of the Netherlands was that of Louvain, founded in 1425. Louvain remained in Spanish and Catholic hands; Leiden was Calvinist.

18. From 1554 to 1644 there were at least 13 editions, 5 in Flemish, 5 in English (*A new Herball*), 2 in Latin, and one in French.

19. There is no full biography of Dodonaeus. The best account is by Emile Varenbergh in the *Biographie nationale de Belgique*, 6: 85-112 (1878). Short account by Cyp. Demars, "R. Dodoens," *IIIe Congrès national des sciences*, Brussels, 1950, 30 pp.

20. I have no space in this book to speak of Guillaume Rondelet (1507-66) or of Pierre Belon (1517-64), both outstanding French zoologists. See *Appreciation*, pp. 55 ff.

21. On the title page of the *Rariorum plantarum historia* (Antwerp: Plantin, 1601), he is called "aulae quondam familiaris."

22. Nicolas Clénard (Cleynaerts), born in Diest, Brabant, 1493/94, taught Greek and Hebrew in Louvain. In 1531 he went to Spain with Christopher Columbus' son Fernando, and taught Greek and Hebrew in Salamanca. While in Spain he studied Arabic. He died in Granada in 1542. His Hebrew grammar (1529) was reprinted 29 times, and his Greek grammar (1530) 300 times! His letters, some of which deal with Islamic matters, were edited half a dozen times. The final edition is that of Alphonse Roersch, *Correspondance de Nicolas Clénard* (3 vols., Brussels, Académie de Belgique, 1940-41). Alphonse Roersch,

Clénard peint par lui même (Brussels: Office de Publicité, 1942; reviewed in *Isis*, 40: 133).

23. *Fungorum in Pannoniis observatorum brevis historia* (in *Rariorum plantorum historia*, 1601), with thirty-two woodcuts. The Ms. disappeared from the Plantin archives but was used by Frans Van Sterbeeck of Antwerp in his *Theatrum fungorum, oft tooneel der campernoelien* (Antwerp, 1675), and is now in the library of the University of Leiden. A facsimile copy of it was published in Budapest, 1896-1900 (Claus Nissen, no. 374, 1951).

24. Wilhelm Jan Lütjeharms, *Zur Geschichte der Mykologie. Das XVIII. Jahrhundert* (284 pp., 2 pls., Gouda, 1936; reviewed in *Isis*, 34: 78).

25. We owe an elaborate biography of Clusius to F. W. T. Hunger: *Charles de l'Escluse* (470 pp., The Hague: Nijhoff, 1927). A shorter life, largely based upon Hunger's, was written by Joh. Theunisz: *Carolus Clusius* (178 pp., 8 figs., Amsterdam: Van Kampen, 1939; reviewed in *Isis*, 40: 363). These two books are in Dutch. The French account by Emile Varenbergh (*Biographie nationale de Belgique*, 5: 383-410 [1876]) is good but obsolete on many points.

26. The convenience of the Latin names is well evidenced in the cases of Clusius and Lobelius, which can be indexed only under C and L, while Charles de l'Escluse (Lecluse) and Matthias de l'Obel might be indexed under D, L, E or D, L, O.

Lobelius and Clusius are immortalized by the names of two botanical families, the Clusiaceae (order Hypericales) and the Lobeliaceae (order Campanules) and of two important genera of these families, the Clusia and the Lobelia.

27. Edward, eleventh Baron Zouche (c.1556-1625), a man of great political and social importance, patron of arts and letters.

28. On the title pages of various editions, Pena is named before Lobelius, against the alphabetical order.

29. Louis Ramond de Carbonnières in his *Voyage au Mont-Perdu* (Paris, 1801). The Mont Perdu is a high mountain (3,353 meters) just south of Gavarnie (Hautes-Pyrénées).

30. There is no full-length biography of Lobelius. Article by Ed. Morren in *Biographie nationale de Belgique*, 5: 452-65 (1876).

31. For example, the garden planned in 820 for the monastery of St. Gall in Switzerland. For other mediaeval botanic gardens see *Introduction*, 3: 224-25, 1177.

32. Let us give a few more dates rapidly. (Those marked with a star below were obtained frrom Charles Stuart Gager, *Botanic Gardens of the World* (Brooklyn, 1937; 2nd ed., *Brooklyn Botanic Garden Record*, 27: 151-406 [1938]). The great majority of the gardens listed in this book date from the nineteenth and twentieth centuries; there are historical notes on ancient gardens, but the author was more interested in those that exist today.) Zurich 1560; Rome, Vatican, 1566;* Bologna 1567/68 (the creation of Ulisse Aldrovandi); Cassel 1568 (by order of the landgrave, Wilhelm IV); Vienna 1573 (directed by Clusius); Leipzig 1579/80 (1542*?); Leiden 1587 (directed by Clusius from 1592 to his death in 1609); Breslau 1587; Montpellier 1593; Heidelberg 1593; Paris 1597; London 1595 or 1596 (this was the "botanic garden" of John Gerarde in

Holborn); Parma 1599.* This list is probably incomplete and the dates are uncertain, for when does the life of a garden begin? The date most likely to be recorded is that of the decision to establish it.

It would appear that the first German botanic garden was that of Cassel or Kassel in Hesse (1568). It has been claimed that gardens were laid out as early as 1490 in Cologne, 1540 in Hamburg, and not much later in Nuremberg. Martin Möbius, *Geschichte der Botanik* (Jena: Fischer, 1937), p. 419. According to Möbius the garden in Cassel was "ein richtiger botanischer Garten," but what does that mean exactly? Wilhelm IV the Wise was landgrave of Hesse-Cassel from 1567 to 1592.

The Paris garden, founded in 1597, was reorganized under Louis XIII in 1626 and 1635, Guy de la Brosse being the first superintendent of the Jardin du Roi (A. Arber, *Isis*, 1: 359-69 [1913]). Later it was called Jardin des Plantes and was part of the Muséum Naturelle d'Histoire (1793).

John Gerarde's garden in London had the earliest printed catalogue of any botanic garden, *Catalogus arborum, fruticum ac plantarum tam indigenarum quam exoticarum in horto Johannis Gerardi . . . nascentium* (London: R. Robinson, 1596; A. Hatfield, 1599). In the seventeenth century and later many other catalogues were published.

33. A number of monographs describe the birth and growth of individual gardens, either in the form of separate books or as chapters in the history of individual universities.

34. It was probably Busbecq who brought back the first tulip bulbs from Constantinople c.1555. For details concerning the early knowledge of tulips in western Europe see *Isis*, 33: 573.

35. Marie de Brimeu was her maiden name. She was the daughter of Charles de Brimeu (c.1525-Zwolle 1572), soldier and statesman; she married Lancelot de Berlaymont, who died young, and then Charles de Croy, prince of Chimay, duke of Aerschot. She was always a Protestant (*Nieuw nederlandsch biografisch Woordenboek*, 7: 217-19 [1930]).

36. It includes a description of the cedar and a picture of it, reproduced by A. Arber, op. cit., p. 235.

37. More details in *Appreciation*, pp. 59 ff.

38. Plants had been dried and preserved for medical or culinary use from time immemorial.

39. See Martin Möbius, *Geschichte der Botanik*, cited, pp. 422-27; Agnes Arber, *Herbals*, cited, 1938 ed., pp. 138-43.

40. According to information kindly sent to me by Dr. Saitta Reugnas, director of the Biblioteca Angelica (letter dated January 24, 1955), two herbaria prepared by Gherardo Cibo are preserved in the library and described in *Inventari dei mss. delle Biblioteche d'Italia* (26: 121-22, Florence, 1948). Otto Penzig, *Contribuzione alla storia della botanica* (Genoa: Ciminago, 1904).

41. *Andreae Caesalpini De plantis libri XVI* (Florence: Marescotti, 1583), p. vii.

42. This John Falconer is not very well known, but he is mentioned in the *Dictionary of National Biography*, 18: 161 (1889). He was a merchant, and "Maister Falkonner's Boke," as William Turner called it, is the earliest English herbarium on record.

43. Montaigne, *Journal de voyage* (edited by Louis Lautrey, Paris: Hachette, 1906), p. 77. Montaigne calls him Foelix Platerus.

44. This herbarium, preserved in the Muséum d'Histoire Naturelle in Paris, was begun by Jehan Girault, medical student in Lyon, in August 1558. It includes 313 plants of southern France. J. B. Saint-Lazer, "Histoire des herbiers," *Annales de la Société Botanique de Lyon*, année 13, pp. 1-120 (1885). J. Camus, "Historique des premiers herbiers," *Malpigli*, anno 9 (pp. 282-314), pp. 306-307. Information kindly sent me by Mrs. A. Arber, January 25, 1955.

45. *Herbals*, cited, 1938 ed., p. 140.

46. This Spigelius was the Fleming Adrian Van der Spiegel (1578-1625), professor of anatomy in Padua in 1617-25. He was born in Brussels, like Vesalius, and completed in Padua the Flemish cycle begun by the latter. His *Isagoge* was published in Padua first in 1606, then in 1608, and in Leiden in 1633.

47. The word herbarium in our sense *(herbier)* first occurs in Joseph Pitton de Tournefort, *Elemens de botanique* (Paris, 1694).

48. Codex Atlanticus, 72b. Jean Paul Richter, *Literary Works of Leonardo* (Oxford University Press, 1939; reviewed in *Isis*, 35: 184-87), no. 16 in vol. 1, p. 359.

49. *Introduction*, 3: 929, 1870.

50. *Materia medica* was the title of Dioscorides' book *(peri hyles iatrices)*. This title meant botany even as the Almagest meant astronomy; Dioscorides' name meant botany even as Euclid's meant geometry.

51. The *lectio simplicium* was followed by the *ostensio simplicium*.

52. Even as late as 1603 or later. I have read of Prospero Alpino, "in 1603 è preposto alla prefettura dell' orto ed alla ostensio dei semplici," in *Gli scienziati italiani* edited by Aldo Mieli, 1: 84 (1921).

53. Richer de Belleval of Châlons-sur-Marne (1564-1632). He obtained his M.D. in Avignon in 1587, and was "professor of botany and anatomy" in Montpellier. In 1593 he received "lettres patentes" permitting him to establish a botanic garden. He published the *Onomantologia seu Nomenclator stirpium quae in horto regio Monspeliensi recens constructo coluntur* (Montpellier: J. Gilet, 1598), listing 1,332 plants. An earlier catalogue of this kind was published by John Gerard in 1596 (see note above). He wrote other pamphlets about his gardening efforts, e.g., *Remonstrance et supplication au Roy touchant la continuation de la recherche des plantes du Languedoc et peuplement de son jardin de Montpellier* (s.l.a.). His *Opuscules* were reprinted in Paris in 1785. He was accused of devoting too much time to his garden, spending too much money on it, and neglecting his courses *(Dictionnaire de biographie française*, 5: 1352, 1950).

54. Arber, *Herbals*, cited, 1938 ed., p. 100.

55. Fuller information on Gesner, Aldrovandi, Belon, and Rondelet will be found in *Appreciation*.

56. The bird books of Gesner and Aldrovandi were followed by many others. Claus Nissen, *Die illustrierten Vogelbücher. Ihre Geschichte und Bibliographie* (Stuttgart: Hiersemann, 1953).

57. The Canary Islands were named after their canaries, and the Azores after their goshawks (*açores* in Portuguese).

58. The herring were one of the best sources of protein for the poorer people. They played an enormous part in popular diet after means had been discovered of preserving them; this discovery was probably made, or considerably improved, in the first half of the fourteenth century (*Introduction*, 3: 821-23). Most of the herring were taken in the Baltic and North Seas. The disappearance of the herring hastened the decadence of the Hanseatic League (*Introduction*, 2: 1063; 3: 1020, *passim*).

59. Morus-Richard Lewinsohn; the words are taken from his book *Animals, Men and Myths* (London: Gollancz, 1954; reviewed in *Isis*, 46: 61-64), p. 151.

60. Pietro Pomponazzi (1462-1525) of Mantua, professor in Padua, author of the *De immortalitate animae* (Bologna: Justinianus Leonardus Ruberiensis, 1516), concluded that the immortality of the soul cannot be proved but is a matter of revelation. His book was burned in Venice but he enjoyed papal protection in Bologna.

61. The Swede, Olaus Magnus (1490-1558), came to Rome in 1527 and lived in the monastery of St. Birgitta (XIV-2); *Introduction*, 3: 1355). His *Historia de gentibus septentrionalibus* (Rome: J. M. de Viottis, 1555; Antwerp: Plantin, 1558; Basel: Henricus Petrus, 1567) was the standard book on Scandinavian history, political and natural.

62. This translation was not published as a curiosity but for actual use. We should not laugh, however, for there are still lapidarists and "gemmologists" today who would praise the *Speculum lapidum*.

63. *Bermannus* (1530), *De ortu et causis subterraneorum* (1546), *De natura eorum quae effluunt ex terra* (1546), *De natura fossilium* (1546), *De veteribus et novis metallis* (1546), *De animantibus subterraneis* (1549). The title of the first was taken from the name of his friend Lorenz Bermann, a prominent miner. Was a play on words intended? *Bergmann* is a mountain-dweller, *Bergmännchen* a gnome.

64. Hoover's edition of Agricola's *De re metallica*, cited, p. 433.

65. The word *fossilis* was applied to every object dug out of the earth. It was only later that it was restricted to organic remains. Until the end of the Renaissance *fossilis* applies to both organic and inorganic matter. *Fossile flumen* is a canal, as opposed to *flumen*, a river.

66. For many more details on Agricola and other mineralogists listed in this chapter see Frank Dawson Adams, *The Birth and Development of the Geological Sciences* (506 pp., Baltimore: Williams and Wilkins, 1938; reviewed in *Isis*, 32: 218-20) and Herbert Hoover's translation of the *De re metallica*, cited.

67. The illustrations of *De re metallica* are so numerous that Herbert Hoover found it necessary to add a special index to them in his translation.

68. Aristotle, *Problemata* (935a35). Berakya ha-Naqdan (XII-2), *Dodi venechdi* (ch. 5). The saltness of the sea was discussed by Roger Bacon (XIII-2) in his *Summa philosophiae* (treatise 18: *Introduction*, 2: 960); in al-Dimashqī's (XIV-1) Nukhbat al-dahr (part 4; *Introduction*, 3: 800); in Giacomo de' Dondi (XIV-2), *Tractatus de causa salsedinis aquarum* (*Introduction*, 3: 1670).

69. Juan de Jarava, *La philosophia natural* (Antwerp, 1546); *Della filosofia naturale* (Venice, 1557), p. 92. René Descartes, *Principia philosophiae* (Amsterdam, 1644), p. 164.

70. One of the many Italian academies of the Renaissance. Valerius' booklet was its last publication. In place of the Aldine anchor it bears the Academy's emblem, a figure of Fame with the motto "Io volo al ciel per riposarmi in Dio." Because of this emblem the academy was often called Accademia della Fama. Valerius' pamphlet being difficult to obtain, Adams gives a long description (*op. cit.* pp. 344-57) and quotes half of it.

71. Adams, *op. cit.*, p. 344.

72. It was included in the collection entitled *De omni rerum fossilium genere* . . . , together with Kentmann's *Nomenclaturae* and other treatises.

73. Sarepta is a place on the Phoenician coast between Sidon and Tyre (*Luke* 4: 26). It is mentioned in the Old Testament under its original name Zarephath (*1 Kings* 17:9-10; *Obadiah* 20). The Hebrew name has a metallurgical meaning, a place of refining or smelting.

74. Richard de Bury (XIV-1) is his *Philobiblon* used the word *geologia* in opposition to *theologia;* he meant earthbound science as opposed to heavenly science, divinity. The modern meaning of geology is no longer earthbound science but science of the earth. The first use of the word in English occurs in the *Panzooryctologia* of Robert Lovell (Oxford, 1661). The word geology was driven out for a while by geognosy, favored by Abraham Gottlob Werner (1774).

75. Sarton, "Simon Stevin," *Isis,* 21: 256, 280 (1934). The historians of geology, Sir Archibald Geikie (1905) and Frank Dawson Adams (1938) do not even mention Stevin, who was better known as a mathematician and mechanician.

76. Leiden, 1605; vol. 1, part 2, pp. 47-67.

77. The barbarous term *hylocinesis* refers to the internal changes of the earth's crust.

78. A summary of views on the origin of ore deposits is given by Herbert Hoover in a gigantic footnote to his Agricola, cited, pp. 43-53.

79. Pietro Martire d'Anghiera (1457-1526), councillor to Ferdinand and Isabella, and later to Charles V. His *De rebus oceanicis et orbe novo decades tres* (Alcalá de Henares, 1516) was one of the first accounts of the discovery of the New World. English translation by Richard Eden, *Decades of the Newe Worlde, or West India* (London: R. Jugge, 1555).

80. Summary of ancient views on the unity of nature in *Introduction,* 3: 211-13.

81. Jacques Aubert, *De metallorum ortu et causis contra chemistas* (Lyon: J. Berion, 1575). Joseph Du Chesne (Quercetanus), *Ad Jacobi Auberti de ortu et causis metallorum . . . explicationem* (Lyon: Joannis Lertotius, 1575).

82. Gabriele Frascata of Pavia, *De aquis Returbii Ticinensibus commentarii mineras, facultates et usum earum explicantes* (Pavia: H. Bartholus, 1575).

83. François La Rue (Rueus), *De gemmis* (Paris: C. Wechel, 1547; 2nd ed., Zurich, 1566), p. 2.

84. Petrus Severinus, *Idea medicinae philosophicae* (Basel: Henricus Petrus, 1571), p. 73.

85. Giov. Batt. Brocchi, *Conchologia fossile subapennina* (2 vols., quarto, Milan: Stamperia reale, 1814), vol. 1, pp. iv ff.

86. Girolamo Fracastoro, *Homocentrica* (Venice, 1538).

87. Girolamo Cardano, *De subtilitate libri XXI* (Nuremberg: J. Petreius, 1550).

Bernard Palissy, *Discours admirables* (Paris: Martin le Jeune, 1580). Andrea
Cesalpino (Caesalpinus), *De metallicis* (Rome: A. Zannetti, 1596).

88. Michele Mercati (1541-93) of San Miniato. His *Metallotheca* was edited
posthumously by Gian Maria Lancisi (ill., Rome: 1717, 1719).

89. Giovanni Battista Olivi, *De reconditis et praecipuis collectaneis ab Francisco Calceolario in musaeo adservatis, J. B. Olivis . . . testificatio* (Venice: P.
Zanfrettus, 1584; Verona: H. Discipulus, 1593).

90. "Ars tam nobilis," *Introduction*, 2: 1040; 3, 171.

91. This institution was a feature of the guild system as it existed in France.
Members of a trade or craft were divided into three groups: apprentices,
journeymen *(compagnons),* and masters. The *tour de France* was a privilege of
the *compagnons,* those who were no longer apprentices but were not yet established on their own account. It was a transitional stage that enabled journeymen to spend as usefully as possible a time of relative freedom. The best
journeymen, like Palissy, managed to improve this golden opportunity. For
guilds see *Introduction,* 3: 152, 325.

92. The *gabelle* was the salt tax established in 1340, but extended to Poitou,
Aunis, and Saintonge only in 1544. Palissy was then about 34.

93. Historians of science will remember that William Smith (1769-1839), nicknamed "Strata Smith," the founder of stratigraphical geology, was also a sur-
veyor, but he worked on a much larger scale than Palissy, making elaborate
surveys for the English canals.

94. Montmorency was an illustrious family already famous in the twelfth
century. This *connétable* was Anne I (1493-1567), marshal of France, who was
killed at Saint Denis in a battle against the Calvinists.

95. "Inventeur des rustiques figulines du Roi."

96. The Palais des Tuileries was so called because it was built in a place occupied by tile-works *(tuileries)* since the thirteenth century. The place was built
for Catherine de' Medici in 1564 ff. by the famous architect, Philibert Delorme
(1515-70), who used Palissy in a subordinate capacity. It was enlarged by other
kings and set on fire by the commune in 1871. The Jardin des Tuileries remains.
Palissy's pottery was established in the Tuileries sometime in 1563/64, for there
are copies of his first book (1563) with a cover dated 1564 in which he is styled
"Bernard Palissy des Tuileries."

Philibert Delorme built the chateau of Anet (near Dreux, Eure-et-Loire) for
Diane de Poitiers in 1548 ff.; very little of it is extant, but he is immortalized
by his *Premier tome de l'Architecture* (Paris: Fréderic Morel, 1567). Edward
Fenton, "Messer Philibert Delorme," *Bulletin of the Metropolitan Museum,*
December 1954, pp. 148-60.

97. Organized by the Ligue, a confederation headed by Henri, duke de Guise
(1550-88) to defend Catholicism against the Huguenots, dethrone Henri III and
replace him by a member of the Guise family. The outburst began in May 1588
with the "Journée des barricades."

98. Or 1590. Paré, who was about seven years younger, died in that year.
Palissy and Paré, two of the greatest French men of science of their age, were
almost exact contemporaries. Henri, duke de Guise, and his brother Louis,

cardinal de Bourbon, had been murdered by Henri III's order on December 23, 1588; Henri III was murdered by a monk on July 31, 1589.

99. Sedan in the Ardennes (now Ardennes Dept.) was then an independent principality ruled by Henri Robert de la Marck, duke of Bouillon, who was a Huguenot.

100. It was customary to deliver series of learned lectures during Lent for the edification of the people.

101. Among them were Petrus Pena, co-author with Lobelius of the *Stirpium adversaria nova* (1570); Germain Courtin, who wrote *Adversus Paracelsi de tribus principiis, auro potabili, totaque pyrotechnia portentosas opiniones* (Paris, 1579); "Monsieur Paré, premier chirurgien du Roy;" Paré's colleague Richard Hubert (d. 1581), who had royal permission to dissect in public the bodies of executed criminals; Abbé Alphonse del Bene (d. 1618), to whom Ronsard dedicated his *Art poétique;* Nicolas Bergeron (d. c.1587), mathematician and chronologist, pupil of Ramus and his editor (1560, 1577, 1579); and the sculptor Barthélemy Prieur (d. 1611).

102. Marl (French *marne*, Latin *marga*), a kind of clay mixed with calcium carbinate, used as a fertilizer for soils deficient in lime.

103. First printed in 1575 and again in 1577(?). I have seen only the third edition, revised by the author, *Academie françoise, en laquelle il est traicté de l'institution des Moeurs et de ce qui concerne le bien & heureusement vivre en tous Estats et conditions: Par les Préceptes de la doctrine, & les exemples de la vie des anciens sages, & hommes illustres* (Paris: Guillaume Chaudière, 1582) with the author's portrait, reprinted 1587, 1598. *Suite de l'Académie françoise* (216 ff., Paris: G. Chaudière, 1580), reprinted 1588, 1591, 1598. *Troisième tome de l'Académie françoise* (165 ff., Paris: Chaudière, 1590), etc. *L'Académie françoise, divisée en quatre livres.* Nouvelle édition revue (4 parts in 1 vol., quarto, Saumur, 1613). English translation by Thomas Bowes (London: Edmund Bollifant, 1586; reprinted 1589, 1594, 1602, 1614. *Second part* (1594, 1605). *Third part* (1601). *The French academie* (four parts, folio, 1618). German translation entitled *Academia gallica* (2 vols., folio, Mümpelgart, 1593-94).

The Académie Française was founded by Richelieu in 1634. Pierre de La Primaudaye's book was fifty-nine years earlier. According to Palissy, Jacques de la Primaudaye was a Vendômois; actually he was an Angevin, but he may have lived in or around Vendôme. The La Primaudayes were one of the leading Protestant families of Anjou. Pierre (b. c.1545) was attached to the courts of Henri III and Henri IV.

For more details on this early Académie Française and on the contemporary "Palace Academy" founded by Jean Antoine de Baif (1522-89) and Ronsard, see Frances A. Yates, *The French Academies of the Sixteenth Century* (London: Warburg Institute, 1947), pp. 105-30, 319-26.

104. He was not the first to think of this. The management of forests was regulated by the Venetian Council of Ten as early as 1475. There were early regulations also in Tuscany and the Papal States (*Nature*, 119: 37 [1927]).

105. Palissy's bibliography is easy because he published only two books, *Recepte véritable* (132 pp., La Rochelle: Barthelemy Berton, 1563) and *Discours*

admirables (362 pp., Paris: Martin le Jeune, 1580). These two volumes are exceedingly rare. They were reissued together with other materials in two volumes, Paris, 1636. Third edition of both by Faujas de Saint Fond (1 vol., 730 pp., quarto, Paris, 1777). This edition was dedicated to Benjamin Franklin, another self-taught man. Franklin's *Expériences et observations sur l'électricité* had appeared in French (Paris, 1752) and he was very much in the public eye. Later editions of Palissy's works by Paul Antoine Cap (Paris, 1844), Anatole France (Paris, 1880), and Benjamin Fillon (2 vols., Niort, 1888).

Henry Morley, *The Life of Bernard Palissy* (2 vols., Boston, 1853). Well written but no longer up to date; it includes long extracts from his works in English translation (vol. 2, pp. 203-347). Ernest Dupuÿ, *B. Palissy* (Paris, 1902). Désiré Leroux, *La vie de Palissy* (126 pp., 8 pls., Paris: Champion, 1927). Palissy deserves a full biography written by a historian of science well acquainted with French politics and religion.

106. Other aspects of the religious intolerance of the sixteenth century have been discussed in my study on Servet and Chateillon, *Cahiers d'histoire mondiale,* 2: 140-69 (Paris, 1954).

107. Michel de l'Hospital (1507-73), jurist and statesman, chancellor of France (1560). He was tolerant and tried in vain to avert the religious wars, but he was driven out of office, witnessed the unbearable tragedy of Saint Bartholomew, and died of grief not long afterward.

108. The five men named by way of example were respectively an artisan, a man of letters, a magistrate, a philosopher, and a historian.

NOTES TO FIFTH WING

1. For Galen see my little book, *Galen of Pergamon* (University of Kansas Press, 1954). The school of Salerno began before the ninth century and its climax came in the twelfth century. *Introduction,* 1: 725, *passim.* George W. Corner, *Anatomical Texts of the Earlier Middle Ages* (112 pp., 3 pls., Carnegie Institution of Washington, 1927; reviewed in *Isis,* 9: 452-56).

2. See dissection scene in the *Fasciculo de medicina* (Venice: Gregoriis, 1493), often reproduced.

3. Between Leonardo and Vesalius one might place Iacopo Berengario da Carpi, who was professor of surgery in Bologna from 1502 to 1527 and died in 1550. The first edition of his *Isagogae breves* (Bologna: Benedict Hectoris, 1523) was the first anatomical treatise illustrated with woodcuts. It included various novelties. Many other anatomists were active during the first half of the sixteenth century.

4. The best tool for the study of Leonardo's anatomy was given us by Charles D. O'Malley and J. B. de C. M. Saunders: *Leonardo da Vinci on the Human Body* (506 pp., quarto, 215 pls., New York: Schuman, 1952; reviewed in *Isis,* 44: 65-66).

5. Copernicus' treatise was brought to him when he was dying; he died on May 24, 1543. Vesalius' *Fabrica* was published in June, less than one month earlier.

6. *Isis,* 44: 66 (1953).

7. G. Sarton, "The death and burial of Vesalius and, incidentally, of Cicero," *Isis,* 45: 131-37 (1954). C. Donald O'Malley, "Vesalius' pilgrimage," *ibid.,* 138-44. O'Malley defends (against Sarton) the reality of this pilgrimage and claims that there are proofs of Vesalius' presence in the Holy Land; he cannot produce them, however.

8. For details see my *Galen of Pergamon,* cited, pp. 43-44, etc.

9. Calcar (or Kalkar) where he was born, near Cleves, in the Rhine province. It is a Dutch enclave of Germany.

10. After William M. Ivins, Jr., "What about the Fabrica of Vesalius?" in Samuel W. Lambert, Willy Wiegand, and William J. Ivins, Jr., *Three Vesalian Essays to Accompany the* Icones anatomicae *of 1934* (New York: Macmillan, 1952).

11. Eustachio was luckier than Vesalius in one respect. The Eustachian tonsil, tube, and valve were named after him; hence every medical student knows of him. Vesalius' name, curiously enough, failed to be attached to any organ.

12. The main biography of Vesalius is still that by Moritz Roth (Berlin, 1892) but Charles D. O'Malley is preparing a new one.

M. H. Spielmann, *The Iconography of Vesalius* (London: Bale, 1925).

Vesalii Icones anatomicae (large folio, New York, Academy of Medicine, 1935; reviewed in *Isis,* 28: 467-69). Reproduction of the illustrations of the *Fabrica* made from the original blocks which were preserved in the University of Munich and were destroyed during the second World War.

Harvey Cushing, *Bio-bibliography of Vesalius* (268 pp., 89 figs., New York: Schuman, 1943; reviewed in *Isis,* 35: 338-41).

Charles Singer and C. Rabin, *Prelude to Modern Science, being a discussion of the history, sources and circumstances of the "Tabulae anatomicae sex"* (144 pp., folio, 59 figs., Cambridge University Press, 1946; reviewed in *Isis,* 38: 109-11). Includes facsimiles of the six tables.

The Epitome of Vesalius translated by L. R. Lind (140 pp., 23 pls., New York: Macmillan, 1949; reviewed in *Isis,* 41: 210-12). The Latin *Epitome* was published by Vesalius at about the same time as the *Fabrica* (August 1543).

As the *Fabrica* was a very expensive book which few doctors could afford to buy, the *Epitome* was more popular, as is witnessed by the number of editions, translations, and borrowings. Students used the *Epitome* and also frequently the *Institutiones anatomicae* (Wittenberg, 1611) of the Dane, Caspar Bartholin, senior, etc.

J. B. de C. M. Saunders and Charles D. O'Malley, *Illustrations from Vesalius' works* (252 pp., Cleveland: World Publishing Co., 1950; reviewed in *Isis,* 42: 53).

Samuel W. Lambert, Willy Wiegand, and William M. Ivins, Jr.: *Three Vesalian Essays* (140 pp., ill., New York Academy of Medicine, 1952; reviewed in *Isis,* 44: 119).

Charles Singer, *Vesalius on the Human Brain* (178 pp., 48 figs., Oxford University Press, 1952; reviewed in *Isis,* 44: 281-83).

13. The number was enormous as compared with the past but very small as compared with our own day. Toward the middle of the sixteenth century Paris

had at least 300,000 inhabitants and only 72 doctors. To these must be added, however, innumerable barbers and irregulars of many kinds.

14. His equivocal nature has been well analyzed by Owsei Temkin, "The elusiveness of Paracelsus," *Bulletin of the History of Medicine*, 26: 201-17 (Baltimore, 1952).

15. The *Labyrinthus* (Karl Sudhoff, *Bibliographia Paracelsica* [Berlin, 1894], no. 30) was first printed in Nuremberg by Valentinus Neuber in 1553. The *Sieben Defensiones* were first printed by Arnold Byrckmann (Cologne, 1564). Karl Sudhoff edited it for his *Klassiker der Medizin* (vol. 24, 1915), and again in the *Sämtliche Werke* (vol. 11, 125-60, Munich, 1928). English version by C. Lilian Temkin in *Paracelsus: Four Treatises* (Johns Hopkins University Press, 1941), pp. 3-41.

16. He played upon the word *Erfahrung*, which means experience (empirical knowledge) but is derived from *fahren*, to move from place to place, to travel (cf. to fare in English).

17. See *Introduction*, 3: 289.

18. Dioscorides, Book V, chapters 84 to 183.

19. For Rupescissa, see *Introduction*, 3: 1572-74 and Robert P. Multhauf, "John of Rupescissa and the origin of medical chemistry," *Isis*, 45: 359-67 (1954).

20. This is Boerhaave's famous textbook on chemistry, the first edition of which was published without his permission. It was reprinted in Venice in 1726, and Boerhaave published in 1732 the genuine edition, *Elementa chemiae* (Leiden, 1732). There are no essential differences between the spurious and genuine editions. In the *Elementa* the history of chemistry covers 24 pages, out of which no less than 4½ are given to Paracelsus. Tenney L. Davis, *Isis*, 10: 33-46 (1928).

21. The adjective Galenic is not well defined, however. See my *Galen*, cited.

22. Henry E. Sigerist, "Laudanum in the works of Paracelsus," *Bulletin of the History of Medicine*, 9: 530-44 (1941).

23. *Ladanon (ledanon)* or *cisthos creticos, gum cistus* (Dioscorides 1: 128). A gum derived from the shrub *ledon* (mastic), still used as an aromatic.

24. A distinction which is still obvious in France, where two professions coexist, that of *pharmacien* (pharmacist or dispenser) and the humbler and less technical calling of *herboriste* (herbalist).

25. Antimony was used mainly in the form of tartar emetic (potassium antimony tartrate, or perhaps potassium tartryl antimonite) and of kermes mineral (antimony trisulphide).

26. Ernst Darmstaedter, *Arznei und Alchemie. Paracelsus Studien* (85 pp., Leipzig: Barth, 1931; reviewed in *Isis*, 17: 494).

27. Original text in the Sudhoff edition (vol. 9, pp. 463-544, 1925). English translation and commentary by Georg Rosen in *Four Treatises*, cited, pp. 43-126.

28. Bernardino Ramazzini (1633-1714), *De morbis artificum* (Modena, 1700). English translation by the late Mrs. Wilmer Cave Wright (600 pp., University of Chicago Press, 1940; reviewed in *Isis*, 33: 260-61; 43: 368).

29. For example, sediments in urine, to the examination of which Paracelsus attached much importance. But he could guess the nature of these sediments, or of any others, very imperfectly if at all.

30. *Tartarische Krankheiten* (Sudhoff edition, vol. 11, pp. 15-122 [1928]). The name was derived from the assimilation of sediments in the body to those found in wine casks, also from the assimilation of pathological pains to the pains of hell (Tartaros).

31. This requires qualification. Jean Riolan the younger was the first (in 1649) to show a relationship between goiter and the thyroid gland. The first description of cretinism was given by the Bavarian Wolfgang Höfer in his *Hercules medicus* (Vienna, 1657). The Savoyard, François Emanuel Fodéré, was the first to establish a relationship between goiter and cretinism (Paris, 1787, 1790). Paracelsus' idea was but a vague adumbration.

32. Goiter is an enlargement of the thyroid gland in the anterior part of the neck. It is not uncommon in mountainous districts and is easy enough to observe; in fact, in some districts (such as those where Paracelsus lived) it was impossible not to notice the ugly deformity. Marco Polo recognized endemic goiter in Chinese Turkestan (*Isis*, 37: 71). Claudius F. Mayer, "History of goiter," *Isis*, 37: 71- 73 (1947).

33. He could not be included because his *Baderbuchlin* was not printed until 1562. It was then edited by Adam von Bodenstein (Mülhausen, 1562). Reprinted in 1563 with the *Buch von den tartarischen Kranckheiten*. Revised edition *Von warmen oder Wildbädern* (Basel: Peter Perna, 1576). Sudhoff nos. 45, 57, 172.

34. Pre-Platonic even. The concept may be found in Hippocratic writings and in Democritos (*History of Science*, 1: 334).

35. Hippocratic and Galenic medicine were psychosomatic too (*History of Science*, 1: 334); hence in this respect Paracelsism was simply a reversion to ancient common sense.

36. For St. Vitus' dance, or the dancing mania, see *Introduction*, 3: 1665-68.

37. Incomplete English translation with commentary by Gregory Zilboorg in *Four Treatises*, cited, pp. 127-212.

38. Original text in Sudhoff's edition (vol. 14, pp. 115-51, [1933]). Henry E. Sigerist's essay and translation of this book is the last in the series edited by him under the general title *Four Treatises* (cited, pp. 213-53).

39. Or Girolamo, another form of the same Christian name, Hieronymus in Latin, Jerome in English or French.

40. In order to prove that he was a scientific doctor Cardano drew the horoscope of his patron, but he did not foretell his atrocious death. The powerful lord archbishop was hanged at Stirling in 1571 on the charge of being accessory to the earl of Darnley's murder (1567) and of complicity in that of the earl of Moray (1570). Did Cardano hear of these terrible events in his old age, when he was himself at the bottom of the wheel of fortune? Could he have foreseen that his patron would fall in so short a time even lower than himself?

41. As quoted by Oystein Ore, *Cardano the Gambling Scholar* (Princeton University Press, 1953), p. 46.

42. Edited by A. G. Little and E. Withington (*British Society of Franciscan Studies*, vol. 14, also Oxford: Clarendon Press, 1928; reviewed in *Isis*, 13: 110-11; *Introduction*, 2: 959, 964). English version by Mary Catherine Welborn, *Isis*, 18: 26-62 (1932).

43. George Sarton, "Deux centenaires, Servet et Chateillon," *Cahiers d'histoire mondiale*, 2: 139-69 (Paris, 1954). This includes a bibliography of recent publications devoted to Servet.

44. That fancy was still accepted by so great a man as Leonardo da Vinci and even by Vesalius in 1543. The latter's statement was somewhat ambiguous. In his second edition of the *Fabrica* (1555) he definitely rejected the invisible holes and explained that his earlier acceptance of them had been *"faute de mieux."*

45. This discovery had been made by Ibn al-Nafîs (XIII-2) and published in an Arabic text which remained unknown in the West until recently. Servet was apparently the first to make it, independently, in the West. For Ibn al-Nafîs, see *Introduction*, 2: 1099-1101; 3: 267; for the history of the discovery of the pulmonary circulation my article, "Deux centenaires, Servet et Chateillon," cited.

46. A short biography of Fernel was written in Latin by his young friend Guillaume Plancy of Le Mans (1514-1568 or later) but printed only in 1607. Plancy lived with Fernel for ten years. Fernel is better known today in the English world than he used to be because he attracted the attention of the English neurologist, Sir Charles Sherrington (1858-1952), who often referred to him in *Man on His Nature* (Cambridge University Press, 1940; reviewed in *Isis*, 34: 48) and later devoted to him a well documented book, *The Endeavour of Jean Fernel*, with a list of the editions of his writings (233 pp., Cambridge University Press, 1946; reviewed in *Isis*, 37: 199; 41: 212). This includes an English version of Plancy's biography (pp. 150-70).

47. Guillaume Budé (1468-1540) was one of the greatest classical scholars of France. The library that he helped to create at Fontainebleau was the nucleus of the Bibliothèque Nationale. It was he who suggested to François I in 1530 the creation of the Collège Royal (now Collège de France).

48. Jacques Lefèvre d'Etaples (in Pas-de-Calais) or Faber Stapulensis (1455-1537) mathematician, theologian, Biblical scholar with affinities to the Reformation. Josse van Clichthove (Niuport 1472-Chartres 1543) was one of Lefèvre's collaborators in Aristotelian commentaries, defender of Christian humanism and orthodoxy, and of peace. *Biographie nationale de Belgique*, 4: 172-74 (Brussels, 1873).

49. Preface to book I of the *Dialogi*, i.e., *De abditis rerum causis* (Paris: Christian Wehel, 1548), as translated in Sherrington, *The Endeavour of Jean Fernel*, cited, p. 17. Two words in this quotation need to be explained. Demetrius is a reference to Demetrios Poliorcetes (337-283 B.C.), son of Antigonos, king of Asia. Early paper mills were located, c.1268-78, in Fabriano, province of Ancona (*Introduction*, 3: 175). The reference to longitude at the end does not give a favorable idea of Fernel's astronomical knowledge.

50. Richard Foster Jones, "Background of Swift's Battle of the Books (1710)" in *The Seventeenth Century* (Stanford University Press, 1951), pp. 10-40.

51. One of the many colleges of the University of Paris. It was founded in 1321. (Cornouailles is French for Cornwall.)

52. See Wing Two. Fernel's measurement was described by Jean Picard, who repeated it with greater precision almost a century and a half later. See Picard's *Mesure de la terre* (Paris, 1671).

53. The *Medicina* consisted of seven books of *Physiologia*, seven of *Pathologia*, and three of *Therapeutica*. The *Physiologia* was a revised and amplified edition of his book of 1542, the *Pathologia* was printed for the first time; the second book (out of three) of the *Therapeutica* was a revised edition of the *De vacuandi ratione*. Posthumous editions of the *Medicina* plus the *Dialogi* were issued under the title *Opera medicinalia* by two Venetian printers in 1565 and 1566, under the title *Universa Medicina* by Andreas Wechel (Paris, 1567), and fifteen more times in the sixteenth century by various printers in France, Germany, Italy, and Switzerland.

54. The *De naturali parte medicinae* (1542) was often called *Physiologia*. It was so called in the *Medicina* (1554), in later editions, and in the French translation *Les VII Livres de la Physiologie* (Paris, 1655). The term physiology was often used in the larger sense indicated by its etymology (science of nature), for example, by Gilbert in the title page of his *De magnete* (1600).

55. Before Fernel the main physiological authorities were Galen, Avicenna, and other Arabic physicians.

56. François, who in 1558 married Mary Stuart, Queen of Scots, who was being educated in France. Under the name of François II he was King of France for seventeen months (1559-60); he died at the age of seventeen.

57. For Henri's death of a tourney wound see Sherrington, *The Endeavour of Jean Fernel*, cited, pp. 54, 180.

58. A curious anatomical discovery may be ascribed to him, however. He was the first to note that the spinal cord is hollow (*De naturali parte medicinae* [1542], VI, c.13; begun in 1538). The same discovery is ascribed to Charles Estienne, who published it three years later. (*De dissectione partium corporis humani*, Paris: S. Colines, 1545). Vesalius failed to mention the fact in his *Fabrica* (1543).

59. Let us recall briefly that Bacon, Galileo, Harvey, and Descartes were born respectively 64, 67, 81, and 99 years after Fernel. Comparisons between them and him are unfair.

60. See the elaborate notes devoted to them in *Introduction*, vol. 3, or the summaries of mediaeval surgery in the same work (2: 73-75; 3: 271-73, 1232-34).

61. *Introduction*, 2: 1080, and better 3: 863-64. Abundant details in Ernest Wickersheimer, *La médecine et les médecins en France à l'époque de la Renaissance* (693 pp., Paris: Maloine, 1906), pp. 128-99. Wickersheimer's book is a mine of information covering every aspect of medical life; its sources are excellent but seldom indicated; very few notes, no index.

62. So called because they wore a long gown like the doctors. On the other hand, the barbers were dressed like artisans.

63. In French *renoueur, rebouteur, rhabilleur*. In Spanish, *algebrista*, from the Arabic al-jābir.

64. Fernel attended Catherine de' Medici in every one of her ten deliveries and was very richly paid for doing so, receiving ten times ten thousand *écus*.

65. Some surgeons apparently obtained a doctor's degree, like Paracelsus, who called himself on the title pages of his books "utriusque medicinae doctor," which meant doctor in medicine and surgery. Was this an invention of his?

66. It is not yet completed in some countries. For example, in Egyptian villages barbers are attached to the health department and have medical duties; they are also "burial brokers." Tawfīq al-hakīm, *The maze of Justice* (London: Harvill, 1947), pp. 74-75, 106.

67. Example of the woodcuts in *Osiris*, 5: 120, 174 (1938). This is the same Brunschwig who wrote the book on distillation, *Kunst zu distillieren* (Strasbourg, 1500; reviewed in *Osiris*, 5: 164-65) dealt with in Wing Three.

68. Julius II (1503-13) was a fighting Pope; like other princes who wanted to extend their territory, he was obliged to employ military engineers and military surgeons. Hence his readiness to patronize Vigo was natural.

69. A monument was erected in Rapallo to Vigo's memory at the time of the 400th anniversary of his death, 1925 (*Isis*, 9: 159).

70. The Hôtel Dieu was then the outstanding hospital of Paris and of France (*Introduction*, 3: 295). It was more hospitable to young surgeons than to young physicians (Wickersheimer, *op. cit.*, p. 134).

71. Happily, various surgical books had been written in French and other vernaculars, because that was the best way of reaching potential readers. Manuscript copies were in circulation. Moreover, many editions of Gui de Chauliac (XIV-2) had already been printed before 1501 in French, Latin, Dutch, and German (Klebs, nos. 494-99). The first edition of John Arderne (in English) was published only in 1588 (London).

72. Apparently Paré had instinctive skill in choosing good ointments. Galen's success as a surgeon of gladiators had been partly due to that kind of skill.

73. Jacobus Sylvius was the Latin name of Jacques Dubois (1478-55), not to be confused with a later Sylvius, François de le Boe (1614-72), physiologist.

74. The others were: *Briefve collection . . . anatomique* (1549), on anatomy and obstetrics, which became the *Anatomie universelle* of 1561; a new treatise on wounds, *La méthode curative des playes* (1561); *Dix livres de la chirurgie* (1564), derived from the preceding items but on a more ambitious scale; *Traicté de la peste* (1568), dealing not only with the plague, but also with smallpox, measles, and leprosy; *Cinq livres de chirurgie* (1572), sometimes called his masterpiece (the material is all new); *Deux livres de chirurgie* (1573), also new, on embryology and monsters; *Discours de la mumie* (1582), a compilation of little if any originality discussing not only mummies but also the unicorn, venoms, and plague. Apropos of the *Traicté de la peste,* Paré's "plague" included many kinds of epidemic diseases, yet he described the typical bubo. Wickersheimer, *La médecine . . . de la Renaissance,* cited, pp. 356-58.

75. An excellent summary of this question is given by Janet Doe in her *Bibliography of Paré's Works* (University of Chicago Press, 1937), pp. 13-17.

76. The best edition of the original French text was provided by Joseph François Malgaigne (1806-65), *Oeuvres complètes* (3 vols., Paris, 1840-41). See also: Claude Stéphen Le Paulmier, *Paré d'après de nouveaux documents* (420 pp., Paris, 1884). Francis R. Packard, *The Life and Times of A. Paré* (310 pp., New York: Hoeber, 1921; reviewed in *Isis*, 4: 326). Dorothea Waley Singer, *Selections from Paré's Works with Short Biography* (248 pp., London: John Bale, 1924; reviewed in *Isis*, 7: 208). Janet Doe, *Bibliography of Paré's Works* (285 pp., University of

Chicago Press, 1937; reviewed in *Isis*, 29: 220; *Addenda* (8 pp., 1940). This is a splendid work.

77. Summaries of mediaeval *regimina* in *Introduction*, 2: 88-89, 93-94; 3: 285-86, 1238-40.

78. See *Isis*, 33: 261.

79. This term was popularized by the treatise of Goethe's friend, Christoph Wilhelm Hufeland, *Die Kunst das menschliche Leben zu verlängern* (Berlin, 1796), often reprinted and translated into many languages. The word *Makrobiotik* first occurred in the title of the third edition, *Makrobiotik oder die Kunst . . .* (1805).

80. He is also called Ludovico and Alvise, which are variants of the same Christian name, our Louis or Lewis. In Venice the family name Cornaro was also spelled Corner.

81. He claimed to have witnessed the arrival in Italy of three great evils: Lutheranism, flattery, and gluttony. The last two, however, were old evils, already well established in Roman days; it is possible that they were especially prevalent in the sixteenth century.

82. This is explained in the *Trattato di acque del magnifico M. Luigi Cornaro* (quarto, 30 fol., Padua: G. Perchacino, 1560).

83. His age is often wrongly quoted because it was assumed that the four essays were published in 1558 at the age of 95. On that basis he was born in 1463 and died at the age of 103. Such mistakes are repeated in various forms; William B. Walker gives the dates 1467-1565, age of death 98 (*Bulletin of the History of Medicine*, 28: 524-34 [1954]).

84. Michelangelo (1475-1564) was almost the exact contemporary of Cornaro, but died two years earlier, at 89. This was in a way more remarkable still because of Michelangelo's arduous life and passions; whatever the exuberance of his youth might have been, Cornaro had become a "cold fish," and such live longer. See my essay on Hoefer and Chevreul (*Bulletin of the History of Medicine*, 8: 419-45 [1940]). Cornaro's longevity was largely due to the fact that his passions were as moderate as his diet.

85. The *Trattato* was translated into Latin at least twice, first by the Flemish Jesuit, Leonard Leys (or Lessius; 1554-1623), in his collection *Hygiasticon* (Antwerp, 1613). The Latin text was put into English by no less a person than the poet George Herbert (Cambridge University Press, 1634). Modern editions are *L'arte di vivere a longo*. Con prefazione di Pompeo Momenti (Milan: Treves, 1905) and *The Art of Living Long*, with other documents (Milwaukee: William F. Butler, 1905; reprinted 1917).

86. *King Lear*, Act I, scene 2.

87. *Introduction*, 3: 929. Steven Runciman, *History of the Crusades* (Cambridge University Press, 1954), vol. 3, p. 273. There is said to be an earlier reference to scurvy in the *Historia orientalis* of James of Vitry (XIII-1) but I cannot locate it.

88. Lord Stanley of Alderley, *The First Voyage around the World* (Hakluyt Society, no. LII, London, 1874), p. 64.

89. James Phinney Baxter, *A Memoir of Jacques Cartier* (New York: Dodd, 1906), pp. 190-91. Some of Cartier's men were cured by the use of a herb or tree

called in Iroquois *annedda,* probably white spruce (*épinette blanche*) or hemlock (*Science,* 98: 242 [1943]).

90. Balduinus Ronssaeus, *De magnis Hippocratis lienibus, Pliniique stomacace at sceletyrbe seu vulgo dicto scorbuto libellus* (Antwerp: M. Nutius, 1564). As the title indicates, Ronsse identified scurvy with a disease described by Hippocrates and Pliny. The Latin *lien,* Greek *splen,* means milt or spleen; *megaloi splenes* means affections of the spleen; could this be scurvy? Ronsse's biography by Paul Bergmans in *Biographie Nationale* (Brussels, 1908), 20: 15-17.

91. Louis H. Roddis, *James Lind (1716-94), Founder of Nautical Medicine* (190 pp., 8 ills., New York: Schuman, 1950; reviewed in *Isis,* 42: 332).

92. Morus, *Animals, Men and Myths* (London: Gollancz, 1954; reviewed in *Isis,* 46: 61-64), p. 146. Morus calls pellagra Columbus' sickness because corn is an American plant and pellagra was an indirect consequence of its importation into Italy. He does not give any reference and his information is very doubtful. For one thing, though maize was introduced into Spain by Columbus as early as 1493, its massive introduction seems to have occurred only half a century later via Turkey and Hungary (hence it was known as Turkey wheat). The Indians did not suffer from pellagra, the disease was not introduced by Columbus, and it did not affect the people of Lombardy until considerably later. The first descriptions of pellagra in medical literature date only from the middle of the eighteenth century. F. H. Garrison, *Introduction to the History of Medicine* (4th ed., Philadelphia: Saunders, 1929), p. 367. Paul Weatherwax, *Indian Corn in Old America* (New York: Macmillan, 1954; reviewed in *Isis,* 46: 64-65).

93. It is derived from Garrison, *op. cit.,* p. 242. Apropos of this I wish to pay tribute to my old friend, Garrison, whose *Introduction* is still the best one-volume history of medicine; I understand that a new revised edition is being prepared by John F. Fulton to be published in 1957. I have added notes of my own to Garrison's account, but have not tried to check his statements on the sources.

94. The Germans called it *Kriebelkrankheit; kribbeln* means to itch, to tingle.

95. Spur is *ergot* in French, hence the name of the disease, ergotism. Spurred rye in French is *seigle ergoté.*

96. For ergotism in the fourteenth century and in general see *Introduction,* 3: 1650, 1668, 1860, 1868.

97. John Caius of Norwich (1510-73) described it in Latin and in English. *A boke or counseill against the disease called the sweate* (London: Richard Grafton, 1552). Facsimile edition with introduction by Archibald Malloch, New York: Scholars' Facsimiles, 1937; reviewed in *Isis,* 34: 429.

98. Reproduced in facsimile with introduction and notes by Charles Singer (48 pp., Oxford: Clarendon Press, 1915; reviewed in *Isis,* 3: 108).

99. The French entered Naples, then in Spanish hands, on February 22, 1495.

100. The French called it *mal de Naples;* the Italians, *mal francese (morbus gallicus),* the Germans, French sickness (or pox); the Poles, German sickness; the Russians, Polish sickness, etc.

101. The literature *ad hoc* is immense and constantly growing, for the riddle cannot be solved. In order to solve it one would have to answer the question,

Did *spirochaeta pallida* exist in Europe before 1495? This is evidently impossible. The organism might have existed, but remained passive.

Among the many publications I should like to mention Karl Sudhoff, *The Earliest Printed Literature on Syphilis, 1495-98,* English translation by Charles Singer (Florence: Lier, 1925; reviewed in *Isis,* 8: 351-54). Heinrich E. Sigerist, "Kritische Betrachtungen über die Frühgeschichte der Syphilis," *Deutsche medizinische Wochenschrift,* Nr. 25, 1926; reviewed in *Isis,* 11: 179). Sigerist favors the non-American theory but with moderation. In his life of Columbus, *Admiral of the Open Sea* (Boston: Little Brown, 1942; reviewed in *Isis,* 34: 169-72), Admiral S. E. Morison favors the American origin with qualifications. See also *Isis,* 29: 406 (1938).

102. In the same way smallpox, introduced by Europeans into the West Indies, Central and South America, caused the destruction of millions of Indians. E. W. Stearn and Allen E. Stearn, *The Effect of Smallpox upon the Destiny of the Amerindian* (Boston: Bruce-Humphries, 1945; reviewed in *Isis,* 37: 124). Many other examples could be adduced concerning not only human diseases, but also plant and animal pests.

103. Yaws or framboesia is a tropical disease very close to syphilis. One of its symptoms is the appearance of raspberry-reddish tumors (raspberry in French is *framboise,* hence framboesia). Gonzalo Hernandez de Oviedo y Valdez (Toledo, 1525) called it *bubas* and Andre Thévet (Paris, 1558) compared it with the French pox. A Dutch physician (W. F. R. Essed, Leiden thesis 1933, reviewed in *Isis,* 43: 199) has argued that the outbreak after 1495 was not syphilis but yaws. The mystery of early syphilis is thus replaced by the mystery of early yaws. J. J. Van Loghen, "Essed's theory on the great pox epidemic in Europe," *Actes du VIᵉ Congrès d'histoire des sciences,* 361-63, Amsterdam, 1950; reviewed in *Isis,* 44: 117. Yaws is still a terrible plague in southeast Asia and the West Indies. Thanks to international help it has been almost eradicated from Haiti (1951-54).

104. *Tractatus cum consiliis contra pudendagram seu morbum gallicum* (Rome: Pietro della Turre, 1497). This is the most valuable of the syphilis incunabula; it is the fifth item in the Sudhoff-Singer collection (Florence, 1925), facsimile pp. 183-232.

105. The book was very popular; twenty editions appeared in the sixteenth century, and more than a hundred in four centuries, most of them in Latin, some in Italian, English, French, German, Spanish, and Portuguese. Leona Baumgartner and John F. Fulton, *Bibliography of the Poem Syphilis* (157 pp., 10 figs., Yale University Press, 1935; reviewed in *Isis,* 24: 437-39). English translation by William Van Wyck, *The Sinister Shepherd* (112 pp., Los Angeles: Primavera, 1934; reviewed in *Isis,* 23: 454). Latin-English edition by *Heneage Wynne-Finch* (London: Heinemann, 1935).

106. Latinized, *guaiacum (guaiacum officinale);* shortened to guaiac. It was thought to be a panacea and was called later *lignum sanctum* (holy wood) or *lignum vitae.* The modern drug *guaiacol,* derived from the herb by distillation, has been used in treating pulmonary tuberculosis. For the use of guaiac at the end of the sixteenth century see my study on Demetrio Canavari, *Journal of the History of Medicine,* 1: 398-416 (1946), pp. 405-14.

107. He has been tentatively identified with Gonzalo Hernandez de Oviedo y Valdez (mentioned in footnote 103), who traveled to the West Indies in 1514 and was back in December 1515. This would date the arrival of guaiac, and the date is plausible.

108. Nicolas Pol, physician and humanist, was born in the Tirol, c.1470. He was in the medical service of Duke Sigismund of Tirol until 1490 and then of the Emperors Maximilian I and Charles V. He collected a rich library, substantial parts of which are now owned by the Medical Library Association of Cleveland, Ohio, and the Yale Medical Library in New Haven, Connecticut; he died in 1532. Max H. Fisch, *Nicolaus Pol Doctor 1494. With a critical text of his guaiac tract,* edited and translated by Dorothy M. Schullian (346 pp., 18 pls., New York: Reichner, 1947; reviewed in *Isis,* 40: 56-58). This is the best source not only for Pol but also for the story of guaiac.

109. He died at the age of 35, presumably of syphilis.

110. For two reasons. It was apparently more virulent than it is now, as one would expect a new disease to be. The period of extreme virulence and epidemic contagion was 1495-1530. In the second place, guaiac and other early drugs were not much of a protection.

111. *Smilaceae* (order *Liliales*). The main genus is Smilax (greenbriers or cat-briers).

112. Popular belief in herbs has continued to this day, except that the favorite herbs are not always the same. The popularity is witnessed by the use of various kinds of teas and root beers. Some of those drinks may be useful; they cannot do any harm.

113. Latin-English edition by Mrs. Wilmer Cave Wright (d. 1951; see *Isis,* 43: 368), *Fracastorii De contagione* (New York: Putnam, 1930; reviewed in *Isis,* 16: 138-41).

114. *Introduction,* 3: 1650-68. This includes a long list of plague treatises of the fourteenth century; a list of those written in the following century would be longer still. The incunabula editions are listed under many headings in Klebs (*Osiris,* 4: 1-359 [1938]).

115. It must be added that Fracastoro's is the only scientific Latin poem that has survived; I can remember offhand only one other, the *Anti-Lucretianus, sive de Deo et natura* by Cardinal Melchior de Polignac (1661-1741), but that is of a later age (posthumously published, Paris, 1747). There were many Latin poets in Renaissance Italy, but they had no interest in science: for example Petrarch (XIV-1), Giovanni Pontano (1426-1503) in Naples, Angelo Poliziano (1454-94) in Florence, Jacopo Sannazaro of Naples (1458-1530), Pietro Bembo (1470-1547) of Venice, Marco Gerolamo Vida (1490-1556) of Cremona, Marc Antonio Flaminio (1498-1550) of Venice, Teofilo Folengo (1491-1544) of Mantua.

116. For the story in the fourteenth century see *Introduction,* 3: 405, 50, 394, 1049, 1338.

117. For more details see Gregory Zilboorg, *The Medical Man and the Witch during the Renaissance* (225 pp., Johns Hopkins University Press, 1935; reviewed in *Isis,* 25: 147-52). The *Malleus maleficarum* was many times reprinted (at least six incunabula editions). English translation by Montague Summers (folio, 291 pp., London: J. Rodker, 1928).

118. This may seem unbelievable, yet see details given by Edward Theodore Withington, "Dr. John Weyer and the witch mania," *Singer's Studies in the History and Method of Science*, vol. 1, pp. 189-224 (Oxford: Clarendon Press, 1917), pp. 196-97.

119. "Historically the Devil is more solidly proved than Peisistratos: We have not a single word from a contemporary declaring to have seen Peisistratos. On the other hand thousands of eye witnesses claim to have seen the Devil. There are few historical facts whch are based upon as many independent testimonies. Nevertheless, we do not hesitate in rejecting the Devil and admitting Peisistratos. That is because the Devil's existence would be irreconcilable with all the laws of science." Ch. V. Langlois and Ch. Seignobos, *Introduction aux études historiques* (4th ed., Paris: Hachette, 1911), p. 177.

120. Wier is the original Dutch name (rhyming with beer); it is often Germanicized Weyer because the Germans annexed him as they did Rembrandt and Vesalius. See Withington's article of 1917 and Zilboorg's book of 1935, mentioned in previous notes. Leonard Dooren, *Doctor Johannes Wier. Leben en werken* (156 pp., Aalten, 1940), in Dutch.

121. Not far from 's Hertogenbosch (Bois-le-Duc), where he received his secondary education.

122. Heinrich Cornelius Agrippa von Nettesheim (born in Cologne, c.1486, died in Grenoble, c.1534), German theologian, physician, and occultist. He was one of the most influential writers of his time and the vicissitudes of his life were many.

123. When I visited the city of Cleves before the wars it looked very much like a Dutch city although it was in German territory (Düsseldorf district). The legend of Lohengrin is related to the ducal castle of Cleves called Schwanenburg. The duchy of Cleves was associated with two neighboring duchies, Berg and Jülich. Anne of Cleves (the fourth queen of Henry VIII) was the daughter of John, duke of Cleves, while her mother was the daughter of William, duke of Jülich.

124. The battle that Wier began was not completely won until the nineteenth century, and there are still among us today some individuals who continue to believe in witchcraft, e.g., the Rev. Montague Summers (*Isis*, 25: 149), as shown in his *History of Witchcraft and Demonology* (368 pp., 8 pls., New York: Knopf, 1926). *Introduction*, 3: 1049, 1051, 1865.

125. When a plague decimated Geneva in 1543-45 it was believed that the disease was spread by plague sowers (*semeurs de peste*); Calvin shared and strengthened that superstition. The same thing happened during the Milan pest of 1630, the one described by Manzoni in *I promessi sposi* (1825-26). G. Sarton, "Beccaria," (Supplement, *Bulletin of the History of Medicine*, no. 3, pp. 283-308, Baltimore, 1944), pp. 301-303; "Servet et Chateillon," *Cahiers d'histoire mondiale*, 2: 140-69 (Paris, 1954), p. 160.

126. He translated it himself into Latin, *De republica libri sex* (779 pp., folio, index, Paris: J. Du Puys 1586). The book aroused considerable attention in Europe. It was the only one of his books to be promptly translated into English, *The six bookes of a commonweale* (London, 1606). Spanish translation (Torino, 1590). For more details see Roger Chauviré, *Jean Bodin, auteur de la République* (543 pp., Paris: Champion, 1914).

127. The book was not published until the last century, first incompletely by

G. E. Guhrauer (Berlin, 1841), then more completely by Ludwig Noack (358 pp., Schwerin, Mecklenburg, 1857).

128. Best informed in social and political matters; he was ignorant of scientific matters and had no scientific training whatsoever. This explains his aberrations without excusing them. Wier was a physician, Bodin a jurist.

129. I say French because I am speaking of Bodin, but these prejudices existed in other countries as well. Their existence is crystallized in the language, e.g., lumbago is called in German *Hexenschuss* (witch-shot).

130. Our readers will recognize the family name. This de Thou (Thuanus) was the first eminent representative of a family of magistrates, the most illustrious member of which was his third son, Jacques Auguste de Thou (1553-1617), author of the *Historia sui temporis*.

131. The "Réfutation des opinions de Jean Wier" is printed on fol. 218-52 of the Paris edition of 1582, the earliest available to me. I do not know whether it was included in the first edition (1580).

132. See *Essai* II, 37 and *passim*.

NOTES TO SIXTH WING

1. This is a free translation of my lecture delivered in French at the Palais de la Découverte in Paris on the Fourth of July, 1952, and published in *Léonard de Vinci et l'expérience scientifique au seizième siècle* (Paris: Presses Universitaires de France, 1953), pp. 11-29. I delivered substantially the same lecture, in English, at the Pierpont Morgan Library on October 16, 1952. I take advantage of this first publication in English to thank the sponsors of these lectures in Paris and New York for the opportunities which they so kindly opened to me.

2. For the reader's convenience, each quotation is identified by the number given to it in Richter's edition. This one is Richter 886. Jean-Paul Richter, *The Literary Works of Leonardo da Vinci* (2d ed., 2 vols., Oxford University Press, 1939; reviewed in *Isis*, 35: 184-87). Richter refers to the original Mss.

3. The fragment is Richter 1363. Sigmund Freud, *Eine Kindsheiterrinerung des Leonardo da Vinci* (74 pp., Leipzig, 1910).

4. In 1916 I was invited to deliver six lectures at the Lowell Institute in Boston on science in Leonardo's age. After that I spent two more years analyzing every one of Leonardo's thoughts. My ideas and plans were then set forth in various writings, such as "Une encyclopédie léonardesque" (*Raccolta Vinciana*, 10: 235-42, Milan, 1919). I then realized that my knowledge of ancient and mediaeval science was insufficient, and I decided to undertake an elaborate study of this subject, which bore fruit in my *Introduction to the History of Science*. I had to end my story not in 1900, as I had planned, but in 1400. In spite of thirty-five years of diligent work, I was not yet back to Leonardo.

5. For a discussion of the birth date see *Isis*, 43: 125 (1952).

6. The best known visitors of Verrocchio were il Perugino, Sandro Botticelli, young Lorenzo di Credi, and the brothers Pollaiuoli.

7. When Cardinal Luis d'Aragon visited Leonardo at Cloux in 1517 his secretary, Antonio de Beatis, noticed that Leonardo could not use his right hand

for painting and concluded that it was paralyzed. Was not that a wrong interpretation of Leonardo's left-handedness?

8. The years between the end of his stay with Verrocchio (c.1477) and the beginning of his residence in Milan (1483) are rather obscure. If Leonardo traveled to the Near East (Egypt, Armenia, Taurus Mountains), it was possibly during this period. Richter, 2: 315-23.

9. Never did the wheel of fortune turn more furiously than in the case of Lodovico Sforza, also called Lodorico il Moro. Born in 1451, he was duke of Milan from 1481 to 1499, a great patron of the arts, but he joined a league against the French in 1495 and was defeated by Louis XII in 1499. He spent the rest of his life imprisoned and died in his last prison, the castle of Loches (23 miles southeast of Tours) in 1508.

10. Luca Pacioli was dealt with in Wing Two, when I spoke of his best known work, the Summa de arithmetica geometria, etc. (Venice: Paganinis, 1494). Another work of his, Divina proportione (same printer, 1509) was illustrated with geometric figures drawn roughly by Leonardo (Richter, 1: 243-44).

11. Marcantonio della Torre (1478-1511); see below, note 30.

12. Giuliano de' Medici (1478-1516), the elder brother of Giovanni de' Medici (1475-1521) who became Pope Leo X (1513-21); they were the sons of Lorenzo il Magnifico and like him great patrons of arts and letters.

13. Raphael was also working in the Vatican at the same time. He was painting frescoes, the Disputa, the School of Athens, etc. Michelangelo was completing the ceiling of the Sistine Chapel. An extraordinary conjunction of major stars! In 1514 Leonardo was 62, Michelangelo 39, and Raphael 31. The oldest and the youngest were nearest to death; they had but 5 and 6 more years to live, but Michelangelo was to live another 50 years, more than the whole of Raphael's span.

14. John the maker of mirrors (Richter no. 1351-53).

15. Cloux was a part of the royal domain of Amboise on the Loire. The congress organized in 1952 by the French government to celebrate the fourth centenary of Leonardo's birth ended on Sunday, July 14, in Amboise. The royal estate now belongs to the Comte de Paris, who offered a dinner; a solemn mass had been celebrated in the morning in the church of Amboise. The main officiant was the parish priest of Vinci.

16. The identification of this portrait with the Mona Lisa cannot be proved but is considered probable by Germain Bazin: Hommage à Léonard de Vinci (Paris: Musée du Louvre: 1952), p. 24. The three paintings have remained together since 1515 and are now in the Louvre.

17. Francesco Melzi was a young gentleman of Milan (Richter no. 1566) born in 1493 (hence 41 years younger than Leonardo). He inherited all of Leonardo's manuscripts and took them to Vaprio d'Adda (Milan), where Giorgio Vasari saw them in 1565. He died in Vaprio, c.1570. Very little of his work is extant. A very attractive portrait of him drawn by Giovanni Antonio Boltraffio (1467-1510), another of Leonardo's disciples, is preserved in the Ambrosiana; the curators of that museum vouch for its authenticity.

18. Shio Sakanishi, The spirit of the brush, being the outlook of Chinese

painters on nature from Eastern Chin to Five Dynasties, 317-960 (Wisdom of the East Series, London: John Murray, 1939; reviewed in *Isis,* 31: 220). See also *The essay on landscape painting (Lin ch'üan kao chih)* by Kuo Hsi (c.1020-90), translated by S. Sakanishi (Wisdom of the East Series, 1935; reviewed in *Isis,* 25: 461-64), and the *Chieh-tzŭ-yüan hua ch'uan,* translated into French by Raphael Petrucci (Paris: Laurens, 1918; reviewed in *Isis,* 4: 345-47).

19. The three outstanding equestrian statues of the Renaissance are: first, the one of Erasmo Gattamelata in Padua, made by Donatello, c.1444; second, that of Bartolommeo Colleoni in Venice, made by Verrocchio after 1479 (Leonardo witnessed its composition and planning); third, that of Francesco Sforza, duke of Milan (1447-66), Lodovico's father, made by Leonardo, who had devoted considerable thought to it. See his notes concerning the casting (Richter nos. 710-15). It was destroyed by Gascon archers during their occupation of Milan (1499-1512).

20. In my *Introduction* (vol. 3) I have given a list of some fifteen authors of technical books of the fifteenth century. Three of these are Italians; it is not necessary to assume that Leonardo had seen their texts and drawings, but he certainly followed the same oral and manual traditions.

21. I do not refer to the observations made in our own time by means of ultra-rapid photography. This made it possible to see details that no human eye could observe.

22. Richter, no. 1155.

23. In my Harvard lectures on the history of science I came back to Leonardo and Vesalius every other year, and tried to explain the technique of their dissections, how they cut and separated integuments and tissues with various knives and sometimes with their nails. I did it one day with so much realism that a student felt nauseated and was obliged to leave the auditorium at great speed. I have often wondered how the early anatomists managed to escape infection.

24. See *Introduction,* 3: 1584. Leonardo's ideas *ad hoc* are shown in his drawing of the Accademia of Venice, often reproduced. The Greek canon was fixed by Polycleitos (fl. 452-412 B.C.)

25. Galen (II-2). See my little book *Galen of Pergamon* (University of Kansas Press, 1954; reviewed in *Isis,* 46: 296-97), p. 47.

26. *Quaderni d'Anatomia* I, 3r; II, 3 (*Isis,* 35: 186). These *quaderni* were very well edited by Ove C. L. Vangensten, A. Fonahn, and H. Hopstock (6 vols., folio, Christiania, 1911-16). Richter, 2: 419.

27. From that point of view the method of *"plis cachetés"* practiced by the Académie des Sciences in Paris seems unfair to me. A member is permitted to announce a discovery in a sealed envelope, the date of which is authenticated, but which will be opened and published only when the member wishes it. Can this establish any valid priority? If the member had no faith in his own discovery until it had been confirmed by later events, he did not really make it. He cannot have it both ways.

28. Richter, 1: 5-7.

29. These figures may not be exact, but they will suffice to prove the point.

30. Vasari defined Leonardo's collaboration with Marcantonio as follows "aiutato e scambievolmente aiutando." Marcantonio, who died at thirty without having given anything to posterity, is immortalized by Leonardo's references to

him and by the bronze bas-reliefs which Andrea Riccio executed for San Fermo Maggiore in Verona (now in the Louvre). See note 11.

31. In fairness to him it must be added that in this case he was the victim of circumstance. The statue was to be of very large size; the model of the horse only was 7.2 meters high and the weight in bronze would have been of the order of 200,000 pounds. The model was destroyed by Gascon soldiers. It would have cost a very large amount of money to cast the monument in bronze, and Leonardo was criticized by many, including Michelangelo. The bronze needed for the statue was given to Lodovico il Moro, but he had it cast into guns (Richter, 2: 3).

Toward the end of his life Leonardo planned an equestrian statue of the famous captain, Gian Giacomo Trivulzio (died Chartres, 1518), but nothing came of this (Richter, 2: 9).

32. Many young painters worked in Leonardo's studio, chiefly when he was in Milan; they were apprentices and servants and their names appear in Leonardo's notebooks in such brief manner (say, Giulio, Bonifazio, Arrigo, Lorenzo, il Fanfoia) that identification is impossible. Others are better known, such as Giacomo Salai, Francesco Melzi, Cesare da Sesto, Ambrogio de Predis (c.1455-1508), Andrea Solario (1458-1509+), Giovanni Antonio Boltraffio (1467-1516), Gaudenzio Ferrari (c.1484-1546). The greatest, or at least the most popular, of those epigoni was Bernardino Luini (c.1475-c.1532). Leonardo's influence was felt not only by Milanese or Lombardese artists but also by other Italians and by some of the Flemish painters who visited Italy.

33. Italian typography began at Subiaco (not far from Rome) in 1465; the first Roman edition dates from 1467, those of Venice from 1469, those of Florence and Milan from 1471. Before the end of the fifteenth century printing was one of the main industries of Venice.

34. He refers to definite books but it is impossible to know whether his references apply to manuscript or printed copies.

35. *Anatomical Mss., A,* 8b, Paris, 1898.

36. Pietro of Arezzo (1492-1557), poet, satirist, and blackmailer.

37. Albrecht Dürer (1471-1528) was a little younger than Leonardo (1452-1519), but he did not live as long (57 years instead of 67). One might compare Leonardo also with Raphael of Urbino (1483-1520), who lived only 37 years, yet produced an incredible number of paintings.

38. The first of these three books (1525) was soon translated into Latin (Paris: C. Wechel, 1532, 1534, 1535) and again by Joachim Camerarius (Nuremberg, 1534); the second (1527) was translated into Latin (Paris: C. Wechel, 1535); the third (1528) was translated into Latin by Joachim Camerarius (Nuremberg, 1532), into French by Loys Meigret (Paris: Périer, 1557) and into Italian by G. P. Gallucci (Venice, 1591-94).

39. There is no absolute incompatibility between art and business, and Dürer was not the only artist to be a good business man; we think of Titian, Rubens, and Van Dyck, or even of Chopin.

40. Drawn with red chalk, kept in the Library of Torino. It is the only portrait of him which I can trust to be genuine.

41. Richter 1210, "l'amore di qualunche cosa è figliuolo d'essa cognitione e l'amore è tanto piu fervente quanto la cognitione è piu certa."

Index

In this index names are, in general, alphabetized as in the index of Professor Sarton's *Introduction to the History of Science*.